THE CHRIST IN THE BIBLE COMMENTARY
Volume Two

THE
CHRIST IN THE BIBLE
COMMENTARY

Volume Two

Joshua
Judges
Ruth
First and Second Samuel
First and Second Kings
First and Second Chronicles

Dr. Albert B. Simpson

CHRISTIAN PUBLICATIONS
CAMP HILL, PENNSYLVANIA

Christian Publications
3825 Hartzdale Drive, Camp Hill, PA 17011

The mark of  *vibrant faith*

ISBN: 0-87509-494-5
LOC Catalog Card Number: 92-070937
© 1992 by Christian Publications
All rights reserved
Printed in the United States of America

92 93 94 95 96 5 4 3 2 1

Cover Design: Step One Design

CONTENTS

Joshua

Judges, Ruth and Samuel

Samuel, Kings and Chronicles

JOSHUA

INTRODUCTION

T he following chapters contain the substance of a series of expositions of
the book of Joshua, designed to unfold the deeper spiritual teachings of this
book as a revelation of Christ and His fullness, and as a type of the higher
inheritance of faith and peace into which our divine Joshua waits to introduce His faithful people.

They do not claim to be so much an exegetical commentary on words and
phrases, as a more comprehensive analysis of the general plan and spiritual
teachings of the volume, and an exposition of the mind of the Spirit, as He,
through these ancient types, unfolds to us our privileges under the gospel
and our full inheritance in Christ.

Other volumes sufficiently expound the questions of history, geography,
textual criticism, skeptical objections and allusions to manners and customs,
and other matters connected with biblical illustration.

Our object, in harmony with the general purpose of these volumes, namely, to unfold "Christ in the Bible," is to bring the hearts of our readers into
touch, at all points, with the Lord Himself and with the lessons which He
designs for their own spiritual life.

There is in all things a good, a better and a best. That is especially true in
our spiritual life. The story of Exodus, Leviticus and Numbers is *the good,*
unfolding Israel's redemption from Egypt, and foreshadowing our salvation
through the Lord Jesus Christ.

Deuteronomy and the earlier chapters of Joshua introduce us to *the better:*
Israel's entrance upon the Land of Promise, the type of our sanctification
through the Lord Jesus, and by the power of the Holy Spirit.

But there is something more than even this, and the later chapters of the
book of Joshua unfold *the highest and the best* possibilities of our spiritual
life.

There were choice possessions in the Land of Promise. There were victories to be won, even after all the land was subdued and the 31 kings were
conquered. Hebron, Kiriath Sepher and Timnath Serah represented something more than ordinary victory, and point us forward to the prizes of the

Christian life and the special inheritance of glory awaiting the few, even in the sanctified host of God, who are willing to be more than conquerors through Him that loved them.

If this volume is used of God to inspire any of God's wandering children to turn from the good to the better, we will feel deeply thankful.

But if we have the joy of finding, in the day of harvest, that it has stimulated some of God's consecrated children to press on from the better to the best, and to win some Hebron of love, or Timnath Serah of cloudless light and incorruptible joy, in the heavenly places which await us even here, we will feel that the highest purpose of this beautiful, inspired volume which we have sought to unfold has been in some measure accomplished, and that we have not been disappointed in our own humble and most earnest hope and prayer.

CHAPTER 1

OUR FULL INHERITANCE IN CHRIST

After the death of Moses the servant of the LORD, the LORD said to Joshua son of Nun, Moses' aide: "Moses my servant is dead. Now then, you and all these people, get ready to cross the Jordan River into the land I am about to give to them—to the Israelites. I will give you every place where you set your foot, as I promised Moses. Your territory will extend from the desert to Lebanon, and from the great river, the Euphrates—all the Hittite country—to the Great Sea on the west." (Joshua 1:1–4)

In the plan of divine revelation there is a deep, logical and Christological order of conception and thought; and while, of course, we find at every step the usual freedom and diffuseness of the Oriental style, yet there is one great definite idea that moves steadily onward in clear development and grand progression.

THE BOOKS OF MOSES

The book of Genesis is the book of beginnings, and everything that comes in the later books has, in some sense, its source and foundation here. Exodus is the book of redemption, and all that the later Scriptures reveal with respect to the grand plan of human redemption, has here its roots and germs. Leviticus is the book of reconciliation, and unfolds the teachings of the Holy Spirit respecting our access to God, and our life in the holy place of His sanctuary. Numbers is the story of the wilderness, and the picture of our wanderings below; and especially of the failure of God's people to enter into their inheritance. Then Deuteronomy comes as the second or new departure of the people of God, after the sad experience of failure and sin, and rehearses afresh God's covenant and His charges to His people, as the second generation looks forward to entering into the rest which their fathers had refused.

JOSHUA

The culmination of all this is reached in the book of Joshua. As Numbers is the story of failure, and Deuteronomy of renewed preparation, so Joshua tells us of the actual entering into the Land of Promise. It marks the highest point in the history of the covenant people hitherto, and necessarily suggests some deeper lessons in its higher spiritual significance as respects the New Testament revelation, and the spiritual people of whom ancient Israel was but the type.

Therefore, we find the apostle in his letter to the Hebrews saying: "For if Joshua had given them rest, God would not have spoken later about another day. There remains, then, a Sabbath-rest for the people of God" (4:8–9). It is evident, therefore, that Canaan was not designed to be the permanent inheritance of Israel, but a type of the higher heritage of faith and holiness which still remained for God's covenant people.

NOT HEAVEN

That inheritance cannot be the heaven that awaits us after death, or even the earthly kingdom of glory and righteousness which the coming of Christ is to bring. Our hymnology is laden with this conception and its appropriate phraseology, but it is all contrary to the real idea of the Holy Spirit; for we shall not find in heaven, or even in the millennial state, anything to correspond with the enemies in the land whom Joshua had to fight, with the years of conflict through which Israel passed, with the shame and sin of Achan or the subsequent backsliding of Israel. Into that land "nothing impure will ever enter" (Revelation 21:27), and there shall be no foe nor fear of conflict; and even Satan, the great leader of all the adverse host, shall be utterly cast out.

The spiritual kingdom must, therefore, be some experience and condition here. What it means the apostle very distinctly expresses when he tells us: "For anyone who enters God's rest also rests from his own work, just as God did from his" (Hebrews 4:10); and yet again, "Therefore, since the promise of entering his rest still stands, let us be careful that none of you be found to have fallen short of it" (4:1). God's rest is something here—a condition and experience of Israel in Canaan; just as the wretched experience of failure and inconstancy so often found in Christians corresponds with the story of the book of Numbers and the 40 years of wandering in the wilderness.

TWO TYPES OF CHRISTIANS

Even the most superficial observer must have noticed in the records of Christian experience, and the observation of life, that there are two very distinct types of Christians in the world, in every age: one representing an experience of despondency, anxiety, doubt, inconstancy and frequent declension—a life so unsatisfying as to make one question whether it is really worth all it costs; and the other full of confidence, victory, joy, satisfaction, power and stability.

The difference between these two types is more marked than even the experience of conversion or the contrast between the man of the world and the professing Christian. Those who have passed into this second stage of Christian life have uniformly testified that their second blessing marked a far greater change in their experience than their first.

There has been no period in the history of the church without these two classes of disciples. Even the apostles themselves passed from one stage into the other. Their experience before the coming of the Holy Spirit was the realization of the book of Numbers; and their subsequent life, after the day of Pentecost, was a repetition of the book of Joshua. There is not a congregation of Christians on earth today but contains the same two classes: the people who have simply come out of Egypt and are wandering in the wilderness, with a hope of salvation and a measure of grace sufficient to separate them from the world; and, on the other hand, the people who have been filled with the Spirit and are walking in the light and joy of the Lord.

Taking the lowest view of it, who is there who has not felt the need for something deeper and higher in his Christian life? Who is there who has not wept over his failures and humiliations, and reached out for a purity and the power worthy of the cost and the grandeur of God's great salvation? Who is there who has not felt that there must be something higher than a life of sinning and repenting, and longed to rise above the evil that he hated and realize the holy aspirations which constantly struggled in his soul?

Sometimes men have grown so weary and dissatisfied that they have thrown up the little religion they possessed, and said: "If I cannot have something better than this, I will have nothing;" and after years of struggling, have found the full salvation of God, and accepted it and been brought into the full experience of the sanctification of the Holy Spirit. It is the natural instinct of a newborn soul to expect such a life from the beginning; and it is a strange disappointment when the first fall comes and the soul is overwhelmed with its insufficiency and helplessness and pours out for the first time the bitter cry, "What a wretched man I am! Who will rescue me from this body of death?" (Romans 7:24).

We read as early as the 13th chapter of Genesis that God gave to Abraham a vision of this Land of Promise, long centuries before it was fulfilled; and so God has been giving to us, all our lives, a vision of a larger, richer blessing than we have ever enjoyed. Sometimes we have seen it in the lives of God's saints with whom we have come in contact, and their shining faces have made us hunger for what we did not possess, and wonder why we did not have it too. Sometimes we have seen it in the promises of God, and asked ourselves why we should not realize these great words, if God really meant them. Sometimes the vision has seemed to be a vague outreaching, quite indefinable. And then sometimes the light has grown clearer, and the land has stood out in its great landmarks and headlands, until we understood more definitely what the promise meant and what the fullness of our inheritance involved. This is the apostle's prayer for his friends in Ephesus; and it is the prayer of the Spirit for each of us, that "the eyes of your heart may be enlightened in order that you may know the hope to which he has called you, the riches of his glorious inheritance in the saints" (Ephesians 1:18). May God so open our eyes that, as we read these lines, we may understand the meaning of the inheritance of the saints and the fullness of the blessing of Christ!

VICTORY

The first definite landmark in the inheritance is *victory*. Canaan meant to ancient Israel triumph over their enemies, and our first great spiritual need is power to overcome the evil within us, and the evil around us. We are not anywhere promised that we shall be delivered from the conflict, but it is our privilege to be victorious in it.

Sin shall not cease to exist, in this present dispensation, but we may be dead to sin, and claim the mighty promise—"For sin shall not be your master, because you are not under law, but under grace" (Romans 6:14). It is the covenant and oath of Jesus that we have "salvation from our enemies/ and from the hand of all who hate us/ . . . to serve him without fear/ in holiness and righteousness before him all our days" (Luke 1:71, 74b–75). Victory over the sin within us, over the self that dominated us, over the temptations that beset us—this is the promise of Christ; this is the purchase of His blood; this is the sanctification which the Holy Spirit comes to give to every surrendered heart.

"And I will put my Spirit in you and move you to follow my decrees and be careful to keep my laws" (Ezekiel 36:27).

REST

Canaan is called "God's *rest.*" Following, as it did, 40 years of weary wandering, it was, indeed, a delightful repose. It tells of something in Christian experience which is as precious as it is rare—deliverance not only from sin and temptation, but from care and fear; the peace that passes all understanding, and garrisons the heart and mind through Christ Jesus; the trust that is not anxious about anything; the confidence that casts all care on Him; the perfect peace in which God keeps those whose minds are stayed on Him; the great peace of those who love His law, and nothing shall offend them. Christ had this perfect peace Himself, and His last bequest to His disciples was: "Peace I leave with you; my peace I give you. . . . Do not let your hearts be troubled and do not be afraid" (John 14:27).

Greater than to be saved from the ills of earth, is it to be kept from their shadow and their fear. This is the privilege of the heart that fully trusts and wholly yields itself to God. It is the heaven of the soul, and the blood-bought inheritance of all who are willing to enter into the promised land.

REALIZATION

The land of Canaan was to them the realization of many former promises. It made actual to them things which had been only hopes. And so to us, in our Christian life, there is a stage of faith and promise, and there is the experience of full realization and blessed satisfaction. "For the law was given through Moses; grace and truth came through Jesus Christ" (1:17).

The Holy Spirit is an earnest and a seal; and these figures express most emphatically the deep impress of living realities in our heart and life. There is for us the actual consciousness of divine things: the personal and intimate knowledge of God; the utter satisfaction of every longing of the soul; love so rooted and grounded that it cannot be moved; and blessings "immeasurably more than all we ask or imagine" (Ephesians 3:20). The inheritance, beloved, is for you. God wants to make the things of the Spirit more actual in your life than the things of sense are in the lower world of the material, and to quicken every inward sense until you shall know and see the invisible realities of the world to come with a vividness that the things of earth can never have.

POWER

How men long for power! How weak and ineffectual are the lives of our Christians; how little they tell for God and man! Christ is the Almighty One, and there is no sphere in which His almightiness should be so strongly felt as in the spiritual realm, where the Holy Spirit supremely rules.

The experience of Joshua in Canaan expresses victorious power. It was the march of God, through His people, in continual triumph, until every earthly foe and every material force acknowledged this supremacy. The same power has been embodied in the Lord Jesus Christ and His Almighty Spirit, and it awaits the trust of every fully surrendered heart. "You will receive power when the Holy Spirit comes on you; and you will be my witnesses . . ." (Acts 1:8). "Anyone who has faith in me will do what I have been doing. He will do even greater things than these" (John 14:12).

YOUR OWN INHERITANCE

But there is something higher than all this. The Land of Promise has a personal meaning for each of us. No man can occupy the whole world, or live in a whole city; there is one spot which each of us calls home. That is a personal location and possession, and expresses our own individual residence. And so there is a sense in which God has a special inheritance for each of His children. God's promises have a meaning for you that they cannot have for me; and God has a plan for you which is distinct and individual.

That plan He is ever unfolding to our faith, as we are able and willing to receive it. This is what David meant when he said, "The boundary lines have fallen for me in pleasant places;/ surely I have a delightful inheritance" (Psalm 16:6).

The inheritance of every Christian is the highest will of God for him. It includes both our internal and our external life and it means for each of us the revelation of Christ in our own heart in all His fullness of grace and power, and the ordering of God's providence in our life, so as to develop us in the highest manner and use us for the greatest good.

All our life long God has been speaking to us about this plan. Some of us remember the distant vision of our childhood, as we knelt in our earliest prayers, and the light of heaven first began to illumine the firmament of our souls and open them to the thoughts and plans of God. More and more clearly, as we have come into His more immediate presence, has He made plain to us His thought for us, and added promise unto promise. And as He has fulfilled them successively, He has led us on to a larger vision, vaster hopes and bolder advances, and we have begun to walk through the land in all the length and breadth of it.

The measuring lines of this land are the promises of God. Every New Year's eve, every day of special waiting upon Him, every time of renewed dedication, every birthday and every anniversary He has enlarged these promises and expanded this vision. And every successive year that faith and expectation have been turned to thanksgiving and praise, as we have found His promises fulfilled and His Word proved sure and true.

THE LARGER LAND

But for most of us there is a larger land than we have yet realized, and God is speaking to us as He did to Abram of old, saying:

"All the land that you see I will give to you and your offspring forever. I will make your offspring like the dust of the earth, so that if anyone could count the dust, then your offspring could be counted. Go, walk through the length and breadth of the land, for I am giving it to you" (Genesis 13:15–17).

And again, He is speaking to some of us in the rich and glorious promises of Deuteronomy:

For the LORD your God is bringing you into a good land—a

land with streams and pools of water, with springs flowing in the valleys and hills; a land with wheat and barley, vines and fig trees, pomegranates, olive oil and honey; a land where bread will not be scarce and you will lack nothing; a land where the rocks are iron and you can dig copper out of the hills.

When you have eaten and are satisfied, praise the LORD your God for the good land he has given you. (8:7–10)

What a glorious land this is: with its springs of spiritual refreshing; its fountains from which these springs all come in the indwelling life and presence of God; its ample provision for all your spiritual need; its wheat, barley, fig trees and pomegranates; its bread without scarceness; its honeyed sweetness; its oil and olives, producing in perpetual freshness the anointing of His gladness and His power. The land whose very stones and hills, with their ruggedness and barrenness, are but mines of brass and iron, enabling us to draw strength out of our very difficulties, and blessing from all our trials.

Beloved, there is such a land for you, if you will but enter in and claim all the fullness of this boundless blessing. We do not need to fear to claim all the fullness of this promised land.

Again, in Jeremiah 32:41, He says: "I will rejoice in doing them good and will assuredly plant them in this land with all my heart and soul."

This was the apostle's prayer for the Thessalonians: "With this in mind, we constantly pray for you, that our God may count you worthy of his calling, and that by his power he may fulfill every good purpose of yours and every act prompted by your faith" (2 Thessalonians 1:11). This was the meaning of the prayer of Epaphras in Colossians: ". . . that you may stand firm in all the will of God . . ." (4:12b). This was the holy confidence of Paul: ". . . that I will in no way be ashamed, but will have sufficient courage so that now as always Christ will be exalted in my body, whether by life or by death" (Philippians 1:20). And this was his one desire in life, and the only thing that he counted dear, as expressed in Acts: ". . . if only I may finish the race and complete the task the Lord Jesus has given me—the task of testifying to the gospel of God's grace" (20:24).

There is for each of us a ministry, according to the will of God, for each of us a plan for reaching His highest thought for us. It is the very best that we can do or be for Him and the world, and to even seem to come short of it will be an everlasting disappointment. And so He calls upon us, "But encourage one another daily, as long as it is called Today, so that none of you may be hardened by sin's deceitfulness" (Hebrews 3:13).

There is nothing in life so important as this; and when the close comes, it will be an unending satisfaction to look back and feel that nothing has failed of all the will of God. But what a bitter disappointment it will be to look back from the light of eternity and realize how very much God had intended for us, and that it is forever lost!

Every moment of our life is adding something to this land or taking something from it. How swiftly the shuttle is flying to and fro with every throb of our heart, and threads are being woven and the pattern being wrought out or ruined. We cannot do it over again; the issues are hastening near, and they are forever. May God help us that we may not even *seem* to come short!

ITS BOUNDARIES

In our text the boundaries of Canaan are given in a very striking manner. They were to extend "from the wilderness unto this Lebanon," and "from the great river Euphrates unto the great sea, toward the going down of the sun" (Joshua 1:4, KJV). The wilderness was its southern limit, and Lebanon the northern boundary. Joshua was standing at the time on the edge of the wilderness, and Lebanon was far away on the extreme north. It seems very strange to call it "this Lebanon." Humanly speaking, it was "that Lebanon." But Joshua was speaking of it in the language of faith, and faith always overleaps distance, and counts the things that are not as though they are. It was by Abram's faith that he saw the promise afar off and ran to meet it and embrace it. He had such faith in God that he saw the land afar off. Faith brings the distant near, and the far-off things that appear unapproachable, the blessings that seem to be beyond our reach, are made so plain to the eye of faith that they are reckoned ours before they come to pass.

So yonder snow-crowned mountain, lost in the clouds, and dim in the distance of more than a hundred miles, is "this Lebanon." The eye of faith loves to gaze upon the distant heights of promise, and say "this Lebanon." One touch of faith will dissolve the spaces that intervene, and cancel the interval of years, and bring us into God's ever present *now*. "With the Lord a day is like a thousand years, and a thousand years are like a day" (2 Peter 3:8). We may get a foretaste of heaven, and dwell in its light, and sing the joyful song of trust:

> Give me the glorious foretaste here, I pray,
> Let faith foredate that everlasting day;
> And, walking in its glory all the way,
> Oh! lead me in the way everlasting.

There is another beautiful suggestion in the description of the eastern and western boundaries. Their line was to extend from the river Euphrates unto the great sea "toward the going down of the sun" (Joshua 1:4, KJV). It was not to reach the going down of the sun, but to be toward it. In this land the sun never goes down. Away beyond the great sea of God's fullness lies the sunset, but our western boundary never reaches it. It is very striking and beautiful that the last picture in the book of Joshua is the inheritance of Joshua himself, which was Timnath Serah, which literally means "the city of the sun." So the picture of Canaan begins and ends with the sunlit sky, whose light and glory shall never fade. This is the inheritance where God's children may all abide. ". . . the LORD will be your everlasting light,/and your days of sorrow will end" (Isaiah 60:20b). Are we dwelling in this light?

Perhaps we might regard all these places as at least symbols, if not types, of some higher spiritual meaning. Shall we take the wilderness where the survey began as a figure of our life of wandering? Shall we take Lebanon to represent the strength and power of God in the truly consecrated and Christ-filled life, endued with the Holy Spirit and filled with the fullness of God? Shall the river Euphrates represent the rich fruitfulness of which it was a type, and shall the great sea speak to us of the larger fullness of God Himself, to whom all these blessings are intended to lead us?

Such is God's great survey of the Land of Promise. Into it He is waiting to bring His consecrated people. Shall we not listen while He says, in solemn earnestness, to each of our hearts: "Therefore, since the promise of entering his rest still stands, let us be careful that none of you be found to have fallen short of it" (Hebrew 4:1)?

CHAPTER 2

THE GRAVES AT THE GATEWAY

Moses my servant is dead. Now then, you and all these people, get ready to cross the Jordan River into the land I am about to give to them—to the Israelites. (Joshua 1:2)

We have looked at the land, now let us look at the gateway. It leads past four solemn graves. Through death we enter into this higher life, and the deeper the death the higher the life will be. There is no principle so profound and so prominent in the plan of redemption as this principle of life through death. Indeed, we find it deeply written in the records of nature. The generations that live today are treading on the dust of former generations. The very plants on which animal and human life is sustained are the outgrowth of death, and they have sprung from the ashes of myriads of beings that once themselves were living creatures.

> Life evermore is fed by death,
> And joy by agony:
> And that a rose might breathe its breath,
> Something must die.

Spring itself, with all its glory, comes from the grave of winter; the waving harvests grow from buried seeds, and the corn and wheat must die before they bear their fruit of golden grain.

TYPES OF DEATH

The rite of circumcision, which was the initiatory ceremony of Judaism, is the symbol of death—the death of our natural life. Baptism has its chief significance in the same idea. All these symbols find their fulfillment in the cross of Jesus Christ, the cornerstone of redemption and the eternal memorial of life through death and salvation by suffering and sacrifice. The profoundest truths connected with our deeper spiritual life are associated with this idea of death. And so, in introducing the subject of sanctification, in the sixth chapter of Romans, the apostle teaches us that we must enter into union with the death of Christ, and thus into His resurrection life. "In the same way, count yourselves dead to sin but alive to God in Christ Jesus" (6:11).

And so, again, in Colossians (2:12), we are represented as dead with Christ, and risen again with Him, by virtue of His resurrection from the dead. It is all summed up in these pregnant words: "I have been crucified with Christ and I no longer live, but Christ lives in me. The life I live in the body, I live by faith in the Son of God, who loved me and gave himself for me" (Galatians 2:20).

This is the truth that lies back of the vivid symbolism of the book of Joshua. The Land of Promise, the great type of our full inheritance with Christ, was entered by the gateway of the grave. Four graves stand out before us in these opening chapters.

THE GRAVE OF MOSES

"Moses my servant is dead. Now then, you and all these people, get ready to cross the Jordan River" (Joshua 1:2).

The death of Moses has something very touching about it. Many of us have wept over that lonely grave on the heights of Nebo, and wondered why it should have been necessary for that brave, true heart to sink on the very threshold of his most glorious hope. And yet the death of Moses was essential to our higher life, for Moses never could lead Israel into the Land of Promise. This was something that Joshua alone could bring about. Moses represented the law, and "the law made nothing perfect, and a better hope is introduced, by which we draw near to God" (Hebrews 7:19). Moses represents human effort and the best that man can do; and man's best can never bring us into the land of victory over sin and full obedience to God. Therefore, Moses must break his own law and sink under its condemning blow, to prove forever to the world that all man's efforts to sanctify the soul are vain. And so in every individual life there must come a point where we pass out from under the law, and it becomes true—"For sin shall not be your master, because you are not under law, but under grace" (Romans 6:14).

There are thousands in the Church of Christ who fully believe in salvation by Christ, but they are struggling after sanctification by works. It is as impossible for man to purify his heart as it is for him to cancel the judgment of God against his sins; and so God has to let us strive and struggle chiefly that we may find out our own inability, and give up the struggle for the better way of Christ and His divine and complete salvation.

Sanctification is the obtainment of grace, not the attainment of effort.

True, it involves the most strenuous and mighty energy on our part, but it is all the divine fruit of God's working in us "to will and to act according to his good purpose" (Philippians 2:13). And we pass out of our works into His working, and from henceforth say: "To this end I labor, struggling with all his energy, which so powerfully works in me" (Colossians 1:29).

But there is a deeper death signified by the river Jordan.

THE GRAVE OF SELF AND SIN

"Now then, . . . get ready to cross the Jordan River" (Joshua 1:2).

We know that the Jordan is the symbol of death and judgment, and the crossing of the Jordan is the symbol of our partnership with the Lord Jesus Christ in that deeper death to self and sin of which the New Testament speaks so fully.

Some very suggestive things are brought out by the detailed account given in these opening chapters of the passage of the Jordan by the children of Israel.

1. We notice that it was a very definite act. They came up to a real river; they stepped in and passed over; they knew when they crossed it, and they knew that they were on the other side. And so this experience in our life must be very definite. We cannot glide into it; we cannot grow into it. We come to a point where we take a definite step that can never be undone, and can never be done over again. This is not a great marsh that spreads over leagues and miles, and in which we wade along indefinitely for half a lifetime; but it is a real river, of which there is no mistaking. There is a moment in every consecrated life when we come to the fords of this Jordan, when we pass sentence of death upon ourselves, and by one blow, by one definite act, forever pass out of ourselves into Christ and His fullness. From that time on our Christian life is as different from its former era as that was different from the time prior to our conversion.

2. It was difficult, as well as definite. We are told that when they crossed the Jordan the river overflowed all its banks, for it was the time of harvest; and it is always floodtime when God calls us into the experience of death. The thing He asks you to do is the most difficult thing He could ask of you, and the time is usually the hardest time when it could happen. When God aims a death-blow at us, He aims at the heart, and His aim is so true and sure that He never wants to repeat the blow. When man tries to crucify himself, he always manages to escape a vital point; but when God undertakes the work He chooses the thing which is the very key to the situation, and requires the sacrifice in which all your life is most intensely bound up. It is your Isaac that He demands; it is your life He seeks. If you are wise you will let Him have it promptly and unreservedly, and by one decisive and final act be done with the agony.

3. It is possible only through divine enabling. You cannot put yourself to

death; God alone can accomplish this work. You are just as unequal to the death as you are to the life. You can mutilate yourself, you can tantalize yourself, you can deny yourself a thousand things, but you cannot slay your sinful self. God must do that. We read in Romans 8:13, ". . . if by the Spirit you put to death the misdeeds of the body, you will live." It must be through the Spirit. And again the apostle says, "May I never boast except in the cross of our Lord Jesus Christ, through which the world has been crucified to me, and I to the world" (Galatians 6:14).

No one but Christ can crucify you. You cannot die alone, but must fall into the arms of Jesus, and hang with Him upon His cross, and let Him love your sinful soul to death.

Now, this is all set forth in the symbolism of Jordan. The people could not enter Jordan until the ark—which is ever the type of Christ—had preceded them. And it had to remain in the bed of the Jordan until they had all clean passed over, and then to follow up and finish the work which it had begun.

Jesus must lead us into the waters of death; He must stand with us through them, and must bring us out on the other side. We are helpless to preform any act of self-surrender or true consecration except by Him. We can pass sentence of death upon ourselves, we can yield up ourselves to the death-blow, but He must strike that blow, and we must trust Him to do it.

4. It must be an act of faith. The symbolism here is very fine. They had to step down to the very edge of the flood. Their feet had to touch the cold waters, and it was not until they were dipped into the brim, that the waters divided and the way appeared. And so our self-surrender must be right up to the edge of death itself. We must go forward until there is no way apparent, and God will not interpose until the very last hour. And then, as we march on right boldly, the sea will divide, and a way will be prepared, even in the midst of the flood, for our feet to walk upon dry ground.

5. It must be a very thorough work. We read that ". . . the priests who carried the ark remained standing in the middle of the Jordan until everything the LORD had commanded Joshua was done by the people, just as Moses had directed Joshua" (Joshua 4:10).

The people were no doubt very anxious to go over quickly. It was an awful journey; it was a terrific pathway; it was a trying hour; but right here, in the midst of the flood, they must stand unmoved, and listen to all God had to say—how long we know not, but long enough to accomplish a thorough and everlasting work.

We are in too great hurry to get through our transactions with God. The Holy Spirit will do thorough work if we will let Him. When God lays you low at His feet He wants you to listen to Him. There are things you can hear in the valley of the shadow of death that never can come to you again, and His word is, "Humble yourselves, therefore, under God's mighty hand, that he may lift you up in due time" (1 Peter 5:6). This is a place that you can never come to again; let nothing be wanting in its completeness. Let your heart answer back, "I will listen to what God the LORD will say" (Psalm 85:8); and the echoes of those messages will come back to you amid the hallelujahs of His coming.

6. Again, it was an enduring act. They brought up from the bed of Jordan memorial stones, and they planted them on the other shore as a memorial of that crossing, so that it could never be forgotten. And so, God wants us to remember this hour, and to be established in this experience forever. He wants you to be dead, and to know it. So He uses the strongest figure of arithmetic when He says "Count yourselves dead"—count by a process which admits of no evasion—"to sin but alive to God in Christ Jesus" (Romans 6:11).

THE GRAVE AT GILGAL

Next, we come to the third grave. It is the grave at Gilgal, which is the place where they were to be circumcised after they had crossed the Jordan. But why is this added symbol here introduced? Is it intended to emphasize especially the death of the flesh, and its affections and passions, as one of the things we need most carefully to watch? Or has it some broader and larger significance? Undoubtedly it does mean that we should be very sure that our self-crucifixion reaches to our natural life, and lays our tenderest affections and all our appetites and propensities at the feet of Jesus for His filling and consecration.

But it means more than this. The crossing of Jordan expresses the faith side of our dying; the circumcision at Gilgal, the experiential side. Jordan teaches us how to count ourselves dead, but Gilgal teaches us how to realize the dying in actual life.

Surely we all have learned the difference between these two things. There is a day in our spiritual life when we yield ourselves up unto God, and pass the sentence of death upon ourselves, and register it in heaven, and begin to count ourselves "dead to sin but alive to God in Christ Jesus." And there is another day when we step out into the battle of life, and find our old self, at the first temptation, rising up in all the strength of self-assertion, and refusing to be counted dead. Then it is that Gilgal comes in, and as we come face to face with the touch of God, He makes the death real. Helpless and distressed, we throw ourselves upon Him and claim the fulfillment and realization of the great transaction which we have so sincerely entered into. Then the Holy Spirit actually touches our inmost life with the sharp knife of His power and the consuming fire of His breath, and withers the evil that we cannot touch, and fills us with the life of purity which excludes the darkness through the coming in of the light. And so, day by day, as we go through the repeated tests, we find the promise holds; the faithful love and power of God continue to meet us, the counting becomes a reality, and the promise tried and proved.

Now all this is beautifully illustrated in the idea of crucifixion. Crucifixion was not an instantaneous dying, but a lingering death. And yet the victim was said to be crucified the moment he was suspended upon the cross.

It was high noon on that Friday which never shall be forgotten, when Jesus was hung by the cruel nails on Calvary's cross, but it was three o'clock in the afternoon before He died. Yet from the very first moment it was said by the sacred narrative: "They crucified him" (Mark 15:25). He was regarded as crucified from that midday hour; but it was not until hours later that He breathed out His glorious Spirit into His Father's arms, and went down amid the regions of the dead.

This is exactly fulfilled in the crucifixion of the believer with his Lord. There is a moment when we yield ourselves to be dead with Christ; and from that moment it is true, "I have been crucified with Christ" (Galatians 2:20). But after this there come hours and days of suffering, during which we are hanging with Him upon that cross, and a thousand voices are saying to us as they said to Him, "Come down from the cross and save yourself!" (Mark 15:30).

Oh, how many do that, and forfeit all they have suffered and done! It is of these that the apostle says: "Have you suffered so much for nothing?" (Galatians 3:4). But there are others who remain unmoved and undismayed through all the severity of the test, and it is to these that the Spirit comes with His love and power in the actual experience of the death.

How long these three hours represent, God only knows. Each life has its dark Friday and its dying day. The first of these is represented by the Jordan, and the second by the circumcision at Gilgal. And as "they remained where they were in camp until they were healed" (Joshua 5:8), so God holds us still until His testing is complete and the work is done. This must surely be the meaning of that passage in Philippians where the apostle prays, "I want to know Christ and the power of his resurrection and the fellowship of sharing in his sufferings, becoming like him in his death," (Philippians 3:10), after which comes the great hope, "and so, somehow, to attain to the resurrection from the dead" (3:11).

JOSHUA'S GRAVE

There is one more death. Even Joshua, the captain of the Lord's host, must die. The picture of his self-surrender is very striking and significant. Standing over against Jericho, perhaps at dead of night, reconnoitering the position, and thinking of the assault which he was about to make, suddenly there stood before him a man with his sword drawn in his hand. Not daunted, but every inch a soldier and a captain, Joshua went to him and asked, "Are you for us or for our enemies?" (Joshua 5:13). The answer came that thrilled his soul and laid him on his face before the supernatural Presence: " 'Neither,' he replied, 'but as commander of the army of the LORD I have now come.' Then Joshua fell facedown to the ground in reverence, and asked him, 'What message does my Lord have for his servant?' The commander of the LORD's army replied, 'Take off your sandals, for the place where you are standing is holy.' And Joshua did so" (5:14–15).

This was no other than the Son of God, the true Captain of the host. Joshua had supposed that he was captain, but henceforth his sword was laid down before the Captain of the Lord's host, and Joshua, with his shoes off his feet, took a servant's place, took his orders from above and followed when the Lord should lead.

This is the secret of Christian victory; this the place where we must come before we can be overcomers. This is the meaning of that sublime announcement of the apostle: "Thanks be to God, who always leads us in triumphal procession in Christ" (2 Corinthians 2:14). It is not our own strength that causes us to triumph. We are not the victors, but simply the followers of the great Commander, as He leads us conquering and to conquer. With such a Leader, we must always be victorious. But to have such a Leader we must die to our self-sufficiency and strength. There cannot be two commanders; you and Christ cannot both rule.

How much there is among consecrated Christians and the best of God's children that needs to be laid down at His feet! How much there is in our Christian service that reflects honor upon ourselves, or springs from self-consciousness! Sometimes it throws around us such a glamor that it dazzles us with its brilliancy, and we do it for the work's sake, rather than for the Lord's sake. All this is false and wrong. To all this we must die, so that our service will not be affected by the approval of others or their neglect, by the pleasantness of the surroundings, or the self-denial it costs us. We should be like the holy angels, of whom it has been said, that if they were sent to sweep a street crossing they would be just as willing as to minister in a palace, or to lead an army into victorious battle. The holy I, the pious I, the useful I, the spiritual I, the ecclesiastical I, the I that says, "I follow Paul, . . . I follow Apollos" (1 Corinthians 3:4)—all these must cease, and Christ alone be known and glorified. Then shall our service abide the testing day; then can Christ lead us through all the land of victory and power, and then shall "your light shine before men, that they may see your good deeds and praise your Father in heaven" (Matthew 5:16).

CHAPTER 3

THE TWO WATCHWORDS OF VICTORY

Joshua 1:1–9

Like the two wings of a bird, like the two oars of a boat, both essential to its proper movement, are the two principles of faith and obedience, which are ever linked together in a rightly regulated Christian life, and which are interwoven in the opening scenes of the book of Joshua. Let us look at them separately and then jointly.

THE WATCHWORD OF FAITH

The Land of Promise was won by faith. Every step was a step of faith: the Jordan was crossed by faith; by faith the walls of Jericho fell down after they had been compassed seven days; by faith Rahab was saved, and perished not with them who believed not. By faith every victory was achieved in their onward progress until at last Caleb had claimed the heights of Hebron, and Joshua had reached his inheritance at Timnath Serah. Here we have some of the features of faith most strongly emphasized.

PRESENT TENSE

1. We have the present tense of faith—Joshua 1:2b: "The land I am about to give to them—to the Israelites." God here speaks in the immediate present. It is not something He is going to do, but something He does do, this moment. So faith ever speaks. So God ever gives. So He is meeting you today, in the present moment.

This is the test of faith. So long as you are waiting for a thing, hoping for it, looking for it, you are not believing. It may be hope, it may be earnest desire, but it is not faith; for "faith is being sure of what we hope for and certain of what we do not see" (Hebrews 11:1).

21

God meets us first in the future tense, as He did Abraham, Genesis 17:2: "I will confirm my covenant between me and you." But He brings us immediately, if we are willing, into the present tense; so we read in Genesis 17:4: "As for me, this is my covenant with you . . ."

There must come a moment in your life when you really receive Christ as your Savior, and in that moment you are saved. There must come a crisis-hour when you yield yourself to Him, and take Him as your Sanctifier, and from that moment you are sanctified.

The command in regard to believing prayer is in the present tense. "Whatever you ask for in prayer, believe that you have received it, and it will be yours" (Mark 11:24). Have we come to that moment? Have we met God in His everlasting *now*?

PERFECT TENSE

2. We have next the perfect tense of faith. We see this in the third verse: "I will give you every place where you set your foot, as I promised Moses" (Joshua 1:3). The present has now become the perfect tense. That which but a moment ago was the present is now the perfect tense. And so in Genesis 17:5b we find the present tense passing into the perfect and God saying: ". . . for I have made you a father of many nations." This is perfectly consistent. God cannot repeat Himself or allow His words to be of no effect. When He speaks it is done; when He commands, it stands fast. And He is pleased to have us recognize His work as perfect and His word as everlasting, and step out upon it in unfaltering confidence.

So we find Him speaking in His own Word, of Jesus as "the Lamb that was slain from the creation of the world" (Revelation 13:8), although it was not actually fulfilled until the world was 4,000 years old; but His purpose and His promise were counted fulfilled, and God speaks in the language of faith and certainty.

IMPERATIVE MOOD

3. We have the imperative mood of faith, Joshua 1:9: "Have I not commanded you? Be strong and courageous. Do not be terrified; do not be discouraged." This is the faith that falters not, fears not, refuses to be dismayed, but with defiant courage goes forth and faces every foe. It says, with Isaiah 50:7: "Because the Sovereign LORD helps me,/ I will not be disgraced./ Therefore have I set my face like flint,/ and I know I will not be put to shame." And with Paul: "However, I consider my life worth nothing to me . . ." (Acts 20:24). ". . . that I will in no way be ashamed . . . so that now as always Christ will be exalted in my body . . ." (Philippians 1:20). "Because I know whom I have believed, and am convinced that he is able to guard what I have entrusted to him for that day" (2 Timothy 1:12).

Our faith must not only be real, but it must be strong; sometimes it must be audacious. The faintest fear will paralyze it. A quiver in that regimental line will bring disaster and defeat to the whole army. There must be unfaltering steadiness and bold defiance throughout. Unbelief always begins in little doubts and fears, and God reiterates the command, "Do not be anxious about anything . . ." (Philippians 4:6). "Therefore do not worry about tomorrow . . ." (Matthew 6:34). Not with the fiery artillery of hell is our faith first assaulted, but by an army of little moths, with their soft touch and velvet wings; and soon our spiritual garment is riddled and ruined before the real fight begins. If we would win in the conflict of faith, we must stand without fear, unfaltering and unmoved, and resist in the imperative mood of victorious confidence.

ACTIVE VOICE

4. Next there is the active voice of faith. True faith expresses itself in action. It reaches the soles of our feet, and steps out in actual movements that prove its reality and sincerity. We read of "the footsteps of the faith that our father Abraham had" (Romans 4:12). Faith has steppingstones. So their faith expressed itself; first, in their stepping into the waters of the Jordan, and next in their circuit of Jericho for seven days. Their faith was not only active, but persistent. They continued to go through the whole testing until it was thoroughly proved and finally triumphant. So our faith must ever step out and claim its blessing until it fully receives it. It was as the lepers *went*, that they were healed. Had they lingered pleading at the feet of Jesus, they never would have been healed; but when they moved forward in obedience to the Master's command, they found His promise awaiting them as they advanced.

It was as Naaman stepped into the Jordan at the command of Elisha, that his healing came. But he had to do it more than once; seven times he had to persevere until his faith was fully proved, and then the answer came. It is in the midst of the proving that faith often breaks down. It is easy to take one bold step, but a patient continuance in the work of faith tries the inmost soul.

Their faith had not only to encompass Jericho seven days, but on the seventh day it had to rise to a height to which it had not before attained, and with sevenfold patience and perseverance complete the circuit over and over again until the trial was complete, and the shout of victory came at last.

It must have been very hard. To their own rational sense it must have seemed strange, and to the people of Jericho, no doubt, it looked contemptible. One can see them gathering on the walls as, day after day, the procession was resumed, until at last it became ridiculous; and doubtless on the seventh day the circuit was scarcely noticed. But on and on those faithful soldiers marched, until at last, their movements became accelerated, and quicker and quicker their footsteps repeated that course until, as the sun went down, the last round was finished, the trumpets gave the signal, the shouts of the people rent the heavens, and with a resounding crash, the walls of Jericho tumbled down before the assault of victorious faith.

Again, we see faith following up God's working, in the story of Jericho. In answer to their advance and their shout of faith, the walls of faith fell down; but this would have been unavailing if they had not at once followed up God's mighty working and marched in at the open gates. And so we read that "every man charged straight in, and they took the city" (Joshua 6:20). So in our lives there is ever a place for the faith which recognizes God's mighty working and advances along the lines which He has prepared.

Once more we have an illustration of faith in the saving of Rahab. We learn that this glorious principle of action is not only for the higher stages of our Christian life, but that the vilest sinner may rise through it into the place of pardon and salvation. Rahab was the vilest of the Canaanites, but that little scarlet cord which she hung from the walls of her house, that crimson sign of her trust in God and the word of His messengers, was sufficient to obliterate the stains of her whole life, and to place her in the very line of His redeemed—yes, among the very ancestors of Christ Himself.

This is the watchword by which we too must enter our land of promise. By the faith that believes and receives forgiveness and salvation, before we feel it, must we pass from condemnation into justification. By the faith that takes Christ as our sanctification and reckons ourselves dead indeed to sin, but alive unto God through Jesus Christ our Lord, must we cross the Jordan and take our inheritance of full salvation. By faith must we receive the Holy Spirit and recognize His indwelling before we feel His touch. By faith must we overcome our enemies, and utter the shout of victory in the thickest of the fight. By faith we must receive the answers to our prayers and turn them into praises and thanksgivings, before we witness their fulfillment. "Now we who have believed enter that rest . . ." (Hebrews 4:3). "See to it, brothers, that none of you has a sinful, unbelieving heart that turns away from the living God" (3:12).

Let us claim the faith that receives the promise in the present tense, that confesses it in the perfect tense, that triumphs in the imperative mood, and that conjugates it through all its moods and tenses, until it can write under every promise, "tried and proved," and over every difficulty, "more than conquerors through him who loved us" (Romans 8:37).

THE WATCHWORD OF OBEDIENCE

This is just as emphatic as the other. "Be strong and very courageous. Be careful to obey all the law my servant Moses gave you; do not turn from it to the right or to the left, that you may be successful wherever you go" (Joshua 1:7).

"Do not let this Book of the Law depart from your mouth; meditate on it day and night, so that you may be careful to do everything written in it. Then you will be prosperous and successful" (1:8).

Here we have the various moods and tenses of obedience.

INTELLIGENT

1. It must be intelligent and diligent. "Be careful to obey" (1:7). It is not merely the blundering and clumsy obedience of careless feet, but the earnest, thoughtful, watchful obedience of the whole mind and soul and heart. It takes pains to find out the will of God, as well as to do it; it heeds and hearkens, as well as runs to do His bidding. How often hearkening is emphasized in the Old Testament! "To obey is better than sacrifice,/ and to heed is better than the fat of rams" (1 Samuel 15:22b). The obedient heart is one that listens for the whisper of His voice, watching daily at wisdom's door to know the heavenly message, and diligently observing that it make no mistake. Most of the failures and faults of our lives arise not from intent, but from culpable ignorance. We ought to have known better, and our ignorance will not excuse us. Therefore, a spirit of meditation upon God's law, and thorough familiarity with it, is required on the part of Joshua. Do we thus study our Bible? Do we meditate on its precepts day and night? Do we thus diligently compare our lives with His Word? Do we regulate our hearts, our homes and our conversations according to His Word? Do we deal with our friends and our foes according to the very Word of God?

A sanctified life is a life conformed to the Scriptures in every particular. It commences with our hearts; it next reaches our ears, and then it is accomplished in our feet. First, we love the Lord our God with all our heart, next we hearken to His voice, and finally we walk in all His ways. Hence, in the anointing of the ancient priest, the thumb of the right hand was anointed as a symbol of the faith that takes God's promises; and the right ear and the right foot as an expression of the obedience that hearkens and follows.

We need a very attentive ear and a very watchful spirit to escape being deceived and to avoid missing the Master's perfect will. There is no more solemn instance in all the Old Testament than the story of the nameless prophet who came from Judah to Bethel, in the days of Jeroboam, and at God's command boldly denounced the idolatry of Israel's king and bore witness for Jehovah with magnificent fidelity, and at the risk of his life. Then he started home, but on his way, disobeyed Jehovah in a very small and apparently trifling thing. God had told him to go home without lingering on the way, and not to enter any man's house until he had left the accursed land. But on his way back, another prophet enticed him by telling him that he also was a prophet, and had received a word from the Lord, bidding him to tarry for a night at this house. He listened to the insidious temptation, went home with the false prophet, and the next day as he was pursuing his way home a lion met him on the way and devoured him because he had broken the command of his God.

God would thus emphasize the meaning of real obedience, and the way He regards the slightest deviation from His perfect law. And though He has in His great longsuffering, often borne with many of us, none the less does He hate our negligence, and sometimes indifference; and none the less does real holiness and obedience involve such watchful and entire regard to His slightest word.

INVARIABLE

2. But our obedience must be invariable and inflexible—"do not turn from it to the right or to the left" (Joshua 1:7). There can be no compromise about it; it is as inflexible with respect to the least as to the greatest command. The highest test of the spirit of obedience is always given in some little thing. When God hung the testing of the human race upon a single act in the garden of Eden, it was not a great act, but a simple abstinence from a single indulgence, so slight as to be in itself unimportant; but for that very reason the greater test of the spirit of obedience. When a thing itself is insignificant we do it not for its own sake, or because of its intrinsic value, but because we have respect for the will of our Master. Therefore, in almost every case, the most fatal acts of disobedience are little compromises. A bold and daring act of wickedness compels us to recognize our awful position and carries with it a certain check; but a trifling compromise escapes the ordinary conscience, and leads on by imperceptible stages to the final and farthest degrees of disobedience and sin. Saul lost his kingdom, not by refusing to do what God commanded him, but by doing nearly all that he was sent to do, and simply compromising on one little detail. He went against Amalek, he took much trouble and underwent many sacrifices, perhaps risked his life in the campaign, defeated armies and destroyed cities, and thought he had done all that he had been told to do; but he simply put aside a little of the spoil for himself and received the awful rebuke, "To obey is better than sacrifice,/ and to heed is better than the fat of rams" (1 Samuel 15:22b). "Because you have rejected the word of the LORD,/ he has also rejected you as king" (15:23b).

David has emphasized in the 119th Psalm this essential quality of true obedience in these great words: "and because I consider all your precepts right,/ I hate every wrong path" (119:128).

And Jesus put it into a still more emphatic sentence in His words to His disciples: "You are my friends if you do what I command" (John 15:14).

TESTED AT AI

As the principle of faith was illustrated in the early incidents of the book of Joshua, by the story of Jericho, so the principle of obedience is exemplified in the failure of Achan and the defeat of Israel at Ai.

Flushed with their first victory, Israel's hosts marched against Ai expecting an easy triumph. But they were surprised to find that their hosts were hurled back in defeat. Joshua threw himself on his face before the Lord. God would not listen to his prayers, but commanded him immediately to arise and put away the sin which had brought dishonor to Israel and separated them from the presence and blessing of God. "I will not be with you anymore" was the awful threatening, "unless you destroy whatever among you is devoted to destruction" (Joshua 7:12b). How solemn the lesson! How fearful the effect of a single sin!

But there was a remedy for their disobedience; the sin was to be acknowledged, brought into the light and put away forever; and then God said, in that wonderful message, "Do not be afraid; . . . For I have delivered into your hands the king of Ai, his people, his city and his land" (8:1b).

REMEDY FOR DISOBEDIENCE

Is there a remedy for the disobedience of the sanctified Christian? Yes! Surely God is not less merciful to His dear children than He is to the ungodly world, and it is graciously true of us, His people, that "if we confess our sins, he is faithful and just and will forgive us our sins and purify us from all unrighteousness" (1 John 1:9). The way is very simple: confess; call the evil by its right name; recognize it in God's light; do not excuse or palliate it, or call it by some complimentary term, but bring it out into full light of God's holiness and forever abandon it as an accursed thing. The blood of Jesus will not only expiate it but will wash away the stain and cleanse you from all unrighteousness, restoring you to more than your former place in God's fellowship and favor.

We have still further illustration in this book of Joshua of the true spirit of obedience in the incident related in the ninth chapter, with respect to the Gibeonites. It will be remembered that these men came in disguise pretending that they were pilgrims from a far country, and by their wiles they inveigled Joshua into a treaty with them which became a permanent snare. This illustrates the spirit of watchful obedience and hearkening to God, and the necessity of constant vigilance, if we would know His perfect will and not be deceived by the wiles of the adversary.

And so these two words—faith and obedience—are interwoven with the story of the first Canaan, even as they are inseparable from any true experience of our higher spiritual inheritance. Indeed, faith and obedience are the reverse sides of the same shield. When Abraham's faith is spoken of in the Epistle to the Hebrews, it is called obedience. "By faith Abraham, when called to go to a place he would later receive as an inheritance, *obeyed*" (Hebrews 11:8). And indeed, the old Saxon word "believe" is just a combination of the two words "live" and "by." To believe is to "live by" the thing you believe; that is, to translate it into your daily life and conduct. Hence the apostle speaks of those who not "holding on to faith and a good conscience . . . have rejected these and so have shipwrecked their faith" (1 Timothy 1:19). You cannot obey rightly without a true faith, and you cannot keep a true faith if you cease to obey. Let us join together the wings of faith and obedience, and so mount up into the heavenly places and press our glorious way into the heights of grace and glory.

CHAPTER 4

THE CONFLICT AND THE CONQUEROR

Finally, be strong in the Lord and in his mighty power. Put on the full armor of God so that you can take your stand against the devil's schemes. For our struggle is not against flesh and blood, but against the rulers, against the authorities, against the powers of this dark world and against the spiritual forces of evil in the heavenly realms. Therefore put on the full armor of God, so that when the day of evil comes, you may be able to stand your ground, and after you have done everything, to stand. Stand firm then, with the belt of truth buckled around your waist, with the breastplate of righteousness in place, and with your feet fitted with the readiness that comes from the gospel of peace. In addition to all this, take up the shield of faith, with which you can extinguish all the flaming arrows of the evil one. Take the helmet of salvation and the sword of the Spirit, which is the word of God. And pray in the Spirit on all occasions with all kinds of prayers and requests. With this in mind, be alert and always keep on praying for all the saints. (Ephesians 6:10–18)

The book of Joshua is a story of conflict and victory. Almost every chapter echoes the thought of this picture in Ephesians of our spiritual warfare with the principalities and powers in heavenly realms.

CONQUERING BUT NOT POSSESSING

But to the Reubenites, the Gadites and the half-tribe of Manasseh, Joshua said, "Remember the command that Moses the servant of the LORD gave you: 'The LORD your God is giving you rest and has granted you this land.' Your wives, your children and your livestock may stay in the land that Moses gave you east of the Jordan, but all your fighting men, fully armed, must cross over ahead of

29

your brothers. You are to help your brothers until the LORD gives them rest, as he has done for you, and until they too have taken possession of the land that the LORD your God is giving them. After that, you may go back and occupy your own land, which Moses the servant of the LORD gave you east of the Jordan toward the sunrise." (Joshua 1:12–15)

Here we have the story of the Reubenites, the Gadites and the half-tribe of Manasseh. They had chosen their inheritance on the wilderness side of Jordan. But they were required by the Lord to leave their wives and children in their inheritance, and pass on with their brethren and assist them in fighting their battles and conquering the western tribes and nations. This they did; and not until Joshua had subdued the whole land did they return to Gilead and settle down with their families on their chosen heritage.

Now this, at first sight, looks like a brave and loyal course. They sacrificed the comforts of home. They separated from those who were dear to them. They risked their lives and exposed themselves to dangers and toils to fight the battles of the Lord. They crossed the Jordan and fought the giants of Canaan. Are they not examples of a high and holy consecration and a most unselfish victory?

This is all true; but back of it the fact remains that they had deliberately chosen their inheritance on the other side of Jordan, in the land that bordered on the world, and they went back to it as soon as they were through their campaign, and made it their permanent home.

They are types of a great many people who believe in the truths of a higher Christian life, who testify for them, who contend earnestly for them, who fight their battles, who help others to enter into them, who lead, perhaps, hundreds of souls into deeper blessing, who pass through, in a certain sense, the experience of Jordan, and live for a time in the Land of Promise and know much of the deeper things of God. But they do not stay there. Their chosen rest is somewhere nearer the world, and they always recognize their home and resting place as on the wilderness side.

It is possible to know all about these things in theory. It is possible to have a certain experience of them for a time, and yet to be sojourners, not residents. It is possible to be working for the truth rather than enjoying it and living it, and to settle down at last, not, perhaps, in the world, but on its borders. But you will have the same results as these trans-Jordanic tribes did in the end: that the world, beside which they so willingly sat down, at last sweeps over them and finally almost blots them out of existence.

Where are we living? Where are our interests and affections invested? Where have you got your money? What is your real home and the center of your life?

It is not enough to be fighting for the truth and helping others to receive it. Are you yourself living it, and wholly committed to it? Which side of Jordan is your home?

FIGHTING AND NOT PREVAILING

"Israel has sinned; and they have violated my covenant, which I commanded them to keep. They have taken some of the devoted things, they have stolen, they have lied, they have put them with their own possessions. This is why the Israelites cannot stand against their enemies . . . because they have been made liable to destruction. I will not be with you anymore unless you destroy whatever among you is devoted to destruction" (Joshua 7:11–12).

We here see the hosts of Israel for the first time turned back before their enemies. There was no lack of faith, apparently, for their confidence was so great that they attacked Ai with a small contingent, and expected it would be an easy victory. But they were ignominiously routed and defeated. The reason was very plain: they had sinned, and sin always brings defeat and failure. Faith cannot live except in an atmosphere of purity; the slightest disobedience will wither it and leave us exposed to the successful fury of our foes. God was obliged to dishonor even His own cause rather than countenance evil. One enemy in the camp is worse than a million in front. We must keep pure and walk in obedience, or we shall always fail. "Holding on to faith and a good conscience . . . some have rejected these and so have shipwrecked their faith" (1 Timothy 1:19).

RISING OUT OF FAILURE AND DEFEAT

"Then the LORD said to Joshua, 'Do not be afraid; do not be discouraged. Take the whole army with you, and go up and attack Ai. For I have delivered into your hands the king of Ai, his people, his city and his land' " (Joshua 8:1).

Here we see the army which yesterday was flying from their pursuers, today marching forward with undismayed, victorious tread, and carrying all before them.

The secret was very simple: they had put away their sin, and God had also put it away; and now He meets them with a yet bolder assurance of victory and blessing.

There is still for us the same remedy. When sin has come between us and the Lord, there is but one thing for us to do: it must be definitely recognized and utterly put away. We must go right back to the very thing, however hard, and deal with it definitely and thoroughly. Then all the train of sins and sorrows that came with it will pass away, and God will start afresh with us, as if it had never been. The simple direction in the New Testament is, "If we confess our sins, he is faithful and just and will forgive us our sins and purify us from all unrighteousness" (1 John 1:9).

This one little word "confess" is explicit and unambiguous. It does not mean merely to ignore it, or even to be sorry for it, but to recognize it, identify it, and call it by its right name.

What God wants is to bring the evil to light, strip it of its disguises, force it out of its hiding place and bring it into the light of His Holy Word, so that it can never again deceive us. And therefore we must confess it to God, to ourselves, and, if any one else has been wronged, to the one we have injured. Then God will immediately forgive it, cleanse it and clear away all the avalanche that has accumulated around it.

If I have a thorn in my finger, it will fester; my hand will swell, my arm will become involved, and gradually my whole body will suffer, and I will die if the trouble continues. What am I to do? Treat the finger, the hand and the arm with lotions and plasters? No, take out the thorn. Until you do that all the treatment is vain; but the moment you remove the irritating thorn the trouble will cease.

Back of all your defects, temptations and wrongs, there is one little fault in which all the trouble began. Go back at once, lay your pride in the dust; don't be afraid to confess that you have lost your sanctification. You have not lost Jesus, but you cannot touch Him again until you recognize this thing and lay it on the sin-offering. Then, in a moment, He will become your righteousness, and go on with you as before.

You may hang on to the fiction of your sanctification all you please, but ever back of it lies the fact of your unconfessed sin, which will explode all your hopes like a sunken torpedo.

A friend said publicly, a few days ago, "Almost all our troubles and spiritual difficulties would be removed if we would just call things by their right names."

There is a whole world of truth in this simple thought. God is utterly upright and honest, and we must deal honestly with Him and with ourselves if we would "walk in the light"—"If we walk in the light, as he is in the light, we have fellowship with one another, and the blood of Jesus, his Son, purifies us from all sin" (1 John 1:7).

We need not be afraid of the light and all its disclosures, because the blood is ever there to cleanse.

Let us welcome our great High Priest, who comes to us with the lamp in one hand and the hyssop in the other, to cleanse the sin that He reveals, and to keep us by the sprinkling of His blood, so cleansed and purified that we shall not fear the light, but gladly come to it, "so that it may be seen plainly that what he has done has been done through God" (John 3:21b).

THE WILES OF THE DEVIL

Our great adversary does not usually make his attacks openly. He is a master of strategy, and his greatest art is to hide his hand and to attack us in disguise.

His choicest argument is to try to prove to people that there is no devil. Nothing pleases him so much as to lose his identity, and when he comes to us, to persuade us that his insinuations and suggestions are the voice of God, or the thoughts of our own minds. He loves "to . . . call evil good and good evil" (Isaiah 5:20). He is adept in mixing moral principles and compromising things. He is a great diplomat, and our greatest need of divine equipment is that we "can take [our] stand against the devil's schemes" (Ephesians 6:11b).

We see all this very finely illustrated and typified in the conduct of the Gibeonites, in the ninth chapter of Joshua. They found they could not resist Israel in open warfare, and so they resorted to subterfuge. Disguised as travelers from a far country, arrayed in old clothes, and carrying provisions that seemed to have been brought from distant lands, they pretended that they were a company of pilgrims from afar. Before Joshua had taken time to counsel with the Lord, he was entrapped into a league with them, contrary to the divine command, and was obliged to keep them in Israel under honorable protection through all the coming centuries. True, they were degraded to the rank of servants, but their presence and influence were there all the same, and they became snares and sources of temptation which eventually led to loss of the national separation, and the judgments of God upon Israel's backsliding.

Oh, how many Christians have been led into similar compromises! Some evil course has been presented to you under the guise of harmless indulgence, or possibly divine revelation. Some compromise with evil has been made under the plea of doing good to someone and obtaining an influence over him for his spiritual benefit. Some business partnership has been formed which has entangled you in all your financial affairs for the rest of your life, and put your money at the disposal of the devil and the world, because you allowed yourself to be drawn into this compromise under some plausible pretext.

How many times a Christian girl has allowed herself to become attached to an ungodly man in order to save him, and given her life to him in marriage, and the result has been that either both are lost, or she is held back and embarrassed in all the future by his unholy influence.

The Church is full of Gibeonites today, and they are leading her into backsliding and imbecility.

What is the remedy? It is very plain. "The men of Israel sampled their provisions but did not inquire of the LORD" (Joshua 9:14).

They are not blamed for exercising bad judgment. They are not condemned for lack of wisdom, for it was a case where their wisdom was wholly unequal to the emergency, and where they were absolutely dependent upon the will of God. Confident in their own good sense, they did as sensible people so often do—they relied upon their own judgment and made a fatal error.

Oh how true it is that "the wayfaring men, though fools, shall not err therein" (Isaiah 35:8c, KJV), but "He catches the wise in their craftiness" (Job 5:13a).

In this heavenly life we are insufficient even to think anything as of ourselves, but we must ever depend upon the mind of Christ and the counsel of the Holy Spirit, or we shall fall into continual error and be involved in the most fatal mistakes.

"Trust in the LORD with all your heart/ and lean not on your own understanding;/ in all your ways acknowledge him,/ and he will make your paths straight" (Proverbs 3:5–6). "He who trusts in himself is a fool" (28:26a), but "whoever trusts in the LORD is kept safe" (29:25b).

TREADING ON CONQUERED FOES

> Joshua said, "Open the mouth of the cave and bring those five kings out to me." So they brought the five kings out of the cave—the kings of Jerusalem, Hebron, Jarmuth, Lachish and Eglon. When they had brought these kings to Joshua, he summoned all the men of Israel and said to the army commanders who had come with him, "Come here and put your feet on the necks of these kings." So they came forward and placed their feet on their necks. (Joshua 10:22–24)

This is a picture of our attitude toward our great adversary. We are not equal to the conflict if we allow him to get on our level. If we meet him breast-high, we shall be struck by his dragon wing. But if we keep him under our feet, we shall be upheld.

"The God of peace will soon crush Satan under your feet" (Romans 16:20). "I have given you authority to trample on snakes and scorpions and to overcome all the power of the enemy; nothing will harm you" (Luke 10:19).

Christ has conquered our enemies and He brings them forth to us and bids us put our feet where He has already put His, and we must not fear to do so. We must boldly take a stand, and we shall have victory.

We must not give place to the devil. Nothing encourages him so much as fear, and nothing dwarfs him and drives him away so quickly as audacity.

If you for a moment acknowledge his power, you give him that power. If you for a moment recognize that he is in you, you will find that he is in you.

If you let the thought or consciousness of evil into your spirit, you have lost your purity. If you "count yourself dead to sin" (Romans 6:11), you will find that you are "dead to sin." If you recognize him as in your heart, he will stay in your heart. If you put your foot upon his neck and stand in victory, shouting, "thanks be to God, who always leads us in triumphal procession in Christ" (2 Corinthians 2:14), you shall hold your victorious stand, and be "more than conquerors through him who loved us" (Romans 8:37).

UNCOMPROMISING WAR

"Except for the Hivites living in Gibeon, not one city made a treaty of peace with the Israelites, who took them all in battle" (Joshua 11:19).

This was a war of extermination, or should have been. These Hivites should never have been admitted to peace. They were the Gibeonites who made the forbidden league with Joshua.

There was no possible meeting ground between Israel and the Canaanites. One was the seed of Satan, the other the seed of God. And so in our spiritual warfare there is no place for compromise.

God can do more with a single, uncompromising Christian than with a whole nation of mixed people.

There is no more extraordinary spectacle than the contrast between the kingdom of Judah and the men of Babylon.

For more than six centuries God tried through Judah's kings and priests and prophets to magnify His name among the heathen, but they always failed Him.

There was much good in them. There was a Jehoshaphat, a Hezekiah, a Josiah, an Isaiah, a Jeremiah, a Hosea, and many a holy prophet; but there was a mixture of worldliness, idolatry and sin which always checked the perfect blessing and qualified the best service.

Consequently, Judah failed, and at last even the temple had to fall. The name of God was blasphemed among the heathen, and Nebuchadnezzar glorified his gods because they had triumphed over the God of Israel.

Then God rejected the nation and selected the individual.

He took out a Daniel, a Shadrach, a Meshach, an Abednego; and, first of all, he separated them from the evil of their time and gave them a purpose and a principle which they refused to compromise with anything contrary to the will of God.

The secret of their victory was all expressed in two single sentences:

> But Daniel resolved not to defile himself with the royal food and wine. (Daniel 1:8a)

> Shadrach, Meshach, and Abednego replied to the king, "O

Nebuchadnezzar, we do not need to defend ourselves before you in this matter. If we are thrown into the blazing furnace, the God we serve is able to save us from it, and he will rescue us from your hand, O king. But even if he does not, we want you to know, O king, that we will not serve your gods or worship the image of gold you have set up." (3:16–18)

This was the challenge, and the battle was short but decisive. Such men must ever be victorious.

Before the story of their life was all told, God had humbled Babylon and Persia, and the two proudest kings of antiquity had issued a decree that there was no God like Jehovah, and even provided for the restoration of Israel and the return of the captives to Jerusalem.

Four uncompromising men were stronger than all the kings of Judah and all the pride and power of Nebuchadnezzar and Cyrus. These are the men that God wants in these last days—wholly consecrated and utterly uncompromising men who will stand where God has placed them, and on whom heaven can wholly depend.

RECOGNIZING GOD'S HAND OVER THE HAND OF OUR ENEMIES

"For it was the LORD himself who hardened their hearts to wage war against Israel, so that he might destroy them totally, exterminating them without mercy, as the LORD had commanded Moses" (Joshua 11:20).

It must often have seemed discouraging to Joshua and his brave followers, after each successive victory, to see still before him fortress after fortress, and foe after foe, and to find the campaign renewed again and again, until slowly the whole land was successfully subjugated. But as each enemy came with fiercest hate and strongest force, we are told that "it was the LORD himself who hardened their hearts to wage war against Israel in battle" (11:20a).

God sent each one of them in turn—not a single one was accidental. Every one of these tests was needed, and, unconsciously to themselves, they were fulfilling the Word of God and becoming tributary to His great purpose.

There are two ways that God can use a man. One is with the intelligent and loving consent of the man, as a fellow worker with God. The other is to be used in spite of himself, by the sovereign will of God overruling his life in mighty power for the glory of God and the good of others.

It is a very awful thing to be used in this way; but God will use everything, even the wrath of man and the hate of Satan.

Some people are called to go as angels on missions of love; some are called to be street scavengers, sewers or files, to keep God's people pure and sweet.

If that is your business, go ahead and do it. God can use you to teach His people patience. But God have mercy on you when He is done with you!

Everything that comes in our life is permitted of God, for our complete training. Everything that reveals itself in your own heart and life is a part of God's final plan, to show you that thing in order that you may be saved from it, be strengthened against it, and be made a better man through the discovery.

When you find anything wrong in your heart and life, rejoice that you find it. Take victory over it, and go on praising God for His faithfulness.

When you meet an enemy that is too strong for you, rejoice and fall back on God, who will give you power to come back a victor, and stronger for that temptation.

"Blessed is the man who perseveres under trial, because when he has stood the test, he will receive the crown of life that God has promised to those who love him" (James 1:12).

Do not attempt to run away from your life, but let it make you run to God for more of His fullness and grace, and you will often sing,

> Happy for me was the thorn that stung,
> And sent my heart crying to Thee;
> Thanks for the sorrow that taught me to find
> Thy grace all-sufficient for me.

THE CAPTAIN OF OUR SALVATION

The secret of victory is all found in the vision of the Captain.

"Now when Joshua was near Jericho, he looked up and saw a man standing in front of him with a drawn sword in his hand. Joshua went up to him and asked, 'Are you for us or for our enemies?' 'Neither,' he replied, 'but as commander of the army of the LORD I have now come.' Then Joshua fell facedown to the ground in reverence, and asked him, 'What message does my LORD have for his servant?' " (Joshua 5:13–14).

We are accustomed to think of Joshua as the type of Christ, and Moses as the type of the law. But I believe this is a mistake. Joshua is simply the pattern of a man of faith, and Christ Himself seems to be revealed, in this book, not in Joshua, but in the Captain whom Joshua met as he stood over against Jericho.

This was none other than the Son of God, our victorious Leader, who wants to bring us also into the Land of Promise, if we, like Joshua, will die to our own strength, and accept Him as our leader and our Lord.

Have we done so?

All our experiences, all our toils, all our failures are meant to teach us our utter insufficiency. It is not His help we need; it is Himself as our All in All.

We have proved the promise, "I will strengthen you" (Isaiah 41:10c), but that is not sufficient.

We have tested the great word, "I will . . . help you" (41:10c), but even His help has not been enough. We have come to the end of all this, and, fainting at His feet, we have sunk in utter despair.

Then it is that the greatest promise comes, "I will uphold you with my righteous right hand" (41:10d).

This is something more. This is His upholding altogether, when He takes us in His very arms and carries us Himself and we just trust and see Him triumph.

Then, indeed, we shall accept the testimony of the apostle, "Not that we are competent in ourselves to claim anything for ourselves, but our competence comes from God" (2 Corinthians 3:5); and of this greater word, "Thanks be to God, who always leads us in triumphal procession in Christ" (2:14).

CHAPTER 5

THIRTY-ONE KINGS, OR THE VICTORY OVER SELF

These are the kings of the land that Joshua and the Israelites conquered on the west side of the Jordan . . . thirty-one kings in all. (Joshua 12:7, 24)

Arba, who was the greatest man among the Anakites. (14:15)

From Hebron Caleb drove out the three Anakites—Sheshai, Ahiman and Talmai—descendants of Anak. (15:14)

For Christ's love compels us, because we are convinced that one died for all, and therefore all died. And he died for all, that those who live should no longer live for themselves but for him who died for them and was raised again. (2 Corinthians 5:14–15)

These words describe the great conflict of the higher Christian life in the Land of Promise. This is not a conflict with the grosser forms of sin, for we leave them behind us when we cross the Jordan and come into the land of holiness, obedience and rest.

Surely it ought to go without saying that no consecrated Christian would dare to indulge in willful disobedience or sin. But there are other foes more subtle, and these are symbolized, we believe, by these kings with whom Joshua made war so long.

They are the various forms of self-life which, while not perhaps directly and willfully sinful, in the grosser sense, are yet as contrary to the will of God, and as necessary to be subdued and slain, before the soul can be in perfect harmony with the divine will. They are all tyrants which, if allowed to remain, will ultimately bring us into subjection to sin and separate us from the Lord.

They belong to one family, and the progenitor of every one of them is

Arba, the father of Anak; and his firstborn son, Anak, has perpetuated his generation through many children. The numerous offspring constitute a line of no less than 31, so that there is a foe for every day of the month, in the Christian's calendar.

The name Arba means "the strength of Baal." This represents the strength of the natural heart. Baal was the ancient Sidonian god of nature, and Arba stands for the natural heart, in all the force of its self-will and self-sufficiency.

The name of his son, Anak, signifies in Hebrew "long-necked," and everybody knows that a long neck suggests pride and self-will; so that these two names express the character of the whole family.

The other three sons whose names are mentioned, Sheshai, Ahiman and Talmai, carry out the family resemblance.

Sheshai means "free," suggesting the idea of the license in which selfishness delights.

Talmai means "bold," representing the independence of the self-life, which brooks no control.

Ahiman means "brother of men," and expresses aptly the humanism which ignores God, and would make humanity a god unto itself, expressing the self-sufficiency of the race rather than of the individual.

Shall we look at these kings of the old Self Dynasty, and see if we can recognize any of them in our own experience?

SELF-WILL

This is old Arba, the head of the dynasty. It expresses its decrees in the personal pronoun and the active verb—I will, I shall. It recognizes no king but its own imperative choice.

Arba must die before Hebron can be won by Caleb. Self-will must be slain before love can reign.

Yield yourself unto God, is the watchword at the gate of holiness and peace.

It is not only the evil will, but the self-will that must die. Things that it would be right for us to have, God cannot give us when we want them willfully, and therefore He has often to crucify us to our own will, for no other reason than to break us, and make us self-surrendered and wholly subjected to His control.

Often, therefore, in our lives, we have had to surrender something to Him which He really wished us to have. Later in our life, when we no longer wanted it because we wanted it, but because it was His will for us, He could trust us with it without harm, and it was freely given, when we could receive it no longer as a selfish idol, but as a divine trust.

So God had to take Isaac from Abraham, and then give him back as no longer Abraham's Isaac, but God's.

The will thus surrendered becomes a stronger will, because it is henceforth not our will, but His within us; and when we choose, we choose with the strength of God, and choose forever.

Have we yielded our will and received His in return? Has the city of Arba become the city of Hebron, and the home of His love?

SELF-INDULGENCE.

This is the gratification of self in any of its forms.

Is it wrong to eat and drink, and indulge our appetites? No, the act may not be wrong in itself, but it becomes wrong when we do it for the sake of the indulgence. I am not to eat because it gratifies me to eat; I am not to drink because I enjoy the act, but I am to eat and drink for the glory of God; that is, with the distinct thought and purpose of pleasing Him and ministering to my bodily wants that I may be strong to serve and glorify Him. It is the thought of self-gratification that defiles the act which in itself is right, but in its motive may be wholly selfish and sinful.

So the commonest acts of life are to be wholly consecrated to Him and done unto Him, and thus they become sacred and holy.

Have we learned the secret of thus living for His glory, and dying unto ourselves?

SELF-SEEKING

This is one of the forms of self-life which must be surrendered. "Love . . . is not self-seeking" (1 Corinthians 13:4–5). Her object is not to accomplish some personal end, but to benefit another and to glorify God.

The great business of the people of this world is to seek their own ends, aggrandizements, honors and pleasures. But a consecrated life has but one purpose: to "seek first his kingdom and his righteousness," and then to rest in His will, knowing that "all these things will be given to you as well" (Matthew 6:33).

SELF-COMPLACENCY

This is the spirit of Anak, the long-necked one. It is the spirit of pride, the pride that takes delight in our own qualities and rests with satisfaction in ourselves.

It is very different from vanity, which seeks the approval of others. Self-complacency is so satisfied with itself that it cares little for the opinions of others, and has a lofty independence about it that even scorns their criticism and rises superior to their praise. It is a god unto itself.

It is one of the most subtle forms of self-life, and has a sort of lofty grandeur which blinds its possessor to its danger and its deep sinfulness.

SELF-GLORYING

Self-glorying is the converse of this. It seeks the praise of others, rather than its own. It may be very small in its own eyes, and for this very reason tries to shine in the eyes of others.

A lady of rank is not dependent upon her dress or her equipage for her position, but is usually very simple. It is the lack of real greatness that makes the society butterfly eager to attract attention by her gaudy display.

Self-glorying vaunts itself and inflates its little bubble because it is so small. There is no creature so diminutive in its real proportions, when really reduced to its actual dimensions, as the dude and the daughter of fashion.

The truly consecrated life wants none of this. It is conscious of its nothingness, and knows that it is dependent on God alone for all it can ever possess. Therefore it covers its face with the veil of His loveliness, and robes itself in His own righteousness, and then hides in His bosom, saying, "I no longer live, but Christ lives in me" (Galatians 2:20).

SELF-CONFIDENCE

This is a form of self-life which relies upon its own wisdom, strength and righteousness. It is Simon Peter, saying, "Even if all fall away, I will not" (Mark 14:29).

This is your man of strong common sense and self-reliance. He believes in his own opinion. He relies upon his own judgment. He laughs at the people who talk about divine guidance and the Spirit's leadings.

This must die before we can become established in the strength of Christ. Therefore, the strongest natures have often to fail in order to bring them to the end of self, and lead them, like Peter, to lean on God, and like Jacob, with wounded thigh, to go forth depending henceforth on the strength of God.

Closely allied to this is

SELF-CONSCIOUSNESS

This is the self that is always thinking of itself and covered with its own shadow.

Every act and look and word is studied. Every feeling and inward state is morbidly photographed upon the inward senses.

Sometimes we become conscious of our own physical organism. We watch our breath, our pulses, our temperature and our physical state. We carry about with us continually a morbid consciousness of our functions and conditions. All the simplicity is taken away. We are bound to ourselves like a man with his hand on his own collar, trying to pull himself along.

This is a dreadful bondage. God wants us to have the freedom of a simple child, that acts without thinking from spontaneous impulses and with a beautiful liberty. He does not want us to see the shining of our faces, to be conscious of our holy acts, or to make a note of every sacrifice and service. But He would have us, when He comes at the last to say, "I was hungry and you gave me something to eat, I was thirsty and you gave me something to drink" (Matthew 25:35), to be so self-forgetful that we shall answer back, "When did we see you hungry and feed you, or thirsty and give you something to drink?" (25:37).

How shall we get out of this wretched self-consciousness?

Only by getting into a higher consciousness, even the presence of our Lord, and a purpose and object beyond ourselves, to live for God and others, and realize that He is living for us, and living in us, in those sweet, spontaneous impulses that are the true springs of action.

An exaggerated form of self-consciousness is

SELF-IMPORTANCE

This is very offensive and yet very common. Some people carry it in their very gait and bearing, as they walk along the street, and almost tempt one to step up to them and ask the question which it is said Sydney Smith used to ask of people whom he saw on the street, "Excuse me, sir, but may I ask if you are anybody in particular?"

This is not the usual accompaniment of true greatness, but it is very common in very small men and women, who make up for their lack of real weight by an immense amount of self-assertion and swaggering assumption.

This is very offensive to a true Christian taste.

Holy modesty will show itself in the very bearing. True humility consists not so much in thinking meanly of ourselves, as in not thinking of ourselves at all. And the ripe head of wheat always hangs down in proportion to its weight.

Closely allied to this is

SELF-DEPRECIATION

This is just a bad as the other. Some people are egregiously conscious of their own shortcoming and inability. It keeps them from useful service and is always thrusting its littleness and nothingness upon every situation.

If it sees its name in print, it is afraid of being puffed up. If asked to be seated on the platform, it will blush and shrink, and hide away. If called upon to do some service, it will refuse on the ground of inability. This is all self.

A truly surrendered heart doesn't have any name to see in print, any person to be conscious of, any power to serve. Its name has been given to Christ, and if He wants it used, let Him have it, and blaze it before the universe in fame or infamy. It hasn't any ability to work, and if Christ wants to send it, He must equip it and supply it with all necessary resources.

Therefore it goes unquestioning and fully assured, because all its strength must come from God.

SELF-VINDICATION

This is the self that stands for its own rights and avenges its wrongs. It is quick to detect an injury or an offense, and to express its sense of it in some marked and unmistakable way.

It believes in receiving the respect and consideration due to it in all cases, and while it asks nothing beyond, yet it insists upon all its rights.

It is not egregious in its own conceit. It does not demand applause beyond its merits, but it asks proper consideration, and is going to have it.

Now, this is a very respectable, but a very real form of selfishness. It is directly contrary to the spirit of Christianity and the Lord Jesus Christ.

The very idea of His incarnation was the renunciation of all His rights. Being in the form of God, He was entitled to be equal with God, but we are told He did not count this a prize, but "made himself nothing,/ taking the very nature of a servant,/ being made in human likeness" (Philippians 2:7).

If God wants to bring you here, it is very easy for Him to empty you and make you of no reputation, and there will be lots of people who will be ready to help Him do it. But it is very lovely to do this ourselves, as Jesus did, and not wait to have it done for us.

The very essence of Christ's humiliation was that He gave up all His heavenly rights, and when He came down to earth He gave up all His earthly rights, and made it the business of His life to let go, until there was nothing left to give up, but even His very life was yielded.

You have not begun to deal with the question of self-surrender until it reaches your dearest rights, and you let them go into His hand as a glorious deposit; and every time you do so, He puts it down in your bank account, and when the interest has all accumulated, O! how He will pay you back—much of it in this world, but how much more in the day of eternal recompense!

I solemnly believe that most of the blessings that have been given to me in my life and ministry have come because of the evil things people have said of me, and because God made me willing to allow them to do it.

"It may be that the LORD will see my distress and repay me with good for the cursing I am receiving today" (2 Samuel 16:12).

SENSITIVENESS

One of the most painful forms of selfishness is sensitiveness.

One day in India I picked up a beautiful little vine that was spreading over the ground. I thought how lovely it would be to press it in my notebook.

But by the time I had taken it up it disappeared, and there was nothing left in my hand but a long string on which the leaves had been. It was as stiff and hard as a leafless stem, and I said, "Why, where has my plant gone?" I looked on the ground, and the other leaves were spreading over the grass as before, but I could see no trace of the one I supposed I had dropped.

I looked at the little dry stem in my hand again, and I found it was the same little branch I had picked from the ground, but its leaves had all folded up as firm and dry as if it had been struck by an autumn blast. And when I touched the other leaves on the ground they disappeared in the same way. Then I said, "Why, it is a sensitive plant!"

I thought of people I had seen who had been all bright and radiant for a time, but something touched them that was offensive, uncongenial or humbling, and they suddenly disappeared and shrank into such hard, dry, leafless sticks that there was no point of contact with them. They seemed to have become all at once like Egyptian mummies, ready for a glass case. What was the matter? Self!

"Great peace have they which love thy law: and nothing shall offend them" (Psalm 119:165, KJV). The Lord bring and keep us there!

There is a place where we can be, or rather where we can cease to be; and Christ become instead of me. And of that place it is true, "The one who was born of God keeps him safe, and the evil one cannot harm him" (1 John 5:18).

SELF-SEEING

There are some people who always see things from their own side. How does this affect *me?*

You see your own side of it. But if you would wait and see your brother's side, if you would be willing to believe that there is another side, you yourself would be saved from a thousand stings and others from a thousand misundings.

"Each of you should look not only to your own interests, but also to the interests of others" (Philippians 2:4). Put yourself in your brother's place. Take into consideration his circumstances, his views. Think how you would act if you felt as he feels, saw with his eyes, were placed as he is placed. You will be surprised to see how differently you will look at things. And yet this is only one of the first things in the holy act of self-forgetfulness.

INTROSPECTION

Our morbid and excessive self-examination is one of the forms of self-life that causes much pain and works much injury in our Christian life.

There is a right, but there is a wrong self-examination. God alone can truly search us. We are very apt, when we attempt it ourselves, to get poisoned with the effluvia of the sepulcher into which we penetrate. Even Paul said, "I do not even judge myself. . . . It is the Lord who judges me" (1 Corinthians 4:3b–4).

Let us commit our own way unto Him and honestly say, "Search me, O God, and know my heart;/ test me and know my anxious thoughts./ See if there is any offensive way in me,/ and lead me in the way everlasting" (Psalm 139:23–24).

Thus let us walk in Him, trust Him to show us all we need to see, and then believe "if on some point you think differently, that too God will make clear to you" (Philippians 3:15b).

SELF-LOVE

Self-love is the root of all these forms of the self-life. It is a heart centered upon itself, and so long as this is the case every affection and every power of our being is turned inward and self-ward, and the whole character distorted by the false adjustment of our nature; just as much as our eye would be if it were ever turning inward upon itself rather than outward upon the objective world which it was made to perceive.

God, who is the type of all true being, is essentially love, and lives not for Himself, but for others, and when we become self-centered we are the opposite of God, and really assume His throne and become gods unto ourselves.

It is the ruin and perversion of a soul to love and live for itself.

SELFISH AFFECTIONS

Selfish affections are the natural fruit of self-life.

We love our own friends and families and the people who minister to our pleasure; and even those we love, we love not so much for the blessing that we can be to them, as for the pleasure that they minister to us.

Love that terminates on ourselves is selfish and degrading. The love that seeks another's blessing is elevating and divine.

SELFISH MOTIVES

Selfish motives may enter into the highest acts and mar and pervert them to their inmost core.

It is not only what we say and do, but why. God sees the very thought and purpose, and He judges the act by its intent.

The natural heart cannot do a good thing without some selfish object which perverts and destroys its purity.

SELFISH DESIRES

Selfish desires are always springing up in the old natural heart, and even if they never reach fruition, or never become choices, acts or facts, we want to be free from the very wish, and have God so give us our desires that they shall spring from Him, and be prompted by His love.

The spirit of covetousness is just a selfish desire, and God has pronounced it idolatry—a most dreadful sin.

SELFISH CHOICES

Selfish choices are still more serious, for the will is the spring of human actions and determines all our words and deeds.

We want a rightly directed will, which chooses not its own gratification, but because of "God who works in you to will and to act according to his good purpose" (Philippians 2:13).

SELFISH PLEASURES

There are two kinds of enjoyment: one, which we seek for its own sake, and this is selfishness; the other is the pleasure that comes to us from doing good, and because we are in harmony with God and with our own being, which is the truest enjoyment.

Selfish pleasure, the desire that seeks its own, and terminates on itself, is earth-born, transitory and wrong.

SELFISH POSSESSIONS

The worldling seeks to gain the world, and calls his possessions his own. The true child of God has nothing for himself, but holds all as a sacred trust for God. "No one claimed that any of his possessions was his own" (Acts 4:32).

The true Christian conception of property is stewardship—the holding of the gifts of God for His service, and subject to His direction, and for His glory.

This is the sovereign remedy for avarice and the grasping spirit of the world. We are never consecrated until all is laid, absolutely and forever, at His feet, and held there subject constantly to His will.

SELFISH FEARS AND CARES

Nearly all of our cares and anxiety spring from pure selfishness.

If we were wholly yielded to God, and recognized our life in its every moment as absolutely His, we would have no anxiety, but would regard ourselves as His property and under His safe and constant protection. The Lord has said, "You cannot serve both God and Money" (Matthew 6:24), and has added, with strange logical suggestiveness, "Therefore do not worry about tomorrow" (Matthew 6:34).

That little word, "therefore," discovers the link between money worship and anxious care.

SELFISH SORROWS

Many of our griefs and heartbreaks spring from the purest selfishness, wounded pride, ambition, self-love or the loss of something which we should not have called our own.

The death of self blots out a universe of wretchedness and brings a heaven of joy.

SELFISH SACRIFICES AND SELF-DENIALS

Selfish sacrifices and self-denials are as real as they are paradoxical.

A man may "give all . . . to the poor and surrender [his] body to the flames, but have not love" (1 Corinthians 13:3). He may do it all for the gratification of his vanity or the display of his orthodoxy, and the propagation of his own beliefs and opinions.

Simon Stylites, after sitting a quarter of a century on the top of a pillar and living on roots and pauper pittances, was perhaps the most egregious embodiment of self-righteousness and self-consciousness in the whole world. He had denied himself to gratify himself, to exalt himself and to save himself. It was simply the old stream of his life turned into a new channel.

And so there may be

SELFISH VIRTUE AND MORALITY

The Pharisees were virtuous, but their virtue was a selfish cloak, intended for display, and therefore worthless, or worse. It was simply an advertisement, and its motive destroyed its value.

The lady who walks the street with her skirts held carefully away from the touch of her fallen sister may be an icicle of selfish propriety; while her poor sister, with all her faults, may have a generous heart, and may even be sinning from some motive of mistaken love, and sacrificing herself for another. And while this does not palliate her sin it may make her a nobler character than even the virtuous one who scorns her.

And so there is a

SELF-RIGHTEOUSNESS

Self-righteousness would even seek to justify itself before God by its own religious works, and thus forfeit His righteousness and salvation. For it is not of our sins alone, but even of our righteousness that He has said, they are "like filthy rags" (Isaiah 64:6), and they must be laid down, and we, as helpless, worthless sinners accept the righteousness of Christ for our justification before God.

SELFISH SANCTITY AND SANCTIFICATION

We may have selfish sanctity and sanctification and be so absorbed in our religious experience that our eye will be taken off Jesus and centered upon ourselves, and thus we shall become offensive exhibitions of religious self-consciousness, and our very good be marred by its indirection and introversion.

True sanctification forgets itself and lives in constant dependence upon the Lord Jesus as its righteousness and all-sufficiency.

SELFISH CHARITIES AND SELFISH GIFTS

So too we may have selfish charities and gifts.

The largest generosity and the most munificent offerings of money may be only an advertisement of ourselves, and prompted by some motive which terminates on our own interest or honor.

Some people give liberally, and then hamper their gifts with so many conditions and get themselves so wrought into the administration of their beneficence that all its disinterestedness is lost, and it looks like the gratification of their own higher pleasure.

OUR CHRISTIAN WORK MAY BE SELFISH

We may preach because of the intellectual pleasure it gives us.

We may work for the church because we like the church, the minister or the people.

We may engage in a benevolent or Christian profession because it enables us to make a comfortable livelihood, and gives us congenial employment.

Or we may do our religious work on selfish principles and from religious selfishness.

The Church of God today is blighted by the selfishness of her evangelistic work. She is spending 700 times as much for her own people as she does upon the heathen world, and the spirit of religious selfishness runs through all her plans.

SELFISH PRAYERS

There is nothing that sounds so selfish as the prayers of many Christians.

They travel in a circle about the size of their own body and soul, their family and perhaps their own particular church. The suffering household of faith and the perishing world are scarcely ever touched by their sympathies or their intercessions.

The highest prayer is the prayer of unselfish love, and as we learn to pray for others and to carry the dying world upon our hearts, we shall find ourselves enriched in return, a thousandfold, and prove indeed that "it is more blessed to give than to receive" (Acts 20:35).

SELFISH HOPES

The future of many persons is as selfish as their present. They live in the dreams of coming joys and triumphs, and their vision is all earth-bound, and often, alas! as baseless as the fading cloudland that floats upon the summer sky.

The true hope of the gospel swallows up all these selfish visions and earthly hopes. Looking for "the blessed hope—the glorious appearing of our great God and Savior, Jesus Christ" (Titus 2:13), we hold all other prospects subordinate and subject to that supreme prospect. Even the old hope of heaven that was sometimes a selfish weariness, and a longing to be at rest, has been exchanged for that high and glorious looking for His coming that lifts us out of ourselves into the greater blessing it is to bring to millions, and nerves us to the highest and noblest efforts to work for the hastening of the coming glory and the preparation of the world to meet Him. God alone can give this new and heaven-born hope, which is as divine as it is lofty and inspiring.

OUR LIFE

Our very life must be held not as a selfish possession, but as a sacred trust.

"I consider my life worth nothing to me" is the true spirit of consecration, "if only I may finish the race and complete the task the Lord Jesus has given me—the task of testifying to the gospel of God's grace" (Acts 20:24).

That is the meaning of life, and the only object for which it should be cherished.

So we find the same apostle saying, "For to me, to live is Christ and to die is gain" (Philippians 1:21); and he adds, "Convinced of this, I know that I will remain, and I will continue with all of you for your progress and joy in the faith" (1:25).

The unselfish life is a safe life, and it is immortal till its great purpose shall be fulfilled.

CONCLUSION

How shall we overcome these giant Anakim? How shall we win the victory over self? How shall we possess Hebron, the city of love?

1. We must definitely and thoroughly enter into the meaning of that mighty word, "You are not your own" (1 Corinthians 6:19b). We must surrender ourselves so utterly that we can never own ourselves again.

We must hand over self and all its rights in an eternal covenant, and give God the absolute right to own us, control us and possess us forever. And we must abide in this attitude and never recall that irrevocable surrender.

2. We must let God make this real in detail as each day brings its tests and

conflicts, and each of these 31 kings comes face to face before us. That which we did in the general must be fulfilled in the particular, and step by step we must be established in the full experience of self-renunciation and entire consecration.

As each of these issues meets us, God is asking us the question, "Are you your own, or are you Mine?" And as we stand true to our covenant, He will make it real.

We must choose that each new Agag shall die, and God will make the death effectual the moment we sign the death warrant.

3. We must receive the great antidote to self—the love of Christ.

We have seen the power of love in a human life transforming a selfish girl, living for the pleasures of society and the gratification of her own self-love, into a patient, self-sacrificing wife and mother, willing to endure any privation and go any length for the man she loved with all her heart.

In a far higher sense the love of Christ, and that alone, can slay the strength of self-love, and enable us to say,

> For Christ's love compels us, because we are convinced that one died for all, and therefore all died. And he died for all, that those who live should no longer live for themselves but for him who died for them and was raised again. (2 Corinthians 5:14–15)

4. Finally, we need not only the love of Christ but the Christ Himself.

It is not a principle, nor an emotion, nor a motive, that is to transform our life and conquer these determined foes, but it is a living Person.

Christ will put His own heart into us and so live in us and we so live in His life, love in His love, and think, speak and act in Him, in all we do, that it shall be "not I, but Christ that liveth in me" (Galatians 2:20, KJV).

So let us receive Him, the Antidote of self, the Lord of love, the Conqueror of the heart.

> There is a foe whose hidden power
> The Christian well may fear,
> More subtle far than inbred sin
> And to the heart more dear.
> It is the power of selfishness,
> It is the willful I,
> And e'er my Lord can live in me
> My very self must die.
>
> There is, like Anak's sons of old,
> A race of giants still,

Self-glorying, self-confidence,
Self-seeking and self-will.
Still must these haughty Anakim
By Caleb's sword be slain,
E'er Hebron's heights of heavenly love
Our conquering feet can gain.

O save me from self-will, dear Lord,
Which claims Thy sacred Throne;
O let my will be lost in Thine,
And let Thy will be done.
O keep me from self-confidence,
And self-sufficiency;
Let me exchange my strength for Thine,
And lean alone on Thee.

O save me from self-seeking, Lord,
Let me not be my own,
A living sacrifice I come,—
Lord, keep me Thine alone;
From proud vain-glory save me, Lord,
From pride of praise and fame;
To Christ be all the honor given,
The glory to His Name.

O Jesus, slay the self in me,
By Thy consuming breath;
Show me Thy heart, Thy wounds, Thy shame,
And love my soul to death.
When the Shekinah flame came down,
E'en Moses could not stay;
So let Thy glory fill me now,
And self forever slay.

O Jesus, come and dwell in me,
Walk in my steps each day,
Live in my life, love in my love,
And speak in all I say;
Think in my thoughts, let all my acts
Thy very actions be,
So shall it be no longer I,
But Christ that lives in me.

CHAPTER 6

POSSESSING THE INHERITANCE

When Joshua was old and well advanced in years, the LORD said to him, "You are very old, and there are still very large areas of land to be taken over." (Joshua 13:1)

How long will you wait before you begin to take posssession of the land that the LORD, the God of your fathers, has given you? (18:3)

We have looked at the conquest of the land and the kings who disputed its ownership. This is over now and the occupation of the conquered territory next engages the attention of the great leader. This is quite different from its subjugation.

It is one thing to fight a decisive battle and disperse the opposing forces of a hostile province. It is another thing to settle down to the employments of peace, and cultivate the conquered territory, covering it with peaceful homes and fruitful fields, and developing its resources.

This was the next business of the conquerors of Canaan, and in this we find a strange and long delay. For a considerable period after the conquest of Canaan we find no less than seven of the great tribes still lingering around the tabernacle at Shiloh, and failing to go forward to claim their respective inheritance, so that God had to reprove them for their negligence and delay, and Joshua had to send forth a special commission to divide the land and apportion it to the tribes that had not yet received their inheritance.

This is all applicable to our special inheritance. There is much more for us than the conflict with temptation and sin. There are positive advances in the Christian life into which God is calling us as well as them, and it is to be feared that a much larger proportion of the spiritual Israel has failed to enter into its inheritance than even the seven tribes who lingered at Shiloh.

God is obliged, after 18 centuries, to send forth His messengers to plead with His negligent and faithless people to take the blessings which He has, at such a tremendous cost, provided and prepared.

He is pleading with us, as He did with them, and saying, "How long will you wait before you begin to take possession of the land that the LORD, the God of your fathers, has given you?" (Joshua 18:3). There are not, perhaps, 10 Christians in a hundred who even claim to have accepted all the fullness of the gospel of Christ; and the people of God as utterly, fail to enter into their inheritance of service in the evangelization of the world. In every direction, "there are still very large areas of land to be taken over" (13:1).

Let us survey this unoccupied territory, and listen to the challenge which is speaking to us from heaven, to arise and occupy it.

POSSESSING THE LAND

It is much more than conquering the land. It is one thing to break down the walls of Jericho; it is another thing to enter in and possess the city.

It is one thing to fight a great, decisive battle with temptation; it is another thing to go on to perfection, and add to our faith, knowledge, self-control, godliness, brotherly kindness, love and all the fruits of the Spirit.

Every word is extremely suggestive. The first thought suggested is appropriating as our own the inheritance. It is one thing to understand the promises, to desire the experience, to purpose obeying the commands. It is another to put our own name in all and claim for ourselves the things promised and commanded. The personal pronouns "my" and "mine" make all the difference in the world.

The second thought suggested by the expression is the actual experience of the thing that we have claimed—the entering upon it and living it out.

The immigrant may go to the land office and put in his name and application for a free grant on the Western Reserve, but that is not enough. It cannot become his property until he settles down upon it, builds a house and lives in it, and begins to cultivate the estate. Then he is the real possessor, and his title cannot be alienated.

This is what God requires us to do. First, by faith, to appropriate the inheritance promised, and then, by actual experience, to settle down upon the promise and take it into our lives.

There is something very real in this idea of appropriating for ourselves a distinct Christian experience. Most people are trying to live somebody else's life. But God has an inheritance for each of us—unique, distinct and personal. He wants us to appropriate it, understand it, catch the vision of it, claim it for ourselves and realize it in our actual life.

The great majority of people are made up of patchwork. They take a rag from one, a piece from another, and they stitch them on as best they can, until they become like a patchwork quilt, and it is little wonder if sometimes it is a "crazy quilt."

God wants you to be yourself, in Him. He has a pattern for you that He has for nobody else. If you will let Him, He will weave it into your life, and work it out in all its unique and beautiful design.

Is not this the meaning of this remarkable and often misapplied verse, "Work out your own salvation with fear and trembling, for it is God who works in you to will and to act according to his good purpose" (Philippians 2:12–13)?

This does not mean that we are to earn salvation by our works, for before the works begin, we are assumed to have the salvation and to have made it "our own." Then when it is our own, when we have claimed and appropriated it, we are to work it out, develop it; we are to enter into it in all its fullness. Work it out as the weaver works out the pattern of his web; work it out as the artist works out the design on his canvas; work it out as the sculptor works out the figure in his marble; work it out as the oak tree is worked out of the acorn; and work it out "with fear and trembling" (2:12), with a sense of the tremendous responsibility, the infinite trust, the mighty possibilities, and the Divine Worker who is working in you and pressing you on to apprehend all that for which you are apprehended in Christ Jesus.

THE UNOCCUPIED LAND

"There are still very large areas of land to be taken over" (Joshua 13:1).

In the Word

1. There is much unoccupied territory in the Word of God. There are promises that we have not yet made our own. There are conceptions of truth that we have not yet grasped with our minds, or translated into our lives. There are commandments whose finer shades of sacred duty we have not yet conceived, far less fulfilled. There are fields of truth into which the Holy Teacher and Comforter is waiting to lead us. There are many things which He would say to us, but we cannot bear them now. But if we will follow on, we will find that

> He who so wondrously hath taught,
> Yet more will have us know;
> He who so wondrously hath wrought,
> Yet greater things will show.

In Christian Experience

2. There is much territory in the land of Christian living to be possessed. The things we know, have we fully believed? The things we believe, have we fully realized? The things we realize, have we fully proved?

We have learned some lessons of love, but have we the love that "always protects" (1 Corinthians 13:7), that "never fails" (13:8)? We have learned to suffer long, but have we learned to "suffer long" and yet be "kind" (13:4, KJV)? And have we come into "great endurance and patience . . . joyfully" (Colossians 1:11)? We have received the white robes, but have we also put on the wedding robes? We have been made holy but have we received "the splender of his holiness" (Psalm 29:2) and the finer touches of His polishing and perfecting hand?

We have known something of the joy of the Lord, but have we learned to "consider it pure joy, . . . whenever [we] face trials of many kinds" (James 1:2) and to "rejoice in our sufferings" (Romans 5:3)?

We have learned something of answered prayer, but have we come into the life of prayer, the prayer of the Holy Spirit and the higher prayer of self-forgetfulness?

We have submitted to the will of God, and chosen it, but have we come to delight in it, and not only to delight in it, but "to test and approve what God's will is—his good, pleasing and perfect will" (Romans 12:2)?

In Christian Work

3. In the realm of Christian work "there are still very large areas of land to be taken over" (Joshua 13:1). What infinite varieties of holy service there are for the consecrated and obedient servant!

Most of us can remember how, within a short lifetime, Christian work has grown in its various phases and opportunities.

Fifty years ago there was usually but one worker in an ordinary congregation—the preacher. His business was to work, and the others were simply worked upon.

After a little while, the Sunday school was added to the machinery of the ordinary church, and there was more work to be done and more workers were required. So the circle increased until there were, perhaps, a dozen workers in the church.

In the past quarter of a century how many new forms of Christian work have arisen—rescue missions, work for the fallen and the suffering, calling out all the varieties of talent and capacity in the Church of Christ, and all the gifts of the Holy Spirit—so that today there are 10 people working in every thoroughly awakened church for one a quarter of a century ago.

But this is only the beginning. And how has this come about? Simply because some of God's children who were walking with Him, and waiting upon Him, caught the vision of His higher will, received His commission to go out in some new field, obeyed, and were used to originate some new department of service for God.

But the day is coming when all this will be multiplied an hundredfold, and when it will scarcely be respectable for anyone to be a member of a Christian congregation for any considerable period, unless he can point to precious souls whom he has led to Christ; and the very least that Christ has suggested as the test of discipleship and the measure of fruitfulness, is thirty-fold.

God is waiting for workers to whom He can commit greater trusts than anything that we have seen. As the [19th] century hastens to its close, everything is moving on accelerated time, and God is going to multiply the agencies for Christian work in a manner that we can scarcely realize. If we are willing to open our ears to His voice, He will speak to us and send us. And we shall wonder at the ways in which He will own and multiply our efforts, if made in the Holy Spirit.

Beloved, "open your eyes and look at the fields! They are ripe for harvest" (John 4:35) and ask the Lord to show you His highest thought and will for your precious life.

THE CAUSES OF FAILURE

"How long will you wait ('are ye slack,' KJV) before you begin to take possession of the land" (Joshua 18:3)? This little word "slack" expresses the secret of all the failure. It is a very difficult word to translate, but many of us will doubtless recognize some of its applications to our own souls.

Indolence

1. It denotes indolence. There is no meaner vice in the world than laziness. Most people would be ashamed to claim it as a relation; but the fact is more people are suffering from it than would be ready to own it.

It is the cause of most of the failures in secular life. God hates it and always blesses the diligent in natural ways.

"Do you see a man skilled in his work?/ He will serve before kings," God has said. "He will not serve before obscure men" (Proverbs 22:29). Even if a man is wrong in many things God will recompense him in natural things, as far as He can.

Many are kept back from spiritual progress by a spirit of indolence and unwillingness to put forth any real spiritual effort. It is so much easier to be content with things as they are, and take the easy way.

One of our missionaries in Peking told me of a Chinese beggar, for whom she got a good situation; but he kept it only two or three days, and then was back on the "Beggar's Bridge" once more. When she asked him why he had given up his job he said, "Well, the truth is, I can stand almost anything; I can bear to be cold and hungry, to be beaten and kicked, to be poor and homeless, but I cannot bear to be tired."

A good many people are like him. It is true of spiritual, as well as natural things, that "diligent hands bring wealth" (Proverbs 10:4). We cannot reach the highest place in heavenly things unless, like the great spiritual athlete of whom we read in the Epistle to the Philippians, we "press on toward the goal to win the prize for which God has called [us] heavenward in Christ Jesus" (3:14).

Indifference

2. Many persons are kept back from the highest blessing by spiritual indifference. They have no intense or holy ambition or desire for the highest things. They are content to be saved any way, and the prizes of the high calling have no attraction for their hearts. Like Esau, they despise their birthright, and do not think it worth the trouble or the cost. They that would enter into that rest must "make every effort to enter" (Hebrews 4:11), and kindle with the holy intensity that "consider[s] everything a loss compared to the surpassing greatness of knowing Christ Jesus my Lord" (Philippians 3:8).

God will never give His prizes to an indifferent heart. He wants them to be prized above all cost, and sought above all treasures.

Self-Complacency

3. This keeps many back. They are quite satisfied with what they have attained. They have received enough blessing to assuage a guilty conscience, and heal the fear of future punishment. And, perhaps, they have gone further, and had some experience in the past on which they are continually lingering, which effectually displaces all true and honest hunger of the heart for the larger life that God can only give to self-emptied souls.

"Blessed are those who hunger and thirst for righteousness,/ for they will be filled" (Matthew 5:6).

"You say, 'I am rich; I have acquired wealth and do not need a thing.' But you do not realize that you are wretched, pitiful, poor, blind and naked" (Revelation 3:17).

Ease and Pleasure

4. There is nothing that so relaxes the cords of spiritual earnestness as the life of the world, the life of ease and pleasure. Men who contend for earthly prizes have to forego the pleasures of earthly indulgence. The trainee for an athletic contest denies himself every gratification that could relax his vigor or weaken his physical energy. Much more must they who strive for an incorruptible crown keep their body under and bring it into subjection.

The cost of holiness is too great for the lover of this present evil world. Many of you, dear friends, who read these lines, are hindered in your holy ambitions and heavenly aspirations because there is some selfish thing in your life which has shorn you of your strength, even as Delilah robbed the mighty Samson of his Nazirite separation, and brought him to disgrace and ruin by the fascination of earthly pleasure.

The Influence of Others

5. There is nothing so depressing as the tendency of some persons to look at things on the average. They say: "Why should I be better then my neighbors? Why should I claim more than my father ever knew? Thousands of good people are content to go on in the old way, and they are all going to heaven; why should not I be content to be as good as they?"

And so, "measur[ing] themselves by themselves and compar[ing] themselves with themselves" (2 Corinthians 10:12), they rise no higher than the human standard, and comfort themselves by the average Christian and the average measure of the gospel, and are slack to go up to possess all the land which the Lord our God has given them.

Beloved, "Let God be true, and every man a liar" (Romans 3:4). You cannot afford to come short of anything which God has prepared for you at such large cost. There is not a promise in His Word, not a command in His precepts, which is not essential to you for your complete Christian life.

If you miss any part of His will, you shall be an eternal loser, and your future will be defective to just that extent. God's faithful people in every age have had to be in the minority. The man who goes with the crowd is invariably wrong.

God is calling you to step out and stand alone, and, putting your fingers in your ears, to press forward in the narrow way, calling, "Life, life, eternal life!"

Unbelief

6. They say, "It is of no use for me to attempt this higher life." Like Israel at Kadesh Barnea, they admit that "the land is a good one, but the enemies are so great and we so little, we shall never be able to enter in." But as old Caleb answered, "The LORD helping me, I will drive them out just as he said" (Joshua 14:12).

Faith in the promises of God and in the power of the Holy Spirit will nerve the feeble arm, steady the relaxed spirit and make us more than conquerors over every obstacle and adversary.

Lack of Courage

7. Some people are moral cowards. They are afraid of self-denial, singularity, criticism, conflict and spiritual hardship. Only spiritual heroes can win the inheritance. Cowards will always fail. God is willing and able to give us true courage, if we will dare to stand where He bids us.

Beloved, let us face the difficulties and the enemies. Let us set our face like a flint. Let us take His own divine courage, and let us go up at once and possess all the land which the Lord our God has given us.

Lack of Power

8. Slackness expresses feebleness. This well characterizes the spiritual condition of the great majority of Christians. They are like a bow so relaxed that the bow-string has no spring, the arrow no momentum. The life that should be an example of the omnipotence of God, and show the credentials of holy energy and divine efficiency, is, in most cases, such a poor, flabby, limp, powerless form that the men of the world despise it and feel that they are better off without it.

Lack of Persistence

9. There are some bows that retain their spring for a short time, but the wood is inferior and after a few hours the spring becomes relaxed.

So many start out for the heavenly inheritance with high ambitions and hopes, but they have no real perseverance. The fair promise of their beginning soon becomes "like the morning mist, like the early dew" (Hosea 13:3).

We are made partakers of Christ if we hold our confidence steadfast unto the end. There can be no allowance anywhere for ease, indulgence or laxity. It is a lifelong way, and every step we must stand with girded loins, "Forgetting what is behind and straining toward what is ahead, . . . press[ing] on toward the goal to win the prize for which God has called [us] heavenward in Christ Jesus" (Philippians 3:13b, 14).

HOW LONG?

This is a solemn and tender appeal to us to act promptly and obey, without a moment's delay, the impulses of the Holy Spirit. If we are disposed to take the easy way this morning, we will be just as likely to do it the next morning.

Besides, time is passing by, and that which is more important, opportunity, is slipping away. There are crisis hours in life when everything concentrates at a solemn focus, and if the decision is not made then it may never be made.

There is something very pathetic in the words, "You are very old and there are still very large areas of land to be taken over" (Joshua 13:1).

There is a spiritual age that comes to people and comes sometimes before their life-work is fulfilled. We have all seen people young in years but old in heart, their pulses benumbed, their spiritual forces paralyzed by disobedience to the voice of the Holy Spirit.

There is such a thing as losing the spring of life, the high and heavenly inspiration that comes from the breath of God, and makes sacrifice and toil luxurious delights.

There is a heavenly glow, there is a divine enthusiasm, which comes from the continual presence of Christ within us and the sweet voice of His approval; and if these are lost, life is drudgery indeed. Every toil will be a task, and every trial a crushing weight of unutterable woe.

And all this comes from disobedience. The Holy Spirit leads us up to the great decisive hour, and then presses us forward to the right decision. If we hesitate, if we shrink, if we refuse, there comes a time when that Presence is withdrawn, and the heart sinks back into a strange heaviness, and life has lost its glow. Temptations overcome us; trials discourage us; joy and gladness leave us; and gradually we sink back into premature old age and yet we know not what is the matter, and perhaps never fully realize where the fatal error was committed.

Oh! what is so sad is to see gray hairs on the hearts of people, and they know it not; to see the loss of spiritual freshness, buoyancy and power gradually creeping over the life that once was all aglow, and to know that another soul has looked back on the way, and another crown has been lost by slackness!

Beloved, do not disobey the voice of God. Cherish the inspiration of the Holy Spirit, and follow on after the hand that is beckoning you to higher things. Lose not a moment; meet every question of God today; or tomorrow you may find yourself unprepared for further advances. If you once begin to lose time on this heavenly highway, you may never make it up again.

There are some railway trains whose schedule time is arranged at the highest possible maximum—there is no room to make up a lost hour. If the train is late at this station, it will be late at the next, and come in late at the end. If it were a freight train or an accommodation train, it might make up what was lost; but the great Limited Express has no room for the recovery of loss.

Beloved, you and I have taken our passage to the heavenly land on God's great Limited Express, and we cannot afford to lose a moment on the way. Let us be true to our high calling, and let us begin today to press forward that we may "take hold of that for which Christ Jesus took hold of [us]" (Philippians 3:12).

CHAPTER 7

THE INHERITANCE OF LOVE

So Hebron has belonged to Caleb son of Jephunneh the Kenizzite ever since, because he followed the LORD, the God of Israel, wholeheartedly. (Joshua 14:14)

The city of Hebron is still one of the most interesting and delightful places in Palestine. It is a highly elevated spot, overlooking a wide extent of country, and even amid the desolations of Palestine it is still a scene of surpassing beauty, fertility and luxuriance. The country is covered with vineyards and plantations. The grapes of Eshcol still grow in the valleys, and the rains and water springs are returning in something like their former fullness.

One cannot wonder that Caleb should set his heart upon this choice inheritance and claim it as his own.

The incident of this chapter is one of the most stirring in the book of Joshua. Caleb was one of the faithful spies who returned from the land of Kadesh. Unlike the rest of his brethren, he encouraged the people to go up and claim their inheritance. But they refused, and for 40 years he waited until that unbelieving generation had passed away. And now, for more than four years, he has stood shoulder to shoulder with his comrades in the conquest of the land and the securing of their various inheritances, until at last the kings were all subdued and the land divided by lot. Then he comes forward and claims his own inheritance and justly receives it.

The whole scene is full of spiritual meaning, and vividly sets forth the higher inheritance which faith may claim from the great Commander in the better Land of Promise.

SPECIAL INHERITANCE

Hebron represents a special inheritance; something more than the ordinary lot of the tribes. Caleb's act expressed a holy ambition which is worthy of our imitation.

God is pleased to have us claim all there is for us in His great redemption. The Master was not angry with James and John when they wanted more than their brethren. The prophet of old was angry with Israel's king when he was willing to take so little, and reproved him that he had not struck five or six times with the arrows of faith upon the ground.

There is more for each of us than an ordinary Christian experience. There is much more than just being saved and sanctified. God has choice possessions for choice spirits, and He lets each one of us decide for ourselves how much we shall have.

He is always watching with loving jealousy to see how earnest our spirit is, and how much of our high calling in Christ Jesus we will claim.

GOD'S BEST

Hebron represents not only a higher inheritance, but the very highest. It was the choicest spot in all the land. Caleb wanted it just because it was the best, and Anak held it for the very same reason. God has for each of us a good, a better or a best. The great majority are languidly content to have the good, a minority choose the better, and one out of myriads occasionally claims the best. But it has been truly said: "The better is the greatest enemy to the best." If we rise a little higher than the average we are apt to rest there in self-complacency, and so miss the highest calling.

Caleb would take nothing less than God's best, and he got it. God wants us to be content with nothing but His highest thought, and to "fulfill every good purpose of yours" (2 Thessalonians 1:11) and "his good, pleasing and perfect will" (Romans 12:2).

HARD

Hebron represents a very hard-won victory. It was not only the highest, but the hardest choice. It is ever true that God's highest gifts are the most costly.

In natural things, value is expressed by rarity and cost. Pearls do not grow on the trees. Sovereigns do not fall like snowflakes. The laurel of fame does not hang on every branch along the way. Success is not a capricious accident.

All these things are the recompense of labor, sacrifice, self-denial and often great suffering. And so the highest spiritual things are costly things, which involve intense labor and self-denial.

Satan does not dispute our way over the plains of average blessing, but when we ascend to higher altitudes we find his principalities and powers disputing our advance, and they are thickest at the end.

The devil is too shrewd to waste his ammunition on ordinary, average things. The reason that Arba, the greatest of the Anakites, chose Hebron was because it was the choicest place in Palestine.

The reason why the best things in your life cost you such great temptations and pressures is because such mighty and unspeakable blessings lie behind the breastworks of your foe. But they are yours if you will only dare claim your inheritance.

If you are to reach the heights of holiness, you will have, like Habakkuk, to have "the feet of a deer" and learn to "go on the heights" (Habakkuk 3:19). If you are to come into the more delicate shades of Christian experience, you will have to know the heaviest touches of the adversary's hand.

If you are to sit with Christ upon His throne, you must go with Him through His Gethsemane. Christ is not holding you back from the highest places at His side, but He is asking you, as He did His disciples of old, "Can you drink the cup I am going to drink?" (Matthew 20:22).

Caleb understood all this when he asked for Hebron, and the reason he wanted it was because "the cities are large, with walls up to the sky. We even saw the Anakites there" (Deuteronomy 1:28). Christ is still looking for men and women of the heroic type, those who will bear the hardest things, and fear not the cost of the highest things in His kingdom.

Once in my life, when almost tempted to discouragement by the temptations and pressures around me, my eye fell on this line in an old book: "The best evidence that you are in God's will is the devil's growl." And so I thanked the devil for his growl, and found that the reason he was there in force was because there was a Hebron just beyond.

THE VICTORY OF FAITH

Hebron represents the victory of waiting faith. The promise claimed at Hebron had been given 40 years before. It was the realization of a lifelong vision. It was the fulfillment of a long deferred hope.

God's richest blessings often require not only sacrifice, suffering and hard conflict, but long delay and patient waiting. But the blessing grows with the delay. The interest gathers with the extended time, and God's ratio is always compound interest.

It is very blessed to receive, in the early morning of life, some precious promise, and then stand, as the years go by, and wait for God to fulfill it, undiscouraged by the lapse of time, but knowing that "with the Lord a day is like a thousand years, and a thousand years are like a day" (2 Peter 3:8).

So God gave all His ancient people the early promise and the waiting years. And oh, how His heart looks down with delight as His children hold fast, amid all the testings, knowing that "though it linger, wait for it;/ it will certainly come and will not delay" (Habakkuk 2:3).

Thus, and thus alone, are the strongest things matured. The basswood tree can grow in a decade, but the mighty oak that lasts for a century takes many years to mature. So God is teaching us to reach our highest blessings. Let us hold fast to all His promises. Let us learn to wait for the best wine at the last.

I am sorry for the man who has all his blessings, and has no unanswered prayers, and no reserve of faith and hope beyond the present hour. Like the painter who wept when he had reached his ideal, because he could never rise beyond the present, so the heart loses its spring when it reaches its full desire.

The Holy Spirit is always pressing us forward in holy aspiration and infinite outreaching after greater things, that He may lure us on by the hopes He sets before us.

Let us store the heavens with these waiting prayers, and let life's perspective be crowned, height above height, with our unrealized blessings; and we shall praise Him as much for what He has not yet given us as for the blessings we have received, and often sing with one of the sweetest spirits of our century:

A sweet new song is in my mouth,
To long-loved music set;
Glory to God for all the grace
I have not tasted yet.

LOVE

Hebron represents especially the inheritance of love and holy friendship. It was the city of Abraham, the friend of God, and its name to the present day is "The Friend." It is the type of love, the highest heritage of Christian faith and experience.

I do not speak of love in its ordinary, natural meaning, as a human instinct, but of the love which is the grace and gift of Christ; and I think that Hebron represents not the commoner phases of Christian love, but the choice and finer shades which the Holy Spirit has to give to those who will "move up to a better place" (Luke 14:10).

We know the Lord Jesus had some disciples who came nearer to His heart than others; and love has still its inner chambers and finer shades. Hebron seems to express these heights of love and heavenly fellowship.

There is "perfect love [that] drives out fear" (1 John 4:18); the perfect confidence in the Father which has no cloud; a fellowship which is eternal and unbroken and covered with His mighty oath. "I have sworn not to be angry with you,/ never to rebuke you again" (Isaiah 54:9). Do we not want this mountaintop of love?

Then there is a love of Christ shed abroad in our hearts, that is the very heart of Christ in us. I cannot sing the song,

> Give me a heart like Thine,
> Help me to love like Thee.

because I am not able to resemble Christ. I must have Christ Himself to live in me. This in my highest Hebron, that "because in this world, we are like Him" (1 John 4:17). "That the love you have for me may be in them" (John 17:26).

Again, there is what we have sometimes called the love-life of the Lord— the blessed tender relationship in which we call Him *Ishi* and He calls us beloved. It is where we are betrothed unto our Lord and He becomes the Bridegroom of the heart, quickening all our being with a touch so real, and so infinitely holy, that it is preeminently true of this as of everything else.

> The love of Jesus, what it is,
> None but His loved ones know.

Do we not want to dwell on this high place of love?

Then there is the love that adjusts all our natural and spiritual relationships, and enables us to love each one in Christ, not with an earthly, sentimental love, a selfish love that often hurts what it would bless, but just as Christ loves each one with perfect, righteous, unselfish love and simplicity.

How our hearts often ache because they are unadjusted! How bone fails to fit bone, in the body of Christ, and joint to fit into its socket, until the whole frame is distorted and diseased!

But Christ has a love for each of us which is stronger than our natural affection, and infinitely sweeter, quieter, more unselfish and blessed than any earthly love.

Some of you would die for your friend today, through your passionate devotion; but tomorrow, if he should slight your corpse, you would instantly rise from the dead to pour upon him your angry recrimination. That is not the Christ-love. It is peaceful and everlasting.

Some of you will fasten on the fault of another until you become blinded to his better qualities and forget his real goodness.

The Christ-love can see the error, but it can see also the other side, and can cover the error with the faith and hope that will claim from Christ its healing, and see him only in the light of Christ's own perfect love and grace.

The Christ-love has no respect for persons. It loves most dearly those whom God has fitly framed into the nearest place, but it loves each in his or her place, simply, wholly, unselfishly, with Christ's own thought and blessing.

The sun looks into the little daisy and gives it all the light the daisy can hold. The same sun looks into the great bosom of the summer lake and gives it a larger, richer glory, because the lake can hold more and reflect back the sun and the glory.

And so the love of God meets each person that comes in contact with your life, and touches each according to the adjustment of God's providence and the principles of His Word.

This Christ-love can love even the unworthy for its own sake and not for theirs. It loves not for the worth of the object, but, like the sunshine, it covers the meanest things with its own glory, "and loves the loveliness itself hath given."

Are not these some Hebron heights we long to climb, where it would be sweet to dwell above the clouds of our murky skies and malarial plains?

FELLOWSHIP

And so we might speak of Hebron as the type of fellowship, as the name expresses. There are heights of fellowship with God into which we need to rise. Do you not want to know the prayer of the Holy Spirit in all its mighty possibilities? Do you not want to know the prayer of faith in God in all its limitless forces? Do you not want to know the prayer without ceasing, and the abiding communion where the curtains are never closed and the Presence is never withdrawn?

Do you not want to know the communion of wordless fellowship which waits upon the Lord, which brings in His very life and fullness, which breathes His breath and lies upon His bosom in perfect rest, without a murmuring wave upon the peaceful shore?

Do you not want the sympathetic intuition that catches the very thought of God, that meets the Spirit's finest touch, that understands the Master's will, that responds to the still, small voice, and reaches out into the very mind of God?

Are these the things that weary you and oppress you and have no charm for you? Or does your spirit cry, "Tell me, you whom I love, where you graze/ your flock and where you rest your sheep at midday" (Song of Songs 1:7).

> I'm leaning close to Jesus' breast;
> So close that I can hear
> The softest whisper of His love
> In fellowship most dear;
> And feel that His almighty hand
> Is with me in this hostile land.

And then this makes the fellowship of others just as close and holy. In this secret place of the Most High, God brings to us the most sacred companionships of love, leads us into their inner lives, lays upon us their needs and makes it a luxury to pray for them. He uses us to carry their work and share in their sorrows, and begins even here the holy fellowships of the world above.

There are none so near to us as those that are far away, across wide seas and distant continents.

> There are cables underlying
> Every ocean wide;
> Cords of love and prayer are stronger
> Than the Atlantic's tide.

These are some of Hebron's heights. Beloved, shall we claim them and dwell there with Caleb, "in the summer-land of love"?

COVENANT BLESSINGS

Hebron was the city of Abraham and of David. As the city of Abraham, it represents the covenant of all the children of faith. It is our right to have their highest blessings.

There is nothing within the limits of the promises of God, or the possibilities of faith and love which we are not entitled to claim through the everlasting covenant, if we will but dare to appropriate it and enter in.

And so David was crowned at Hebron before he reigned at Jerusalem. So Hebron is a royal city, and so the place of love is always the place of kingliness. If we would rule in human hearts, and influence human destinies, we must have the heart of love. As I watch people in the work of God, I always see the loving heart go out in advance. And just as certainly the souls that have not won the highest victories of love, notwithstanding the most brilliant gifts, will become disqualified for the highest service.

If God is to make you a king, and crown you for the highest place in His work, you must get settled at Hebron, and begin your kingdom there, in the place of perfect love. Sensitiveness, selfishness, irritability, censoriousness, lack of sympathy, gentleness and infinite compassion, will bar you from the highest work and the grandest compensation.

FAITH

Hebron represents the victory of faith. How did Caleb win this mighty citadel? "The LORD helping me, I will drive them out just as he said" (Joshua 14:12).

It was all of faith. And so every victory must be one of faith. When Jesus told the disciples of the vast requirements of love for the erring, requiring forgiveness even unto 70 times seven, they might well have cried, "Lord, increase our love!" But their Spirit-prompted prayer was wiser than this. It was, "Increase our faith!" (Luke 17:5). They were right, and Jesus well said in reply, "If you have faith as small as a mustard seed, you can say to this mulberry tree, 'Be uprooted and planted in the sea,' and it will obey you" (17:6).

The mightiest mountain of unbelief and alienation will yield to one germ of divine love. We cannot grow into faith. It is not a plant indigenous to the soil of earth, but it must be claimed in the name of Jesus, on the ground of the covenant, through the Holy Spirit, as the direct obtainment of His grace.

And if today you have seen any lack of love in your heart and life, you have but to appropriate it according to your covenant right, to put down your name there, and then to put down your foot upon it and believing that you do receive it, step out into the testing of that love, insisting upon it as your right, and it will come into your life through His faithful and all-sufficient grace.

OBEDIENCE

Once more, Hebron represents the recompense of obedience. Hebron became the inheritance of Caleb because he "followed the LORD [his] God wholeheartedly" (Joshua 14:9).

Human love gives its rewards capriciously. That mother will hug her child almost to death this moment, and an hour hence may beat it almost to death.

But God loves on principle, and His caresses are always given for something. It is when we obey Him, when we please Him, when we stand fast in some place of testing, when we sacrifice some selfish thing at His bidding—it is then that we hear the sweet words, "Well done, good and faithful servant! . . . Come and share your master's happiness" (Matthew 25:21).

Like a loving mother, He takes up His child in His tender embrace, and lavishes upon him the fullness of His affection. It was when Abraham had proved his fidelity by the sacrifice of his son that God met him with that sweet testimony, "Now I know that you fear God, because you have not withheld from me your son, your only son" (Genesis 22:12).

This is what Jesus means in these wonderful words: "Whoever has my commands and obeys them, he is the one who loves me. He who loves me will be loved by my Father, and I too will love him and show myself to him" (John 14:21).

This is something more than He says to the ordinary Christian. This is His special love for the always-obedient heart. So struck were the disciples with it that they asked Him again concerning it. And He repeated the same promise in still stronger language: "If anyone loves me, he will obey my teaching. My Father will love him, and we will come to him and make our home with him" (14:23).

This is the pathway to Hebron. Shall we walk obediently in it, and so enter into all the joy of our Lord?

And now, in conclusion, God has been calling us in these lessons to the highest things. Do we realize that in these waiting years Caleb had already accomplished much more than an ordinary life? He had reached nearly a century of years. He had seen two generations pass away. He had been a slave amid the brickfields of Egypt. He had crossed the Red Sea, had stood under Sinai's awful cloud, had crossed the borders of Canaan, and stood on Hebron's heights nearly half a century before, and had afterwards traversed the whole round of the wilderness, without once turning from his God, following like a faithful dog, as his name signifies, and obeying all the will of his Master.

And now he had gone through the whole campaign of the conquest of Canaan, had marched around Jericho and entered through the breaches of its walls, had triumphed at Beth Horon, and walked through the length and breadth of the land. As his gray hair streamed in the wind that day, a man nearly a century old, almost anyone would have said that he, at least, might well deserve to claim a release from work and toil and enter the richest inheritance his Commander could give him. But we find him instead just stepping out on the threshold of his greatest life work, and, like a young man of 21, begging for the privilege of fighting the hardest battles that remained and conquering the mightiest giants of the Anakites.

Glorious Caleb! Inspiring leader! Bright example! Speak to the men and women that have been sanctified and called to meet the mighty opportunities of these momentous days.

As we stand on the threshold of the coming kingdom and await the first beams of the millennial dawn, Lord, send us out to higher, diviner, more victorious achievements of faith and love than we have yet experienced, for the glory of our Master's name. Amen.

CHAPTER 8

KIRIATH SEPHER, OR THE MIND OF CHRIST

And Caleb said, "I will give my daughter Acsah in marriage to the man who attacks and captures Kiriath Sepher." Othniel son of Kenaz, Caleb's brother, took it; so Caleb gave his daughter Acsah to him in marriage.

One day when she came to Othniel, she urged him to ask her father for another field. When she got off her donkey, Caleb asked her, "What can I do for you?"

She replied, "Do me a special favor. Since you have given me land in the Negev, give me also springs of water." So Caleb gave her the upper and lower springs. (Joshua 15:16–19)

The conquest of Hebron by Caleb was followed a few days afterwards by the capture of Kiriath Sepher, also known as Debir. For its capture Caleb offered as a prize the hand of his daughter Acsah; and Othniel, Caleb's own nephew, took up the challenge and won both the city and the maiden.

She brought her husband not only her fair self, but a still richer dowry from her father, who gave her, at her request, not only the splendid inheritance looking toward the south, but also the upper and the lower springs.

All this is full of holy suggestiveness and sacred teaching in connection with our higher inheritance in Christ.

KIRIATH SEPHER

Kiriath Sepher and Debir suggest the victory of faith over the natural mind and the wisdom of the world. Kiriath Sepher means "the city of the oracle, or the book," and Debir means "the speaker."

One is the fitting symbol of the natural mind, and the other of its most powerful instrument and expression, the tongue, and both together represent the hardest victory of the spiritual life, the conquest of our thoughts and our words.

Human nature is threefold, and consists of the spirit, soul and body. We have not only a spiritual nature, but we have an intellectual being, the seat of reason, mind and intelligence.

THE CARNAL MIND

This has been blighted by the fall, and requires to be renewed through the blood and Spirit of Christ just as much as any other part of our being.

Our mind influences our whole character and life. "For as he thinketh in his heart, so is he" (Proverbs 23:7, KJV), and intelligence without character is the most dangerous of created powers. Satan himself is just a great unholy intelligence. In one of the versions of the Bible his name is translated "the knowing one."

He is a being of transcendent brightness, but utterly without any right principle, his whole moral and spiritual being perverted and corrupted. Like the serpent—his scriptural image—his life is all centered in his head. You cannot kill a serpent until you strike its head. You may bruise its whole body, but if you leave the head intact it still lives. Hence the first promise of redemption was "he will crush your head" (Genesis 3:15).

He came to our first parents' intelligence. There was one tree in the garden that was prohibited to them. Everything else that could constitute happiness was theirs. All possible delights were given to them without stint. But there was one little bit of knowledge they must not claim, one single tree whose fruit they must not taste, one secret that must remain unknown; and it was with this that he tempted them, and with this that he destroyed them. He lured them on to enter the forbidden precincts. He attracted them by the dazzling promise of divine wisdom. He covered the forbidden prize with the glamor of his false light until everything else seemed eclipsed by its delusive brightness, and they reached forward over the precipice to grasp it. When they claimed it, they found it was but an empty bubble—but it had cost them an eternity of ruin for all their race.

And so still the tree of forbidden knowledge is the mystery with which he lures men and women on until they venture beyond God's holy prohibitions and sink into the depths of ruin.

OUR THOUGHTS

Temptations still assail us chiefly through our thoughts. In speaking of the depths of corruption in the days of Noah, God said, "Every inclination of the thoughts of his heart was only evil all the time" (Genesis 6:5). It is through imagination that sin approaches. Floating like a beautiful vision through the mind, the evil thought at first seems harmless, but if entertained and allowed to lodge, it becomes the seed that springs up into a living plant of unholy desire, which quickly bursts into blossoms of unwholesome fragrance, and if they are permitted to fertilize and linger, the fruit of evil choice—sinful yielding and actual transgression—follows with awful certainty and rapidity.

We must meet temptation, therefore, in our thoughts. We are so constituted that if we dwell on an evil thought it creates its own character within our spirit. The man of old who looked on the Gorgon's head was instantly turned into stone, and the soul that complacently and willingly indulges the thought of evil absorbs the evil into his own nature.

Walk down the street and let your eyes be fixed for a moment on a picture of obscenity, and you will immediately find your whole soul clouded by spiritual darkness and defilement. Although your spirit may revolt from it, still you will be conscious of a horrible fascination, and if you allow it to linger it will overpower your better feelings and change your nature into that of another man. Even your very body will be affected, and you will be conscious of being benumbed with the draught from the fountains of the pit.

The inventive genius of modern literature has given us the picture of a man who, by a certain draught, could be changed from one man into another of higher, nobler character. But he would immediately fall back from the nobler man into the lower ideal the moment he thought of it, feared it and recognized it. There is a strange truth here. The consciousness of evil creates evil, the thought of good becomes the fertile soil of good.

Christian Science, which is itself one of Satan's false and unholy thoughts, has one truth in it, as all lies have. That truth is that the thought of evil creates evil, and the thought of good has a tendency to produce good.

THE MIND OF CHRIST

Not only do we need to correct our thoughts, but we must go farther and actually crucify the old natural mind and receive an entirely new mind in Christ. The sanctification of the spirit is not the improvement of the old natural spirit, but the renouncing of it and the receiving of God's Holy Spirit instead. So the sanctification of our mind must be just as radical. We must recognize that our natural mind is wrong and must be laid wholly down, and we receive the mind of Christ instead, to think in us God's thoughts after God. So that our first experience is not the correcting of our thoughts, but the entire surrender of our mental being to the Lord Jesus Christ, to be crucified with Him.

The apostle has said that the wisdom of this world is entirely wrong in its principles and nature. His language is exceedingly strong. He says, "The world through its wisdom did not know him" (1 Corinthians 1:21). Its *very wisdom* kept it from God. "If anyone of you thinks he is wise by the standards of this age, he should become a 'fool' so that he may become wise. For the wisdom of this world is foolishness in God's sight" (3:18–19).

David says, "I hate thoughts" (Psalm 119:113, KJV); not only vain thoughts, but all thoughts that are human. This is the source of all our unbelief, our anxious care, our doubts and fears, our envies, jealousies, irritations, seditions, strifes, controversies—all have their seat in the strong intellectual life of the human heart; the willfulness of our opinions and the entertaining of thoughts, questionings, evil surmisings and imaginings that disquiet and defile the soul. From all these Christ wants to save us, to give us the mind which "is steadfast" (Isaiah 26:3); "the peace of God, which transcends all understanding" (Philippians 4:7), and garrisons the thought and the heart through Christ Jesus; the heart so subdued that every evil argument is demolished, and every pretension that sets itself up brought low, and every thought taken captive to make it obedient to Christ (2 Corinthians 10:5).

In the picture given of the works of the flesh in Galatians (5:19–21), dissensions, selfish ambition and controversies are spoken of in the same category as sexual immorality, impurity and debauchery. All these things are just as unholy in God's sight as the things that we call immoral.

THE TONGUE

Thus, Kiriath Sepher not only represents the mental source of evil thought, but the outward expression of it, the tongue. The control of the tongue, James says, is the rarest form of practical righteousness, and he adds that he who wins this victory will have little trouble in living a triumphant life in every other direction. "If anyone is never at fault in what he says, he is a perfect man, able to keep his whole body in check" (James 3:2).

The awful evils of the tongue are well described by the same apostle in language of terrible strength. "The tongue also is a fire, a world of evil among the parts of the body. It corrupts the whole person, sets the whole course of his life on fire, and is itself set on fire by hell" (3:6).

This is the Kiriath Sepher and the Debir that the Lord Jesus Christ is calling on us to smite and take. When we win this citadel of Canaan, we receive in Christ a divine inheritance in the very thing that we have surrendered. Instead of our own mind, we have the mind of Christ. Instead of our foolish and restless thoughts, we have the thoughts of God. Instead of our vain imaginings, we have the vision of His light and glory. Instead of our limited knowledge, the eyes of our understanding are enlightened, and we are able to know the "hope to which he has called [us], . . . and his incomparably great power for us who believe" (Ephesians 1:18–19).

Instead of the profoundest thoughts of man, we are led into "the deep things of God."

"No eye has seen,
no ear has heard,

> no mind has conceived
>   what God has prepared for those who love him"—
>
> but God has revealed it to us by his Spirit.
>   The Spirit searches all things, even the deep things of God.
>   (1 Corinthians 2:9–10)

God will open His glorious Word to us, and give the revelation and il-lumination of the Holy Spirit, and "your eyes will see the king in his beauty/ and view a land that stretches far" (Isaiah 33:17).

The tongue that has learned to be silent for self and Satan will become the instrument of God's messages and the channel of His glorious power.

The very symbol of the Holy Spirit at Pentecost was a cloven tongue. The very member He wants to use most is our voice and our power of utterance, but He will not use it until He has its absolute control and He can stamp it with His own signature and monogram, as His exclusive property and His own living voice.

Beloved, is not this a glorious possibility? Is not this a choice possession? Shall we go up and smite Kiriath Sepher and take it, to be henceforth owned and occupied by the Holy Spirit, to the glory of God alone?

It will be noticed that Kiriath Sepher comes after Hebron. It is love first, and then light. It is only as we learn the love life of the Lord, and get out of self and all its sensitiveness, that we can do rightly, speak rightly, think right-ly and know rightly.

We want to get the seat of life centered not in the brain, but in the heart and spirit; in love, and not in truth only. Then we shall understand the meaning of "Speaking the truth in love, we will in all things grow up into him who is the Head, that is, Christ" (Ephesians 4:15).

OTHNIEL

Othniel is the type of the secret victory over the natural mind. The word Othniel means "the lion of God," or "the force of God," as Dr. Young trans-lates it. He represents the power of the Lord Jesus Christ and the Holy Spirit in a courageous spirit.

Nothing less than omnipotent power can overcome the pride and strength of the carnal mind. It needs the very "force of God." "But no man can tame the tongue. It is a restless evil, full of deadly poison" (James 3:8). "The sinful mind is hostile to God. It does not submit to God's law, nor can it do so" (Romans 8:7).

It is a wild and desperate rebel; your own resolution never can control it. But if we will be brave enough to choose to die to it Christ is able to subdue it.

The weapons we fight with are not the weapons of the world. On the contrary, they have divine power to demolish strongholds. We demolish arguments and every pretension that sets itself up against the knowledge of God, and we take captive every thought to make it obedient to Christ. (2 Corinthians 10:4–5)

We are so glad that God put these words "divine power" or "mighty through God" (KJV) there. Every one who has tried to still the over-active brain, to subdue the flood of thought, to drive out the burning image from the imagination, to cleanse the foul picture from the chambers of the heart, to think calmly, or better, cease thinking altogether, knows how useless the endeavor in the strength of the human will.

But there is a voice that says to the wildest tempest of the heart and brain: "Quiet! Be still!" (Mark 4:39); and lo! there is a great calm! There is a power that can keep every thought, like handmaids and servants, waiting outside the inner chamber to come at call—a troupe of obedient servants, not a horde of wild disturbers—waiting for the call of will and conscience, and utterly controlled by the voice of the Holy Spirit.

Oh, this indeed is peace! Happy are they who know it! Thank God, it waits for all who are willing to yield themselves in complete surrender to the mind of Christ and the thoughts of God.

ACSAH

Othniel's victory was accepted as the price of Caleb's daughter, the fair Acsah, whose name signifies grace, and who may be regarded as the type of the special grace which Christ will give to victorious souls, and especially to those who have overcome the carnal mind.

GRACE

There is a grace that saves the sinful soul; but there is a deeper, richer grace that sanctifies and fills it with all the fullness of God.

"We have gained access by faith into this grace in which we now stand" (Romans 5:2). "God is able to make all grace abound to you, so that in all things at all times, having all that you need, you will abound in every good work" (2 Corinthians 9:8). "Those who receive God's abundant provision of grace and of the gift of righteousness reign in life through the one man, Jesus Christ" (Romans 5:17). "From the fullness of his grace we have all received one blessing after another" (John 1:16), the grace that meets the need of every moment, and supplies the lack of grace in us for every emergency.

Do we need the grace of faith, of love, of patience? There is grace for this, grace to supply it in abundance; so that we shall be patient in His patience, gentle in His gentleness, strong in His strength, and loving in His love.

This is the grace that Jesus has to give the souls that have become victorious over their own self-will and self-sufficiency, and are content to take Him as their strength and wisdom.

Acsah moved her husband to ask great things of her father. And so the grace of God moves us to the highest, mightiest prayers and to take the riches of divine grace and blessing.

Acsah, it would seem, moved Othniel to ask even more than Othniel asked for himself. We find her going to her father with a large prayer for him and for herself. And so grace asks for us even more than we ask for ourselves.

She brought her husband a rich inheritance, the south land, lying toward the warm sunshine; then she claimed for herself and him an added and double blessing.

It is very beautiful to see her getting off her donkey, before she approaches her father with her great request. Grace stoops to plead, and the lower it goes, the more it can ask and recieve. Abraham got on his face when he asked the everlasting covenant from Jehovah. The Syrophoenician woman rose to the very highest faith in the New Testament from the deepest humiliation, accepting even the terrible word the Master spoke about her sin and willing to count herself a "dog" (Matthew 15:27), yet claiming and receiving all the fullness of His infinite grace.

And so grace can stoop to the very depths of self-abasement, and yet rise to the heights of glory to claim all the fullness of God.

What she asked her father for was springs, and this grace always has for thirsting hearts. The life of works is a life of constant labor and painful effort, and the life of grace is a perpetual spring of spontaneous fullness and freedom.

It is so delightful to live and work for God from impulses that carry us beyond ourselves. There is a place in the midstream of human life where the current sweeps us along in the infinite fullness of God. But there is a place where we have to contend with eddies and cross-currents, to row and struggle against the stream and to press our way through the greatest difficulties.

Oh, it is so blessed to be carried on the current of His love and fullness and say continually, with an overflowing heart: "All my fountains are in you" (Psalm 87:7).

Acsah asked for springs, and her father gave her more than she asked: "So Caleb gave her the upper and lower springs" (Joshua 15:19).

FULLNESS OF GRACE

This beautiful figure tells us that the glorious fullness of the grace of God sweeps the whole circle of our being, "holding promise for both the present life and the life to come" (1 Timothy 4:8).

There are upper springs—springs of faith, that keep us trusting in the face of every discouragement; springs of prayer, that come from the promptings of the Holy Spirit, and carry our petitions straight to the throne with a consciousness of acceptance; springs of love that leap up to God, and enable us to say, "For Christ's love compels us" (2 Corinthians 5:14); springs of joy that burst from the eternal hills, a joy so inexpressible that it is glorious (1 Peter 1:8); springs of hope that reach out to the yet unseen and invisible, anticipating all that shall yet be revealed in our future inheritance; springs of power, that make our service a delight, our testimony a great overflow from a heart that cannot be silent, because it is so full. These are some of the upper springs.

But there are lower springs which we value even more. There are springs that flow in the low places of life, in the hard places, in the desert places, in the lone places, in the *common places* which seem farthest removed from all that is sacred and divine.

How blessed it is to drink from the springs of health, and find our strength "renewed day by day" (2 Corinthians 4:16), and the life of God flowing into even our physical organs and functions!

How delightful it is to have His gladness in the low places of sorrow, and to be able to "rejoice in our sufferings" (Romans 5:3).

How precious the springs that flow into the places of temptation, for there is nothing in life so trying as the touch of Satan's hand and the breath of the destroyer.

Oh, how sweet it is even there to find that the light is as deep as the shadow, and heaven is nearest when we are hard by the gates of hell; so that we can "consider it pure joy, my brothers, whenever you face trials of many kinds" (James 1:2), and say "Blessed is the man who perseveres under trial, because when he has stood the test, he will receive the crown of life that God has promised to those who love him" (1:12).

SPRINGS IN THE DESERT

There are springs that flow amid the places of toil and secular business. It is possible to be filled amid the common things of life with the conscious presence of God. It is possible to work in the shop and the kitchen with a zest as sweet as that which inspires the preacher in his sublimest flights of thought, the singer in her highest notes of devotion, the saint in his most blessed moment of communion.

God loves to cheer those that toil in lowly places, and we can hear the sweet bells of the high priest's garment within the veil and the echoes of the harps of God even amid the din of the busy streets and the rattle and roar of the 10,000 hammers and the whirling wheels of the factory.

The heart that has its spring within can be happy anywhere. The soul that is set to heavenly music can never be out of tune. The light that is kindled from above can shine in darkness, though "the darkness has not understood it" (John 1:5).

Beloved, God has for us these springs, and we need them every day. Let us drink of the living waters. Nay, let us receive them into our very hearts, so that we shall carry the fountain with us wherever we go, that it may be true of us as He said of old, "But whoever drinks the water I give him will never thirst. Indeed, the water I give him will become in him a spring of water welling up to eternal life" (John 4:14).

CHAPTER 9

THE DISCIPLINE OF HARD PLACES

"If you are so numerous," Joshua answered, "and if the hill country of Ephraim is too small for you, go up into the forest and clear land for yourselves there in the land of the Perizzites and Rephaites." (Joshua 17:15)

This chapter gives us three instructive lessons on the meaning of hard places and the discipline they should bring us.

THE CASE OF THE DAUGHTERS OF ZELOPHEHAD

"Now Zelophehad son of Hepher, the son of Gilead, the son of Makir, the son of Manasseh, had no sons but only daughters, whose names were Mahlah, Noah, Hoglah, Milcah and Tirzah. They went to Eleazar the priest, Joshua son of Nun, and the leaders and said, 'The LORD commanded Moses to give us an inheritance among our brothers.' So Joshua gave them an inheritance along with the brothers of their father, according to the LORD's command" (Joshua 17:3–4).

Half a century before, Moses had made special provision for the daughters of the tribes inheriting their portion, under certain circumstances equally with their brethren, when there was danger of their patrimony being alienated to another tribe, through intermarriage. The five daughters of Zelophehad came to Joshua and claimed their inheritance, in accordance with this provision of the Mosaic statute, and they received it at the hand of the great leader.

FAITH TRIUMPHING

This is a fine example of faith triumphing over difficulties and claiming its promised rights. This was the faith of Ruth, the Moabitess. She had found, through Naomi's teachings, that there was an ancient provision of the Mosaic law entitling her to claim the protection of Boaz, as her nearest of kin; and although it cost her the sacrifice of her sensitiveness, and the risk even to her reputation, yet this daughter of faith dared to go forward and claim her rights and place herself at the feet of Boaz.

The consequence was that she became one of the honored line of the Savior's ancestry and the aristocracy of the kingdom of God.

So God has given to us the redemption rights in His covenants of promise, and it is the part of faith to press through every difficulty and, claiming our full inheritance, we shall receive it.

This is the ground on which we claim our temporal blessings, our physical healing, and 10,000 things which so many allow to go by default. They are ours by right of promise, and there is no generosity in giving them away, or letting them be lost, for they have already cost our Savior His precious blood, and the only recompense He asks is that we claim them and enjoy them. Let us press forward and claim all our great bequest.

THE PLACE OF WOMAN

There is a special suggestion in this passage of the rights of woman under the gospel. We little realize, in western lands, how much Christianity has done for our sisters, and how high and glorious the equal place of honor and privilege which Christ has given to every daughter of faith.

Has woman a right to speak in the Church of God? Certainly, if she has anything worth saying, and if she is living what she says.

We believe she has no right to exercise the special ministry given to man as the ruler and pastor of the Church of God. But the New Testament Scriptures have given her undoubted freedom to the ministry of testimony to the gospel of Christ both in public and private, provided she does it in the modest way becoming to her holy womanhood.

These five dear girls in ancient Canaan were pioneers of the great army of brave and holy women whom Christ is sending forth today to minister to Him in the fields of Christian service, both at home and abroad.

Their names are suggestive of the highest womanly qualities.

Mahlah means "melody" or "song." She represents the spirit of praise, which should always go in front of Christian life and spiritual movement.

Noah means "rest," and implies that spirit of gentleness, stillness and peace which is woman's peculiar adorning, even "the unfading beauty of a gentle and quiet spirit, which is of great worth in God's sight" (1 Peter 3:4).

Hoglah, the third, means "festival," and fittingly expresses the spirit of joy which is the strength of every Christian life, and peculiarly the fruit of woman's sweet ministry. Every true Christian woman should be a joy-bringer and make life a festival of gladness wherever she goes.

Milcah means "counsel," and suggests the spirit of wisdom, propriety and good sense, without which all other womanly qualities fail of their object.

The true woman never speaks an indiscreet word, or does a thing which is out of place; but she moves with such a sense of propriety and the fitness of things, such true instincts of rightness, tact and holy wisdom, that she is a sort of balance-wheel in the mechanism of life. The picture of Solomon in his ideal woman is sweetly fulfilled in her, "She speaks with wisdom,/ and faithful instruction is on her tongue" (Proverbs 31:26). Some of our sisters, I am sure, know women who do not meet this ideal.

Beloved, shall you be a true Milcah, and claim as your inheritance the mind of Christ and the wisdom which is from heaven, which is "first of all pure; then peace-loving, considerate, submissive, full of mercy and good fruit, impartial and sincere" (James 3:17b)?

Tirzah, the last of these five blessed women, means, "benevolent," and represents the spirit of unselfishness, without which no woman can be true to her mission, or anything but a disappointment to herself and everybody else.

Selfishness is bad in anybody, but it is intolerable in a woman, for it is a perversion of the center of her being, and the primary object of her existence—love. If a woman is not love, she is a fallen angel and a melancholy wreck.

Dear sisters, shall you ask the Lord to give you, as your inheritance among the daughters of Zelophehad, this glorious life of praise, of peace, of joy, of wisdom and of heavenly love?

THE CHILDREN OF MANASSEH

We have next an example of slothfulness and sinfulness, compromising with difficulty and yielding to defeat. We read in the 12th verse that "the Manassites were not able to occupy these towns, for the Canaanites were determined to live in that region" (Joshua 17:12).

This seems very strange. They could do much harder things. They could cross the Jordan at floodtide. They could break down the walls of Jericho before the trumpet blast of faith. They could conquer 31 kings in five years, and subdue all the strongholds of Canaan. They could conquer Kiriath Sepher, drive out Arba and Anak, and the giant races; and yet they could not dispossess a few Canaanite hordes in the small towns and villages of their inheritance.

This is passing strange. Alas! the secret is revealed in the next verse, and it is a very humbling one: "However, when the Israelites grew stronger, they subjected the Canaanites to forced labor but did not drive them out completely" (17:13).

THE SECRET OF FAILURE

Ah! that is the secret; there was some tribute in the question! There was some advantage to be gained by compromise. There was some loss or pain to be incurred by a brave, determined effort. And so they gave the Canaanites the right of way, with the understanding that they should pay for it. And they fancied for a while that they had made a good bargain.

But the day came when the Canaanites put them to tribute, crushed them beneath their feet, and placed them in an intolerable bondage, so that the Israelites became the slaves of them they had conquered. And not only so, but they were led into terrible sins which brought upon them the displeasure and judgments of God, through the allurements and temptations of the tribes which they had tolerated.

This is just what Satan is doing today. He is getting people to compromise, for the sake of some benefit. God is trying to raise up a few uncompromising men. Half a dozen such men in Babylon were sufficient to shake the whole Babylonian Empire. One such man in Persia was stronger than Haman and all his plotting. And today, a handful of whole-hearted, uncompromising Christians would do more to revolutionize society and evangelize the world than 10 million half-hearted professors.

THE WILL

We learn from this chapter the real nature of our inability. The children of Manasseh could not drive out the Canaanites because they *would* not. Inability is usually unwillingness. Christ summed it all up when He said: "Yet you refuse to come to me to have life" (John 5:40). It is true there is a place which says: "No one can come to me unless the Father who sent me draws him" (6:44). But we must not forget it is added, "Everyone who listens to the Father and learns from him comes to me" (6:45).

The Father is always teaching, and those who are willing to learn will find no difficulty in coming. The unwilling heart does not want to learn, and is unable, because of its unwillingness.

Any soul that will choose to come to Christ will find Christ there to enable him to come.

Any Christian who desires to take any advance step in spiritual life has but to choose to take this step, and Christ will enable him to do so.

God will give you just as much as you really choose to take, and He will not only do this, but He also "works in you to will and to act according to his good purpose" (Philippians 2:13).

If you really want to choose the right and holy, God will enable you to do so.

There is a beautiful expression in the story of Nehemiah, full of encouragement to timid hearts: "Your servants who delight in revering your name" (Nehemiah 1:11). Nehemiah was a little afraid to say he revered the Lord's name, but he could honestly say that he desired to revere it, and God accepted that choice, and enabled him to make it. Our gracious and all-sufficient Savior asks no more of us than we are really able to give. He puts His grace within reach of every human being, and if you will take it you can, and He will do the rest. The chariot of grace is passing by, and He is saying, in the language of one of old, "Is thy heart right with My heart, as My heart is with thy heart? Come into My chariot." And He will carry you in the chariot of His grace above all your trials, conflicts and difficulties, and make you more than conqueror, through His all-sufficient grace.

THE CHILDREN OF EPHRAIM

In the closing incident we have a picture of the way to reach the highest things. The children of Ephraim came to Joshua with a special request for a double inheritance.

Their plea was that they were a great people, and that the Lord had blessed them hitherto. Their request was that they should receive part of the fertile valleys adjoining them, and held by the native tribes; and it seems to be implied that they expected their brethren to help them to drive them out. It really amounted to a request that they might receive a larger share from the inheritance of their brethren, and the help of the other tribes to win this inheritance.

Joshua's reply is full of keen sarcasm and shrewd wisdom. He does not deny their claim; he does not discourage their ambition. He says, "You are numerous and very powerful" (Joshua 17:17), and then he bids them to go and prove their greatness by doing something great, and thus conquering the enemy over against them.

The mountain, he adds, is there, with its powerful Canaanites and its chariots of iron. They can have no grander opportunity than to conquer these hordes. And they can have just as much as they can take and prove their right to by valorous conquest.

They seem to have disliked his sarcastic and practical message, and they came back the second time. But he only sharpened his caustic words a little more, and repeated his former challenge—that if they were as great as they claimed to be, they must prove it by some great achievement, and they could have all they could conquer.

They seem to have dropped out of the drama at this period; and, as we learn from a former verse, they could not drive out the people of the land, but the Canaanites should dwell in the land. We have reason to fear that the greatness of Ephraim faded away "like the morning mist,/ like the early dew" (Hosea 6:4).

But the words remain for us, and a grander inheritance still awaits every brave heart that is willing to take up the challenge and climb the mountain heights of hardship and opposition.

There are several things in the plea of the Ephraimites that are fitted to fill us with humiliation. The first is their consciousness of their own greatness. This is very humbling and discouraging. "We are a numerous people" (17:14)! It is a good deal better to have somebody else say this than to say it ourselves.

SELF-IMPORTANCE

We are all in danger of getting self-conscious. It is not only a blemish upon a noble character, but it is a source of great weakness. In conscious nothingness alone lies our strength and security evermore.

The next serious criticism is the reference to their claim for superior blessing. "The LORD has blessed us abundantly" (17:14). Well, He has blessed other people, too. And if He has blessed you more than others it is only a stronger reason why you should do more than others, and it gives you no claim for a special possession or an easy inheritance won for you by others.

A true servant—like the Seraphs—hides his feet as well as his face with his wings, and presses forward to the things that are yet undone.

The third fault of the Ephraimites was that they looked for others to help them. They wanted somebody to give them an inheritance, and Joshua told them they could have it for the taking.

How much would any of us amount to if we were separated from the people that surround us and uphold us, and, stripped of our props, were sent out to stand alone?

Take you out of this assembly, with its hallowed associations, and send you out to stand alone with God in some lone field, at home or abroad, and how much faith and courage would you have left?

These are tests that have to come to us sooner or later. Every one must learn to lean upon God, and then God can trust him with human surroundings and supports, without the danger of his leaning upon an arm of flesh.

Ephraim wanted other people to conquer his inheritance for him, and there are lots of people today willing to accept the prizes of grace if somebody will give them without effort. They will allow the Lord to heal them if somebody will pray it into them and believe for them. They want to have sanctification and the baptism of the Holy Spirit, but they want to get it from somebody's hands or prayers. They are willing to work for Christ, but they want someone to prepare the work for them, and give it to them, like a piece of machinery, all wound up and ready to go.

Put them into the pulpit, with a nice congregation, choir and salary, and they will go with considerable regularity for awhile.

Start them in some routine of Christian work, and buoy them up with sympathy, appreciation, encouragement and praise, and they will do nicely.

But send them out to the regions beyond, set them down, like Paul and Silas in the prison of Philippi, plant them in a wilderness of isolation and desolation and they will shrink into nothing, and wither like a fading flower.

There are people who are as tall as church spires now, who will scarcely be fit for doorsteps in the temple yonder. Thank God that He does send us out alone sometimes, and prove how much of Himself we really possess.

But there are, on the other hand, some very cheering things in this message.

RIGHT AMBITION

The first is that God is not displeased with our holy ambition, and does not discourage our high aspiration. If we want a larger work, God will give it to us. We may step out into the regions beyond and conquer as much territory as we dare. There is nothing to hinder any ambitious Christian starting out tomorrow and starting a mission in Central China that will be as much blessed as the China Inland Mission, if he dare to take it from the Lord.

There is nothing to hinder any earnest Christian, who has the call, from starting a work in the slums that will be as fruitful as the Water Street Mission. That began with nothing, and you can begin with just as much capital if you take the Lord for it.

When James and John came to Christ with their mother, asking Him to give them the best place in the kingdom, He did not refuse their request, but told them it would be given to them if they could do His work, drink of His cup and be baptized with His baptism.

Do we want the competition? The greatest things are always hedged about by the hardest things; and we, too, shall find the mountains, the forests, the Canaanites and the chariots of iron, as well as the Ephraimites.

HOW TO WIN A CROWN

Hardship is the price of coronation. Triumphal arches are not woven out of rose blossoms and silken cords, but of hard blows and bloody scars.

The very hardships that you are enduring in your life today are given by the Master for the explicit purpose of enabling you to win your crown. Do not wait for some ideal situation, some romantic difficulty, some faraway emergency; but rise to meet the actual conditions which the providence of God has placed around you today.

Your crown of glory lies imbedded in the very heart of those things—those hardships and trials that are pressing you this very hour, week and month of your life.

The hardest things are not those that the world knows about. Down in your secret soul, unseen and unknown by any but Jesus, there is a little trial that you would not dare to mention, that is harder for you to bear than martyrdom. There, beloved, lies your crown. God help you to overcome, and some time to wear it!

Oh, how the days are telling as they pass by! The Spirit is testing us and trying our fitness for something beyond.

Each of us is conscious, as we meet people, of measuring them mentally and physically, and determining their character and weight, and what they are fit for. And how disappointed we are when those whom we have trusted do not come up to our standard for them, and we feel that they are not fitted for the place we had given them in our thought! And how pleased we are when they do come somewhere near our ideal of them!

Beloved, this may help you to understand how God is watching you from the heights above, not with the eye of a critic, but as a loving Master, and when we rise to His standard how His arms will enfold us! How He will press us to His bosom, and rejoice as He can say: "Well done, good and faithful servant! . . . Come and share your master's happiness!" (Matthew 25:21). "Sit with me on my throne, just as I overcame G and sat down with my Father on his throne" (Revelation 3:21).

God grant we may all press forward to the high places He has prepared for us, and meet the moments that come as witnesses that shall come back some day to testify either for or against us in the great day of eternal recompense!

CHAPTER 10

TIMNATH SERAH, OR THE CITY OF THE SUN

When they had finished dividing the land into its allotted portions, the Israelites gave Joshua son of Nun an inheritance among them, as the LORD had commanded. They gave him the town he asked for— Timnath Serah in the hill country of Ephraim. And he built up the town and settled there. (Joshua 19:49–50)

This was the last of the special inheritances in the Land of Promise. Joshua, the unselfish leader, left his own inheritance until the last, and even then it was his people who gave to him his portion, and he accepted it only when they pressed it upon him. It is no wonder that it was the highest and best of all the choice possessions of the land.

Its name is suggestive of its value and significance. Timnath Serah in Mount Ephraim means "the city of the sun," and it speaks to us of the highest and best possibilities of our own Christian life.

SPIRITUAL JOY

1. The city of the sun is a place of delightful happiness, for the sun is the type of the Lord Himself, our Light and our Salvation—"you will fill me with joy in your presence,/ with eternal pleasures at your right hand" (Psalm 16:11b). "Blessed are those who have learned to acclaim you,/ who walk in the light of your presence, O LORD./ They rejoice in your name all day long;/ they exult in your righteousness" (89:15–16).

The figure speaks of gladness and sunshine. Are we living there?

There is no better way for us to glorify Him than to be happy in Him, and "be glad all our days" (90:14).

This will be a witness to the world that they cannot resist, and it will give a strength and energy to our own life and service which cannot be exaggerated.

Oh! you downcast souls, you children of anxious care and gloom, come up

91

into the city of the sun and dwell in the light of the Lord! There is a heaven below in which victorious souls may dwell before they reach the heaven above.

GLORIOUS GRACE

2. The city of the sun is a place of abundant and glorious grace, for "the LORD God is a sun and shield;/ the LORD bestows favor and honor;/ no good thing does he withhold/ from those whose walk is blameless" (84:11).

Its inhabitants have the immunities and privileges of heavenly citizens, and dwell continually in the presence of their King, and all the riches of His grace are their free inheritance.

He gives them not only His grace, but His glory, and withholds from them no good thing. They have His resources for all their undertakings, and out of His fullness do they receive even grace for grace.

Beloved, are we dwelling in this city of the sun? Have we received this abundance of grace, and are we reigning in the light and joy of Jesus Christ? Can you say with a glad and rejoicing heart, "My God will meet all your needs according to his glorious riches in Christ Jesus" (Philippians 4:19), and "Surely goodness and love will follow me/ all the days of my life,/ and I will dwell in the house of the LORD/ forever" (Psalm 23:6)?

CHRIST'S PRESENCE

3. The city of the sun is the place of Christ's manifested presence. In the 14th chapter of John, Jesus said to His disciples, "Whoever has my commands and obeys them, he is the one who loves me. He who loves me will be loved by my Father, and I too will love him and show myself to him" (14:21).

This word "show" in the original involves the figure of the brightest sunlight, and it literally means the outshining of the sun, and expresses the glory of Christ's inward revelation of Himself to the trusting and obedient heart.

Brighter than the noonday sun, more real than the effulgence of the orb of day, is the light with which Christ makes Himself known, ofttimes, in the inner sanctuary of the consecrated soul.

It was foreshadowed in the Shekinah glory, that lit up, in ancient times, the Holy of Holies and hovered above the mercy seat. Speaking of it, the apostle says: "For God, who said, 'Let light shine out of darkness,' made his light shine in our hearts to give us the light of the knowledge of the glory of God in the face of Christ" (2 Corinthians 4:6).

The Holy Spirit is spoken of as having "poured out" (Romans 5:5), or shined abroad, the love of God in our hearts. Do you know the vision of His glorious face? Have you seen Him in the revelation of His inward glory: "His face was like the sun shining in all its brilliance" (Revelation 1:16), and of whom you can truly say, "[he] is . . . outstanding among ten thousand . . . he is altogether lovely" (Song of Songs 5:10, 16)?

DIVINE LIGHT

4. The city of the sun is a place of light and guidance. For again the Master has said: "I am the light of the world. Whoever follows me will never walk in darkness, but will have the light of life" (John 8:12). The Light of life is the light that shines upon our daily life.

There is a place where we may walk continually in the light of the Lord, and receive habitually the guidance that will guard us from serious error, and keep us in the light of God.

There is a way of coming to God occasionally for direction in great crises, and then doing the best you can on ordinary occasions. But it is possible to have our whole life so possessed by the Holy Spirit that our very thoughts and intuitions will come to us in quietness and simplicity, with the consciousness that they have been touched by His thought and illumined by His light, that we are walking continually with our Father, and receiving constantly the testimony that we please God.

This is a very beautiful freedom which He has promised to the meek and consecrated spirit. "I will instruct you and teach you in the way you should go;/ I will counsel you and watch over you" (Psalm 32:8). "Whether you turn to the right or to the left, your ears will hear a voice behind you, saying, 'This is the way; walk in it' " (Isaiah 30:21).

Beloved, are you dwelling in this city of light, walking continually under His directing eye, and with the consciousness of being in His blessed light?

LIFE AND POWER

5. The city of the sun is a place of quickening life and power. The sun is the source of life and force. As it ascends the higher meridian of spring and summer, how the pulses of nature revive, until every tree and plant is throbbing with new vitality, and all the forces of nature are stimulated and vivified!

How easily the sun holds this world and all the train of planets and satellites in their circling orbits, without a quiver of restlessness or a flutter of decaying strength! How mighty the force of gravitation that sweeps from yonder ball of fire and holds the solar system in harmonious activity!

Christ is our Sun and Source of life and power. As we dwell in His presence we are quickened into resurrection life and animated with His own almighty power.

The joy of the Lord is our strength, and they who dwell above the clouds and mists of earth's lower planes know "his incomparably great power for us who believe" (Ephesians 1:19), and are used by His Spirit as the instruments and vessels of His mighty plans.

Are we dwelling in this city of life and working in His all-sufficiency?

LOVE

6. The city of the sun is a place of warmth and love. It is a summer clime, where the frosts and chills of selfishness and bitterness never come, where the warm atmosphere of God's everlasting love melts every ice bond, dissolves the wintry chains, and brings all hearts into the family relationships of the heavenly world, and we are one, even as the Father is in the Son and the Son in the Father (John 17:21), and "the whole building is joined together and rises to become a holy temple in the Lord" (Ephesians 2:21).

We cannot know anything about love unless we dwell in God and God in us. All true love must come from Him, and as we live in the light of His presence and the warm atmosphere of His fellowship, we shall love even as He loves, and we shall reflect on others the radiance which is shining in our hearts from His.

DIVINE HEALING

7. The city of the sun is a place of divine healing.

Let us look again at His own words: "But for you who revere my name, the sun of righteousness will rise with healing in its wings. And you will go out and leap like calves released from the stall" (Malachi 4:2).

In the natural world sunlight is essential to health, and darkness and shadow create a congenial atmosphere to disease. Good light and pure air are agencies of health.

Still more is the life and joy of the Lord essential to spiritual healthfulness. The light of Christ is the true source of physical strength and the joy of the Lord is the best of all medicines. The inflowing and indwelling of the Holy Spirit brings quickening strength to every fiber of our being.

If you would rise above the depressing influence of climate, contagion and natural infirmity, build your house in Timnath Serah, and dwell continually in the loving presence and cloudless communion of the Holy Spirit.

COMMUNION

8. The city of the sun is a place of cloudless and unbroken communion.

There is a place in Northern Europe which they call "The Land of the Midnight Sun." There, as the months pass by, the sun completes its circle above the horizon, and it is one continual, cloudless day.

There is such a land in our higher inheritance of grace. There is a promise which we may prove and claim even in this life. "Your sun will never set again,/ and your moon will wane no more;/ the LORD will be your everlasting light,/ and your days of sorrow will end" (Isaiah 60:20).

There are human friendships, especially those that are very intimate, whose exquisite delight is this, that they have never been clouded, and that these friends could not ever imagine the shadow of a cloud passing over them. The very thought that you could be alienated from your friend would at once place that friendship on a different plane and make it common.

It is its exquisite prerogative that you cannot even conceive of its being clouded by a doubt or a breach of confidence. And there is a friendship with Christ so exquisite and true that it not only has no severance or interruption, but we cannot even conceive of any breach or suspension.

In its very nature, the love is everlasting, infinite, unconditional and capable of no separation. He has given to us His eternal oath: "So now I have sworn not to be angry with you,/ never to rebuke you again" (54:9). And you would as soon think of blaspheming Him to His face as of even imagining the shadow of a doubt of His perfect and everlasting love.

Beloved, have you come into this high place of unclouded light and love? Have you tasted the exquisiteness of that communion which you know will never be interrupted? It is for you. "The city does not need the sun or the moon to shine on it, for the glory of God gives it light, and the Lamb is its lamp" (Revelation 21:23).

HOW DO WE GET TO THIS CITY?

1. We get there through Jesus Christ, the only Mediator (1 Timothy 2:5). There are two sides to a mountain. If you attempt to ascend you will be hurled from dizzy heights and slippery places to awful chasms, or wrapped in veils of impenetrable mist, through which you cannot find your way.

But there is another way, up a gentle incline, where a pathway has been prepared, and you can safely reach the loftiest heights.

And so there is a way by which we cannot find God—the way of mere research, human wisdom or moral righteousness. In vain have the ages sought to find the seat of His gracious presence, and gaze upon His countenance in light and live. It is like ascending Sinai through the thick darkness and the angry fire.

But there is a way which Jesus has prepared and of which He says: "I am the way . . . No one comes to the Father except through me" (John 14:6); "no one has ever seen God, but God the One and Only, who is at the Father's side [in the bosom of the Father, KJV], has made him known" (1:18). Not only *was* He in the bosom of the Father but He *is* in the bosom, and when we come into His bosom we are in the Father's bosom, too. It is like the ascent of the ancient Mount, when Moses took the elders of Israel up to meet God, and they carried in their hands the atoning blood. As they went up into that glorious Presence-Chamber, we are told with exceeding beauty,

Under his feet was something like a pavement made of sapphire, clear as the sky itself. But God did not raise his hand against these leaders of the Israelites; they saw God, and they ate and drank. (Exodus 24:10–11)

This is the way to Timnath Serah. "Since we have confidence to enter the Most Holy Place by the blood of Jesus, by a new and living way opened for us through the curtain, that is, his body, . . . let us draw near to God" (Hebrews 10:19–22), and we shall find ourselves in the city of the sun.

2. Let us build there. Joshua not only chose Timnath Serah, but he ascended to the mountain-height, and he built the city. Now there are a good many ways to build a city, especially with reference to the sun. We can build so as to shut out all the warmth, or we can turn its face toward the sunshine and open all the windows to the light. Some people seem to be constituted so as to catch every shadow and cloud that comes, and some seem to focus every ray of sunshine at their own door.

Were I building a city of the sun, I should make all the gates of praise and the walls salvation. The houses should be of transparent glass, that the sun might shine through them every day, and the outlook for every window should be toward the rising sun.

There is a story of an Oriental king who worshiped the sun, and he wanted to build a temple to it. He sent for three architects and asked each to give him a model of the temple. After many days they returned to submit their models.

The first prepared a temple of stone, beautifully carved. The king admired it and called for the second. His was of pure gold, and the walls were polished and burnished until they reflected the sun from every side. The king was delighted with it, and the architect thought he had won the prize. But the third brought his little model, and, lo! it was all of glass, so that the sun could come in every side and fill it spontaneously with its light and glory.

"Ah," said the king, "this is the true temple of the sun; this is his own fitting shrine, letting him into every chamber, and having no glory but his own perfect light."

Beloved, shall we be such temples of the Sun of Righteousness, open to Him in every avenue of our being, and filled in the inmost part with His glorious light and presence? He will come wherever there is an opening to receive Him.

3. But Joshua not only built there but dwelt there. He did not visit Timnath Serah occasionally to get mountain views from the sunlit hills, but he made it his abiding home.

Are we dwelling in Timnath Serah? Are we abiding in the light and love of

God? Have we come to that settled place where "your sun will never set again,/ . . . the LORD will be your everlasting light" (Isaiah 60:20)?

And now there are two more words that tell us how we may obtain this blessed portion.

The first is, Joshua received this inheritance. "Do what the LORD has commanded" (Joshua 8:8). God provided it for him in His Word and so He has provided it for each of us. It is not only God's promise, but His command for us, that we shall rise to the fullness of His blessing.

"Therefore, since the promise of entering his rest still stands, let us be careful that none of you be found to have fallen short of it" (Hebrews 4:1).

But there is another word. We are told that Joshua also asked it. God gave it and Joshua asked it; and we shall receive what we ask for, and take.

There are many things in the commands of God for you, which are missing by simple default. "You do not have, because you do not ask God" (James 4:2).

How sorry you would be if you found, after spending a lifetime of poverty and toil, a will had been left by a friend providing you with affluence and wealth, and you had simply neglected to prove it and claim it!

Your bountiful Father has left you a city of glory and joy. Do not let it be lost through your default, but claim your inheritance, enter upon it, build it and occupy it, and you, too, shall be able to sing,

> I am dwelling on the mountains,
> Where the golden sunlight gleams,
> O'er a land whose wondrous beauty
> Far exceeds my fondest dreams;
> Where the air is pure, ethereal,
> Laden with the breath of flowers,
> They are blooming by the fountains,
> 'Neath the amaranthine bowers.
>
> Is not this the Land of Beulah,
> Blessed, blessed Land of Light,
> Where the flowers bloom forever
> And the Sun is always bright?

CHAPTER 11

THE CITIES OF REFUGE, OR THE SINNER'S INHERITANCE

We who have fled to take hold of the hope offered to us may be greatly encouraged. (Hebrews 6:18)

T his chapter describes the arrangements in ancient Israel for the protection of persons accused of murder or manslaughter. It was no unusual thing in ancient times to provide asylums for such persons.

It is said that the city of Rome was ordinarily peopled by refugees from all countries, who were promised immunity by Romulus, and who came to the asylum established for them, and afterward became citizens of Rome.

The arrangements made by God through Moses and Joshua were of much wiser and more righteous character. It is very significant that God should so emphasize His care for the sinner in this book, which is so specially devoted to typify the principles of the higher Christian life.

GOD'S LOVE FOR SINNERS

At the very threshold of the land we meet Rahab, of Jericho, a woman representing the very worst class of society; and we find her not only saved by the grace of God, but introduced into the ancestral line of David and of Christ Himself, and one of the mothers of the royal family of the eternal ages. And here at the close of the book, in the most careful provision which Jehovah made for the protection of the manslayer, we see a very emphatic hint of God's gracious care for the sinful and the lost.

Surely, it is meant to teach us that the higher we rise in the experience of God's grace, the lower we will stoop in the exercise of His mercy toward the fallen, and the more will we labor and care for the recovery of the lost.

Let us never get so sanctified that we shall be out of reach of poor sinners, or lose our sympathy for them or cut ourselves off from them. The nearer we come to our Master, the more frequently will we be found by His side in the company of publicans and sinners.

I should greatly suspect my sanctification if it led me to lose my interest in the salvation of men, and my love for the souls of the lost and the unworthy. Thank God that in these days the men and women that are going deepest into the slums and searching farthest for the sheep that have gone astray, are those who believe in the fullness of Christ, and live in His abiding love, and in all the higher things which we have been studying in this wondrous book!

In this connection it is very noteworthy that all the cities of refuge were placed under the care of the Levites, and, in fact, were Levitical cities.

The Levites, as we know, were the types of the highest consecration; and the lesson is, that God has given the sinful world in trust to His true Levites, and as His consecrated people fulfill the mission of the Levites they will be found seeking and saving the souls that have gone astray.

In the ancient cities of refuge there is a beautiful type of God's provision in the gospel for the salvation of men.

THE LEGAL AND DIVINE PROVISION

It was guarded and sanctioned by divine enactment, and it was as secure as the will and power of God could make it.

If the law of the land stands behind you, you are stronger in your humble home, with a simple thread to hold the door, than you would be in a fortified castle, if you were contrary to the law.

Entrenched behind the right, you can fold your arms and defy all the power of man to disturb you. But against the law, and in a position of wrong, you may be barricaded and defended by walls of stone and bastions of steel; but the law will break through your defenses, drag you from your hiding place and consign you to the dungeon of a criminal in spite of all your fancied security.

The protection which God gave to the ancient manslayer was a legal and divine protection. Asylums were provided under special laws, to which he might flee and defy the avenger to touch him. Within that sacred enclosure it would be a crime to shed his blood, and every law and power in the land were bound to protect him.

And so the salvation which God offers to the sinner is not a mere adventitious escape from punishment, but a security so divinely arranged, so justly secured, so eternally guaranteed, that "we who have fled to take hold of the hope offered to us may be greatly encouraged" (Hebrews 6:18).

If you accept the gospel of Jesus Christ, you will have all the power of God back of you to defend you; all the will of God on your side; all the justice and righteousness of God pledged to your defense, as well as all the infinite love and mercy of God to welcome and bless you.

It is not a mere caprice of conditional clemency, which He may change at will, but an everlasting protection, based upon the principles of right, and immovable as the throne of God.

Every debt is not merely forgiven, but paid absolutely and forever by a just equivalent fully accepted by the offended party. The atonement of Jesus Christ has met every requirement of justice, and it would be wrong on the part of God to punish one who has availed himself of this divine provision. Therefore, we are told that "if we confess our sins, he is *faithful and just* and will forgive us our sins and purify us from all unrighteousness" (1 John 1:9).

He is bound by the very attributes of justice to save the soul that accepts the atonement of Jesus, and His word is pledged as one that cannot lie, to save and keep the trusting heart.

Oh, sinner, if you come within this enclosure you are as safe as though you were in heaven! That word—"Whoever comes to me I will never drive away" (John 6:37) will be a wall of stone against your guilty conscience and all your foes. That mighty promise—"I give them eternal life, and they shall never perish; no one can snatch them out of my hand" (10:28), will hold you as "an anchor for the soul, firm and secure. It enters the inner sanctuary behind the curtain" (Hebrews 6:19).

A JUST AND RIGHTEOUS PROVISION

It was not indiscriminate immunity from punishment for all classes of criminals, but it was a place of safety for the man who had accidentally, or without intent of evil, taken the life of his neighbor. He was sheltered and guarded until his case could be investigated, and if he were found to be innocent of any intent of evil, he was allowed to remain in safety in this refuge until the death of the high priest.

And so the gospel of Jesus Christ is not a premium on vice, or an excuse for license. It does not say to man, "commit all the sin you please, and you shall have plenary indulgence." But it is God's provision for men who sincerely desire to be delivered from sin, and be right with God and man.

If you really want to be saved and cleansed, and to live a right and true life, and will honestly choose it, the blood of Christ and the grace of the Holy Spirit will instantly and fully save you, no matter who you are, or what you have been or done.

But if you do not want to do right, if your intention is to commit sin; if your purpose is to do evil, and you only want the gospel to shelter you in it, you shall find it the most terrible place beneath the heavens for a false heart to stand. No man dare trifle with the precious blood of Christ.

It says to the sinner, "Then neither do I condemn you" (John 8:11); but it says just as solemnly, "Go now and leave your life of sin" (8:11). "But with [God] there is forgiveness" (Psalm 130:4); not that He may be trifled with, but "therefore you are feared" (130:4).

THE DEATH OF CHRIST

The manslayer abode in the city of refuge until after the death of the high priest; then he was free to return to his home.

This very significantly points to the death of Jesus Christ, as the ground of our deliverance from guilt and sin, and our acceptance into the favor of God and the liberty of His sons.

More specifically it points, perhaps, to the difference between the Old Testament saints and those under the gospel. Under the Old Testament, the sins of believers were forgiven, and they were accepted into the favor of God, in anticipation of the redemption which was to be accomplished in the future, but they did not enter into heaven, but were held until the Ascension of Christ, under a certain reserve, in Hades, or Paradise. But after Christ's resurrection they ascended with Him into heaven, and now the souls of believers at their death immediately pass into His glory, and enjoy the fullness of the purchase of His blood, as those of the past dispensation did not.

Therefore, we find that David "rested with his fathers" (1 Kings 2:10), but Stephen said, "I see heaven open and the Son of Man standing at the right hand of God" (Acts 7:56) as he enters His immediate presence. Lazarus is carried, not to the side of Jesus, but "to Abraham's side" (Luke 16:22), with the Old Testament saints. But Paul expects to "be with Christ" (Philippians 1:23), and "the spirits of righteous men made perfect" (Hebrews 12:23).

The death and resurrection of Jesus Christ have discharged us from every claim, and given to us the glorious liberty of the sons of God in this world, and the heirs of His glory in the world to come.

ACCESSIBLE TO ALL

The ancient cities of refuge were accessible from all places, and to all classes. There were no less than six of them distributed throughout the land; three of them on the west side of the Jordan, about equal distances apart, and three on the east side; and none farther than a day's run from any point in the land.

The roads that led to them were always kept in good repair, at the expense of the government. The way was always open, both day and night, for any fugitive that should fly to the asylum. The gates of the city were continually open, and persons there to welcome the fugitive the moment he might arrive, and to provide him with every necessity of life. No one was allowed to obstruct his progress on his journey. Everybody made way for him, and there was no possibility of mistaking the way, for at every crossing, and often along the way, were mile posts and inscriptions, pointing in the right direction, and the word "Refuge" written on each post, so that he could read even while he ran. This is the meaning of that expression: "He that runneth may read."

So the way to Christ and the salvation of the gospel is just as open and just as plain. Christ is accessible to every sinner who wants Him, and the gates of mercy are never farther than a day's run—nay, a moment's look—from the most hopeless heart.

The way of salvation is so plain that it is impossible for an honest inquirer to mistake it. There may be differences of opinion about doctrines. There may be variations about sanctification, healing, the Lord's coming and the doctrines of theology, but they are all one about the way of salvation.

In the missions and in the inquiry meeting there is but one gospel and one salvation; and you could never find out, if you tried, what church that Christian worker belongs to, when he is pointing souls to Christ. Praise God for the simplicity of the gospel.

No man need ever be lost through ambiguity or uncertainty about this. God has left the highway always open; the gates are never closed; and He wants us to keep all obstacles out of the way of the sinner, and speed him on his way to the hope set before him. Oh come and enter in!

SAFE

The fugitive was perfectly safe in the city of refuge, and all his wants were supplied at the public expense. There was not even a weapon of war to be found within its gates, and there was no lack of anything which he needed for his comfort or maintenance.

And so with the provisions of the gospel. We are eternally secure and amply supplied. "We have gained access by faith into this grace in which we now stand" (Romans 5:2). God has provided in Christ for the supply of all our needs. There is grace for our daily cleansing and constant keeping, and our God has declared that He will supply all our needs "according to his glorious riches in Christ Jesus" (Philippians 4:19); and from "the fullness of his grace we have all received one blessing after another" (John 1:16).

FLY

There were two things which the manslayer must do, and which the sinner must also do. The first was to fly, and never to stop until he got within the precincts of the refuge. The second was to stay, and never venture beyond those precincts until he was publicly released.

And so for us there is a refuge, there is salvation, there is abundant grace; but we must fly to it. We must claim it. We must take it, or we shall perish.

There is no safety on the way. There is no safety, almost there. The manslayer could have perished even on the very steps of its portals. And so we must not linger or delay a moment until we have crossed its threshold and are safe within its doors.

God's words are awfully urgent. "Flee from the coming wrath" (Matthew 3:7). "Take hold of the life that is truly life" (1 Timothy 6:19). "Flee for your lives! Don't look back, and don't stop anywhere in the plain" (Genesis 19:17b). "I tell you, now is the time of God's favor, now is the day of salvation" (2 Corinthians 6:2).

Outside of Christ, everything in heaven and earth is against the sinner. Destruction pursues him in every breath, element and force about him. His only safety is to *fly* to Christ without a moment's delay, and then when he enters that sacred refuge, stay there.

STAY

There was a small circle around its walls within which the inmates could have freedom, and it was large enough to give them all the freedom they needed; but beyond that there was no safety.

And so God has circumscribed our refuge. Within its precincts, within the Holy Bible we are absolutely safe; but beyond His Word there is danger, and there may be destruction. Let us abide in Him and under His commandments, and we shall be safe and happy in His infinite protection and everlasting love.

The ancient cities of refuge also set forth the *fullness* of Christ's salvation for the sinner.

It is not enough to be merely saved. God has a boundless progression of blessing through which He wants to lead us. And as we press forward into the fullness of Christ, we are not only safe and secure, but we are guarded from falling, and led on to all the heights of His grace and glory.

A wise Christian worker will never be content with simply leading a soul to Christ, and will never rest until he has introduced him to the fullness of His grace, the baptism of His Spirit and the blessings of a consecrated life.

All this is finely set forth in the ancient cities of refuge. There were six of them, and their names are significant of the fullness of Christ.

SIGNIFICANT NAMES

The first was Kedesh, in the northwest, signifying "righteousness." The second was Shechem, in central Palestine, west of the Jordan. This name signifies "a shoulder," and will stand for strength. The third was Hebron, in southwestern Palestine; and this, we know, means "friendship and love." On the other side of the Jordan was Bezer, signifying "security." Next is Ramoth, which means "heights." And Golan, the last, means "a circle," and of course signifies the everlasting things.

Now, these six names, with their beautiful significance, furnish a glorious progression in the blessings of the gospel and the grace of God.

The first thing Christ brings to us is righteousness, making us right with God, right with our own selves and right with everybody else. This is Kedesh.

Next, He gives us His strength to keep us and help us, carrying us upon His shoulders, helping us in our helplessness, and bearing our burdens and us as well. This is Shechem.

The next is Hebron, where He brings us into the experience of His love, and unfolds to us the fullness of His grace and the love-life of the Lord, filling us with His love for others and binding us to Himself forever.

Then we come to Bezer, the place of establishing, settling and security, where we are confirmed in our faith and hope, and established in our life and love immovably.

Now we are ready to make a further advance, and so we come to Ramoth, and all the heights of His grace and glory, the resurrection and ascension life of Christ, the place where we dwell on high, and seek the things that are above, and look on all things from the heaven side and the throne life.

And, finally, the series closes with Golan, the circle that never ends, the way everlasting, where we have the faith that falters not, the love that changes not, the peace that abides, the health that is divine, the joy that remains in us—in short, the indwelling Christ, who is in us, "Jesus Christ . . . the same yesterday and today and forever" (Hebrews 13:8). This is an experience in which we anticipate even now the glory which is to come, and enjoy a foretaste of what awaits us in its fullness at His blessed coming.

Beloved, have we come along the whole of this glorious progression? Have we His righteousness, His strength, His love, His security, His heights of grace and glory, and do we know His everlasting way?

If not, the doors are all open. Perhaps you have entered Kedesh, but you may enter Shechem, too, and Hebron waits to welcome you, and Bezer to establish you, and Ramoth to exalt you, and Golan to bring you into the life eternal in which we may live, even before we reach eternity. Oh, let us enter and dwell there!

> There safe shall we abide,
> There sweet shall be our rest;
> And, every longing satisfied,
> With full salvation blest.

CHAPTER 12

THE INHERITANCE OF THE LEVITES, OR ALL IN GOD AND GOD IN ALL

Therefore, I urge you, brothers, in view of God's mercy, to offer your bodies as living sacrifices, holy and pleasing to God—this is your spiritual act of worship. (Romans 12:1)

The 21st chapter of Joshua gives us an account of the inheritance of the Levites. They were the official tribe in ancient Israel, and entrusted with all the services of the sanctuary, the work of education and the religious culture of all the tribes.

They were the types of Christian service, and represented the principles of true consecration.

REDEMPTION

They represented the principle of redemption as the basis of consecration.

In the eighth chapter of Numbers and the 17th and 18th verses, we read, "Every firstborn male in Israel, whether man or animal, is mine. When I struck down all the firstborn in Egypt, I set them apart for myself. And I have taken the Levites in place of all the firstborn sons in Israel."

They were thus substituted for the firstborn who had been doomed to death, and saved by the blood of the Paschal lamb. The Levites stood for these, and thus represented the idea of redemption. They were as men who had been bought with a price and whose lives were not their own. But God did not require their death, but took their lives instead.

Our service as consecrated Christians and our consecration should likewise spring from the redemption of Christ's blood. This is the basis which the apostle presents as the ground of our surrender to God. "You are not your own; you were bought at a price. Therefore honor God with your body" (1 Corinthians 6:19–20).

There is no credit or merit in our consecrating ourselves to God, because we already belong to Him and have no right to retain ourselves. He has purchased every power of our being and every possibility of our existence. When we yield ourselves to Him, we simply recognize the fact that we are already His, and that He has a right to all that we can give or be.

"When you have done everything you were told to do, [you] should say, 'We are unworthy servants; we have only done our duty' " (Luke 17:10). Let no man think, therefore, that because he has made a complete surrender of himself to God, he has put God in any sense in his debt, or has aught whereof to glory. He has simply paid his honest debts and taken his true place in the divine economy, that is all. And he may well say with David, "But who am I, and who are my people, that we should be able to give as generously as this? Everything comes from you, and we have given you only what comes from your hand" (1 Chronicles 29:14).

SEPARATION

The Levites represented the principle of separation as the element of consecration.

We read again in Numbers 8:14, "In this way you are to set the Levites apart from the other Israelites, and the Levites will be mine."

Our consecration separates us from the world and sin, and brings us out from our natural life to be exclusively the Lord's. Therefore, we read in the 12th chapter of Romans immediately after the command to present our bodies a living sacrifice:

> Do not conform any longer to the pattern of this world, but be transformed by the renewing of your mind. Then you will be able to test and approve what God's will is—his good, pleasing and perfect will. (12:2)

It is not merely an outward separation, but a separation which transforms us by a new spirit and a disposition which separates itself from evil, by natural detachment.

The Pharisees separated themselves outwardly from sinners, but in spirit they were identical. Christ Jesus mingled with sinners, but in spirit, He was as distinct from them as light from darkness and oil from water.

The little plant may grow out of a manure heap, and be surrounded by filth, and covered very often with the floating dust that is borne upon the breeze, but its white roots are separated from the unclean soil, and its leaves and flowers have no affinity with the dust that settles upon them. After a shower of summer rain they throw off every particle of defilement, and look up as fresh and spotless as before, for their intrinsic nature cannot have any part with these defiling things.

This is the separation which Christ requires and which He gives. There is no merit in my staying from the theater if I want to go. There is no value in my abstaining from the foolish novel or the intoxicating cup, if I am all the time wishing I could have them. My heart is there, and my soul is defiled by the desire for evil things. It is not the world that stains us, but the love of the world. The true Levite is separated from the desire for earthly things, and even if he could, he would not have the forbidden pleasures which others prize.

DEDICATION

The Levites represented the principle of dedication, as the essence of consecration.

The Levites were presented to the Lord by Moses as a living sacrifice.

> Have the Levites stand in front of Aaron and his sons and then present them as a wave offering to the LORD. . . .
> After you have purified the Levites and presented them as a wave offering, they are to come to do their work at the Tent of Meeting. They are the Israelites who are to be given wholly to me. I have taken them as my own in place of the firstborn, the first male offspring from every Israelite woman. (Numbers 8:13, 15–16)

And again, Numbers 3:6, 13:

> Bring the tribe of Levi and present them to Aaron the priest to assist him. . . . For all the firstborn are mine. When I struck down all the firstborn in Egypt, I set apart for myself every firstborn in Israel, whether man or animal. They are to be mine. I am the LORD.

And so it is required of us, as God's spiritual Levites, that we shall present our bodies a living sacrifice. We are already the Lord's by right of purchase, but now we must acknowledge that right and make a personal surrender, and when we do this He is pleased to accept it from us. It should be unconditional, unreserved and irrevocable, giving Him the right to own us and control us as He shall see best, and renouncing the right to self-control and self-ownership forever. And not only so, but we must do it gladly, and without regret or apprehension.

What would you think of a girl who was shrinking and hesitating whether to commit her life to the man she loves, and saying: "How can I leave my mother and go with this man?" If she loves him, she is only too glad to go with him. She loves to put herself entirely under his control, and trust all her happiness to his keeping, for she knows that he will only seek her good, and she feels safer in his hands than in her own, if he really has her affection.

And so God requires of us not only perfect surrender, but joyful surrender. If we hold anything back in our spirit, He will not accept us. He does not need us. He could create a million souls in a minute that would serve Him better. He only takes us because of what He can do for us. He only wants us unreservedly, so that He can be able more fully to bless us, and true consecration counts it an honor and a privilege to be able to give all and receive all in return.

It is because He wants to do so much for us that He demands the absolute control of all our being, as the foster parent who adopts a child insists on having it take his name, and give him its full control, because he wants to make it the heir to his fortune.

So God demands that we shall be His, and His alone, and then He gives to us as wholeheartedly as He expects us to give to Him.

Have we accepted this claim? Have we responded to His call? Have we made this unreserved, unconditional surrender? Have we presented our bodies a living sacrifice, our spiritual act of worship?

SERVICE

The Levites represented service as the fruit of consecration.

The ministry of the Levites is thus described:

> I have given the Levites as gifts to Aaron and his sons to do the work at the Tent of Meeting on behalf of the Israelites and to make atonement for them so that no plague will strike the Israelites when they go near the sanctuary. (Numbers 8:19)

They were divided into several families: the sons of Gershon, Kohath and Merari.

The Gershonites had charge of the tabernacle, the tent, the covering, the hangings, the curtains and the cords. The Kohathites had a still more sacred ministry: they had charge of the ark, the table, the lampstand and the altars and the vessels of the sanctuary—the most sacred things. The Merarites had charge of the boards of the tabernacle and the bars, the pillars, the sockets and the vessels thereof.

These ancient Levites set up the tabernacle, took it down, carried it from place to place and guarded it and waited upon the priests in their ministry. Later they were the teachers of the people, and looked after all the educational and social work of the tribes, and especially had charge of the cities of refuge and the reception and protection of the manslayer that fled from the avenger.

Thus they represented our Christian service in all its varieties as we are called to build up the spiritual house of the Lord, and to carry forward His kingdom in all places and among all nations, bearing the burdens of His sanctuary and ministering in sacred things.

The high inscription on the crest of many a noble family consists of the two words, "I serve." No nobler dignity can be conferred on a man than to make him a servant. The minister of the gospel is just a servant, and this is the true meaning of the word.

James and Paul loved to call themselves "your servants for Jesus' sake" (2 Corinthians 4:5). Moses and Joshua were servants in the Lord's house, and David "served God's purpose in his own generation" (Acts 13:36).

The general commanding the army is but the servant of his country and his sovereign. The statesman bears the insignia of public service. The Lord Jesus Himself loved to say, "I am among you as one who serves" (Luke 22:27); and God is ever ministering to the whole creation.

We are called to be the servants of God, and our ministry is to set up the true sanctuary, and to wait at the unseen altar whose incense reaches within the veil. In the ages to come, we shall have still higher service. The present is but an apprenticeship for the more glorious future, and God is but schooling us for higher and nobler employments in the new earth and new heaven which are to come.

This is the purpose of our consecration, that God may use us, and that we may be a blessing. It never was intended that one tribe out of 12 should do all the service of the house of God. They were but types of all the rest, and today, under the gospel, we should all be Levites. "[Jesus Christ] has made us to be a kingdom and priests to serve his God and Father" (Revelation 1:6). There are no proxies in this army, and no substitutes accepted in this draft, but each must take his place, and God expects service and fruit from every follower of Christ. "This is to my Father's glory," He has said to every one of us, "that you bear much fruit, showing yourselves to be"—wonderful disciples? No; but to be "my disciples" (John 15:8). We have no reason to consider ourselves His disciples, unless we are bearing "much fruit."

There are great varieties in the service of God. A few are called—like the Kohathites—to enter the sanctuary, and bear the more sacred vessels of the Lord, to take the holy ark and touch the sacred symbols of the mystic cherubim. Theirs is the ministry of prevailing prayer, and theirs is to hear the secret of the Lord, to know His highest thought and catch the very whisper of His will.

Others are called to bear the boards and the rougher and heavier burdens. But to all it is enough to know that they are bearing the burdens of the sanctuary, and ministering to Him upon whom the angels wait, and at whose bidding the heavens hasten to obey.

> We have different gifts, according to the grace given us. If a man's gift is prophesying, let him use it in proportion to his faith. If it is serving, let him serve; if it is teaching, let him teach; if it is encouraging, let him encourage; if it is contributing to the needs of others, let him give generously; if it is leadership, let him govern diligently; if it is showing mercy, let him do it cheerfully. (Romans 12:6–8)

PRACTICAL WORK

The Levites represented the principle of practical service in all the ordinary walks of life.

They were not shut up in Jerusalem in the tabernacle, but we find them distributed throughout every portion of the land, for the obvious purpose of diffusing the principles which they represented among all sections of the people.

Beautifully this represents the application of the principles of consecration to all the ordinary occupations and walks of life. God does not want consecration bound up with our prayer book, folded away in our Bagster Bible, left in our pew between Sabbaths, or brought out for an airing at the weekly prayer meeting. He does not want our religious phrases and tones for holy days and special times. He wants every place sacred, every time Sabbatic, and everything inscribed, "Holy To The LORD" (Exodus 28:36).

He wants us to sit at our dinner table, and eat and drink to the glory of God, to talk with our families in simple happy fellowship, having our speech always "seasoned with salt" (Colossians 4:6).

He wants all our life to be as holy as our communion services, and even our buying and selling to be like a sacrament of sweetness and sanctity.

In the coming age, every pot will be inscribed with "Holy To The LORD" (Exodus 28:36), every cooking utensil will cook for Christ, and even the bells on the horses will chime out glory to Immanuel's name.

I heard the other day, of a company of Christians who came together for a season of waiting upon the Lord, in which they would not allow any of the party to talk on any ordinary subject, or go out to purchase any article in the stores, or to engage in any business which could be avoided. Every moment was supposed to be set apart for some sacred exercise.

This is essentially the idea of monasticism, and it is unwholesome. It is just as holy to laugh as to cry, and to use your handsaw as your prayer book.

We can bring Christ into common things as fully as into what we call religious service. Indeed, it is the highest and hardest application of divine grace to bring it down to the ordinary matters of life, and therefore God is far more honored in this than even in things that are more specially sacred.

Therefore, in this wonderful chapter of Romans which is the manual of practical consecration, just after the passage that speaks of ministering in sacred things the apostle comes at once to the common, social and secular affairs into which we are to bring our consecration principles. We read: "Be devoted to one another in brotherly love. Honor one another above yourselves. Never be lacking in zeal, but keep your spiritual fervor, serving the Lord" (Romans 12:10–11).

God wants the Levites scattered all over the cities of Israel. He wants your workshop, factory, kitchen, nursery, editor's room and printing office, as much as your pulpit and closet. He wants you to be just as holy at high noon on Monday or Wednesday as in the sanctuary on Sabbath morning, and to have your consecration as much in Wall Street's whirlpool of trade and business, as in the cathedral aisle or the quiet closet.

May God give to us this holy priesthood, and make us the light of the world and the salt of the earth!

ALL IN GOD

The Levites represented the principle of finding all our resources in God Himself.

In the 13th chapter and 33rd verse of Joshua we read: "But to the tribe of Levi, Moses had given no inheritance; the LORD the God of Israel, is their inheritance, as he promised them."

This is very significant. God gave the land to the other tribes but He gave Himself to the Levites. There is such a thing in Christian life as having an inheritance from the Lord, and there is such a thing as having the Lord Himself for our inheritance.

Some people get a sanctification from the Lord which is of much value, but which is variable, and often impermanent. Others have learned the higher lesson of taking the Lord Himself to be their Keeper and their Sanctity, and abiding in Him they are kept above the vicissitudes of their own states and feelings.

Some get from the Lord large measures of joy and blessing and times of refreshing from His presence that are very gracious.

Others, again, learn to take the Lord Himself as their Joy; and then it is true, as He promised: "That my joy may be in you and that your joy may be complete" (John 15:11).

Some people are content to have peace with God, but others have taken "the peace of God, which transcends all understanding, [which] will guard your hearts and your minds in Christ Jesus" (Philippians 4:7).

Some have faith *in* God, while others have the faith *of* God. Some have many touches of healing from God; others, again, have learned to live in the very health of God Himself, and to say: "For we who are alive are always being given over to death for Jesus' sake, so that his life may be revealed in our mortal body" (2 Corinthians 4:11).

Some are always wanting to be strengthened and helped by the Lord; others have learned to take the Lord Himself as their strength, and to find His strength made perfect in their weakness.

Some are trying to serve God and to use His Holy Spirit as their Helper and Strength for service; others have so yielded themselves up to God that He just uses them, and they are the channels and vessels of His life and strength.

Such a life leads us constantly to the end of ourselves, and as we grow less He increases and becomes our All in All. True Levitical service is to be lost in God, and find in Him our wisdom, our faith, our love, our power, our peace, our joy, our portion and our all.

Such a life lifts us above surrounding circumstances, and even inner states, and connects us with the Infinite Source of all supplies, the heart of God Himself. We are like the old Norwegian knight, who drank from a horn that was never dry, because a little tube connected it with the river. As fast as he drank, it kept full from its unfailing source. Happy they who can sing:

> I have come to the Fountain of life,
> A fountain that never is dry;
> A life that never can die;
> And I drink of the boundless supply
> In God, my Fountain of life.

GOD IN ALL

The Levites represented the principle of finding God in all. We read in one place that they had no inheritance, and yet we read in the 21st chapter of Joshua, that God gave them the choice cities among all the 12 tribes. They gave up all, and they received more than any of the tribes.

Ephraim had but one inheritance, Judah had but one; but Levi had the choice cities in every one of Israel's estates. This is very wonderful and instructive. The tribe that let all go, and chose God alone, received in return the fairest cities in every corner of the land: Hebron, in the tribe of Judah; Gibeon and Anathoth, in Benjamin; Shechem and Beth Horon, in the tribe of Ephraim; Aijalon, in Dan; Taanach and Golan in Manasseh; Kishion and Jarmuth in Issachar; Rehob in distant Asher; Kedesh out of Naphtali; Jokneam and Kartah in Zebulun; Bezer and Kedemoth in Reuben; Ramoth,

Heshbon, Mahanaim and Jazer in Gad; and many others in the north and the south, and east and the west. The choicest cities—48 in all—of the land, including all the cities of refuge, were given to the tribe of Levi. Who will say that they lost by giving up all for God?

Yes, Lot can have his choice. Take the best, Lot, even all the valley of the Jordan. But wait! God said to Abraham, "Lift up your eyes from where you are and look north and south, east and west. All the land that you see I will give to you and your offspring forever" (Genesis 13:14–15). Because you gave it up for God you shall have it back in God, and more.

Ah, friends, it is a great thing to learn to take God first, and then He can afford to give us everything else, without the fear of its hurting us.

As long as you want anything very much, especially more than you want God, it is an idol. But when you become satisfied with God, everything else so loses its charm that He can give it to you without harm. Then you can take just as much as you choose, and use it for His glory.

There is no harm whatever in having money, houses, lands, friends and dearest children, if you do not value these things for themselves.

If you have been separated from them in spirit, and become satisfied with God Himself, then they will become to you channels to be filled with God to bring Him nearer to you. Then every little lamb around your household will be a tender cord to bind you to the Shepherd's heart. Then every affection will be a little golden cup filled with the wine of His love. Then every bank stock and investment will be but a channel through which you can pour out His beneficence and extend His gifts.

The day is coming when "all these things will be given to you as well" (Matthew 6:33), and you shall have the riches of the universe at your feet, and perhaps be able to create a world, in the power of Christ; but you would not exchange for all the glory of your kingdom one throb of His loving heart or one glance of His countenance.

Yes, "all things are yours, whether Paul or Apollos or Cephas or the world or life or death or the present or the future—all are yours" (1 Corinthians 3:22), on one condition—not that Christ is yours, but that you first belong to Him. "You are of Christ, and Christ is of God" (3:23).

Beloved, shall we learn the twofold lesson, and ask God to translate it into every moment of the coming days and years; first, to have ALL IN GOD and then to have GOD IN ALL!

CHAPTER 13

THE TRANS-JORDANIC TRIBES

Joshua 22:1–34

Therefore judge nothing before the appointed time; wait till the Lord comes. He will bring to light what is hidden in darkness and will expose the motives of men's hearts. At that time each will receive his praise from God. (1 Corinthians 4:5)

The 22nd chapter of Joshua adds a very striking picture to the incidents which preceded in the conquest of the Land of Promise and the division of Israel's inheritance.

We have already referred to the inheritance of the two and a half tribes on the east side of Jordan, and to the mistake that they made in choosing their portion on the world-side of the Land of Promise. In this, undoubtedly, they were types of those who make a similar mistake in the present day, in choosing their portion too near the edge of the world.

At the same time, there are such beautiful lessons connected with their example, that we can but rejoice at the compensations which the sacred story has placed over against their error.

If they did not have the highest inheritance in the land, they had the spirit of the land in themselves, at least, and in the beautiful disposition of which this chapter is such a fine example.

UNSELFISH SERVICE

We see in them an example of the most unselfish service and sacrifice.

They had just spent seven years in helping their brethren of the other tribes to pursue their inheritance on the west side of Jordan. Indeed, they had gone before them in the hardest places and the hottest battles, and had been the real pioneers in all these long campaigns.

The command had been, "But all your fighting men, fully armed, must cross over ahead of your brothers. You are to help your brothers until the LORD gives them rest, as he has done for you, and until they too have taken possession of the land that the LORD your God is giving them. After that, you may go back and occupy your own land, which Moses the servant of the LORD gave you east of the Jordan toward the sunrise" (Joshua 1:14–15).

They had faithfully obeyed this command, and kept themselves. They had fought the battles of their brethren and won for them their heritages of blessing. They had marched around Jericho, stormed the heights of Beth Horon, pursued in the long day at Gibeon, triumphed by the waters of Merom, and been valiant and true until all the 31 kings had been subdued, and the whole land had been won for the Lord of Israel. It was entirely disinterested; not one stroke had they done for themselves. There is no nobler example in all the book of Joshua then their high and unselfish devotion. This is the noblest quality and the rarest among Christian workers.

How pathetically the Apostle Paul exclaims, "I have no one else like him, who takes a genuine interest in your welfare. For everyone looks out for his own interests, not those of Jesus Christ" (Philippians 2:20–21).

The world instinctively does homage to unselfish love. A little fellow was boasting the other day about his wages. "I get two dollars a week," he said, "and I run errands. My father works in the factory and he gets two dollars a day. My brother works in the office, and he gets five dollars a week, and mother, she gets up in the morning about five o'clock, makes the fire, gets breakfast for father and us, and does the work of the house all day, gets our supper at night, and after we go to bed she does the darning, mends our clothes and fixes up things generally."

"Yes, and what does mother get?" "Oh, mother? Well—why, she does not get anything. She does all the jobs of the house, but you know there is no money in it."

It was a boy's thoughtless testimony to the noblest heroism of common life. Hundreds of such heroines are suffering and toiling unmarked and unhonored.

But this is true of Him who came not to be ministered unto, but to minister, and to give His life as a ransom for many, and of whom it has been said that "when they hurled their insults at him, he did not retaliate; when he suffered, he made no threats. Instead, he entrusted himself to him who judges justly" (1 Peter 2:23). "Instead, whoever wants to become great among you must be your servant, and whoever wants to be first must be slave of all" (Mark 10:43–44).

RECOMPENSE

The day of recompense comes at last to the unselfish worker.

These brave men at length received their rich reward. The long weary marches were over at last, and as they stood before their commander, it repaid them for all, to hear Him say,

> You have done all that Moses the servant of the LORD commanded, and you have obeyed me in everything I commanded. For a long time now—to this very day—you have not deserted your brothers but have carried out the mission the LORD your God gave you. Now that the LORD your God has given your brothers rest as he promised, return to your homes in the land that Moses the servant of the LORD gave you on the other side of the Jordan. (Joshua 22:2–4)

And then he added, "Return to your homes with your great wealth—with large herds of livestock, with silver, gold, bronze and iron, and a great plunder from your enemies" (22:8).

It was reward enough to have the "Well done" of the captain, but there was much more. There was the rich inheritance, the ample spoil and the glad homecoming to the children, wives and friends so dearly loved.

Then when we hear the "Well done" of our faithful Master, we shall not regret one tear or toil, but many would give the whole world for the privilege of going back once more to win the crown by earthly sacrifice and service. But it is not only at the end of life that this glad recompense awaits the faithful servant, but even here God has His compensations and rewards for the self-denying and the pure-hearted.

There is a day of toil and sacrifice, and waiting. And there is a day when the harvest is gathered in, and we bring our sheaves with rejoicing and wonder at the full reversions that have followed the years of tearful sowing, and what seemed hopeless waiting.

But even in the days of recompense we must not forget the old spirit of self-denying love. As they came to their inheritance, they were to divide the spoil with their brethren. There is to be no selfish hoarding. They are still to live the same life of love, even in their inheritance and home.

There are Christian workers who begin in the spirit of self-denial and win their success by sacrifice and noble heroism. Then, later in life, when their work is crowned with success, they fall into the snare of selfishness and ease, and allow the very reward, which God gave them, to benumb their holy energies, and turn aside the edge of their consecration and power.

It requires much more grace to know how to abound than to know how to be abased. Even when we reach our millennial glory, it is not to be a selfish life. The highest aspiration of a noble spirit is to rise to a higher service in the life beyond, of unceasing ministries. This is the life of God, and it is the only heaven that God can give.

GOD FIRST

We see in these two and a half tribes, a beautiful example of putting God first before their own inheritance.

When they reached the fords of the Jordan, they paused awhile before turning to their home, and built a great altar there as a tower of witness and an altar of worship. They feared that in coming days their children would forget the service of the true God, and might let their isolation on the further side of Jordan separate them from the common faith. Therefore, to keep in remembrance, and to bind their children to the same faith and worship, they reared this altar of witness.

It would have been natural for them to have hastened home. Long years had passed since they had looked in the faces of those they loved. Throbbing hearts were drawing them to their loved ones, but they paused and remembered God first, and set up this memorial that coming generations might remember His name and maintain His honor and worship.

This is, indeed, a bright and beautiful example. This is the true secret of all blessing and happiness. God first, should be the watchword and keynote of every plan and purpose and enterprise, in the consecrated life. Then He will delight in all our service and blessing, and will love to think of us as generously as we have thought of Him.

MISUNDERSTANDING

And now we see a very beautiful act misunderstood and misjudged.

We read with astonishment that "when the Israelites heard that they had built the altar . . . the whole assembly of Israel gathered at Shiloh to go to war against them" (22:11–12). They seem at once to have begun to think they knew all about it. It was an act of treason and rebellion, and that it must be promptly and severely put down.

Very fortunately, they sent a delegation before proceeding to actual hostilities, to charge them with their crime, and at once began to upbraid them for their trespass.

> The whole assembly of the LORD says: "How could you break faith with the God of Israel like this? How could you turn away from the LORD and build yourselves an altar in rebellion against him now? Was not the sin of Peor enough for us? Up to this very day we have not cleansed ourselves from that sin, even though a plague fell on the community of the LORD! And are you now turning away from the LORD?
>
> "If you rebel against the LORD today, tomorrow he will be

angry with the whole community of Israel. If the land you possess is defiled, come over to the LORD's land, where the LORD's
tabernacle stands, and share the land with us. But do not rebel
against the LORD or against us by building an altar for yourselves, other than the altar of the LORD our God. When Achan son
of Zerah acted unfaithfully regarding the devoted things, did not
wrath come upon the whole community of Israel? He was not
the only one who died for his sin." (22:16–20)

This is truly very humbling, and very much like the rest of us. How often
we have passed these hasty judgments upon our brethren! How many of us
have been alienated for years by some rash conclusion, and found at last that
we had misunderstood the friend and misjudged the act which, if we had
only understood, we would have honored its motives and spirit, and recognized it as worthy of all praise.

Therefore, the Master has said: "Judge nothing before the appointed time;
wait till the Lord comes" (1 Corinthians 4:5), and then He will not only
look at the act, but "he will bring to light what is hidden in darkness and
will expose the motives of men's hearts. At that time each will receive his
praise from God" (4:5). All that can be recognized He will cherish, and all
that He can forget, He will love to leave in oblivion.

MEEKNESS

We see, at the same time, a beautiful example of meekness on the part of
the Reubenites and their brethren. They did not fire up and resent the cruel
misjudgment. They did not retaliate with vindictive words and bitter strife,
but they meekly and gently assured their brethren of their innocence and
honest intent, and their loyal devotion to the common faith and the sacred
altar of the Lord, in the tabernacle.

How much grace it requires to bear a misunderstanding rightly, and to
receive an unkind judgment in holy sweetness! Nothing tests a Christian
character more than to have some evil thing said about you. This is the file
that soon proves whether we are electroplate or solid gold. If we could only
know the blessings that lie hidden in our wrongs, we would say, like David,
when Shimei cursed him, "Let him curse, . . . it may be that the LORD will
see my distress and repay me with good for the cursing I am receiving today"
(2 Samuel 16:11–12).

Some people get easily turned aside from the grandeur of their life-work
by pursuing their own grievances and enemies, until their life gets turned
into one little, petty whirl of warfare. It is like a nest of hornets. You may
disperse the hornets, but you will probably get terribly stung, and get nothing for your pains, for even their honey is not worth the search.

Wiser and happier are they who, like old Nehemiah, say to all the Sanballats, "I am carrying on a great project and cannot go down. Why should the work stop while I leave it and go down to you?" (Nehemiah 6:3).

The gentleness and meekness of the Reubenites and their brethren averted a great catastrophe and turned a curse into a blessing. So, "a gentle answer turns away wrath" (Proverbs 15:1), and a spirit of gentleness will avert many a sorrow.

May God give us more of His Spirit, who, "when they hurled their insults at him, he did not retaliate; when he suffered, he made no threats. Instead, he entrusted himself to him who judges justly" (1 Peter 2:23).

MISUNDERSTANDING HEALED

We see a very beautiful example of a misunderstanding healed, and a curse turned into a blessing. Instead of a fratricidal war, there is reconciliation and love, and they joyfully exclaim: "Today we know that the LORD is with us, because you have not acted unfaithfully toward the LORD in this matter" (Joshua 22:31).

There is no greater evidence of the presence of the Lord in His people than the spirit of love, and there is no sweeter testimony to God and His glorious grace than the reconciliation of strife and the healing of mutual wrongs.

"How good and pleasant it is/ when brothers live together in unity" (Psalm 133:1). "For there the LORD bestows his blessing,/ even life forevermore" (133:3).

When the Lord wants to make "an everlasting sign, which will not be destroyed," this is the way He does it: "Instead of the thornbush will grow the pine tree,/ and instead of briers the myrtle will grow" (Isaiah 55:13).

God's sweetest memorial is the transformed thorn, and the thistle blooming with flowers of peace and sweetness, where once grew recriminations and maledictions. Beloved, God is waiting to make just such memorials in your life, out of the things that are hurting you most today. Take the grievance, the separations, the strained friendships and the broken ties which have been the sorrow and heartbreak of your life, and let God heal them, and give you grace to make you right with all with whom you may be wrong, and you will wonder at the joy and blessing that will come out of the things that have caused you nothing but regret and pain.

"Blessed are the peacemakers,/ for they will be called sons of God" (Matthew 5:9). The everlasting employment of our blessed Redeemer is to reconcile the guilty and the estranged from God. And the highest and most Christlike work that we can do, is to be like Him in this regard.

Shall we go forth to dry the tears of a sorrowing world, to heal the brokenhearted, to bind up the wounds of human lives and to unite heart to heart and earth to heaven?

CHAPTER 14

WARNINGS AND COUNSELS

Joshua 22–24

These chapters contain the parting charges of Joshua to Israel at Shechem. He reviews the faithfulness of God, and all His gracious promises and leadings, and then solemnly pledges them to fidelity to Him and His holy covenant. And when they respond to His appeal and promise to serve the Lord with faithfulness, he reminds them that they are unable to serve Him in their own strength, and then reiterates his own determination for him and his household to serve the Lord, whatsoever others may do.

The chapter closes with a very humbling statement that the children of Israel served the Lord faithfully during all the days of Joshua and the elders who survived him, and the generation that had known the works of the Lord in Canaan, but we learn from the later book of Judges, that before the third generation they were sunk in apostasy and captivity, and the glory of their early victories had been exchanged for a declension and degradation far more terrible than the story of Israel's wanderings for 40 years in the wilderness.

For us there is the solemn lesson that, notwithstanding all the promises of the gospel and the abundant grace of Christ, there is need of the humblest vigilance and the closest abiding, even in the highest places of our Christian life. The greater the height, the greater the fall and the deeper the degradation.

Israel's wanderings in the wilderness after they came out of Egypt lasted only 40 years, but Israel's declension and degradation, under the Judges, lasted over 400 years.

For an ordinary Christian to go back from God is a very serious thing; but for one who has known Him in all the fullness of His grace, to turn aside from the higher pathway of a life of consecration, is a far more serious and dangerous thing; and the Word of God is full of the most faithful and solemn warnings and admonitions to even those who have entered into the fullness of Jesus, to watch and stand fast, lest, being led away by the error of the wicked, they fall from their own steadfastness.

While on the one hand, we have the most gracious promises of our Father keeping us, yet at the same time, we have the most faithful warnings to abide and obey.

The echoes of this chapter ring through the New Testament, and especially those chapters that speak of our higher Christian life. When John tells us, "The anointing you received from him remains in you" (1 John 2:27), he also adds, "And now, dear children, continue in him, so that when he appears we may be confident and unashamed before him at his coming (2:28). While Paul says, "I know whom I have believed, and am convinced that he is able to guard what I have entrusted to him for that day" (2 Timothy 1:12); yet he also adds, "Guard the good deposit that was entrusted to you—guard it with the help of the Holy Spirit who lives in us" (1:14). While in one breath, the Spirit says, "No temptation has seized you except what is common to man. . . . But when you are tempted, he will also provide a way out so that you can stand up under it" (1 Corinthians 10:13). He also adds, "So, if you think you are standing firm, be careful that you don't fall" (10:12).

God's Word is not a castiron system of theology, proclaiming infallible security for any man, irrespective of his own attitude. But it is the wise and loving touch of a mother's hand, on the side of our spiritual life that needs adjustment, whether it be encouragement to lift us up, or admonition and warning to hold us back from presumption and disobedience.

It would have been as cruel and unwise to encourage David, in the time of his disobedience, as to have discouraged Simon Peter, when his heart was breaking with remorse and sorrow.

The one needed stern rebuke, to let him see his sin, and the other needed hope and comfort, to reveal to him his Savior's mercy.

Therefore, let us not think it strange, if at one time we hear the Holy Scriptures saying, "They shall never perish; no one can snatch them out of my hand" (John 10:28); and at another time, "If anyone does not remain in me, he is like a branch that is thrown away and withers" (15:6).

The very warning is designed to prevent the peril to which it refers.

What were some of the causes of Israel's declension?

DEPENDENCE ON OTHERS

1. The first was, perhaps, their undue dependence upon Joshua and the fathers who had brought them into the land. "Israel served the LORD throughout the lifetime of Joshua and of the elders who outlived him and who had experienced everything the LORD had done for Israel" (Joshua

24:31). But when these had passed away and they were thrown upon their own strength, resources and character, they did not have those elements of stability, principle and permanence which were sufficient to preserve them from the unholy influence of the surrounding nations, and so they gradually sank back again into heathenism.

There are many persons whose religious character is a reflection of the influence of others. Like young Joash, who served the Lord during the days of Jehoiada, his adopted father, and turned back to evil when he was gone, so these persons manifest much sympathetic goodness under the influence of favorite teachers and high examples, and in seasons of deep religious excitement, they may even seem to pass through an experience of great spiritual life, exhibiting many of its emotions and some of its fruits; but when these influences are withdrawn, it becomes evident that there was no real conviction of purpose and will, and no radical transformation of character.

The test will come to all such souls; they will find these favorable influences withdrawn, and these helpful surroundings changed, and they will be compelled to fall back on their own resources and their own direct knowledge of God and His sustaining grace. And when no longer pressed forward by stronger spirits and upheld by helpful hands, but met by opposition, misunderstanding, uncongenial associations, and, perhaps, direct persecution, they will soon find whether their purpose is rooted in God, and their spirit united to the living Christ and whether they are abiding in Him as the source of their strength and service.

If this, indeed, be so, they will continue even in isolation and opposition, and Jeremiah's picture of the man "whose confidence is in [the LORD]" (Jeremiah 17:7) shall be gloriously fulfilled in them. "He will be like a tree planted by the water/ that sends out its roots by the stream./ It does not fear when heat comes;/ its leaves are always green./ It has no worries in a year of drought/ and never fails to bear fruit" (17:8).

The secret of Joshua's victory was that he had long before this learned to stand alone. To him the day had come, more than half a century before, when the unfaithful spies and the whole congregation turned against him, refusing to follow him, and even threatening to destroy him, while he and his faithful companion stood fast to their principles at Kadesh Barnea. His purpose was not affected by the failure of the multitude to follow him. It was not much more affected by the enthusiasm of the second generation to enter with him the Land of Promise. And even now, as he stood on the height and glorious elevation of an accomplished and victorious life, he was still as ready as ever to stand alone, and his lofty independence expresses itself in the heroic words: "Choose for yourselves this day whom you will serve, . . . But as for me and my household, we will serve the LORD" (Joshua 24:15).

This must ever be the secret of steadfastness in the consecrated life. You must know the truth of the Lord for yourself, and commit yourself to it and to Him, even if you have to stand alone. You must be so persuaded of it that you cannot surrender it even if you die. And you must know the Lord so definitely for yourself, and not for another, that even if all the Christians in the world should fail, and all your friends forsake you, you must still stand and exclaim like Martin Luther, "Here I stand; I can do no other, so help me God."

Stronger than all the power of Babylon is the spirit of the men who stand in the fiery furnace, and say, "O Nebuchadnezzar, we do not need to defend ourselves before you in this matter. If we are thrown into the blazing furnace, the God we serve is able to save us from it, and he will rescue us from your hand, O king. But even if he does not, we want you to know, O king, that we will not serve your gods or worship the image of gold you have set up" (Daniel 3:16–18).

IMPERFECT WORK

2. The second cause of Israel's declension was their failure to do thorough work, especially in separating from and exterminating their enemies. We read in the beginning of the book of Judges of many of the tribes of Canaan, whom they should have thoroughly subjugated, that the children of Judah could not drive out of the valley (1:19); and that the children of Benjamin did not drive out the Jebusites that inhabited Jerusalem (1:21); nor did Manasseh drive out the inhabitants of Beth Shan and her towns, but the Canaanites would dwell in the land (1:27); nor did Ephraim drive out the Canaanites in Gezer, but the Canaanites dwelt in Gezer among them, and so of many of the other tribes. Not only so, but Israel, in some cases, put the Canaanites to tribute (1:28–30), making it even a profitable business, and a source of income to have them remain, when the Lord had commanded their utter extermination.

And still worse, we find them even entering into forbidden alliances with them, and also intermarrying among their sons and daughters (3:5–6). God's command to them had been, "You shall break down their altars" (2:2). "When . . . you have defeated them, then you must destroy them totally. Make no treaty with them, and show them no mercy. Do not intermarry with them. Do not give your daughters to their sons or take their daughters for your sons" (Deuteronomy 7:2–3).

But here we read, "The Israelites lived among the Canaanites, Hittites, Amorites, Perizzites, Hivites, and Jebusites. They took their daughters in marriage and gave their own daughters to their sons, and served their gods" (Judges 3:5–6). Israel had become content with the victories which had subdued their more formidable foes, and given them the chief strongholds of the land, but in a thousand little places the enemy still lurked and lingered, and gradually became tolerated. the danger of their continuance did not seem very great, and the trouble and cost of their extermination seemed greater than the courage and patience of Israel. Thus they were suffered to remain, half conquered, and for the time, wholly subordinate. In a little while it became a source of profit to collect tribute from these bold giants, and so, many of them were made tributary to Israel, contrary to the divine command.

A little later, relations of friendship and fellowship began to be established, and before long they were intermarrying with the tribes of Israel and raising a mongrel race in which the true seed would soon be wholly extinguished. Then to crown all, they naturally began to serve the idols of their heathen friends, and to mingle in all the abominations of their unholy religion, thus becoming in the end, really apostate from the worship of the true God altogether.

This is the sad story of the development of evil in many a life which once seemed wholly consecrated. Little sins are left unsubdued. Like Saul they destroy the Amalekites, but they spare Agag, their king, for some good purpose, as they suppose, and keep the best of the spoil with the idea that they are going to sacrifice it unto the Lord. They have not the courage to deal bravely and firmly with evil. After awhile they begin to turn it to profitable account and tolerate certain forms of sin and worldliness because of advantage. Their business interests would be ruined by too rigid a conscientiousness, for some of their investments are not wholly separated from forbidden associations; the profits, at least, will be divided with the Lord, and the end will sanctify the means. A thousand specious and plausible excuses are made for things that ought to be thoroughly put aside and which, like the Canaanites, they put under tribute, and try to justify because of some advantage that can be brought out of them.

By and by, the social element is introduced. Families that were separated from unholy friendships and ungodly alliances become mixed with the world in social reception, the promiscuous dance, or perhaps, in the milder form of the church entertainment. The old people still retain their separation, yet they let their sons and daughters mingle with the Canaanites. They do not shrink from even permitting the marriage of a Christian girl with the godless man, or receiving into this consecrated home, as the bride of a son, devoted in infancy to God, some bright and fascinating daughter of fashion, who soon succeeds in subverting all the separation to God that has been left, until it is not far now to the last step of the worship of idolatry, the unrestrained career of worldly amusement, covetousness which is idolatry, and the carnival of godless selfishness and pleasure.

Dr. Livingstone tells of a singular creature which he found in Africa, called the ant lion. It attacked and destroyed the strongest victims by a masterful piece of strategy. Excavating a little pit in the form of an inverted cone, running to a point at the bottom, it sits down at the base of its little pitfall and waits for some unsuspecting beetle or insect to tread too near the edge of the crumbling sand. The unhappy victim at last approaches, and perhaps prompted by curiosity, looks over the edge of this strange excavation, and lo! in a moment it has lost its balance and rolls down the side of the little pit where the ant lion waits for its prey.

Not, however, directly and instantly does the destroyer attack its victim; this might be too unequal a contest for the little strategist, but it suddenly opens its sharp little mouth, formed like a pair of powerful scissors, and with one quick movement it cuts off a limb from the unsuspecting victim and then disappears out of sight. Slowly the mutilated creature recovers itself, and climbs up the slippery side of the pit; but just as it reaches the summit its footing slips again and it tumbles once more into the jaws of the little monster. Another quick movement and another limb is gone; and again the wounded insect gathers up its remaining strength and makes another ascent of the side of this death trap, but the result is the same as before; again it sinks to receive a fresh blow, and the process is repeated until at length it is so dismembered that it has not strength enough even to attempt to escape, but sinks, a bleeding, suffering mass, into the hands of its enemy, who devours at leisure the antagonist that it would not have dared to approach directly.

This, alas, is the story of many a defeated and ruined life. Some little adversary that was not even dreaded has been the final destroyer, not only by one bold attack, but by a thousand little wounds that, at last, have left the victim helpless to resist or to return.

Saul's career is a sad example of a noble beginning, ending in mournful disaster; and the saddest part of it is the very smallness of the cause where the pathway of declension and ruin began. It was simply in this very thing of refusing to deal firmly with the enemies of God. The reason of his failure was because of his deeper fear to deal firmly with the sin and self-will of his own heart.

Saul's failure to slay Agag and his soft dealing with the Amalekite chief, were but the outward type of his tolerance of a greater giant in his own heart, even his own self-will, and the spirit of disobedience which, Samuel tells him, was expressed by his conduct in this case, and was the ground of his rejection and the secret of his final ruin. But not all at once did Saul go down. For nearly 10 years did he still sit upon Israel's throne and work out the dreadful proceeds of sin's development, leading from step to step, until at last a branded murderer, a slave of blind and furious passion, and an awful instrument of Satan's very possession, he closed his wretched life in tragedy almost as dark as the story of Judas.

Oh, let us beware how we tolerate a single sin, how we leave an enemy in the land, how we make terms with any forbidden thing, how we enter into alliance with the world, or let its spirit touch our fondest affections. "You cannot serve God and Money" (Matthew 6:24). We cannot compromise with any evil thing and remain in the Land of Promise. We cannot abide in His love without keeping His commandments.

"Therefore come out from among them and be separate, says the Lord./ Touch no unclean thing,/ and I will receive you./ I will be a Father to you,/ and you will be my sons and daughters,/ says the Lord Almighty" (2 Corinthians 6:17–18).

SELF-CONFIDENCE

3. Perhaps the most serious cause of their failure was their inability to understand their own weakness. It was the spirit of self-sufficiency and self-confidence that brought about their ruin. There was a deep meaning in the words of Joshua which they could not understand. "You are not able to serve the LORD" (Joshua 24:19), said their faithful leader. He knew better than they the weakness of their own hearts.

They were ready enough to promise and to purpose, but they knew not how certain they were to go back again to the forbidden sin. Their fathers at Sinai had been as ready to answer, under the terrors of the mount, "We will do everything the LORD has said" (Exodus 19:8), but before the month was ended they were dancing around the golden calf. Peter was ready enough to promise, "Even if all fall away on account of you, I never will," (Matthew 26:33), and yet, before the next noonday, Peter was among the enemies of his Lord, a blaspheming, brokenhearted man.

The deepest need of our spiritual life is to know our utter helplessness, weakness and liability to err. Then we shall lean on His stronger arm, and in self-distrust abide in Him, knowing that apart from Him we can do nothing.

This was the great lesson of the Old Testament discipline. "For the law made nothing perfect" but, praise the Lord, "a better hope is introduced" (Hebrews 7:19). "For what the law was powerless to do in that it was weakened by the sinful nature, God did by sending his own Son in the likeness of sinful man to be a sin offering. And so he condemned sin in sinful man, in order that the righteous requirements of the law might be fully met in us, who do not live according to the sinful nature but according to the Spirit" (Romans 8:3–4). "Because through Christ Jesus the law of the Spirit of life set me free from the law of sin and death" (8:2). "Live by the Spirit, and you will not gratify the desires of the sinful nature" (Galatians 5:16).

The secret of victory is the profound consciousness of our utter inability and helpless nothingness. Our insufficiency is measured by His all-sufficiency, and as we decrease, He must increase. Most of our failures are meant to teach us our inability and worthlessness, that we may learn that apart from Him we can do nothing.

GOD'S FAITHFULNESS

4. The review of God's faithfulness and grace is fitted to establish us and encourage us in fidelity and steadfastness. Joshua led them back over the history of the past, and recalled to their mind the marvelous dealings of Jehovah with them and their fathers. Then he reminded them of the good land into which He had brought them, and all the blessings with which He had surrounded them. By all these considerations He called them and bound them to remember their covenant obligations, and be true to their faithful God.

And so, God holds us to Himself by the memory of His grace and love. What marvelous promises He has given us, and how vast are the prospects and the recompenses that He has in store for us! By all these things, let us be true to our covenant and faithful to our heavenly Friend.

God would awaken us to a sense of our true dignity and our glorious future, that we might "live a life worthy of the calling [we] have received" (Ephesians 4:1). Behind us there lies a high and heavenly calling and a past full of His faithful love. Before us is a kingdom of incomparable and everlasting glory, and both are calling us to "stand firm. Let nothing move you. Always give yourselves fully to the work of the Lord, because you know that your labor in the Lord is not in vain" (1 Corinthians 15:58).

CHAPTER 15

FOUR MIGHTY ALLS

So the LORD gave Israel all the land he had sworn to give their forefathers, and they took possession of it and settled there. The LORD gave them rest on every side, just as [according to all, KJV] he had sworn to their forefathers. Not one of their enemies withstood them; the LORD handed all their enemies over to them. Not one of all the LORD's good promises to the house of Israel failed; every one was fulfilled. (Joshua 21:43–45, bold added)

What a glorious collection of majestic and magnificent *alls!* Four *alls,* four glorious *alls!*—*all* the land, *all* the rest, *all* the victory and *all* the promises.

ALL THE LAND

First, the Lord gave them all the land of their inheritance. The Lord gave them *all* their inheritance. Has He given it *all* to you? Have you got *all* of your inheritance? Have you accepted it? And when the close comes shall you be able to look back and say, "I have had all that the Lord meant to give me, *all* that He created me for, all that He redeemed me for, all that He sanctified me for, all that was purchased for me in Christ, all that was revealed by the Spirit, all that He ever made me think of, long for, expect and claim, all that was meant for me to be. I have had all.

"That thing which even my brothers could not be, that thing which was specifically my part in the Redemption of Christ. God gave it *all* to me, not mutilated, not abridged, not in the slightest diminished; but like the full-orbed sun, largest at its setting, my sun is going down a perfect sphere. I have had *all* my inheritance." That is what God wants for you. That is what God meant for you. Are you going to have it? Have you got it *all* now? Your sun may go down today, there is no time to waste in dreaming. Haste to make sure of that higher calling to which you are chosen, the calling which He has set His heart upon for you, more than you have yourself. Have you got all your land?

Your land is not mine, remember. There is something for each—your own inheritance. There is something for you nobody else can fill. No garment will fit you but your own. You have a service which no one can perform but you. There is a joy no one can have but you. There is a white stone with your name written on it. Are you going to have it? That is what God wants for you. He wants to give you the land. He has taken you up to the mount of vision and shown it to you. Will you take it?

ALL THE REST

Then He speaks of all *the rest,* according to which He had sworn to their forefathers. Have you got the rest? Have you got that perfect peace which the Lord says He will keep him in whose mind is steadfast on Him (Isaiah 26:3)? The "peace of God, which transcends all understanding" (Philippians 4:7)—rest round about, as well as rest inside. The whole horizon clear, the whole sweep of life free from an anxious thought. The "great peace which nothing can offend." That is what God means by the Land of Promise, the type of perfect rest.

There are some things good, without being perfect. You don't need to have a whole regiment cannonading outside your room to keep you awake. It is quite enough that your little alarm clock rings its little bell. It is not necessary to fret about everything. It is quite enough if the devil gets your mind rasped with one little worry, one little thought which destroys your perfect peace. It is like the polish on a mirror, or an exquisite toilet table, one scratch will destroy it; and the finer it is the smaller the scratch that will deface it. And so your rest can be destroyed by a very little thing. Perhaps you have trusted in God about your future salvation; but have you about your present business or earthly cares, your money and your family, your reputation, your own spiritual keeping or your future in this life? God wants you to take the perfect peace He gives.

What is meant by the peace that transcends all understanding? It does not mean a peace no one can comprehend. It means a peace that no amount of reasoning will bring. You cannot get it by thinking. There may be a perfect bewilderment and perplexity all round the horizon, but yet your heart can rest in perfect security because He knows, He loves, He leads. He fills your heart with his own perfect love, with His infinite peace. He gives perfect rest round about.

According to *all* which He swore to give them. Have you ever noticed that? God not only promised, but swore. God's mighty oath is pledged to give it. His honor is involved in its fulfillment, and though heaven and earth pass away He will fulfill it. How condescending! He binds Himself to show that He will not evade the responsibility of keeping His great word to us and giving His mighty blessing to those that will hold Him to it.

He gave them the land which He swore, the rest which He swore to give unto their fathers. Do you realize, beloved, what this means? Many of you are accustomed to thinking this is a sort of extra for a privileged few, and that once in a while someone else may get rest. But it is not so. God has bound Himself to sanctify and fully save every soul that will claim salvation and rest through Jesus Christ. He has bound Himself to do more than merely forgive you your sins. The oath which He swore unto Abraham is expressed so beautifully in that chapter in Luke, that He would grant us, that we, being delivered from all our enemies and the hand of all that hate us, "to serve him without fear/ in holiness and righteousness before him all our days" (Luke 1:74–75). God has sworn that He will give this inheritance of rest to all who claim it.

ALL THE ENEMIES

Then we come to that other "all"—victory. One by one their enemies were permitted to confront them that Israel might gain a great victory. There was no other way of bringing them into the fullness of their conquest. Thirty-one kings had to be successively subdued; the most difficult citadels, fortresses and fastnesses of the land had to fall into their hands. But not a place could resist them, victory floated on their banners until they waved triumphantly over all the land and the whole of Canaan lay at their feet. Not one of their enemies remained: the mighty Hittites, the giant Anaks, the Amorites and the people of the Heshbon. He never once failed them when they were right with Him. Once they were beaten, but the failure of Ai was due to His absence, and the scar of the single failure was more than wiped out.

And so, beloved, God calls us to victory. Have any of you given up the conflict? Have you surrendered? Have you said, "This thing is too much"? Have you said, "I can give up anything else but this"? If you have, you are not in the Land of Promise. God means you should accept every difficult thing that comes in your life. He has started with you, knowing every difficulty. And if you dare to let Him, He will carry you through not only to be conquerors, but "more than conquerors." Are you looking for all the victory?

God gives His children strength for the battle and watches over them with a fond enthusiasm. He longs to fold you in His arms and say to you, "I have seen your conflict, I have watched your trials, I have rejoiced in your victory; you have honored Me." Not in one place was there a failure; "not one of their enemies withstood them" (Joshua 21:44). You remember what He told Joshua at the beginning, "No one will be able to stand up against you all the days of your life. As I was with Moses, so I will be with you; I will never leave you nor forsake you" (1:5). and again He says to us, "So do not fear, for I am with you;/ do not be dismayed, for I am your God./ I will strengthen you and help you;/ I will uphold you with my righteous right hand./ All who rage against you will surely be ashamed and disgraced" (Isaiah 41:10–11a).

He wants to give you victory—victory over yourself, over your own heart; we must all begin there. You must conquer yourself first. God wants victory over your heart; not a victory that will crush you, I don't mean that; but a victory, a triumph through Jesus Christ.

There are three great victories that God wants to give to every one of us. The first is victory over ourselves; the second, victory over our circumstances; and the third, victory over our enemies and all those who rise up against us.

Look at Joseph, the type of all these. It was not easy for him to turn away from his father and his home, to go into the kitchen as a slave, and then to be thrown into prison as a criminal, unjustly charged with the sin of another and forced to languish there for long months, with no one to plead for him until the iron entered into his soul, and it seemed as if God had forsaken him. But Joseph endured all this, quietly learning the secret of victory over himself.

Then came the victory over others. God brought his brothers who had wronged him to his feet, and gave him the power—if he had wanted it—to have sweet revenge. Oh, how natural it would have been to have reminded them of their cruel crime and made them feel the bitterness they had caused him long days before!

But no, Joseph had a greater victory. He would not even allow them to feel too keenly the sense of their wrong, but longed to forgive them and make them feel his love, and throw his arms about them with all a brother's forgiving tenderness.

Ah! That is the victory that satisfies a Christlike heart. It is heaping coals of fire on the heads of those who have wronged us. And yet there is a way of putting coals of fire on others' heads that has more meanness in it than an open revenge. There is a way of doing another a kindness in such a manner as to make him feel that we are doing it just to make him feel badly.

Sweeter by far is the revenge which God has promised to the overcomer: "I will make them come and fall down at your feet and acknowledge that I have loved you" (Revelation 3:9), and to acknowledge you as the instrument of the highest spiritual blessing.

Beloved, God is bringing all these things into your life, in order to give you an opportunity of making eternal history. There is a day coming, when your biography will be written in the Bible of the eternal ages the same as Joseph's; that is to say, if it is worth writing.

Ages to come will read the story of your trials and your triumphs, and glorify your Savior for what He has done in you.

ALL THE PROMISES

The last "all" includes all God's promises. "Not one of all the LORD's good promises to the house of Israel failed; every one was fulfilled" (Joshua 21:45). Blessed be His name for that glorious promise! How it sweeps out to the far horizon, and reaches the length and breadth of meaning beyond all that we can ask or think!

How it speaks of a finished life, of an accomplished career, of a homecoming for us, too, that will have no regret in it, and no abatement from all His highest, greatest will!

It is the spirit with which God wants each of us to finish our earthly career. When life's battle is over, and life's mystery about to end, oh, that each of us may look back from the closing portals of the past and say: "Not one of all the LORD's good promises to the house of Israel failed; every one was fulfilled" (21:45).

It is so blessed to feel and to know that God wants to give us this. We are not holding a reluctant heart to an unforced obligation, but we are simply cooperating with our truest Friend to bring about that on which He has set His own heart for us.

Beloved, there is not a promise in your catalogue of promises, there is not a thought of blessing in your inmost heart, there is not a purpose of victory in your soul, which did not originate with Him. You can depend upon His love and His loyalty. His great heart is set upon blessing you, if you will only let Him; nay, we may almost say, upon blessing you in spite of yourself.

I do not know that there is a more inspiring study than to trust the exact fulfillment of the very words of God. There is nothing more wonderful than to take the ancient prophecies of this book and read them along with the parallel columns of human history and see how they correspond in their minutest details.

Take, for example, the first chapter of Genesis and the story of the creation. Four thousand years ago Moses wrote the record that light was created on the first day, and the sun on the fourth day.

The scientists used to love to laugh at that incongruous statement and say that it was impossible to believe the story of creation, and the existence of light before the sun.

They had their day and their laugh—and then it was God's turn. A few years ago, science discovered the solar spectrum. The fact was declared, on scientific authority, that light could exist apart from the sun, and Moses' record was shown to be scientifically true as well as divinely in advance of the times in which it was written.

The Word of God was right, after all, and even more right than all the modern ideas of the age, perhaps even before the days of Moses.

Job in one of his sublime flights, spoke about "the sweet influences of the Pleiades" and "the bands of Orion." (Job 38:31, KJV). Until very recently no one could imagine what was meant by "the sweet influences of the Pleiades," but modern astronomy has discovered the fact that the Pleiades are probably the physical center of the whole universe, and that all the stars and constellations are perpetually moving around that distant spot in far immensity, where mighty Alcyone, the chief of the Pleiades, 12,000 times larger than our own sun, reaches out his tremendous force of gravitation, and holds all these constellations in their orbits.

Again, we read in ancient prophecy two strangely contradictory announcements regarding Zedekiah, the last of Judah's kings—one to the effect that he would go to Babylon, and the other to the effect that he would never see Babylon. They looked like contradictions until the fact was brought out, in the fulfillment, that after the fall of Jerusalem, Zedekiah's eyes were blinded by the cruelty of Nebuchadnezzar, and he was carried in chains to Babylon, but he never saw it, although he ended his days in one of its dreary dungeons.

Thus every jot and tittle of this faithful word shall stand, and the day will come when wondering angels and saints will exclaim again, "Not one of all the LORD's good promises to the house of Israel failed; everyone was fulfilled" (Joshua 21:45).

Even His very judgments are an evidence of the faithfulness of His everlasting word. Two Hebrew rabbis were standing on Mount Zion, looking at the desolations of Jerusalem, and the very foxes that ran on the ruined walls. One of the old men wept, and his brother smiled. Then they looked at each other, and one asked, "How can you weep?" and the other asked, "How can you smile?" One answered, "I weep because I see how God has fulfilled His word, spoken by the mouth of the ancient prophet, that 'the foxes shall run upon the wall of Zion.' " "Ah," said the other, "that is just why I smile, because the same prophet has said, 'Zion shall be restored,' and I know therefore, that as one word has been fulfilled, the other shall also come to pass."

Rabinowitz has told us that the ancient Hebrew Bible has the letters Alpha and Omega, just after the prophecy in Zechariah, "They will look on me, the one they have pierced, and they will mourn" (Zechariah 12:10). For long ages, Israel's rabbis could not understand that Alpha and Omega; but even those two little words were not in vain, and if you turn to the book of Revelation, you will find John recalling the prophecy and applying it to Christ: "Look, he is coming with the clouds,/ and every eye will see him,/ even those who pierced him" (1:7), and then Christ, applying it to Himself, and saying: "I am the Alpha and the Omega, . . . who is, and who was, and who is to come" (1:8).

No! not a single *yod*, the smallest letter in the Hebrew alphabet, shall pass away until all be fulfilled (Matthew 5:18).

And so, beloved, it has been fulfilled and yet will be fulfilled in your own heart and life. You may trust His faithful promises. He will bring it all to pass. You can send up the prayer of David, and say: "Remember your word to your servant,/ for you have given me hope" (Psalm 119:49).

Yes, if He has even caused you to hope in it, He will not disappoint you. His heart is so true that He will not let you trust a misleading word.

With infinite delicacy and confidence He says: "If it were not so, I would have told you" (John 14:2). You may not understand all the promises or their fulfillment; you may not understand all the trials of the way; you may not quite understand all the meaning of His words. They may mean to you what they mean to no one else; they may speak to your thoughts and hopes, what your own circumstances suggest; but all that He has meant for you and all that He has let you claim in the spirit of humble trust, He will weave into the pattern of your life; He will work out in the claim of His providence, and He will cause you to say, with rejoicing heart as you look back from the heights of eternal recompense, "Not one of all the LORD's good promises to the house of Israel failed; every one was fulfilled." (Joshua 21:45).

What He said to Jacob of old, on the stony pillow, He will fulfill to your trusting heart: "I will not leave you until I have done what I have promised you" (Genesis 28:15).

Yes, He will be faithful even to the erring. "If his sons forsake my law/ and do not follow my statues,/ . . . / I will punish their sin with the rod,/ their iniquity with flogging;/ but I will not take my love from him,/ nor will I ever betray my faithfulness" (Psalm 89:30, 32–33).

Even your faith may sometimes falter and seem to fail. But, above all your sighs and tears, the promise will often come ringing back: "if we are faithless, he will remain faithful,/ for he cannot disown himself" (2 Timothy 2:13).

Blessed be His name for all the faithful words He has kept to us hitherto, but He will lift up the vision of our faith to the greater things which He has yet in store for us.

His eye is upon the glorious ending. He wants to have you enter in, saying: "I have fought the good fight, I have finished the race, I have kept the faith. Now there is in store for me the crown of righteousness" (4:7–8a).

Some day, even you, trembling, faltering one, shall stand upon those heights and look back upon all you have passed through, all you have narrowly escaped, all the perils through which He guided you, the stumblings through which He guarded you and the sins from which He saved you; and you shall shout, with a meaning you cannot understand now, "Salvation belongs to our God,/ who sits on the throne,/ and to the Lamb" (Revelation 7:10).

Some day He will sit down with us in that glorious home, and we shall have all the ages in which to understand the story of our lives. And He will read over again this old marked Bible with us; He will show us how He kept all these promises; He will explain to us the mysteries that we could not understand; He will recall to our memory the things we have long forgotten; He will go over again with us the book of life; He will recall all the finished story, and I am sure we will often cry: "Blessed Christ! You have been so true, You have been so good! Was there ever love like this?" And then the great chorus will be repeated once more: "Not one of all the LORD's good promises to the house of Israel failed; every one was fulfilled" (Joshua 21:45).

Beloved, will you take these old promises afresh? Will you make an edition of your Bible not printed by the Bible Society nor the Oxford Press, but a Bible written by the Holy Spirit upon your heart, and translated into the version of your life? And some day He will let us write upon its last page, this glorious inscription: "Not one of all the LORD's good promises to the house of Israel failed; every one was fulfilled."

CHAPTER 16

THE CHURCH'S INHERITANCE

Then Jesus came to them and said, "All authority in heaven and on earth has been given to me. Therefore go and make disciples of all nations, baptizing them in the name of the Father and of the Son and of the Holy Spirit, and teaching them to obey everything I have commanded you. And surely I am with you always, to the very end of the age." (Matthew 28:18–20)

The whole story of the book of Joshua may be applied, in a broader sense, to the people of God collectively, and especially to the New Testament church. In an important sense the whole body of Christians may be called the spiritual Israel. And the history of God's ancient people is full of interesting parallels and lessons for us, even if they may not be exact types in this respect.

ISRAEL'S FAILURE

1. The failure of Israel to enter into the Land of Promise through unbelief had its parallel in the rejection of Christ by His own countrymen, and the consequent rejection of the Jewish people from the privileges of the gospel. But as for ancient Israel there was still a period of probation and long-suffering which lasted for 40 years, affording individuals the opportunity of entering into the spiritual blessings of God's covenant, so there intervened a similar period after Christ's rejection by His own people, before the final destruction of Jerusalem, and the dispersion of the Jews. And as there were some of even the first generation of Israel who believed, so there were exceptions in the ministry of Christ and His disciples, from among even that unbelieving nation, who gladly accepted their Messiah, and entered into their spiritual inheritance.

APOSTOLIC TRIUMPHS

2. The glorious career of Joshua, the crossing of the Jordan, the conquest

139

of Canaan and the dividing of the inheritance among the tribes of Israel, find their striking parallel likewise in the death and resurrection of Jesus, the descent of the Holy Spirit at Pentecost and the triumphs of Christianity, when the Church, to a very great extent, claimed her inheritance of power, purity and blessing, and entered upon the conquest of the world for Christ, until there was scarcely a region of the globe where the gospel was not at least planted and the strongholds of Satan challenged and shaken.

The crossing of the Jordan may well illustrate the cross of Calvary, and the experience of death and resurrection which was so emphasized in primitive Christianity. The new covenant has its counterpart in the coming of the Holy Spirit, and the gospel of full and free salvation.

The death of Moses and the advent of Joshua, whose very name is suggestive of Jesus, suggest the transition which then actually came, from the law to the gospel. The victories of Canaan had their counterpart in the triumphs of Christianity. Dividing the inheritance foreshadowed the various gifts of the Holy Spirit distributed to the Church.

The supernatural element which runs through the entire story of the conquest of Palestine, was more than realized in the first centuries of Christianity in the manifestations of the divine presence and power, in signs and wonders and mighty deeds. And the choice possessions won by Caleb, Othniel, Acsah and others, remind us of the transcendent examples of piety, faith, love, knowledge and holy power and usefulness, which adorned the annals of the early Church.

FAILURE OF THE CHURCH

3. The failure of Israel to enter promptly and fully into their whole inheritance, also finds its counterpart in the church of the New Testament. With all its fresh beauty and divine glory, still there was much of human imperfection and melancholy failure.

The old cry, "There are still very large areas of land to be taken over" (Joshua 13:1), "How long will you wait before you begin to take possession of the land that the LORD, the God of your fathers, has given you?" (18:3b) is echoed back in more than one of Paul's sorrowful admonitions to the churches he loved; and still more strongly in the appeals and warnings of the Son of God to the seven churches of Asia, through the last messages of the Holy Spirit, 60 years after His ascension.

There we find Him saying to the strongest of these churches, "I hold this against you: You have forsaken your first love" (Revelation 2:4). And to another, "You have a reputation of being alive, but you are dead. Wake up! Strengthen what remains and is about to die, for I have not found your deeds complete in the sight of my God" (3:1b–2). And yet again, "You say, 'I am rich; I have acquired wealth and do not need a thing.' But you do not realize that you are wretched, pitiful, poor, blind and naked" (3:17).

Already, even in the lifetime of Paul and John, the primitive church had allied itself sufficiently with the world to open the door for many of the errors which afterwards entered and overwhelmed the purity of the early Church.

THE DARK AGES

4. The fearful declension of ancient Israel, leading ere long to the dark chapter of the book of Judges, and their shameful compromise with the heathen world and subjugation to its power, is more than paralleled in the story of the dark ages of medieval Christianity, through the same cause, namely, the failure of God's people to separate themselves from sin and worldliness, and to enter into their full inheritance. The purity and strength of apostolic Christianity were speedily lost in the unspeakable corruptions of an apostate church, with all the errors and abominations of that anti-Christian system which took the place of the Church of God for 1,200 years, and has been well called a "baptized heathenism."

Many of the pictures of the book of Judges might find a vivid counterpart in the story of the Middle Ages. The graphic picture of Micah and his mother, with its strange intermingling of dishonesty, religion, the ritualism, almost seems like a parable of much of the religious life of such a period, and, indeed, is not without its parallels in our own days. Like Micah's sanctuary, many a formalist has folded his arms in the midst of violence and sin, and said, "Now I know that the LORD will be good to me, since this Levite has become my priest" (Judges 17:13).

Notwithstanding these there were many exceptions in ancient Israel—a wise and patriotic Deborah, a brave and faithful Barak, a divinely called Gideon, a single-hearted Jephthah and a mighty Samson. And so, even in the darkest ages of Christianity there have not been wanting those who have not defiled their garments, and who at times have dared to rise up for God against those that did wickedly, and shed a divine luster on their times and names. Such were the noble army of the martyrs and confessors—a Waldo, a Wycliffe, a Huss, a Savonarola, a Bernard and a Bede.

At length the time of reformation came to ancient Israel, when Samuel, the prophet, arose to recall his people to their ancient faith and prepare them for the coming kingdom. Such a ministry of our own time was that of Luther and the Reformation, calling back the Church of God to her ancient faith, and arousing her to claim her lost inheritance. But, as even Samuel's mighty work was in a measure ineffectual, and was followed for a time by the counterfeit kingdom of Saul, and the false and worldly aims of his countrymen, which led them into a separation from God that left its effects for half a century, so even the revived Christianity of the Reformation has not been perfect; and, like ancient Israel, the Church, delivered from her immediate foe, has given herself up, to a great degree, to a spirit of worldliness, and to look for her kingdom in a forbidden world.

There is much today of the spirit of Saul in nominal Christianity; the pride that finds its satisfaction in earthly gifts, talents and successes, and fails to recognize the true King, who, like the rejected David, waits for His throne as One "despised and rejected by men" (Isaiah 53:3).

The kingdom of David seems to prefigure the true triumphs of our coming King, and the ushering in of His dominion in the final victory of Christianity.

MILLENNIAL VISIONS

5. The peaceful and splendid throne of Solomon completes the picture of the millennial glory which is to be the consummation of the Christian age.

Then will come the full inheritance of grace and glory, both for God's ancient people and the Church and the Bride of the Lamb.

THE TEACHINGS OF JOSHUA

What, then, for us, in the Church of God today, is the teaching of this ancient book?

1. It summons her to her glorious crusade of conquest against the enemies of Christ. Never was there an age more full of encouragement for the good fight of faith and the conquest of the world for Christ. The whole land is before us; every avenue of influence at home, every missionary field abroad, is open for the Church's zeal and holy enterprise. The triumphs of the gospel in the past 50 years have not been unworthy of comparison with Pentecost, or even with Joshua's campaign. True, it has been but a small section of the Church that has dared to claim these victories, but the recompense has been sufficient to call forth far higher achievements and aspirations.

Especially should the near prospect of the coming kingdom arouse us to go forth and win for our glorious Captain the crown of all the world, until every citadel of heathendom, and every stronghold of sin shall have become a monument of His grace and power.

More emphatically still, let the tender lesson of Rahab in the beginning, and the Cities of Refuge at the close, remind us that our supreme conflict is for the souls of sinful men. And beyond all the questions of dogmas, and the discussion of principles, and the undermining of systems of error and iniquity, let our objective point be individual men and women, and our highest and brightest trophies, the transformed lives of the most helpless and degraded of our race.

2. Let us, like Joshua and Israel, go in and possess all our inheritance. The Church has been slack to do this, and is still slack. She has not claimed her

full inheritance of knowledge and truth, nor entered into all the fullness of God's precious promises.

She has not entered into her full inheritance of holiness, but has been content to look upon a life of sanctity and devotedness as an exceptional exhibition of individual temperament rather than as the duty and privilege of every child of God.

She has not entered into her full inheritance of faith, nor recognized the power that lies latent in taking God at His Word and daring to claim all that He has spoken. A life of becoming faith and remarkable answers to prayer is regarded as something special and wonderful, a sort of peculiar calling on the part of some individual of exalted piety.

She has not entered into her full inheritance of love and unity, but has been rent with strifes, divisions, jealousies and controversies, which have left Hebron in the hands of the Anakim and her Lord "wounded in the house of [his] friends" (Zechariah 13:6, KJV).

And she has failed to enter into her full inheritance of supernatural power. The gifts of Pentecost have never been recalled, but have only been imperfectly claimed, and natural talent, human learning and worldly influence have been their weak and insufficient substitutes. Let us go in and possess all the land. All authority is given to our Joshua in heaven and on earth, and surely He is with us always (Matthew 28:18–20).

"God did not give us a spirit of timidity, but a spirit of power, of love and of self-discipline" (2 Timothy 1:7). Let us, therefore, "fan into flame the gift of God, which is in [us]" (1:6); let Zion hear her Master crying, "Awake, awake, O Zion,/ clothe yourself with strength./ Put on your garments of splendor" (Isaiah 52:1); "Arise, shine, for your light has come,/ and the glory of the LORD rises upon you" (60:1).

The Almighty Presence of our risen Lord is sufficient for any obedient service which we will dare to attempt in His strength and name. Let us put on the full armor of God (Ephesians 6:11); "be strong in the Lord and in his mighty power" (6:10). And clothed in all the fullness of the unchanging Paraclete, let the Church of God go forth to the last campaign of the great conflict.

3. Let the Church remember the necessity of separation from sin and the world if she would overcome her enemies and possess her full inheritance. She must cross the Jordan and let its unbridged torrents roll between her and the world. She must know the true meaning of circumcision and let Gilgal roll away the reproach of Egypt from her spirit and person. She must watch against the sin of Achan, and not let the accursed thing touch her spotless hands. She must take no tribute from the Canaanites, nor lean upon the world in the slightest measure for her support.

She must separate from forbidden alliance with the ungodly, and stand "like the dawn,/ fair as the moon, bright as the sun,/ majestic as the stars in procession" (Song of Songs 6:10). Alas, this is the secret of her weakness and failure; she has gone, like Israel, into a forbidden league with the tribes of the land. She has put her head, like Samson, in Delilah's lap, and her locks are shorn, and all her shaking of herself will not renew her strength until she has taken the place of the Nazirite and separated herself from a defiling and hostile world. "Come out of her, my people" (Revelation 18:4) is the Master's call; and as the Church obeys it, will she stand forth in her primitive purity and power and draw all men unto her Lord (John 12:32).

CHAPTER 17

THE MILLENNIAL INHERITANCE

At that time his voice shook the earth, but now he has promised, "Once more I will shake not only the earth but also the heavens." The words "once more" indicate the removing of what can be shaken—that is, created things—so that what cannot be shaken may remain.

Therefore, since we are receiving a kingdom that cannot be shaken, let us be thankful, and so worship God acceptably with reverence and awe. (Hebrews 12:26–28)

Christian hope has always loved to link the Land of Promise with our heavenly inheritance. The sacred poetry of the past is full of this sweet imagery. Jordan is the swelling flood of death, and the sweet fields beyond are the images of that heavenly land,

> Where everlasting spring abides,
> And never withering flowers,
> And death, the narrow stream, divides
> That heavenly land from ours.

The vital objection to this theory is that heaven essentially differs from the earthly Canaan in most of the features which chiefly distinguished the latter. That was a land of conflict and hard-won victory, while heaven shall have no foes to overcome, and all its crowns shall be those of accomplished triumph and peaceful recompense. Heaven will have no Jericho, no valley of Achor, nor failure such as that of Achan, and no sad declension such as that which followed Israel's entry into Canaan.

And yet, there are some points in which the misinterpretation is not without its lessons. Canaan was Israel's home, their place of rest after the conflicts in the wilderness, and the realization of long-deferred hopes and promises.

And so, there remains a rest for the people of God (Hebrews 4:9) on the heaven side of the grave, where they shall be at home, and "they will rest from their labor, for their deeds will follow them" (Revelation 14:13b), and where the long-deferred hopes and expectations of life shall be realized at length, and all their wanderings and trials shall forever cease. God forbid that we should abate aught of the blessed meaning of heaven, where all the ransomed wait in unspeakable felicity for the greater inheritance that lies still farther beyond!

It is of this better inheritance that the ancient Canaan was really the type; for there is a better inheritance even than heaven. Christian hope is always connected in the New Testament Scriptures, not with death and the state of the departed, but with the second coming of the Lord Jesus, and the millennial glory which is then to be ushered in. Even the earthly Canaan itself was but the transient home of the seed of Abraham; it looked forward both in type and promise to the future age when Israel shall inherit their full patrimony, and when all the children of faith shall possess, through the age of glory, their true Land of Promise.

CHRIST WILL BRING IT IN

1. Like the ancient Canaan, it is to be introduced by the true Joshua, the Lord Jesus Christ. There is no millennium promised in the Scriptures apart from His personal coming. The heavens have received Him, according to the language of the apostles, "until the time comes for God to restore everything" (Acts 3:21); but He is coming again, and His appearing and His kingdom will be simultaneous.

There came a day, in Scotland, when the great heart of the reformers went out to John Knox. They felt it was he whom they needed, and his coming would settle every question.

When at last the tidings went abroad, over hill and valley, and hamlet and city, "John Knox has come!" all hearts were thrilled with confidence that the crisis was passed, and strong men gathered at the rallying places, and tyrants trembled on their thrones; for they knew that his single presence was worth the combined strength of all their armies.

And so, the need of our people is not institutions, and organizations, and people, but the coming of the King Himself.

THE CHILDREN OF FAITH AND OBEDIENCE

2. Like the ancient Canaan, only the children of faith and obedience will possess this inheritance. Perhaps many of the ancient Israelites were saved who never entered the Land of Promise; and so it is possible to belong to the people of God and yet lose much of the glory and recompense connected with the hope of His appearing. "And he will appear a second time, not to bear sin, but to bring salvation to those who are waiting for him" (Hebrews

9:28b). "And with him will be his called, chosen and faithful followers" (Revelation 17:14b).

There is a faith that brings salvation; but there is a faith that will bring the recompense promised at His coming, and there will yet be a generation whose faith will keep them from the power of death, and bring them the translation glory.

Often have we seen the children of God struggling through some tremendous trial of soul or body, and it seemed as if their faith did not quite win the victory here. But it was sweet to believe that what they had missed in this world would be given as the recompense of their faith, at His coming.

Not one single grain of true faith is ever lost. Although it may seem to have missed its mark on this side, it is all reserved for His coming, and many a soul that has wept and wondered will wonder yet more, when it beholds the crown laid up for it there when the tears shall have long ago been forgotten.

But obedience is as necessary as faith. They who are to be among the first fruits of His appearing have followed the Lamb wherever He goes (14:4). "You are my friends," He says, "if you do what I command" (John 15:14).

MUST BE WON

3. The millennium, like Canaan, must be conquered, too. Not without resistance shall He enter upon His kingdom. The world's greatest conflict will just precede its millennial Sabbath. The mighty Captain of the millennial armies sits upon a white horse with garments dyed in blood and a name upon His vesture and upon His thigh, King of kings, and Lord of lords; and comes forth as a mighty Conqueror, treading under His feet the hosts of the antichrist and the powers of hell, and scattering His enemies at the feet of Nebuchadnezzar's image, like the chaff of the summer threshing floors; for "he must reign until he has put all his enemies under his feet" (1 Corinthians 15:25). The battles of Joshua and the conquests of David are the living types of the advent struggles and the Armageddon war.

The promises of His coming are all given to the overcomer. God is not going to throw away His crowns and thrones on those who have lived for earthly rewards. He has a "little flock" to whom He will "give . . . the kingdom" (Luke 12:32), and He is picking them out every day, through the tests that come to them and the victories which they win.

Gideon started with 30,000 men, but God only took 300 of all that army. They were not only picked, but they were picked again and again. The first 30,000 were taken out of Israel, then 10,000 were taken out of the 30,000, and then 300 were taken out of the 10,000, and with these 300 the victory was won.

Day by day, each of us is meeting the enemies who come to prove whether we can be trusted with a crown.

UNIVERSAL VICTORY

4. The Lord's coming will bring not only conflict, but victory. Joshua's campaign was an uninterrupted and complete triumph until it was finished. There was no king in all the Hittite confederacy that had not been overthrown; and so our Lord is to put down all authority and opposition and reign without a rival over the millennial earth. The day is surely coming when every evil thing that lifts its head in proud defiance shall be laid prostrate at His feet. Not forever shall right be on the scaffold and wrong upon the throne. "God [will] bring about justice for his chosen ones" (18:7).

Error shall at length cease to delude, selfishness to prey on holiness, and injustice, vice and crime to defile and destroy the creation of God. The hour is coming when the adversaries of the Church and of the soul shall be remembered only as a vanished dream. We shall seek for them and they shall not be found. The proud empires of the world, the blasphemous and defiant power of the antichrist, and even Satan himself shall be given to the saints of God and the Prince of Peace. The conquests of Canaan were not a truce with the adversary, nor an attempt to transform their adversaries to peaceful friends, but their utter extinction.

And so the coming of the Lord is to involve the destruction of His enemies. The gospel age is the time for evangelization and the day for the world's peaceful submission and conversion, but when the Master comes it will be to "overthrow with the breath of his mouth and destroy by the splendor of his coming" (2 Thessalonians 2:8) everything that exalted itself against the obedience of Christ (2 Corinthians 10:5).

OUR INHERITANCE

5. His coming will bring us to our inheritance. Then will Abraham and David possess the literal fullness of their ancient covenants, and the land on which their feet rested for a time shall be their own and the home of their offspring. Then shall the disciples who followed Jesus in His days of rejection "sit on twelve thrones, judging the twelve tribes of Israel" (Matthew 19:28). Then shall we possess our complete redemption—spirit, soul and body perfectly restored to the image of God, and our lost dominion over the earth given back through our exalted Head. Then shall the saints of God receive the recompense for their lives of service and suffering, and those who have overcome shall wear the crowns of victory and glory which He has promised to the faithful and triumphant. Then shall each soul find its perfect sphere and enter upon the service for which its earthly training has qualified it; and doubtless there will be a Hebron of exalted fellowship and love for every brave Caleb; a Kiriath Sepher of boundless knowledge for every conquering Othniel; a fountain of life, with its upper and nether

springs, for every true Acsah who has dared to claim her full inheritance; a double inheritance for every true Ephraimite that has dared to conquer it in the days of earthly battle; a city of honor and service for every Levite who has been true to his consecration; and a Timnath Serah of everlasting light and glory for every faithful Joshua.

Our full inheritance is yet to come. All we know of Jesus in His indwelling fullness and victorious life is but the type of the glory that awaits us at His advent. All we know of truth here is but through a poor mirror refection, then "I shall know fully, even as I am fully known!" (1 Corinthians 13:12). All we know of holiness here is but a shadow of that hour when "we shall be like him" (1 John 3:2), as we see Him as He is. All we know of physical redemption is but a prophetic foretaste of the glorious life that will thrill every frame with the resurrection joy. All we know of service for the Master is but the blundering attempt of the schoolboy as he learns the mere alphabet of knowledge, compared with the mighty faith and divine power with which we shall be workers together with Him in the transformation of the millennial earth, at the inauguration of His glorious kingdom.

He is educating us to bear "an eternal glory that far outweighs them all" (2 Corinthians 4:17). Let us be apt learners and by and by we shall look back with amazement to our earthly childhood and scarcely recognize the trembling and blundering beginner who once struggled through the years of time, and claimed the inheritance that was to be so much more vast and transcendent than his brightest earthly dream.

HIMSELF

6. And best of all, He will be Himself our Eternal Inheritance. "Now the dwelling of God is with men, and he will live with them. They will be his people, and God himself will be with them and be their God" (Revelation 21:3).

How much is meant by the presence of Jesus! How much it used to mean in the old apostolic times! What a difference it made to that little company when suddenly He stood in their midst and thrilled their hearts with the sweet words, "Peace be with you" (John 20:19). "The disciples were overjoyed when they saw the Lord" (20:20b).

Only four or five times did that wondrous Presence appear to Paul, but oh, the power of one such moment upon his life!

What cared he, that day, as he rode into Damascus, for any earthly or heavenly power? What to him was the name of Jesus? But suddenly, like a flash of lightning from a clear sky, the face of Jesus blazed out from the glory, the voice of Jesus spoke to him, and Paul was prostrated upon the ground broken and subdued, and crying, "Lord, what wilt Thou have me to do?" (Acts 9:6 KJV). One moment with Jesus had transformed the mightiest will of the age.

Look at him again, crushed and discouraged, in that dungeon in Jerusalem, wondering if he had made a fatal mistake, and sinking, doubtless, in deep depression. But suddenly the Master appears, and with one word assures him. "Take courage! As you have testified about me in Jerusalem, so you must also testify in Rome" (Acts 23:11). Instantly Paul's heart was on the heights of glory, even as the one flash the sailor gets from the sky and the one observation he takes of the sun, will carry him through long weeks of clouds and storms.

Look again a that little company on the stormy Adriatic. For days the ship has tossed on the wild Euroclydon, but, suddenly, Jesus appears to Paul. One single message is all: "Do not be afraid, Paul. You must stand trial before Caesar; and God has graciously given you the lives of all who sail with you" (27:24).

Paul is a victor again, and standing on that tossing vessel, he inspires with his own courage the sinking hearts of the men with him. They reach the shore, and by and by, the capital of the world.

Oh, what will it be to have that wondrous Presence with us forever, and every moment be able to look into His face, to hear His voice, to have Him with us, and to be "even as He"? Thank God that blessed Coming is near at hand! God is saying to many hearts today, as He has said so often in His Word: "In a little while I will once more shake the heavens and the earth, the sea and the dry land. I will shake all nations, and the desired of all nations will come" (Haggai 2:6–7a).

Surely He is shaking the nations today. Surely this terrible financial trouble that is distressing all the world, making hundreds of thousands of paupers, bringing distress of nations and perplexity, surely this is one of the harbingers of the coming of the Son of man, and the quaking earth is keeping time to the tread of the heavenly march.

Only a few days ago, tidings reached us from across the ocean and the continent, that the very heart of Asia had been shaken by the most significant earthquake of modern times. Surely, if there is one place on earth that is the seat of heathenism and the very citadel of its strength, it is Tibet, and that great monastery, where thousands of priests surround the Grand Llama of Buddhism, the Pope of five million Asiatic people; and yet, a few weeks ago, that very spot was shaken by the hand of God, that great monastery crumbled into a heap of ruins, and the Grand Llama himself has disappeared, with hundreds of others, and filled the minds of his followers with consternation.

God help us to understand the meaning of our times, and to hear Him saying to us, "And who knows but that you have come to royal position for such a time as this?" (Esther 4:14).

JUDGES, RUTH AND SAMUEL

CHAPTER 1

THE CAUSE OF SPIRITUAL FAILURE

And they called that place Bokim. (Judges 2:5)

T he book of Judges has a very important place in the plan of divine revelation. It expresses a great truth and teaches a deep and solemn lesson: the danger of spiritual declension after great spiritual blessing.

A LONG DECLENSION

The book of Numbers is a sad book, because it tells of the wanderings of Israel in the wilderness for 40 years after God brought the people out of Egypt. But Judges is a sadder and more solemn book—it tells of the failure of Israel after they had entered the Land of Promise, a failure that lasted not 40 years but 400. It represents the danger of backsliding after a person has received the Holy Spirit and known Jesus in His fullness—a danger most real and alarming.

The author of Hebrews warns against the same thing: "We want each of you to show this same diligence to the very end, in order to make your hope sure" (6:11).

There is a place in the discipline of the Christian life and in the wise and faithful dealing of God with His people for both warning and promise, for both hope and fear. No one is so unsafe as he who recklessly dreams of safety without vigilance and obedience. God has planted beacons all along the way, not to discourage us with needless fear, but to save us with wholesome caution and vigilant obedience.

Judges stands in a larger sense for the declension of the Church of Christ after the apostolic age, and it represents the dark ages of Christian history. But in its personal application it may also represent the danger of retreating from the baptism of Pentecost and the deepest and highest experiences of the Holy Spirit.

153

BEGAN WITH VICTORY

The book begins with a record of victory.

> After the death of Joshua, the Israelites asked the LORD, "Who will be the first to go up and fight for us against the Canaanites?"
>
> The LORD answered, "Judah is to go; I have given the land into their hands."
>
> Then the men of Judah said to the Simeonites their brothers, "Come up with us into the territory allotted to us, to fight against the Canaanites. We in turn will go with you into yours." So the Simeonites went with them.
>
> When Judah attacked, the LORD gave the Canaanites and Perizzites into their hands and they struck down ten thousand men at Bezek. (1:1–4)

This was all as it should be, and manifested the spirit of faith, obedience and humble dependence upon God. Further on we read that they even took Jerusalem and that they captured Hebron and other strongholds. They pressed down to the country of the Philistines, driving them from most of their strongholds. It seemed as if they still possessed the victorious faith of Joshua and had in their midst the same Almighty Presence of their divine Leader.

BEGINNING OF FAILURE

But we soon begin to see the first indications of the coming failure. First, the men of Judah began to pause in their career of triumph. We see the first word of defeat and discouragement in verse 19: "they were unable to drive the people from the plains, because they had iron chariots." Soon after we read of the partial failure of the tribe of Benjamin: "The Benjamites, however, failed to dislodge the Jebusites, who were living in Jerusalem; to this day the Jebusites live there with the Benjamites" (1:21). It was not that they "were unable," but that they "failed to" dislodge them.

Next we find Manasseh failing to drive out the inhabitants of Beth Shan and the neighboring towns: "for the Canaanites were determined to live in that land" (1:27). Next, Ephraim becomes discouraged and fails to drive the Canaanites from Gezer (1:29). Zebulun also allows the enemy to remain in his town (1:30). Asher yields to the inhabitants living in his region (1: 31). Naphtali fails to drive out the inhabitants of Beth Shemesh (1:33). And Dan flees before the Amorites of his mountain land (1:34). So there was scarcely a tribe of Israel that had not in some degree compromised with the enemy and given place to their foes, whom God had ordered to be completely extirpated from the land. The steps of their failure are very striking as we follow them in detail.

TOLERATING THE ENEMY

First, the Israelites simply *let* the enemy remain. They seemed to have no fear of the Canaanites and just failed to exterminate them.

Second, we find the Israelites deliberately putting the Canaanites under their control and keeping them there for the purpose of making a profit from them and getting something out of them. This is where the world gets into our Christian lives today. We compromise with evil; we not only allow it, but we use it for our own purposes. We think there is no harm in taking money from wicked men for religious purposes and meeting them halfway. We are willing to be agreeable to the world in order to have a good influence over it. But in the end we fall completely under its power.

Third, we find the Canaanites living alongside the Israelites (1:27). Then, a little later, we find Israel living with the Canaanites (1:33). Israel began by treating the Canaanites as guests or slaves, but ended by finding that they had become their masters and conquerors.

CONQUERED BY THE ENEMY

Next we see the Canaanites driving the children of Dan into the mountains. They now have grown strong enough to dictate and demand, as evil always does after we have given it standing room for a little while.

INTERMARRIAGE

Next comes the intermarriage of God's people with the enemy. They meet in the social intimacies of life. They find the people of the world agreeable and profitable, and they consent to the forbidden fellowships and intermarriages of the godly and the ungodly, which in every age have preceded a time of corruption and great wickedness. No child of God has any right to intermarry with the ungodly, and a true parent dare not consent to such a union without involving the eternal well-being of the child. It is never safe to disobey God, and I have no hesitation in saying that I would not perform such a marriage ceremony.

IDOLATRY

The next step is partnership in idolatry and the forsaking of Jehovah's worship for the shameful rites of heathenism. In chapter 3 we read: "They took their daughters in marriage and gave their own daughters to their sons, and served their gods. The Israelites did evil in the eyes of the LORD; they forgot the LORD their God and served the Baals and the Asherahs" (3:6–7).

GOD'S ANGER

The culmination of all this soon came in the anger of Jehovah and His severe and righteous judgment upon His disobedient people:

> In his anger against Israel the LORD handed them over to raiders who plundered them. He sold them to their enemies all around, whom they were no longer able to resist. Whenever Israel went out to fight, the hand of the LORD was against them to defeat them, just as he had sworn to them. They were in great distress. (2:14–15)

What a dreadful thing it is to have God against us and to know that He who controls the breath of our lives and all the elements of destruction around us is compelled by His nature to deal contrary to us and to consume us—even as fire consumes every combustible thing it touches! God is compelled to be against sin, and while He pities the sinner, He hates the sin. While we are against God, His presence must be to us a consuming fire. We would fly from the awful blaze of His holy glance as from a lightning flash and long to hide ourselves in hell.

GIVEN UP

But there is something even sadder than this. We read that God gave them up to the power of their enemies and allowed the Canaanites, whom they themselves had trifled with and taken into covenant, to be the thorns and snares of judgment and temptation to them.

There is nothing more terrible in all the judgments pronounced against Israel than this: "Now therefore I tell you that I will not drive them out before you; they will be thorns in your sides and their gods will be a snare to you" (2:3).

And later we read:

> Therefore the LORD was very angry with Israel and said, "Because this nation has violated the covenant that I laid down for their forefathers and has not listened to me, I will no longer drive out before them any of the nations Joshua left when he died. I will use them to test Israel and see whether they will keep the way of the LORD and walk in it as their forefathers did." (2:20–21)

God allowed them to be filled with their own devices and tempted and tried by the results of their own disobedience. He even sold them into the hands of their enemies and gave their foes a power to subdue and enslave them (3:8), which they could have never claimed without divine permission. From that time forward, the Canaanites, Philistines, Syrians, Assyrians, Babylonians and Romans were but the executioners of divine judgment. They succeeded in their conquests and captivities by direct divine permission.

All of this represents an awful truth which the New Testament undoubtedly confirms: God's last and most terrible judgment is to allow the devil to have power over the disobedient soul and to permit temptation to overcome, torment and punish him because of his willful disobedience to the will of God and his rejection of the grace that would have saved him. The saddest thing about the condition of the sinner is that while he thinks he is free and has the power to reform and do as he pleases, he is the helpless slave of Satan, who has "taken them captive to do his will" (2 Timothy 2:26). He can never be free until he repents and renounces the dominion of God's great enemy and appeals to the blood of Jesus Christ and the power of the Holy Spirit to break the fetters of his captivity.

THE HARDENED HEART

There may come a time in the life of a wicked man when, through persistent rejection of light and right, he shall be given over, as we read in Romans, "to a depraved mind," and "to shameful lusts" (1:28, 26). He shall find within him a power compelling him to evil and possessing him with the devil just as one can be possessed and constrained by the Holy Spirit.

This explains the hardening of Pharaoh's heart. This is the last stage of impenitence and despair, and it never comes to any person until he has rejected and refused the mercy of God and has deliberately chosen evil instead of good, Satan instead of God. God punishes him by letting him have Satan to the full, or as it is expressed so graphically in Proverbs:

> Since they hated knowledge
>   and did not choose to fear the LORD,
> since they would not accept my advice
>   and spurned my rebuke,
> they will eat the fruit of their ways
>   and be filled with the fruit of their own schemes.
>   (1:29–31)

It is possible even for the child of God to be delivered over to the power of temptation through a continuance in willful and persistent disobedience. The very things that we choose become our punishment, and through our own deliberate disobedience, we find ourselves under temptation that we cannot resist. The reason is that we are in a place where God never wanted us to be. We have brought upon ourselves our own torment. The grace of God is equal to all His will for us, and He knows how to deliver the godly out of temptation. But He has not promised His grace for self-imposed burdens, dangers or situations that are contrary to His divine purpose.

There is nothing sweeter in life than to be conscious of being so encased in the armor of the Holy Spirit that Satan cannot touch us. Every fiery shot glances off, as the shot and shell are repelled by the armor plate on the battleship, and we walk through the hosts of hell as safe and unscathed as if we were treading the courts of heaven.

But there is also an experience where we are conscious that Satan has a power over our hearts; that the fiery darts do penetrate and stain the sensitive soul; that the evil instigation does become a part of our thoughts and feelings; and that we are not in perfect victory over the power of evil. This is the meaning of the Master's prayer: "Lead us not into temptation,/ but deliver us from the evil one" (Matthew 6:13).

This is the meaning of hell, the beginning of torment, the retribution of sin. This is something even more bitter than the wrath of God. It is the culmination of the first step of unbelief, disobedience and spiritual declension. Let us guard against the first step, and let us ask Him to save us from the causes that led His people of old into these depths of wretchedness and sin.

THE CAUSES OF ISRAEL'S FAILURE

The first cause was incomplete and unfinished work. The Israelites did not thoroughly finish the battle. They entered into compromises with evil. They failed to be thorough and wholehearted in their dealing with God. Let us make sure that we give no place to the devil and that we allow the world and the flesh no standing ground. All Satan asks is toleration of a single root of bitterness, unbelief or self-indulgence. As surely as God is true, however, that single sin will destroy us in the end.

Second, the Israelites failed to recognize their temptations as God's tests to see what they would do. He allowed the things to come so that He could test their obedience. Similarly, He lets temptations come to us, not so that they may overcome us, but so that they can establish us. If we would recognize them as God's tests and rise above them to meet His higher will, they would become occasions for grander victories and higher advances.

But third, the real secret of their failure was the lack of a true, personal and independent hold upon God as the Source of their strength. There is one passage in the opening verses of Judges that explains the situation: "The people served the LORD throughout the lifetime of Joshua and of the elders who outlived him and who had seen all the great things the LORD had done for Israel" (2:7).

Here we see the cause of the whole trouble. The Israelites leaned upon

Joshua and Joshua's immediate successors more than they leaned upon God. They got their ideas and inspiration from human leaders, but they did not stand personally rooted and grounded in God. When the shock of conflict came, they failed. Indeed, their own language on a previous occasion shows that they did not really understand their own helplessness and their utter need of Jehovah.

SELF-CONFIDENCE

In the closing chapter of Joshua we read that when that great leader had gathered the people together at Shechem and given them his parting charges, they answered with unreserved assurance, " 'We too will serve the LORD, because he is our God.' Joshua said to the people, 'You are not able to serve the LORD' " (24:18–19).

What Joshua meant was that they could not in their self-confident strength do anything but fail and sin. But they had not learned the lesson, and confident in their self-sufficiency, they did fail and sink into the depth of sin and misery. The triumphs of Jericho, Beth Horon, Hebron and Gibeon ended in the tears of Bokim and captivity by their foes.

Thank God there is another side to Bokim, the place of which the inspired prophet said, "No longer will they call you Deserted,/ or name your land Desolate./ But you will be called Hephzibah,/ and your land Beulah" (Isaiah 62:4). Bokim is the place of weeping; Beulah is the place of love and joy. Bokim means failure of our strength; Beulah means married to Him and kept by His power from stumbling and from failure.

Let us go to Bokim and learn our helplessness. And then let us go forth to Beulah and, leaning upon His love and strength, go forward singing: "But thanks be to God! He gives us the victory through our Lord Jesus Christ" (1 Corinthians 15:57). "I can do everything through him who gives me strength" (Philippians 4:13).

CHAPTER 2

SINNING AND REPENTING

In his anger against Israel the LORD handed them over to raiders who plundered them. He sold them to their enemies all around, whom they were no longer able to resist. Whenever Israel went out to fight, the hand of the LORD was against them to defeat them, just as he had sworn to them. They were in great distress.

Then the LORD raised up judges, who saved them out of the hands of these raiders. Yet they would not listen to their judges but prostituted themselves to other gods and worshiped them. Unlike their fathers, they quickly turned from the way in which their fathers had walked, the way of obedience to the LORD's commands. Whenever the LORD raised up a judge for them, he was with the judge and saved them out of the hands of their enemies as long as the judge lived; for the LORD had compassion on them as they groaned under those who oppressed and afflicted them. But when the judge died, the people returned to ways even more corrupt than those of their fathers, following other gods and serving and worshiping them. They refused to give up their evil practices and stubborn ways. (Judges 2:14–19)

This, in a few sentences, is the story of the whole book of Judges. It is a story of sinning and repenting. It is a picture of the Church and the Christian in a state of deep declension. It is a declension more deep and dark because it followed a condition of the highest spiritual blessing. It came not as the wandering in the wilderness did, after their deliverance from Egypt, but it came after their victorious entrance into Canaan and their enjoyment of the life and victory and the fullness of God's blessing.

THE DARK AGES

Its historical parallel is the story of the Dark Ages in the history of Christianity, when for centuries the Church sank into apostasy and worldliness;

and for a thousand years the light of truth and holiness was almost wholly blotted out—and this after the story of Pentecost and the light of apostolic days. It has its individual parallel in the experience of the child of God, when, after the baptism of the Holy Spirit, he falls back into spiritual declension and disobedience and returns to a life of sinning and repenting. It is a far sadder experience because of the light and the power he has known before. The lessons of this book may well warn every one of us to give all diligence to "hold firmly till the end the confidence we had at first" (Hebrews 3:14).

OTHNIEL AND EHUD

Let us look at the first two examples of God's dealing with this sinful people.

The first is the story of Othniel:

> The Israelites did evil in the eyes of the LORD; they forgot the LORD their God and served the Baals and the Asherahs. The anger of the LORD burned against Israel so that he sold them into the hands of Cushan-Rishathaim king of Aram Naharaim, to whom the Israelites were subject for eight years. But when they cried out to the LORD, he raised up for them a deliverer, Othniel son of Kenaz, Caleb's younger brother, who saved them. The Spirit of the LORD came upon him, so that he became Israel's judge and went to war. The LORD gave Cushan-Rishathaim king of Aram into the hands of Othniel, who overpowered him. So the land had peace for forty years, until Othniel son of Kenaz died. (Judges 3:7–11)

Next, is the story of Ehud:

> Once again the Israelites did evil in the eyes of the LORD, and because they did this evil the LORD gave Eglon king of Moab power over Israel. Getting the Ammonites and Amalekites to join him, Eglon came and attacked Israel, and they took possession of the City of Palms. The Israelites were subject to Eglon king of Moab for eighteen years.
>
> Again the Israelites cried out to the LORD, and he gave them a deliverer—Ehud, a left-handed man, the son of Gera the Benjamite. The Israelites sent him with tribute to Eglon king of Moab. Now Ehud had made a double-edged sword about a foot and a half long, which he strapped to his right thigh under his clothing. He presented the tribute to Eglon king of Moab, who

was a very fat man. After Ehud had presented the tribute, he sent on their way the men who had carried it. At the idols near Gilgal he himself turned back and said, "I have a secret message for you, O king."

The king said, "Quiet!" And all his attendants left him.

Ehud then approached him while he was sitting alone in the upper room of his summer palace and said, "I have a message from God for you." As the king rose from his seat, Ehud reached with his left hand, drew the sword from his right thigh and plunged it into the king's belly. Even the handle sank in after the blade, which came out his back. Ehud did not pull the sword out, and the fat closed in over it. Then Ehud went out to the porch; he shut the doors of the upper room behind him and locked them.

After he had gone, the servants came and found the doors of the upper room locked. They said, "He must be relieving himself in the inner room of the house." They waited to the point of embarrassment, but when he did not open the doors of the room, they took a key and unlocked them. There they saw their lord fallen to the floor, dead.

While they waited, Ehud got away. He passed by the idols and escaped to Seirah. When he arrived there, he blew a trumpet in the hill country of Ephraim, and the Israelites went down with him from the hills, with him leading them.

"Follow me," he ordered, "for the LORD has given Moab, your enemy, into your hands." So they followed him down and, taking possession of the fords of the Jordan that led to Moab, they allowed no one to cross over. At that time they struck down about ten thousand Moabites, all vigorous and strong; not a man escaped. That day Moab was made subject to Israel, and the land had peace for eighty years. (3:12–30)

These two incidents, following each other in direct succession, illustrate the progression of evil and at the same time the progression of God's grace.

REPEATED SIN

We cannot fail to notice here the aggravation of repeated sin. We read in verse 7 that "the Israelites did evil in the eyes of the LORD." And we read the same thing in verse 12: "the Israelites did evil in the eyes of the LORD." In the second passage, however, we see that the effects of their sin were much more serious than in the first instance.

After their first disobedience we are told that God sold them into the hands of the enemy, and they served them eight years. But in the second instance the Lord not only gave them into the hands of the enemy, but He gave "Eglon king of Moab power over Israel." And this time they served the enemy 18 years!

Here we find God working on the side of Israel's enemies, giving them power to afflict His people. We see that the effect of continued sin is to prolong the period of our chastisement and fix the habit of evil until it becomes almost permanent. It is an awful truth that evil men and women grow worse and worse, and the power of sin to hurt them and to hold them increases with every repetition. It was not merely that God prolonged the Israelites' captivity by His arbitrary will, but it seems as if they themselves had been so paralyzed by their sin and judgment that they did not even think of turning to Him for help for 18 years.

It would seem as if God always listened to Israel when they cried to Him. But the saddest effect of their sin was that they forgot His former mercy and failed to lift up to Him their penitent cry. Over against their sin, though, is the mercy of a long-suffering God! The moment they turned to Him in prayer and penitence, He heard their cry and sent them help. How striking is the expression, "Again the Israelites cried out to the LORD, and he gave them a deliverer." His mercy was instant, and His deliverance was complete.

Then, when He restored them from their captivity, the duration of the blessing was in proportion to the length of the judgment. When He saved them from the captivity of Cushan-Rishathaim, eight years long, He gave them rest for 40 years. When He saved them from the captivity of Eglon, 18 years long, He gave them rest for 80 years. It would seem as if His mercy was graduated in contrast to their sorrows and their sin. The days of blessing were more than four times as long as the days of punishment and pain.

Has God caused you to look back at some dark chapter of backsliding and spiritual loss? If so, take comfort from the story of Israel's sin. Turn to God in true-hearted repentance and obedience, and He "will repay you for the years the locusts have eaten—/ the great locust and the young locust,/ the other locusts and the locust swarm—/ my great army that [he] sent among you" (Joel 2:25).

How beautiful to observe in the story of Simon Peter that when the Lord restored him after his threefold sin, He gave him a threefold blessing and commission—as if He would put a mark of honor over against every scar that the disciple had brought upon himself. "Make us glad for as many days as you have afflicted us,/ for as many years as we have seen trouble" (Psalm 90:15).

That is the mercy of God. But how much better and sweeter is the grace of God that is able "to keep [us] from falling and to present [us] before his glorious presence without fault and with great joy" (Jude 24).

A DEPENDENCE ON HUMAN LEADERS

There are some further lessons in connection with these incidents that are well worthy of our careful attention. Notice how all through this period the people were dependent upon human leaders. Indeed, this seems to have been their bane throughout the whole period. They were faithful to God as long as Joshua lived, but they had no direct dependence on Joshua's God.

Theirs was a reflected goodness, derived from the circumstances and the people that surrounded them. They were true to God while their judge led them on to victory and ruled over them afterward. But when he died, their hearts, like the sapling that has only been bent, sprang back again to their natural willfulness. The writer has so well expressed it: "the people returned to ways even more corrupt . . . following other gods and serving and worshiping them. They refused to give up their evil practices and stubborn ways" (Judges 2:19).

Here we see the whole root of bitterness—a superficial experience, influenced by persons and circumstances, while our natural heart still remains and we are not personally united to the Lord Jesus Christ and filled with the Holy Spirit for ourselves. The promise of this dispensation, thank God, is not that we shall have Othniels and Ehuds, Joshuas and Calebs to lead us, but that the Holy Spirit shall be poured out "on all people" (Acts 2:17), and "no longer will a man teach his neighbor/ or a man his brother, saying, 'Know the LORD,'/ because they will all know me,/ from the least of them to the greatest" (Jeremiah 31:34).

PATTERNS TO FOLLOW

We are, therefore, to look for our spiritual examples not in the condition of the people of that time, but in the spirit of the leaders. These men were patterns of what each of us may be today in the power of the Holy Spirit.

In Othniel we see, according to the literal meaning of his name, the lion-hearted man, the man of faith and holy courage. We have heard of him before. It was he who, at Caleb's challenge, had dared to assault the stronghold of Kiriath Sepher (Judges 1:12). As a reward for his victory, Othniel won the hand of Acsah, the daughter of Caleb, whose name means "grace." And with her he received a dowry of special grace and blessing.

Othniel stands for the faith that in the first lessons of our Christian life dares to take the victory and receives the fullness of grace. And then, later, when others need our help, we are prepared to lead them into the same victory that we have won.

There is a story behind every story. There is a life behind every public record of triumph and distinction. The Othniel who led Israel to victory against the mighty emperor of the East was not the creation of a moment or the accident of a great occasion. He was the outgrowth and development of a long-past history, when as a young man he met the crisis hour of his own life and dared to believe God and overcome his enemies in the strength of the Lord. He won the blessing that enabled him to meet the greater occasion and to stand as the first of Israel's judges and conquerors.

His story is an example of what we will encounter. There will come a moment when we meet life's issues all alone, and as we stand true and triumph over self and sin, God's mark is placed upon us. He puts us aside for the day when He will need a brave leader and a chosen instrument for some of the great occasions of the world's history. And it will be found true again, as it ever has been true, that "the LORD has set apart the godly for himself" (Psalm 4:3).

A DIVINELY APPOINTED JUDGE

The implication for us from the second account is not quite so clear as the first. Ehud stands before us, apparently, in the light as a secret assassin. By deep subtlety, and in the disguise of a friend, he gains access to the presence of Eglon, the oppressor of his country. He then tells the king he has a secret message for him. The king grants him a private audience, and Ehud tells him it is a message from God. Then swift as the lightnings flash, he pierces him to the heart with the hidden dagger, and strikes down the life of his country's oppressor.

Many commentators have tried to excuse Ehud's act, or at least to exonerate God from all responsibility for it, by calling attention to the fact that it is not said, as in the case of Othniel, that the Spirit of God came upon Ehud. They seem disposed to apologize for him or to make him responsible for his own act, leaving it as a doubtful thing. But a candid reader cannot fail to notice that the inspired writer made no such attempt to evade responsibility. He frankly speaks of Ehud as the deliverer whom God raised up to save His people. He further recognized his whole career as that of a divine leader and judge.

How then shall we justify his act of apparent murder? Surely, the answer is plain. It was not Ehud's act; it was not an act of private vengeance or even patriotic fervor. The answer is found in Ehud's message to Eglon: "I have a message from God for you" (Judges 3:20). He was acting as a divinely appointed judge and executioner of God's sentence against a wicked and condemned man. "I have a message from God for you" is his solemn word as he suits the action to the word and strikes down the bold and impious transgressor at his feet. He was simply acting as the judge upon the bench when he sentences the murderer to his doom, or as the public executioner when he fulfills the decree of the State and takes the life that has been forfeited by law for a public crime. Ehud acted by divine command and in the divine name.

His victim stands before us as the type of our spiritual oppressor. And Ehud stands as the example of the faith that meets the enemy, not in its own name or strength, but in the name and strength of Jehovah, triumphing even as He did.

AN INSPIRING LESSON

There is an inspiring lesson in this attitude. Is it not our privilege to identify ourselves with God in all we say and do, to go forth in victory in His name? Is not this the meaning of that strong expression, "whatever you do, whether in word or deed, do it all in the name of the Lord Jesus" (Colossians 3:17)?

Is it prayer? As we pray let us identify ourselves with Him until it shall not be our prayer, but God's prayer in us, and we shall know that the answer must be given. Is it temptation? As we are tempted let us meet the devil as a conquered foe. Standing in the Person of our victorious Lord, let us say to him, "I have a message from God for you. He bids you flee. Get behind me, Satan, in the name of Jesus." In that mighty name we shall cast out demons and tread upon serpents and scorpions and upon all the power of the enemy.

Or is it service? Are we called to speak for our Master to our fellow men? Let it be not our message, but His; not our ideas and opinions and pleadings, but the word from the throne, delivered to men with the authority of God. Let us look into their conscience and say in the name of our Master, "I have a message from God for you." Our words will be clothed with power, and the Holy Spirit will convict men of sin and righteousness and judgment and seal our message with precious souls and lasting fruits.

This is the true spirit of ministry: "If anyone speaks, he should do it as one speaking the very words of God. If anyone serves, he should do it with the strength God provides, so that in all things God may be praised through Jesus Christ" (1 Peter 4:11).

CHAPTER 3

SHAMGAR, DEBORAH AND BARAK

And what more shall I say? I do not have time to tell about Gideon, Barak, Samson, Jephthah, David, Samuel and the prophets, who through faith conquered kingdoms, administered justice, and gained what was promised; who shut the mouths of lions, quenched the fury of the flames, and escaped the edge of the sword; whose weakness was turned to strength; and who became powerful in battle and routed foreign armies. (Hebrews 11:32–34; compare with Judges 3:31 and 4:14–15)

The darkness of night allows us to see the stars. Similarly, it seems that the darkest times of national and church history are always occasions for the best types of genius and character to shine. The long, sad story of the judges revealed a Deborah and a Barak, a Gideon and a Samson, an Othniel and a Jephthah. The times of Ahab and Jezebel were made illustrious by the ministry of Elijah and Elisha. The dark night of the Middle Ages was made luminous by the testimony of a Wycliffe, a Luther and a Knox.

The story of divine mercy and Christian faith is written on the dark background of human sin and crime. We are to look at a few of these stars of the night as they shine in the firmament of the book of Judges.

SHAMGAR AND AN OXGOAD

The story of Shamgar (Judges 3:31 and 5:6) introduces us to a humble farmer in Southern Palestine. His only weapon was the implement of his daily toil and his battlefield was a country road, but he stands forever illustrious among the heroes of faith and the saviors of his country.

One day he was following his simple plow and oxen and carrying in his hand the rude oxgoad—a long, wooden rod that was often tipped with a piece of metal and was used for driving draft animals. Suddenly, he found himself confronted by a large group of Philistines—possibly the precursors of another invasion of Israel. Seizing his oxgoad by the small end and turning it into a formidable club, he suddenly charged his foes. As they turned and fled before his fierce attack, he pursued them with such resistless fury that before the day was over 600 of them lay dead around him. Doubtless it was more than human prowess. But like David's battles it was one of those times of supernatural inspiration, when God Himself took possession of His chosen instrument and one was able to chase a thousand, and send dismay into the hearts of a host of enemies. Doubtless this battle was a crisis in the history of the country, and stayed some greater invasion. For as these men went back to tell the tale of their strange disaster, their neighbors began to think that if one man could do such wonders, it would scarcely be safe to meet an army of such men.

Shamgar represents in some very striking ways the spirit of Christian faith and victory. Here we see a man standing in the ordinary walks of life, and meeting an emergency as it comes to him without stepping aside from the path of ordinary duty. He does not need to mount a pedestal or be placed in some illustrious position to be a hero. He simply stands in the place where God has put him and there becomes illustrious through the force of his own personal character and conduct. He does not go out of his way to find a mission, but he meets the events that come to him in the ordinary course of life, and turns them into occasions for faith and victory.

PEOPLE IN SECULAR CALLINGS

He represents the men and women who stand in secular callings, and who find a pulpit and a ministry just where God has placed them, amid the tasks and toils of daily life. He stands for the businessman at his office, who finds a thousand opportunities for fighting the battle of the Lord and doing good to his fellow men in the course of his routine.

I know a humble shoemaker in a New England town who finds in his little shop every day a dozen opportunities for preaching Christ, as well as living the gospel. God has used him to lead many of his customers to the Person who transformed his own heart and life. I know a captain on a passenger ship who preaches the gospel in his plain and modest way to tens of thousands of his passengers every year. His cabin has been the birthplace of hundreds of precious souls for whom he lies in wait with ceaseless, watchful tact and love. I know more than one businessman whose office is an object lesson of Bible texts and divine messages, and who never meets a caller without some hint of eternal things, and who never writes a letter without some little enclosure which can speak for God and salvation.

OUR PRESENT RESOURCES

Shamgar did not have to wait until he had a sword or a spear or a battle-bow to fight. He took as a weapon the thing that was in his hand and turned it against the enemy. Similarly, God wants your real resources just as they are, to be used for Him. He is asking you, "What is that in your hand?" (Exodus 4:2). Moses' rod, Dorcas' needle, Shamgar's oxgoad, David's sling and stone, Joshua's ram's horn, the lad's five loaves and two fishes and the widow's little can of oil are all that He requires for His mightiest victories and His grandest ministries. Give Him what you have, be faithful where you are, do what you can and He will do the rest.

> If you want a field of labor,
> You can find it anywhere.

Shamgar's victory may seem small compared with Gideon's. If we just look at numbers, we could say that was true. But we have to see the larger picture. God used it to prevent a major invasion and to render needless some more costly victory afterward. Likewise, the little things we do, the faithfulness with which we meet some trifling opportunity, may prevent some greater disaster or be the occasion of some mightier blessing than we can see at the time.

It may seem a small thing for a woman on a dark and stormy night to dash along the railroad track and signal the rushing train to stop before it reaches the broken bridge, but that single act of heroism saved a hundred lives. It may seem a little thing for a small group of heroes to hold a pass against an army, but that was the key to the whole battle.

It may be a trifling thing for a quiet English girl to find a ragged street urchin and induce him to go to Sunday school by giving him a suit of clothes. Then, when he did not show up, she hunted him up weeks afterward and gave him another suit of clothes, only to find that he did not come to church. Refusing to be discouraged by the boy's deception, she found him a third time. Her patience triumphed and that boy was won for Christ. To most it was a small thing; they surely felt the boy was not worth pursuing. But the day came when that act of tireless love was God's first step in the evangelization of China. That boy was Robert Morrison, the pioneer of modern missions in the Far East.

These are the little things that God loves to glorify! God help many of us to watch for these wayside opportunities and win these battles of faith and fortitude.

THE MINISTRY OF A WOMAN

Our next illustration is the story of Deborah and Barak. Here we are introduced to a new instrument in the work of God—the ministry of a woman.

Deborah stands before us in strong contrast to the customs and prejudices of her time. She is called to lead in a national crisis, to stand in the front of both statesmanship and war as the head of the nation. This is an unqualified recognition of the part women play in ministry. With such an example, backed up by so many honored successors, let no man deny the place of women in the history of nations and the ministries of Christianity.

At the same time, the story of Deborah is as clear in limiting as it is in permitting the ministry of women. It gives no encouragement to the "new woman" in her absurd attempt to usurp the place of men. A mannish woman is an outrage upon her own sex and a caricature of the other sex. She falls between two fires, for she falls short of manhood and she falls out of womanhood. Christ has established the natural and spiritual law that the head of every woman is the man, and the head of the man is Christ (1 Corinthians 11:3). This is the type of womanhood that Deborah represented.

Though she knew that she was called by her spiritual qualifications to lead her people to deliverance from the enemy, Deborah took particular pains to find a man to be the executive officer of her plans and the leader of God's hosts in the divine campaign. Her chief business was to put Barak in the front, and then stand by him with her counsel, prayers, faith and wholesome reproof.

Deborah was a practical and sensible woman. Her name signifies "the bee," and she possessed the sting as well as the honey. She knew how to stir up Barak by wholesome severity as well as encourage him by holy inspiration. He is a very foolish man who refuses to be helped by the shrewd, intuitive wisdom of a true woman. While her head may not be so large, its quality is generally of the best; her conclusions, though not reasoned out so elaborately, generally reach the right end by intuitions that are seldom wrong. A woman's place is to counsel, to encourage, to pray, to believe and preeminently to help.

This was what Deborah did, and in this Deborah was the type of woman's scepter, which is that of yieldedness and love rather than dogmatism and defiance.

MAN'S HELPMATE

We see in the story of Barak a man of weak and timid faith, losing much by his diffidence, and yet used of God and lifted to a more divine faith by the inspiration of Deborah.

Barak shrank at first from the unexpected call to lead an army of 10,000 men against the large army of Sisera. He finally consented when Deborah agreed to go with him, but his timidity cost him the honor he would have won and his sharp and penetrating monitor, Deborah, plainly told him: "But because of the way you are going about this, the honor will not be yours, for the LORD will hand Sisera over to a woman" (Judges 4:9). There were really two women in this case, and Barak was sandwiched in between them, with Deborah in the front and Jael in the rear.

Despite his hesitancy, even poor, weak Barak became one of the heroes of faith who shine in the constellation of eternal stars, upon which the Holy Spirit has turned the telescope of the 11th chapter of Hebrews.

Yes, God can use the weakest instruments, and He generally does choose the poor in spirit and the temperaments that are naturally the opposite, to clothe them with His supernal might.

> God chose the foolish things of the world to shame the wise; God chose the weak things of the world to shame the strong. He chose the lowly things of this world and the despised things— and the things that are not—to nullify the things that are, so that no one may boast before him. (1 Corinthians 1:27–29)

Look at Isaiah when God called him to his splendid ministry. How little he thought of himself. "Woe is me! . . . I am ruined! For I am a man of un-clean lips," (Isaiah 6:5). Yet God used him to unfold the majestic visions of messianic prophecy.

Look at Jeremiah as he shrank back into his conscious nothingness, and cried, "LORD, . . . I am a child," (Jeremiah 1:6). But God took that trem-bling reed and made him a pillar of strength and a fenced, brazen wall of resistance against the kings, the prophets and the priests of Israel. He was the grandest figure of the last days of Jerusalem.

Yes, God can take us in our weakness and nothingness and make us strong in His might to the pulling down of strongholds.

DEBORAH'S MESSAGE

Barak was not always weak. There came a time when he responded to the inspiring call of faith and became a hero. Deborah's message to him is all alive with the very spirit and innermost essence of the faith which counts the things that are not as though they were.

"Go!" Deborah cries, as she rouses him by a trumpet call from his timorous inactivity. "This is the day," she adds as she shakes him out of his procrastination. "The LORD has given Sisera into your hands," she went on to say, as she counted the victory as already won. "Has not the LORD gone ahead of you?" (Judges 4:14), she concludes as she commits the whole mat-ter into Jehovah's hands and tells Barak to simply follow on and take the vic-tory that is already given.

Is it possible for faith to speak in plainer terms, or language to express with stronger emphasis the imperative mood and the present tense of that vic-torious faith to which nothing is impossible?

COOPERATING INSTRUMENTS

Another lesson we see here is that of mutual service. This victory was not won by any single individual, but God linked together, as He loves to do, many cooperating instruments in the accomplishment of His will. Deborah represents the spirit of faith and prophecy. Barak exemplifies obedience and executive energy. There were the people that willingly offered themselves— the volunteers of faith. There were the noble men of Zebulun and Naphtali who jeopardized their lives—the martyrs of sacrifice who are the crowning glory of every great enterprise. And there was Jael, a poor heathen woman out on the frontiers of Israel, who gave the finishing touch to the victory. She struck the last blow through the temples of proud Sisera (Judges 4:17– 24). And high above all were the forces of nature and the unseen armies of God's providence; for the stars in their courses fought against Sisera, and the flood of the Kishon rolled down in mountain torrents and swept the astonished foe away.

Still again, we see the curse of neutrality and the pitiful spectacle which seems always to be present—the unfaithful, ignoble and indifferent ones who quietly looked on while all this was happening. They not only missed their reward, but justly received the curse of God's displeasure and judgment.

And so in the Song of Deborah (5:1–31), we hear of Reuben's enthusiastic purposes, but ultimate debates and doubts, so that he does nothing. We see her sarcasm strike the selfish men of Gilead who abode beyond the Jordan; the careless Danites, who remained in their ships. We see the men of Asher who, secure in their naval defenses, lingered by the seashore and took refuge in their ports and inland rivers. But above all the echoes of her denunciation, rings out the last awful curse against the inhabitants of Meroz, a little obscure city that probably had taken refuge in its insignificance, because its inhabitants had refused to come up to the help of the Lord against the mighty.

God's mighty warfare is raging still. Let us beware lest we, too, hide in vain behind our littleness and meet at last the same curse the city of Meroz received because they refused to help fight:

> "Curse Meroz," said the angel of the LORD.
> "Curse its people bitterly,
> because they did not come to help the LORD,
> to help the LORD against the mighty."
> (5:23)

In these last days, when millions are dying without the gospel and the coming of our Master waits but a few short years, perhaps we shall hear Him say, "Curse the servant who refused to use his single talent and his single pound—because it was so small—to the help the LORD against the mighty."

The final thing we see in this scene is a pattern page from God's book of remembrance. Some day we shall read the other pages and find our names recorded either with the inhabitants of Meroz and Reuben or with the victors of faith who stood with Deborah and Barak in the battles of the Lord. Will we shine like stars in the night now, and then like the sun in the kingdom of our Father?

CHAPTER 4

GIDEON, OR THE STRENGTH OF WEAKNESS

God chose the foolish things of the world to shame the wise; God chose the weak things of the world to shame the strong. He chose the lowly things of this world and the despised things—and the things that are not—to nullify the things that are, so that no one may boast before him. (1 Corinthians 1:27–29)

When the angel of the LORD appeared to Gideon, he said, "The LORD is with you, mighty warrior."
The LORD turned to him and said, "Go in the strength you have and save Israel out of Midian's hand. Am I not sending you?"
The LORD said to Gideon, "You have too many men for me to deliver Midian into their hands." (Judges 6:12, 14; 7:2)

The strength of weakness leaning upon God, and the weakness of human strength—this is the paradox; this is the spiritual truth that Gideon's life illustrates.

We see this principle illustrated in Gideon's call. While Gideon was hiding behind his winepress and seeking by stealth to thresh a little wheat for his family without being discovered by the Midianites, the angel of the Lord suddenly appeared before him with the startling greeting, "The LORD is with you, mighty warrior" (Judges 6:12). Gideon felt anything but a mighty warrior. He must have looked it, too, since he immediately began to apologize and explain to the angel the helplessness and distress of his people.

But the answer came as the Lord looked on him and said, "Go in the strength you have and save Israel out of Midian's hand. Am I not sending you?" (6:14). Gideon questioned God, saying his clan was the weakest in Israel and that he was the least in his family. Again the Lord told Gideon that He would be with him. And Gideon finally understood that it was not his strength that would save his country but God's. It was the strength of faith that is always the strength of weakness, because it is the strength of God.

A PARADOX TO THE NATURAL MIND

This is the story of grace and the secret of supernatural power. It is a paradox to the natural mind. "When I am weak, then am I strong" (2 Corinthians 12:10) is the proper inscription of every victorious saint.

God comes to the sinner and by a word of sovereign grace pronounces him forgiven, and that word makes him what it declares. He comes to the sinful person and says, "You are already clean because of the word I have spoken to you" (John 15:3), and that word creates the fact of his sanctification. He comes to the struggling Jacob and by a word transforms him into conquering Israel. He comes to the stormy Boanerges, and he is henceforth the gentle John rising above all human probabilities and natural causes. Grace speaks and it is done, and faith counts the things that are not as though they were. And because of this we see Gideon, the trembling fugitive from his foes, stand panoplied the next hour in the strength of God, the mighty victor.

We see this principle in the test of Gideon's faith as he is transformed from the natural man to the man of faith. But how weak his faith is, and how slowly it develops into maturity and confidence.

First, Gideon asks for a sign from his supernatural visitor that he may know for a certainty that it is the Lord. So Gideon prepares an offering and brings it to the angel. As Gideon presents the kid and unleavened cakes, the staff in the angel's hand touches the offering and immediately fire flares from the rock and consumes the meat and bread.

No sooner had Gideon's test been granted than he breaks down with a cry of fear: "Ah, Sovereign LORD! I have seen the angel of the LORD face to face!" (Judges 6:22). Gideon is reassured by the comforting message of the Lord: "Peace! Do not be afraid. You are not going to die" (6:23). So he builds an altar to God and goes forth to take his first step of faith and obedience.

This begins at his own home, his father's house, for there altars to Baal and an Asherah pole (a symbol of the goddess) are erected and the worship of the false gods of the Canaanites is carried on beneath his own roof. God commanded Gideon to tear down the altar and cut down the pole and use the wood to build a proper altar to Him, offering up his father's second bullock.

Still we see the timid man and the trembling faith even in his obedience. He takes 10 of his servants and, waiting until night, did as God told him. In the morning his neighbors look with astonishment and anger upon the wreck of their shrine and the evidences of Gideon's bold rebellion. They soon find out who the guilty party is, and their cries are loud and unanimous that he should die.

But Joash, Gideon's shrewd father, tactfully turns aside the anger of the people by suggesting that if Baal was a true god he would deal with Gideon himself. "If Baal really is a god, he can defend himself when someone breaks down his altar" (6:31). The father's brave attitude turns the tide, and God sustains His obedient child, as He always will for those who trust in Him.

No sooner has Gideon begun his task than the devil also begins to stir up his forces and resources. The Amalekites and Midianites assemble a mighty army of 135,000 men and pitch their camp in the valley of Jezreel. Then the Spirit of God comes upon Gideon, and he blows a mighty trumpet call to summon the people of his city, and his clan gathers around his standard. From Manasseh, Asher, Zebulun and Naphtali volunteers pour in, until Gideon stands at the head of an army of 30,000 men.

A REASSURING SIGN

Again we see that Gideon's faith began to falter, and once more he came to Jehovah for a reassuring sign. God was gentle with his trembling servant; He saw the true purpose of obedience, and He gave him time to be sure. He always does. When God commands us to take any important step, He always will grant us all the certainty and all the strength we need.

Gideon suggested that he would place a wool fleece on the threshing floor. If the next morning the fleece was wet with dew and the floor around it was dry, then he would know that God was going to save Israel by his hand.

The next morning Gideon went to the barn. He picked up the fleece and wrung a bowlful of water out of it. The ground all around was completely dry.

Still Gideon shrank from going forward. Once more he asked God to give him a sign—that the token of the previous night be reversed. The fleece should be dry and the ground wet with dew. Again God delivered the asked-for sign.

There was one good thing about Gideon's second request. He was willing to have his sign turned upside down. Sometimes when we are asking for guidance, we want it all one way, and this is usually the reason why we are so often misguided. We are biased in our preference. We want the dew always in our fleece, and we are not willing for it to be dry. But Gideon's will was so fully surrendered to God that he was ready to take His answer either way. As a result, God could teach him.

WE HAVE THE BIBLE AND THE HOLY SPIRIT

It is different for us today. God does not direct His children by this type of sign. He has given us His holy Word and His Holy Spirit to show us the way we ought to go.

We should be careful in resorting to deciding things by chance, or by opening our Bibles at random. We should shy away from a presumptuous and superstitious dependence upon omens and portents that have led so many astray.

In the Bible we have a standard of right and wrong upon which we can always depend for general principles to direct our actions. In the voice of the Holy Spirit, we have the special guidance that we need in particular circumstances. But there are certain conditions that we must always observe: "He guides the humble in what is right/ and teaches them his way" (Psalm 25:9). The yielded and willing heart will find His way. The selfish will, the heart that chooses its way and then comes to God to have Him endorse it, will be very likely to go astray.

We know from reading the New Testament that the apostles, when there was an important decision to be made, gathered and prayed and waited for the Lord's direction. So the wise man today will always bring to every question not only the general principles of the holy Scriptures and the special whisperings of the Holy Spirit, but also a sanctified judgment and a calm, deliberate consideration of all the circumstances and providences concerned. He will then hold these humbly before the Lord in prayer, suspending all action until impressions become absolute convictions. At that time, he can go forth with certainty and rest to follow the path that has been indicated and leave the results with God.

LISTEN AND OBEY ALONG THE WAY

Next, we see the principle of our text illustrated in the selection of Gideon's men. It was a good thing for Gideon that he was weak and timid enough to wait at every point for God's next word. It is quite possible for us to receive a command from the Lord and then to go forward blindly to obey it and really find ourselves at last out of step with God's order. Even though we were seeking to obey Him, we were failing because we did not stop and listen along the way for His further orders.

God guides us step by step and day by day. And it is necessary for us at every moment to listen and obey. Had Gideon gone out with his 32,000 men and all the trappings of a large army—floating banners, blaring trumpets and patriotic enthusiasm—he would surely have been defeated, and all God's promises would have failed. But he wisely waited for his Leader to point every step of the way.

We do have a manual of instructions in the Bible, but we also have a living Lord, a Leader to help us carry out our instructions. Let us walk closely with Him. For while with one breath He says, "Obey everything I have commanded you," in the other He says, "And surely I am with you always, to the very end of the age" (Matthew 28:20).

This is the mistake the Church has often made: it has taken a set of doctrines and rules and bound them up in a volume of instructions, principles, rules, creeds, confessions and doctrinal principles, and then gone forth to carry them out itself. We have no hesitation in saying that even the Bible without the Holy Spirit is not sufficient for the true Christian.

SIFTING OUT

As Gideon waited on God, another message came: "You have too many men for me to deliver Midian into their hands" (Judges 7:2). So God began to sift them, and as Gideon watched, his splendid army melted away until two out of three had gone back at the bidding of their fears.

Similarly, God tests us and lets us retire from the tasks for which He knows we are inadequate. God lets us abandon them because He sees that we are afraid and would fail. But had we dared more, we might have had more.

But even the 10,000 men that were left were still too many for Gideon to accomplish his task. So there was a second test, and God thinned the group even further. How solemn it is to know that in every step we take, we are weighing our own lives, writing our own record and fixing our own place of service and reward!

Gideon brought his men to a brook and simply watched while they drank. Most of them, intent only upon drinking, knelt down and drank as a dog would, lapping the water with their tongues. They never gave a second's thought that the enemy might be waiting to attack them. These men would not do for God's work, so He put them aside.

But there were a few, 300, who drank in a different fashion. With eyes alert, they brought handfuls of water up to their mouths. They satisfied their thirst, but they also remained alert against a surprise attack. These are God's men, and Gideon set them aside while the others went home with the timid ones.

How solemn, how true this is for you and for me! God is always bringing us to the valley of decision, to the test place of life. He gives us some blessing, some water from the fountain of love and prosperity, and He watches to see how we will drink. Often, we become so absorbed in the blessing that we forget everything else. By doing that, we show where our hearts really are, and God cannot trust us in His enterprises.

Perhaps He gives you money, and immediately you become absorbed in business or pleasure. Then when He calls with a sudden emergency, you are not ready. Perhaps He gives you a friend, and that friend becomes more to you than Christ or the call to duty. Perhaps it is some special service that is the test. He lets you disciple a new Christian or gives you a special position, but you become so absorbed in the task that you cannot hear His voice or watch His hand or be adjustable to His will. As a result of your failure, He has to set you aside, not from heaven, perhaps, but from His highest will.

He says, "Go home, drink all you want to. Sleep on now, and take your rest, the opportunity is passed."

WEIGHED IN THE BALANCE

Oh, how the days are telling! Oh, how God is testing! Oh, how unconsciously to ourselves, each of us is being weighed in the balance! God help us to "be very careful, then, how you live—not as unwise but as wise, making the most of every opportunity, because the days are evil" (Ephesians 5:15–16).

God does not give us notice of these tests before they come. This is an examination where the questions are not submitted to the candidates beforehand. We understand it all afterward, and how we wish that we had watched. The testing is not only for rewards of glory, but it is for the sake of higher service here. "If a man cleanses himself from the latter [from ignoble purposes], he will be an instrument for noble purposes, made holy, useful to the Master and prepared to do any good work" (2 Timothy 2:21).

I heard a phrase that well illustrates Gideon's story. It was the expression, "out and out." God wants us to be "out and out." Gideon's men were "out and out." First, they were picked out from the 32,000. Then they were picked out from the 10,000.

So today God is picking out a people from even His professed followers. And from these—yes, even from the consecrated ones—He is picking those who have not only received the Holy Spirit, but have followed Him through all the tests and all the deaths, all the way, so that He can say of them, as we read of the followers of the Lamb in the day of His appearing, "and with him will be his called, chosen and faithful followers" (Revelation 17:14).

CHAPTER 5

THE WEAPONS OF OUR WARFARE

The weapons we fight with are not the weapons of the world. On the contrary, they have divine power to demolish strongholds. (2 Corinthians 10:4)

The three companies blew the trumpets and smashed the jars. Grasping the torches in their left hands and holding in their right hands the trumpets they were to blow, they shouted, "A sword for the LORD and for Gideon!" While each man held his position around the camp, all the Midianites ran, crying out as they fled. (Judges 7:20–21)

This is the crowning illustration of the supreme lesson of Gideon's life, the strength of weakness. In the weapons of Gideon's warfare as well as in Gideon and his followers, we see how God can use the weak things of this world to confound the strong. We see how He uses the things that are not to bring to nothing the things that are (1 Corinthians 1:27–28).

GIDEON'S FEARS

Before the assault we again see the timidity of Gideon. As God sends Gideon forward for the final attack upon the Midianites, He recognizes the fears of His timid servant. He tells Gideon,

> Get up, go down against the camp, because I am going to give it into your hands. If you are afraid to attack, go down to the camp with your servant Purah and listen to what they are saying. Afterward you will be encouraged to attack the camp. (Judges 7:9–11)

We see that God encourages the trembling faith of His child by giving him another sign. Stealthily, Gideon and his servant creep down to the edge of the Midianite camp, arriving just in time to hear one of the soldiers telling his friend about a dream he had. "A round loaf of barley came tumbling into the Midianite camp," the man said. "It struck the tent with such force that the tent overturned and collapsed" (7:13).

The man's friend immediately interprets the dream. "This can be nothing other than the sword of Gideon son of Joash, the Israelite. God has given the Midianites and the whole camp into his hands" (7:14). That was enough to satisfy Gideon that God was already working. The enemies' fears are prophetic of their fate.

Likewise, God is working for those who trust Him. He can fight our battles for us in the hearts of our enemies and strike fear in them before the conflict begins. Let us have the faith to recognize our unseen Ally and the forces and resources that are waiting at His command to assist those who trust and obey Him.

The person you want to see accept Jesus as his Savior, and to whom you may speak the final word that leads him to a decision has no doubt been under a preparation for that word through a whole chain of divine providences with which you have had nothing to do. And when you pass on, God still has other agents and influences to take up your work and carry it on to consummation.

When Elisha stood at Dothan surrounded by Syrian armies, it seemed to his frightened servant that all was lost. But there were armies in the sky and on the mountain tops ready to fight the battle for him.

In Gideon's case we see faith that reckons on the unseen and steps out into the darkness alone with God to find that He is just as able to turn the Midianites against each other as to strike them down by His sword. Indeed, He was already beginning to melt their hearts like wax and prepare them by their dreams for the panic and disaster that was to follow.

It mattered not that Gideon had only 300 men and that the enemy had 135,000. It did not matter that their weapons were lamps, pitchers and trumpets, for they did not need to strike a blow in this great battle. Jehovah was going to turn the Midianites against the Amalekites, while Gideon's army stood waving the torch and blowing the trumpet of victory, shouting, "For the LORD and for Gideon!" (7:18). These simple and apparently foolish weapons are fitting for our warfare, which "are not the weapons of the world. On the contrary, they have divine power to demolish strongholds" (2 Corinthians 10:4).

THE PITCHER

The pitcher was a clay vessel. It did not need to be strong or beautiful. If it had been made of iron or of brass, it would have been useless. Its fragility was its best attribute, because it was of no use until it was broken. How well it represents our bodies, vessels of clay as it were, through which God is pleased to work and about which He says, "Offer your bodies as living sacrifices, holy and pleasing to God" (Romans 12:1). "Offer yourselves to God, . . . and offer the parts of your body to him as instruments of righteousness" (6:13). These members of our body are represented here as weapons. Our hands, feet, lips, eyes, ears and physical senses are all weapons to be used against evil and for the Lord.

Gideon's vessels had to be empty. Similarly, God requires our bodies and spirits to be given to Him exclusively and to be emptied of all our willful, selfish and absorbing desires, ready at any moment for His use and service. Then, when they are filled with His indwelling life and broken like Gideon's pitchers so that the light may shine through, God will use them in their weakness for the revelation of His glory and the accomplishment of His plans.

We need not be troubled about the breaking of the pitchers. God will do that or, at least, will allow it to be done. The circumstances and trials that come to us will furnish the occasion for the victory of His grace. I have seen a child of God standing unmoved amid intense provocation when the natural impulse would have been to speak out and take action and resent the wrong in a manner that might have seemed to the world more dignified and becoming. But instead there was nothing but the flushing crimson of the brow, the starting tear in the eye, the self-suppression that cost a moment's effort, and then the gentle silence and a sweet smile. I have seen a strong man broken down by that victory of love and led to seek the grace that enabled that Christian to triumph over unkindness and to let the light of God's love flash through a broken vessel and shine out because of the cruel wrong. I have seen some worker for Christ stand in silence and misrepresentation and wrong and wait for God to vindicate, and in the waiting days exhibit the patience as no self-vindication could ever have done. And then in the end I have seen the worker come forth with God's own Spirit of Christ and glorify God by that silence the seal of approval and a vindication that human words could never have afforded.

God lets these things come into our lives so that we may reveal the light of His grace and the Spirit of Him whose agony in Gethsamane and shame upon the cross were but the background on which the glory of His grace shone out with a luster transcending even the transfiguration light.

THE LAMPS

Gideon's lamps represented not only the light of truth and the source of all light, the Holy Spirit, but they also stood for the light of the indwelling Christ. The lamps were inside the pitchers, and Christ must be in us if we would shine. I have heard that travelers in the Arctic can take a piece of ice and shape it so that the sun's rays can be concentrated to start a fire. Unfortunately, the same is not true for human hearts. We must be on fire for God before we can set others on fire.

> Thou must thyself be true,
>   If thou the truth would'st teach.
> Thy heart must overflow, if thou
>   Another heart would'st reach.

In speaking of the true seed of the kingdom, Christ says the good seed are the children of the kingdom. And so again He says, "You are the light of the world," (Matthew 5:14). It is not what we say, but what we are and what Christ is within us that constitutes the strength of our testimony and the power of our life. It is the life of Christ within shining through the broken vessel in a suffering saint, a feeble instrument, that most honors God and most effectively works for His kingdom and glory.

THE TRUMPETS

The trumpet represents the gospel message. A trumpet is just an artificial voice proclaiming a loud and startling message of alarm, or warning, or of command. How perfectly it represents the message of the gospel. The trumpet was not used as a musical instrument. It had no fine inflections of tone or sweet cadences of elocution. No, its sound was loud; its summons was meant to arouse and to move.

The word from which "preaching" comes is based on this figure: the trumpet of the herald. When Christ sent out His disciples to preach, He did not say, "Go, and give eloquent orations and artistic speeches." No, He said, "Go, and proclaim as a herald the glad tidings of salvation."

Likewise, our message should be as clear and as urgent as the herald's trumpet. And it should be so simple that no one can misunderstand it. This was what John the Baptist said he was, "a voice." There was not much honor in being a voice to express another's thought and message.

This is the chief business of the missionary of Christ. Let us not be misled by our own reasonings. Let us not be led into believing that we are sent overseas simply to gather about us bands of little children and to train them in the truths of Christianity, thus gradually preparing a Christian community, giving up as hopeless those who are more mature in years and more steeped in sin. God sends us to these sinful and hardened lives—to men and to women, to homes and families, to the cannibal chief and the stone age savage. We are to flash before them the light of the living Christ and proclaim in their ears the message of God, believing that He who spoke to Midian's myriads in their dreams and filled their hearts with fear, can still speak to the hearts of men and arouse them to repentance and obedience by the power of the Holy Spirit.

Let this be the aim of our work and the claim of our faith, and we shall still find that the weapons of our warfare are as mighty as Gideon's. We need not be "ashamed of the gospel, because it is the power of God for the salvation of everyone who believes: first for the Jew, then for the Gentile" (Romans 1:16).

THE BATTLE CRY

The battle cry of Gideon's band is full of instructive meaning. "For the LORD and for Gideon!"—what a startling battle cry! There was no waste of words, but there could be no heightening of emphasis. The very words were almost as startling as the blast of the trumpet, loud and long. "For the LORD and for Gideon." How they must have rung out over the midnight air until they echoed back from the hills and ravines! And what shrieks and groans of the terrified and wounded men answered them!

These were fitting watchwords, linking together the two great principles of divine operation and human cooperation. God comes first, for the battle is the Lord's. It is He who strikes down the enemy. It is He who uses and prepares the instrument. It is He who turns foes upon each other and fills their hearts with fear, deciding the battle before it even begins. It is He who is still present in all His unchanged omnipotence, who looks for opportunities to show Himself upright in behalf of those whose hearts are perfect toward Him.

It is He who saves us. It is He who sanctifies us, who is our Healer and Deliverer in temporal distress. It is He who, as the God of providence, still works in the events and circumstances of life in answer to His people's prayers. It is He who sits upon the throne—an everpresent God, making all things work together for good to them who love Him (Romans 8:28). It is He who by the Holy Spirit convicts the world of sin, of righteousness and of judgment (John 16:8).

He can break the hardest heart. He can change the most stubborn will. He can break down the iron walls of Hindu caste and bring tribes and nations to seek and acknowledge Him. He changed the persecuting Saul into a humble apostle of Jesus Christ. He can prompt the hearts of men to lay their treasures at His feet for the needed resources for the work of the gospel and the evangelization of the world.

He does not need our religious tricks or our shameful compromises with the world in order to gain the favor of the rich and win the popularity of the crowd. Christianity is supernatural power. And the same God who led Israel with pillar of cloud and fire, who spoke at Pentecost through the tongues of flame, who opened Peter's prison door, is waiting to work the greater wonders of His grace for us. Oh, for the sword of God! Oh, for the faith to claim it! Oh, for the proof of the promise, "Commit your way to the LORD;/ trust in him and he will do this" (Psalm 37:5)!

THE SWORD

There is Gideon's sword, too. There is a place for man's obedience as well as for man's faith. So Gideon must be true, and his 300 men must be adjusted and ready. They must follow him just as closely as he followed Jehovah. His command was urgent, "Watch me, . . . Follow my lead" (Judges 7:17). There must be perfect unity and precision of action.

There is not much for us to do; but what He does ask us to do, we should do, and do it exactly as He says. And then, when the victory is won, there is still something to do. The foe must be followed up and pursued; the battle must be completed; the enemy must be cut off in its retreat. In the case of Gideon the enemy was cut off at the fords of the Jordan by the very men that had been rejected the day before. The 9,700 who had been sent home because of their failure at the testing waters, were permitted to come in at the finish and cut off the fleeing foe. And so there was a part for all.

This was the part of Gideon and this is the object of our obedience and fellowship in the gospel. God, teach us to trust as if all depended upon You, and to obey as if all depended upon us.

CHAPTER 6

SELF-RENUNCIATION AND
SELF-AGGRANDIZEMENT

I have been crucified with Christ and I no longer live, but Christ lives in me. The life I live in the body, I live by faith in the Son of God, who loved me and gave himself for me. (Galatians 2:20)

If you keep on biting and devouring each other, watch out or you will be destroyed by each other. (5:15)

The Israelites said to Gideon, "Rule over us—you, your son and your grandson—because you have saved us out of the hand of Midian."
But Gideon told them, "I will not rule over you, nor will my son rule over you. The LORD will rule over you." (Judges 8:22–23)

One day the trees went out to anoint a king for themselves. (9:8)

These various passages constitute a composite picture representing with peculiar vividness the nature and malignity of self.

SELF-RENUNCIATION

The first thing we see is self-renunciation. This stands out in the last chapter of Gideon's life. After defeating Israel's enemies, Gideon, by the world's standards, deserves the honor of a crown. But he had the grace and humility to refuse it. As a result, his life ended as it began. It started in nothingness and ended in self-abnegation.

That is not the case with all Christians, though. Some start with God's glorious blessing, then they begin to heap upon themselves honor and glory because of His blessing. In the end their lives become consumed with self-consciousness and fleshly pride.

Saul is an example of this kind of person. His life began in modesty, but it ended in stubborn pride. He stands as a monument of humiliating failure and irretrievable ruin.

The same thing can happen to some noble Christian enterprise we decide to undertake. In the beginning, when it is weak and dependent upon God, it is blessed. But when it becomes strong and successful, it is apt to rise into self-sufficiency and end in world conformity and selfishness. This has been the bane of Christianity in every age.

Peter crucified with downward head became Peter the Pope and Prince of Christendom. And Prelacy has followed Papacy as far as it dared, and now ecclesiastical pride in a thousand new forms threatens the purity and simplicity of the Church of Christ with the same peril.

A republican form of government does not save a people from the kingship of human selfishness. The spirit of social preeminence, political bossism and personal ambition runs through all our institutions and social life. Similarly, the Church has lost her power because the disciples are still disputing who should be the greatest. Christ's answer is forever unequivocal and plain, "whoever wants to be great among you must be your servant, and whoever wants to be first must be your slave" (Matthew 20:26–27).

Nothing is more important today than to guard the Church of God against the preeminence of men. No wise Christian worker will want to throw the shadow of his own personality too strongly across his work, or become necessary to the success of his cause. God wants no Popes, whether they be on Caesar's throne, in St. Peter's Palace, Episcopal Sees, Salvation Army Dictators or Christian and Missionary Alliance leaders. Let the secret of our strength be the simple apostolic rule, "you have only one Master and you are all brothers" (Matthew 23:8). "Honor one another above yourselves" (Romans 12:10).

SELFISHNESS LEADS TO RUIN

Set off against self-renunciation is self-aggrandizement. If we see self-renunciation in Gideon, we soon find the opposite in his son. The story of Abimelech and the parable of Jotham stand out forever as portraits of self in its most subtle and destructive forms. Abimelech was the illegitimate son of Gideon, born of a Shechemite mother. He seems to have been ostracized in some measure from the family and lived at Shechem with his mother's relatives, while the other 70 sons of Gideon dwelt at Ophrah, their father's home.

After Gideon's death the spirit of selfish ambition seized Abimelech, and playing on the clannish jealousies of his Shechemite relatives, he persuaded them to crown him as their king. He took the devil into partnership with him by going into the idolatrous temple of Baal-Berith and taking out of the treasury money with which he hired a bunch of mercenaries as the nucleus of his army. With these he attacked his father's home and murdered all his brothers except Jotham, his youngest brother, who succeeded in escaping. After this, he assembled all the people in the valley of Shechem for his coronation.

There, in the historic Vale of Ebal and Gerizim, with glorious pageantry the coronation ceremonies were opened. Suddenly, Jotham appeared from an overhanging crag about 800 feet above the valley and shouted at the crowd, "Listen to me, citizens of Shechem, so that God may listen to you," (Judges 9:7). He then proceeded to tell them the parable of "The Thornbush King" (9:7–20), startling the crowd and the king with his sudden apparition and strange and sarcastic message which all could not fail to understand, and then, just as suddenly, he disappeared into the mountain recesses.

Jotham's parable was a portrait of the meanness and fleshliness of selfishness. At the same time it told in unmistakable language the sequence of events that were sure to follow the crowning of Abimelech as king.

After Abimelech had governed Israel for three years, the prophecy began to unfold (9:22-57). Abimelech and his Shechemite friends became estranged and became more and more obnoxious toward each other. Treachery met treachery and hate met hate until it culminated in a revolution against Abimelech by the men of Shechem. This was followed by warfare until the Shechemites were murdered by the thousands and their city razed.

Abimelech pressed on against his enemies, ravaging with fire and sword until at last he brought his foes to bay in the stronghold of Thebez. Some of this city's people managed to escape to a tower and there made their last stand. Abimelech led the final attack, and as he approached the tower, one of the women defenders dropped a rock on him, crushing his skull. Not wanting his enemy to say that a woman had killed him, Abimelech called for his armor-bearer and told him to kill him with his sword.

Thus, God repaid Abimelech's wickedness. Truly, as Jotham prophesied, fire had come out from the bramble of Abimelech to consume the men of Shechem and, at last, Abimelech.

THE FRUIT OF THE CARNAL NATURE

1. The Flesh

We see the origin of self-aggrandizement in this account. It is born of the flesh, even as Abimelech was born of the strange woman of Shechem. Self in all its forms, however subtle and disguised, is the fruit of the carnal nature, and it is the root and center of the sinful life. It is no use to cut off our sinful acts, habits and propensities until we strike the very heart of evil, our self-life, where the little "I" is exalted and made king and everything else made tributary to our own will, pleasure and honor.

2. Human Selfishness

We see, too, that self lives on the selfishness of others and uses the same principle in them for the gratification of its ends. Abimelech appealed to the men of Shechem by ties of race and blood and by the inducements of their own self-interest. And so self-aggrandizement becomes a web of countless coils woven and interwoven with the selfishness of others, until hand joins hand, and a thousand chords of mutual self-interest bind together political parties, commercial monopolies, criminal confederacies and the baneful associations of evil men which so largely constitute human society. Each is bound to the other by his own selfishness, and the man who knows best how to play with the selfish passions of others makes them all tributary to his own needs, while the devil sits supreme as king over all. When you see a man appealing to the selfishness of others you may be very sure that he is selfishness incarnate.

3. Devilish Partnership

We see self in partnership with Satan. Abimelech went to the house of idols and got the means for his unholy war from the temple of Baal. The devil is always ready to advance the funds to carry out any scheme of human selfishness. He is a liberal investor in selfish trusts and sinful monopolies. You can always get money for a political campaign and a whiskey trust even when missionary societies are threatened with bankruptcy. Millions and millions of dollars are being thrown away every day in Satan's investments and sin's cooperative societies, and the cause of Christ is languishing by reason of the selfishness of its followers. The devil has his providences as well as the Lord, and the man who wants to plunge into the depths of Satan will find plenty of capital waiting his call and wonder often at his own success.

4. The Instruments

We see also that the devil not only provides the means but also the men. Abimelech soon found a group of rascals ready to follow him and do his bidding. Unfortunately, there are plenty of such men still to be found. They swarm on every side waiting for employment. They are recruiting by thousands; a hundred to one they can be found on every corner, as compared with the volunteers we seek for Christ. They are the peril of modern society. Some day they will rise in myriad swarms, like the Vandals who swallowed Rome, and in the dark tribulation days will capture this world for Satan. And selfishness is ever ready to use them as its minions, and things that some men would not do themselves, they are willing to let these sons of Belial do. There are many that sit in the high places with kid-gloved hands and polished manners who never perhaps shed a drop of human blood, nor soil their feet and hands with the grosser forms of crime; but they are murderers and criminals all the same, and they do not hesitate to use the basest tools to carry out their purpose. Some day they will stand red-handed and pale with agony as David in the hour when God proved him guilty of another's crime.

5. Its Cruelty

Next we see self unmasking itself and sinking to the depths of cruelty to accomplish its purpose. Abimelech never stopped until his hands were drenched in the blood of his own brothers. Sixty-nine of his own father's children, boys that played with him in childhood, he butchered on the very stone where the angel half a century before had accepted Gideon's offering. Perhaps Abimelech had no idea, when he began, of committing fratricide, but he did all the same.

When a burglar enters the house of his victim, his direct object is not to murder, but he is armed for the worst, and if murder is necessary to accomplish his design or to protect himself, he is not going to shirk it. Likewise, when we start out on the pathway of selfishness and sin, only the mercy of God can keep us from doing evil. Well may we all thank God that we have not been allowed to go further than we have.

6. Shortsighted

The sixth thing we see is the foolishness and shortsightedness of selfishness. How vividly Jotham brought this out in his exquisite parable of the Thornbush King! The olive tree did not want to be king because it would cost too much to leave the fatness of its fruit and the richness of its soil for the empty honor of waving over the other trees.

The fig tree, too, had no desire for a glory that would rob it of its sweetness. The vine was too sensible to sacrifice its luscious grapes and its reviving wine, which even God appreciated and which was a blessing to man, for the sake of a brief preeminence over the other trees. The only shrub that was willing even to consider the proposition of royal honors was a thornbush, which had no fruit to sacrifice, no blossoms to lose and no real business in life but to be a nuisance and torment to others.

So the bramble entered into negotiation with the trees. It expressed a little courteous surprise and skepticism about their sincerity in appealing to it, and almost suggests that they would not have come if they could have gone anywhere else, and then adds, with a touch of sarcasm, "If you really want to anoint me king over you, come and take refuge in my shade" (Judges 9:15a).

The thornbush meant business. If it was to be king, it insisted on the complete subjection of all the other trees under its thorny scepter. If a thornbush could smile, this one must have smiled at the mention of its own "shadow." But in the next phrase we see that it spoke out its honest thought and intention, "if not, then let fire come out of the thornbush and consume the cedars of Lebanon" (9:15b).

We see how little attraction supremacy had for the olive tree, the fig tree and the vine. They had something better to do than rule over others. They had a mission of beneficence, sweetness and service.

A man anointed by the Holy Spirit, fed on the sweetness of Christ and bearing fruit for God and man, is not craving after self-aggrandizement. Empty glory can never fill the human heart; vanity and pride are no substitutes for the joy of the Lord, the fullness of the Spirit and the sweet rest we find at Jesus' feet. A life of holy service for others is much more delightful than receiving and seeking their honor.

Let us not be so foolish as to waste our lives in the same pursuits as the thornbush wasted its life. The society queen is earning a broken heart. The ambitious political leader is laying up for himself the disappointments of a baffled ambition, and perhaps the curse of an evil conscience and an avenging God. God made us for Himself and for the ministry of love. Let us give no place to self, which is but a sapling out of Satan's root. A thornbush by nature, self has been a curse to us as it will be to everybody else.

7. Self-Destroying

We see the evil fruition of self as it works out in the destiny of others and then reacts in our own destruction. Abimelech's life was the historical fulfillment of Jotham's parable. For a little while the thornbush king seemed like an olive or a fig tree. His thorns were not yet fully grown. For three years Abimelech seemed to do well.

Similarly, self hides its sting for a while, and under its nice manners and winning smile, it almost looks like an angel. But when the test comes the sheathed claws appear. The slumbering serpent awakes with its poisonous sting. The men of Shechem had harbored a serpent in their bosom who was going to sting their lives to death. What an awful picture of treachery and destructiveness!

Abimelech oppressed the Shechemites, and they attempted to dethrone him. In turn they were consumed and destroyed by his vengeance. And in the final turn of the wheels of retribution, Abimelech was killed.

How true are the apostle's words, "If you keep on biting and devouring each other, watch out or you will be destroyed by each other" (Galatians 5:15). A selfish spirit is a torment to everybody and at last the greatest curse to itself. Like the scorpion, it spends its life in stinging others, and then at last gathers up itself and with one last effort stings itself to death.

So many a woman has destroyed the honor and purity of others and then has hurled herself into the dark abyss. So many a man has gone on corrupting innocence with his heartless selfishness and then become himself the avenger of his crimes.

It is not possible for selfishness to make anybody else happy, and it is still less possible for it to make its possessor happy. It is a thornbush by nature, and its end will be the crackling thorns and the consuming flame.

One of Aesop's fables illustrates this point. A fox fell off a cliff. He reached out and grabbed a thornbush to break his fall and found that it had injured him worse than the fall. He turned to it in anger and disappointment and reproached it for its deceitful cruelty. The bramble honestly replied, "How can anybody expect to catch hold of me, when the business of my life is to catch hold of others?"

May God open our eyes to see the curses of selfishness! If there is one thing in us that seeks for honor and glory, it is a thornbush. And it can only bring us misery and the flames of judgment. Let us repudiate it and follow the life of holy service, finding our rich reward in the sweet, divine joy of holy usefulness.

TWO PICTURES

How can we be saved from the curse of selfishness? Let us gaze on two pictures.

1. The Curse Of Eden

Let us look back at Eden's gate and see the thornbush. It is the symbol of our curse; it is the fruit of sin; it is the first outcome of man's sad fall.

> Cursed is the ground because of you;
> through painful toil you will eat of it
> all the days of your life.
> It will produce thorns and thistles for you,
> and you will eat the plants of the field.
> (Genesis 3:17–18)

The thornbush still stands as a representation of man's sin and God's curse. Will we make it our king? Will we join hands with Satan, whose own fall began with selfishness and pride? God forbid! Let us turn our backs on it and seek the Tree of Life in the midst of the paradise of God.

2. The Cross Of Calvary

Then let us take another look and gaze on Calvary. What is this that lacerates our Savior's brow and wreathes His gentle face with such a rude, tormenting crown? It is the old thornbush again—a crown of thorns. What are those drops of blood that stain His face and the tears that mingle with them and flow down His cheeks? They are the brambles of my selfishness; they are the thorns of my pride. It was this selfish "I" that I let not only crush my fellows, but even murder my Lord. It was not only for our sins He died but also for our selfishness. And in that death we die.

That is the secret of victory over self. "We are convinced that one died for all, and therefore all died. And he died for all, that those who live should no longer live for themselves but for him who died for them and was raised again" (2 Corinthians 5:14).

We see, too, the vision of hope in that thorny crown. We see the thorns of our selfishness fastened to His cross, and we know that we as well as our sin are dead indeed. The people we were now no longer exist. They have been nailed to the cross with Christ Jesus. There they hang on the bowed head of our Redeemer. We are new men and women, born out of heaven and united with the risen Christ. "I have been crucified with Christ and I no longer live, but Christ lives in me. The life I live in the body, I live by faith in the Son of God, who loved me and gave himself for me" (Galatians 2:20).

And now, like Christ, our place is to live the life of self-renouncing love, and win the highest place by forgetting all about place and seeking only to serve and bless. Blessed Master, help us thus to cease to be, and let your Spirit be in us instead of us, so that it will be truly no longer us living, but Christ living in us.

CHAPTER 7

JEPHTHAH, OR THE FAITH THAT LEADS TO FAITHFULNESS

His master replied, "Well done, good and faithful servant!" (Matthew 25:21)

And Jephthah made a vow to the LORD: "If you give the Ammonites into my hands, whatever comes out of the door of my house to meet me when I return in triumph from the Ammonites will be the LORD's, and I will sacrifice it as a burnt offering."

Then Jephthah went over to fight the Ammonites, and the LORD gave them into his hands. He devastated twenty towns from Aroer to the vicinity of Minnith, as far as Abel Keramim. Thus Israel subdued Ammon.

When Jephthah returned to his home in Mizpah, who should come out to meet him but his daughter, dancing to the sound of tambourines! She was an only child. Except for her he had neither son nor daughter. When he saw her, he tore his clothes and cried, "Oh! My daughter! You have made me miserable and wretched, because I have made a vow to the LORD that I cannot break."

"My father," she replied, "you have given your word to the LORD. Do to me just as you promised, now that the LORD has avenged you of your enemies, the Ammonites." (Judges 11:30–36)

The story of Jephthah illustrates with great power two important principles in the divine economy. The first is that God "chose the lowly things of this world and the despised things—and the things that are not—to nullify the things that are, so that no one may boast before him" (1 Corinthians 1:28–29). The second is that God not only wants men who can trust Him, but men whom He can trust.

HIS BIRTH

Jephthah was born a child of misfortune. His father slept with a prostitute, and Jephthah was the result. However, his father was married and had other sons by his wife. Evidently, Jephthah lived with his father's family, because we read in Judges 11:2 that when these other sons grew up, they forced Jephthah to leave. " 'You are not going to get any inheritance in our family,' they said, 'because you are the son of another woman.' "

In most persons this engenders a spirit of misanthropy and bitterness, and often develops into hard and heartless unbelief and ungodliness.

How natural it is to say, "What is the use of trying? Everything and everybody is against me. The very heavens are hostile, and either there is no God or there is no God for me. Religion is for the fortunate and favored ones. I am a child of cruel fate. Because everyone is against me, I will be against everyone, except if I can use them for my own advantage."

This would be the typical reaction of human character apart from the grace of God. But grace always proves an exception to every ordinary and natural law. And so we find Jephthah, this poor little child of shame and wrong, rising above the unfavorable circumstances of his life and developing into a person with character. He wrung strength and success out of the difficulties that threatened to crush him. And he did it not through his own strength but through the grace of God. As we shall see, Jephthah was a man of deep devotion and intense fidelity to God.

His life resembles another eccentric one—Jabez in First Chronicles 4:9–10. Jabez's name signified "sorrow." That is because he was such a tiny, wizened baby at birth that his mother called him "Jabez," expressive of the sorrow that he had caused her. And so Jabez was thrown into life as a little miserable good-for-nothing, but when he grew old enough to think and pray, he turned from his distressing circumstances to his God. We read of him this glorious chapter: "Jabez cried out to the God of Israel, 'Oh, that you would bless me and enlarge my territory! Let your hand be with me, and keep me from harm so that I will be free from pain.' And God granted his request" (4:10).

So it was with Jephthah. When all else forsook him then the Lord took him up and, trusting in Jehovah, he lived to have a glorious revenge upon his unkind people by bringing them a blessing instead of the curse that they had given him.

We see a bit of Jephthah's character in the name he gave his new home. He called it Tob, which means "good." We read of another man later in Hebrew history who called a certain land that Solomon gave him, "Cabul," which means *disagreeable.* Poor Hiram looked at his country through the green glasses of discontent, and everything was dark; while Jephthah looked at his land in the golden light of faith and hope, and all was bright.

Likewise, God wants His people today to be delivered from sorrow just as much as from sin. Israel's long and sad failure in the wilderness all began in the spirit of discontent and murmuring. From this point they went on to rebellion and judgment—the loss of Canaan and the curse of God.

There is in the spirit of discontent a morbid and unwholesome touch, which is just as defiling as if a person actually had committed a sin. It chills the temperature of the spiritual life and hurts every plant of faith and love. It only takes one frost to destroy the orange crop in Florida; likewise, one touch of morbidness and selfish, sentimental sorrow will not only chill our own spirit, but it will depress everyone with whom we come in contact. It will lower the temperature of a whole community of happy Christians. Let us live in the "land of Tob," and let us accept the fullness of His atonement. Christ not only bore our sins and sicknesses but our sorrows, too.

HIS NAME

Jephthah's name is significant. It means "God opens," and it expresses the kind of trust that looks to Jehovah to open his way and to clear the path of all difficulties and trials. The valley of Achor became the door of hope and the thorns and thistles of sorrow became the myrtles and the palms of victory.

As we continue in our passage, we read that "a group of adventurers gathered around [Jephthah] and followed him" (Judges 11:3). Because Scripture calls these men "adventurers," we can be sure that they were not the "cream" of society. They were the outcasts of society, and men who had been thrown as waifs upon the current of life and left to sink or swim. And they naturally gravitated to a stronger center like Jephthah. Such companions are not usually conducive to the development of high, moral character.

How often do we hear people complaining that others have led them astray? But in the Bible we read that the lives of many of God's noblest people were molded through the very influence of uncongenial associations. Joseph grew to honor and obey the Lord despite the godless people around him. David, in his exile years, was surrounded by the outlaws and outcasts of Israel. But through the power of their own personality and the grace of God, these men became transformed into his noblest followers and friends and, afterward, were made the princes of his kingdom.

That is how the Lord Jesus takes us. We were a company of poor, worthless sinners, and things that were despised; but by the transforming power of His grace, He lifts us into His own likeness and crowns us with His own glory.

But we have to go back into the world, into a society of evil men. Instead of letting them draw us down, it is our task to lift them up to the mounts of blessing, where God has set us, in order that we may be the lights of a dark world and shine the brighter through the very darkness that surrounds us.

I once heard a story of a Methodist preacher in England who was arrested and put in jail because of his street preaching. He prayed so loudly that the authorities were glad to get him out. There is no place, and there is no society where we cannot live the life of Christ and receive the glory of His indwelling. There is no depth of sin and misery so great but that He can lift us up, and turn our sorrow into joy and our curse into a blessing.

Still, He uses "the lowly things of this world and the despised things—and the things that are not—to nullify the things that are, so that no one may boast before him" (1 Corinthians 1:28–29). And so the day came when Jephthah's brothers were glad to send for him to be their deliverer, and Jephthah had the high honor of returning good for evil, and saving the people that once despised him.

This is the way that God loves to vindicate us—by making us a blessing to those who hated and wronged us. His promise is, "I will make them come and fall down at your feet and acknowledge that I have loved you" (Revelation 3:9).

HIS FAITH

When Jephthah responded to their appeal and came to their aid, we see in his very words and acts the spirit of godliness and a lofty faith. We are told explicitly that all his words to the people were "repeated . . . before the LORD" (Judges 11:11). He spoke as if he were in Jehovah's presence. And when he sent his challenge to the enemy, it was couched in the language of the loftiest faith. He repelled their claim to some of the land Israel possessed by reminding them how they had treated Israel in the wilderness and had forced a conflict. Then God had taken their land and given it to His own people and destroyed the power of Og and Sihon, their giant kings. "What right have you to take it over?" (11:23) he finally asked them. "Whatever the LORD our God has given us, we will possess" (11:24). Jephthah refers the impending conflict once more to Jehovah God.

The battle was not the Israelites' but the Lord's and such faith can never be confounded. It was not long before Jephthah returned in triumph from the slaughter of his enemies. His country was delivered, his claims vindicated and his enemies destroyed.

HIS FAITHFULNESS

But now we see in Jephthah another lesson, not only of the loftiest faith, but the sublimest faithfulness. Before he went into the conflict, he vowed to Jehovah that when he returned in victory, "whatever comes out of the door of my house to meet me . . . will be the LORD's, and I will sacrifice it as a burnt offering" (11:31).

"When Jephthah returned to his home in Mizpah, who should come out to meet him but his daughter, . . . She was an only child" (11:34). Now came the test of faith. As Jephthah realized all that his vow meant, he was overwhelmed with grief. But he did not hesitate in his firm and high purpose, nor did his daughter shrink back from the sacrifice imposed upon her. Even she demanded that he fulfill his vow to the Lord.

HIS VOW

There have been several interpretations concerning the real meaning of Jephthah's promise to God and the real fate of his daughter. There are several passages and constructions which can leave no doubt in the mind of a candid reader that it was not a literal human sacrifice that Jephthah offered. His dear child was not slain on the altar like the Ammonites sacrificed their children before their god of fire. In Deuteronomy 18, Israel is warned against imitating the cruel and wicked rites of the Ammonites, especially in offering human sacrifices.

The Ammonites were the very people against whom Jephthah had gone to war. As a godly follower of Jehovah, Jephthah must have been familiar with the commandments of the book of Deuteronomy. For him to directly disobey these solemn injunctions would have been to prove false his character and the meaning of his victory in the name of Jehovah. No, his vow was fulfilled by giving his daughter in all her purity as a living sacrifice of separation and service to Jehovah.

In the 12th chapter of Exodus it is clearly taught that all of the firstborn of Israel were to be recognized as the Lord's, and liable, therefore, to death like the Egyptian firstborn. But instead of their lives being literally required, they were redeemed by the blood of a lamb. The Paschal lamb was offered instead of the life of the Hebrew. But that life was still regarded as wholly the Lord's, given to Him in living consecration, of which the whole tribe of Levi was regarded as the type. Therefore, the life of the lamb was separated unto the service of the Lord as a substitute for the lives of the firstborn.

A LIVING SACRIFICE

The lesson we see here is that what God requires from His people is not a dead body, but a living sacrifice. It is much harder to live for God than to die for Him. It takes much less spiritual and moral power to leap into the conflict and fling a life away in the excitement of the battle than it does to live through 50 years of misunderstanding, pain and temptation.

It would have been far easier for Jephthah's daughter to die and be buried among the flowers of spring, the chants and songs of a religious ceremonial and the tears and tributes of the people who loved her, knowing that her name would be forever enshrined, than it would have been for her to go out from the bright circle of human society and all the charms of youth and beauty and domestic and social delight, and live as a recluse for God alone, giving up the dearest hope of every Hebrew woman, not only to be a wife and mother, but to be the mother of the promised Christ. She was also giving up, as was her father, the fond desire of a son to share his honor and his scepter, to prolong his name. All this it meant. This was the sacrifice she made. And so we read that she did not go aside to bewail her approaching death, but she went aside for two months to bewail her "virginity," the loneliness of her own life. Then she gladly gave her life a living sacrifice to God.

There are several other considerations that might be added if necessary to establish this construction of the passage. It is enough to refer briefly to the fact that the phrase in verse 39 is in the future tense, and refers to her future virginity and not her past. Also, the translation of the 40th verse in some versions is that the daughters of Israel went yearly "to talk" with the daughter of Jephthah four times a year. It is not necessary to pursue the argument that the sacrifice was not literal any farther. It is enough for our present purpose that we catch the inspired lesson. That lesson is supreme, unqualified, unquestioning fidelity to God. Jephthah is the man that can depend upon God, but Jephthah is also the man upon whom God can depend.

God is looking for people on whom He can depend. He will put the weight of His highest service and His eternal glory on such men. God help us to be people who, as the Psalmist says, "despises a vile man/ but honors those who fear the LORD,/ who keeps his oath/ even when it hurts" (Psalm 15:4).

HIS DAUGHTER

How tender and beautiful the lesson which this passage gives to the young as well as the old! Just as Isaac stands out in the older story in a light as glorious as Abraham in the sacrifice on Mount Moriah, so Jephthah's daughter's sacrifice must not be forgotten in the honor we pay her father. Sweet child of single-hearted consecration! God help her sisters and her followers to be true. Don't wait until desire will fail and age chill the pulses of ardent youth and the world will fall away from you itself. Rather, consecrate yourself when the flowers are blooming and the cup is brimming and the heart beats high with earthly love and joy and hope. Then it is so sweet, it is so wise, it is so rare, to pour all at His blessed feet, as Mary poured her ointment on His head. Some day you will receive it back amid the bloom and joys of heaven, where they that have forsaken friends and treasures, fond affections and brightest prospects for His dear sake, will receive a hundredfold, and will have the still richer joy of knowing that they have learned His Spirit and understood His love.

CHAPTER 8

SEPARATION AND STRENGTH—A LESSON FROM THE LIFE OF SAMSON

Judges 13–16

Therefore come out from them
and be separate,
*   says the Lord.*
Touch no unclean thing,
and I will receive you.
(2 Corinthians 6:17)

The story of Samson is an illustration of this text. The principle of which Samson's life is a sad embodiment is set forth in the symbol of Nebuchadnezzar's dream: the iron and clay mixed together and the image partaking of the strength of iron, but also, of the weakness of the clay. This is the story of Samson—divine strength mingled with human weakness, supernatural power hindered by the touch of earth and the taint of sin.

THE VISION

The story of Samson forms one of the closing chapters of the period of the judges. He had godly parents. The angel of the Lord appeared in a vision and promised the birth of a son, accompanying it with the most solemn injunctions: First, that the mother should be separated according to the law of the Nazirites before his birth; and, then, that the child that should be born should also be a Nazirite from his birth and separated unto God from his mother's womb. "Now see to it that you drink no wine or other fermented drink and that you do not eat anything unclean, because you will conceive and give birth to a son. No razor may be used on his head, because the boy is to be a Nazirite, set apart to God from birth, and he will begin the deliverance of Israel from the hands of the Philistines" (Judges 13:4).

THE NAZIRITE

In due time the child was born and carefully brought up according to the divine command. His hair was allowed to grow in perfect naturalness, and he abstained from wine and all strong drink and lived a life of abstinence and purity. When he reached manhood the Spirit of God began to move upon him in the form of extraordinary physical strength. But along with this came the peculiar temptation of his life—a tendency to self-indulgence and unhallowed associations with the daughters of the Philistines. This, at last, became the snare that ruined him.

HIS FIRST ERROR

His first error was to set his affections upon a Philistine maiden of Timnah and to marry her contrary to the advice and wishes of his parents. On his way to her home he performed the first great exploit of his life—the slaying of a lion in a thicket by the road. This marriage was a sad one, and ended in the murder of his bride and the family by the Philistines, followed by Samson's retaliation with the burning up of their grain fields by sending an army of blazing foxes across the country.

HIS TRIUMPHS AND FAILURE

For 20 years he was the terror of his enemies. He used to boldly visit their towns and hamlets, usually in some doubtful association with one of their women. He defied their attempts to take him—until he fell into the snare of Delilah. After winning his confidence, she tricked him into revealing the secret of his strength. Delilah then cut off his hair and delivered him to her countrymen, who bound him, put out his eyes and then placed him for the rest of his life in a solitary dungeon.

There he deeply repented of his sin and folly. God heard his prayer and gave him one more opportunity to use his colossal strength for God and his country. His hair began to grow again, and the strength of the Lord returned to him. Some time later, the Philistines gathered to offer a great sacrifice to their god, Dagon, and to celebrate the capture of Samson. They mocked him, making him perform for them. As he stood among the pillars of the temple, he asked the servant who led him around to place him next to the two main columns that supported the temple. Then he prayed to God, "O Sovereign LORD, remember me. O God, please strengthen me just once more, and let me with one blow get revenge on the Philistines for my two eyes" (16:28). Samson then pushed the columns with all his strength and the temple came crashing down, killing more people with this one blow than he had done in his entire life.

And so he passed out of Jewish history—a marvelous example of what God might have done with a thoroughly separated man, and yet of what self-indulgence and sin can do to hinder the glorious promise and the gracious purpose of God.

A GOOD BEGINNING

Samson's life had a bright beginning, full of promise and possibility. We see God choosing a human life and revealing a high and mighty purpose for a human career. But we also see all this hindered and defeated by earthliness, selfishness and sin.

What more could God have done to show His purpose of love and blessing? Twice He sent His angel to announce the birth of Samson. Time after time He manifested His supernatural power in the life of His servant and the mighty possibilities which He was ready to accomplish if He could only have found an obedient and faithful instrument. Yet all this was brought to nothing by the disobedience and folly of the man whom He had sought to bless and use.

It is a very solemn and awful thing to think how we can hinder God's purposes of love for us. This is an important lesson. Despite the fact that we may have been born to Christian parents who brought us up to fear God; despite the fact that our early days were overshadowed by the Almighty and our consciousnesses felt the touch of heaven and heard the whisper of His calling on our lives; we may, by our willfulness and folly, destroy all this. Sad will be the day when we hear our Master say, as He said of Jerusalem, "how often I have longed to gather your children together, as a hen gathers her chicks under her wings, but you were not willing" (Matthew 23:37).

SEPARATION

We see in Samson's story the necessity for a life of separation and consecration if we would become the vessels of the Holy Spirit and the instruments of God's highest blessing.

The Nazirite, under the Mosaic institutions, was the peculiar type of a life of separation. He was set apart from his childhood to be dedicated to the Lord and separated from all earthly and sensual indulgences. Just as the priest represented the idea of nearness to God, the Nazirite represented the idea of separation to God.

This is one of the profoundest principles of God's whole plan of redemption. From the very beginning God purposed to separate a peculiar people to Himself. We see this in the separation of Abel, Noah, Abraham, Isaac, Israel and others down to the Church of Christ, which just means the called-out ones. The word *ekklesia* means "the separated ones." Man's failure to meet God's ideal has been the cause of all the failures and disasters of the past.

The awful wickedness that preceded the flood was brought about from the intermingling of the holy seed with the people of this world, the intermarriage of the children of God with the daughters of man. And today the same cause is about to produce similar effects. There is a melting away and a breaking down of all barriers between the Church and the world, and the end of it is going to be conditions as shocking and terrible as those of Noah's day. The progeny of such frightful and monstrous unions will once more bring upon the earth a deluge—not of water, but of fire—and the godless will be swept away.

God must have separated vessels. He will not drink out of the devil's cups. We must be His and His alone. We must bear His monogram and be His peculiar people.

If you who bear the name of Jesus are still playing with the world, receiving its attentions, intermarrying with its people, allowing it to invade the very Church of Christ and in the name of religion turn God's holy sanctuary into a place of social entertainment and sometimes indecent exhibitions that would even disgrace a theater, you are opening the floodgates for a coming judgment. You are contaminating the Body of Christ with the poison of your sin. You are draining the fountains of spiritual life and power and, in effect, repeating the story of Samson. And the end can only be the same as his—blindness, bondage, paralysis and death. " 'Therefore come out from them/ and be separate,/ says the Lord./ Touch no unclean thing,/ and I will receive you.'/ 'I will be a Father to you,/ and you will be my sons and daughters,/ says the Lord Almighty' " (2 Corinthians 6:17–18).

DIVINE LIFE FOR THE BODY

We see in Samson a picture of the supernatural life and power that God can give to a consecrated human body. There is no reason to suppose that Samson was a physical giant. The Philistines could not understand his supernatural strength. If he had been like Og or Sihon or Goliath—men of gigantic stature—they would easily have comprehended it. But he seems to have been a man of ordinary appearance and his power was entirely superhuman. It did not come through brawn or bone, but it was because of the divine life that possessed his being and filled his frame with the very strength of God.

THE ILLUSTRATION OF DAVID

Just as the electric wire, when filled with the current, has in it the whole power of the battery and can turn the huge wheels of a mighty factory, so a human frame may be so possessed with the Holy Spirit that the feeblest may be like David, and David like the angel of the Lord.

There is no doubt that David attributed his stupendous exploits entirely to the abilities that came to him from Jehovah. His battles were battles of faith, and he could literally say, "He trains my hands for battle;/ my arms can bend a bow of bronze" (2 Samuel 22:35). We have seen the power of demon possession in a human body so that such a person had the strength of a dozen men. Why should not the Holy Spirit be able to give the same power to a human arm?

And so Samson was able to tear apart a lion with his bare hands, to carry on his shoulders the pillars and city gate of Gaza with their weight of tons and walk with them 10 miles to Hebron and to lift up the pillars which supported the vast amphitheater and literally tear the building to pieces by his arms.

So still, God is able to put His strength into a human frame if it is wholly separated unto Him. He could endue us with the power to resist disease, to persevere under the influence of a harsh climate, to endure hardship and suffering and to go through life, like Moses, with unabated strength until our work is finished.

The Holy Spirit has this for His separated ones in these last days. It is part of the purchase of Christ's redemption and the partnership of His resurrection and ascension power. And if we are empty of all that hinders and open to His unrestricted life and power, He will dwell in us and fill us with His great power. That power is "for us who believe. That power is like the working of his mighty strength, which he exerted in Christ when he raised him from the dead and seated him at his right hand in the heavenly realms" (Ephesians 1:19–20).

But not only was Samson an example of physical power, but also of God's supernatural working in the circumstances and providences of life. When Samson was ready to faint from thirst after his victory over the Philistines (Judges 15:18–19), he cried to God, and God opened a fountain of water from which Samson could drink until he was satisfied.

There is a realm of natural forces and providential surroundings where faith may still claim the interposition of our Almighty Lord in all the emergencies and circumstances of life. While the Spirit dwells within us as the Source of every needed grace, the Son of God is reigning at His Father's right hand. He said to His disciples, "All authority in heaven and on earth has been given to me. . . . And surely I am with you always, to the very end of the age" (Matthew 28:18, 20). This mighty Christ is able to do anything for us that we really need in the line of His purpose for us and the work He has committed to our hands. Are we proving all the power of Jesus' name and all the possibilities of the Spirit-filled life?

THE TOUCH OF EARTH

We see, too, the withering touch of earthliness and sin. Very gradually did the poison insinuate itself into Samson's life; very gradually did he allow the snare of temptation to weave its meshes around him, until at last he was a bound and helpless captive in the power of his destroyer.

His first offense was a visit to the enemy's country. He had no business in going down to Timnah to start with, except as God might send him as a soldier or as a judge. But he went, and then he looked, and then he loved, and then he longed, and then disobeyed his parents' counsel, and then he took the fatal step that linked his life with the daughter of his enemy.

Yet God did not forsake Samson immediately. Again and again He showed His power through His servant over a number of years and helped him out of a multitude of troubles. No doubt God often spoke to Samson and warned him of his folly. But Samson continued down the same self-indulgent path, getting deeper and deeper into sin. At last we find him at Gaza in the house of a prostitute, Delilah, who represents the world's delights and abandonment to selfish pleasure.

Even there an instinct of self-preservation and peculiar sacredness seems to have lingered with Samson. This evil woman, Satan's masterpiece of temptation, had been urged by the enemies of God and of Samson to find out the secret of his strength. They offered her a bribe of $3,000, which in those days was worth 10 times that sum. Using her female charms, she begged Samson to tell her his secret. "How can you say, 'I love you,' when you won't confide in me?" she said to him (Judges 16:15). At last, Samson gave in. It was his heart that betrayed him in the end.

Perhaps you have found yourself in a similar situation. You never intended to yield your principles, your virtue, your conscience, but this person convinced you to do just that. And in one impulsive moment, you were lost. That is how Samson fell. So it is that the lost sheep ever goes astray. It is just a foolish sheep. It wanders, it forgets, it dallies and it perishes all the same.

> Evil is wrought by want of thought
> More than by want of heart.

Oh, how tragic is the picture of Samson's last temptation and fatal fall! Oh, how the fingers of the devil felt for his very heart, closer and closer, until at last they stole his secret and crushed out his life. He knew there was danger, and he played with it, day by day, putting it off and still holding the citadel. But each day letting the enemy come nearer and nearer. First, he told Delilah that if he were to be tied with seven fresh thongs then he would be as weak as any other man. Then she betrayed her true character, and he might have seen the fiend in the fond lover, as she called his cruel foes. Hastily, Samson sprang to his feet, tore his bonds asunder and drove them from his presence in dismay. Next, he told her it actually took new ropes. Again, in the test, the cords tore asunder and she fell, hysterically weeping, and told him that he did not love her, and pleaded for his confidence. And then his heart was touched, and, how near he grazed to the very edge of the precipice! One trembles when one hears him talk of his Nazirite locks and tell her he would be helpless if she braided his hair into a loom. Now she thinks she has him, and, again, the ambush of men is sprung upon him, and again Samson springs through the meshes of his snare and, perhaps, seizes the pin of the loom to beat them from his presence. How narrowly he has escaped! If he had but taken the warning! Oh, if he had but listened to the throbbings of his heart when the Spirit knocked. But a woman's tears and a woman's hysterical pleadings at last conquered Samson's own weak heart. God's hour of longsuffering had reached its margin, not through Samson's triumph, but through Samson's failure. The man who might have been a lighthouse on the shores of time must become a beacon on the sunken rock and the dangerous reef, warning others to avoid the place where he was lost.

In the end, the strong man bowed, the surrender was made and the secret was told. Doubtless, he extracted from her the most sacred pledge, and she vowed she would never tell it. Doubtless she swore all that he wanted—she would keep his secret. But she had him lulled to sleep and the locks were shaven. The bribe had been taken and the enemy was upon him. Samson rose, as before, and shook himself as at other times, and thought he was as strong as ever. He knew not that the Lord had departed from him. The awful progression was completed. Lust had been conceived and brought forth sin. And sin, when it was finished, brought death (James 1:15).

THE RETRIBUTION

Samson's retribution was as terrible as his sin.

1. He lost his strength; and spiritual paralysis always follows surrender to temptation and compromise with evil.

2. Next, he lost his liberty. He was bound and helpless in the hands of his foes. When once we yield to the enemy, we have no power to keep from yielding again. Our defense is departed from us, and we are given over "to a depraved mind, to do what ought not to be done" (Romans 1:28). Eternal sin is the most terrible part of eternal punishment.

3. Samson lost his sight. When we yield to sin and to Satan, our spiritual eyes are blinded, and we cease to know the difference between right and wrong. Our once clear conceptions of God's will are blurred and blotted out, and we wander in the darkness not knowing what we stumble over.

4. He became a sport and spectacle for his enemies. They used him to grace their entertainments, to be a public mockery at their revels, to honor false gods and put to shame the very name of the God he loved. And the most terrible part of Samson's punishment was to hear the shouts of his enemies as they boasted of the triumphs of Dagon over Jehovah and the defeat of Samson and Samson's God. All the while, though, Samson knew it was his sin and folly that caused this shame to the name of Jehovah—the name he, above all men, was sent to uphold.

HIS RESTORATION

In the end, Samson was repentant. In his humiliation, bondage and sorrow, he awoke at last to the meaning of his life, and he asked God for one more chance to be true. To prove his sincerity, and the deep reality of the death of self, he was willing to sacrifice his life in his last exploit. He asked of God that he might die in the service of his country and in the destruction of his enemies.

He was like the Roman nobleman who plunged full armored into the chasm at the city gate, which none but he could fill. He was like the soldier, who, having betrayed his colors, asked only that he might once more lead the forlorn hope on the battlefield, and die with his colors in his bloody hand—his life laid down in the midst of his enemies.

Our service is never worth anything until our life goes along with it and everything is laid down, even life itself if God requires it. Samson had sought only his own pleasure his whole life. But in the end he died to self and, in doing so, accomplished the noblest achievement of his life.

One day in the height of a great national carnival, while hundreds of thousands of Philistia's nobles are crowding the galleries of the vast amphitheater, God takes him at his word. All are waiting for Samson to come forth and make sport for them in his blindness. But Samson's strength is given back to him for one last achievement. Gripping the mighty pillars, which support the immense building, with one stupendous effort he tears them from their foundations and with a crash of thunder and 10,000 cries of terror, the building is in ruins and the proud boast of the Philistines is turned into a death shriek of despair. Samson is victor in his death and accomplished more by dying than he had done in all his 20 years of living.

Let us learn from this story to die to self and sin. If we can do so, then we will be like those individuals of the Old Testament "whose weakness was turned to strength; and who became powerful in battle and routed foreign armies" (Hebrews 11:34). Let us see in Samson's death the type of a greater than Samson, whose death accomplished also the destruction of His enemies and ours, and taught us both how to live and how to die. He died for us that we might live, but He also died for us that we might die. In the power of

His cross, with its holy sign translated into every fiber of our being and every service of our life, let us go forth to live for Him who died, in "the power of his resurrection and the fellowship of sharing in his sufferings, becoming like him in his death" (Philippians 3:10).

CHAPTER 9

RELIGIOUS COMPROMISES—THEIR FOLLY AND FRUIT

Judges 17–18

No one can serve two masters. Either he will hate the one and love the other, or he will be devoted to the one and despise the other. You cannot serve both God and Money. (Matthew 6:24)

The remarkable incidents of Judges 17 and 18 illustrate with great vividness the principles found in Matthew 6:24. They contain the story of Micah and are a medley of sin and crime that condemn with the bitter irony of truth the follies and sins of the dark ages of the judges. And they apply to the social and religious abuses of our own times.

DISHONESTY

First, we see a picture of dishonesty. Micah, a young man of the hill country of Ephraim, stole 1,100 shekels of silver from his mother and, for a time, hid the money from her. Finally, alarmed by her angry curses, he confessed that he had taken the money, and he gave it back to her.

This a common happening—dishonesty and crime beginning at home with the first penny stolen from mother's drawer. From this the person goes on to lead a life of lawlessness and crime.

Absolute righteousness even in the smallest of things is essential to all religious character. We find a lack of righteousness today in society's concepts of right and wrong. There are men and women who can speak of deep religious experiences and extraordinary public services, who yet seem to be unable to appreciate the absolute necessity of strict integrity and uprightness in the matter of property, debt and business transactions.

PASSION

Next, we see a picture of passion. When Micah's mother found that her money was missing, she became angry. She cursed so loud and long that it seemed to be the only thing remembered about the transaction. Her curses made such an impression on Micah that he didn't get over it until he had restored the money. The moment the shekels were returned, she forgot about her passion, and even about the crime of her boy. She fell into another passion of delight and blessed him as extravagantly as she had cursed him before. "The LORD bless you, my son!" (Judges 17:2) she said. The old lady had a little streak of religion running through it all, and probably thought that she was a very good sort of woman. It never occurred to her to sit down, and tell her boy about his wickedness and lead him to true repentance. All she could think of was that she had got the shekels back.

How like many a mother, alternating between the passionate love and the passionate anger, which are both alike natural, animal and devilish!

FALSE CONSECRATION

As we continue in the account, we see a picture of counterfeit consecration. "I solemnly consecrate my silver to the LORD for my son to make a carved image and a cast idol" (17:3). What a strange medley of religion and idolatry! Micah's mother had plenty of "religion," but it was not good because it was mixed.

The world's need is not religion; all people have religion, and the less a man has of God the more he has of religion, as a rule. Animists in Africa or Hindus in India have far more religion than Christians in North America. They sacrifice, give and do more in the service of their gods than we do for Christ—but theirs is the devil's religion.

Back of all their idolatry they, like Micah's mother, have a dim idea of the Lord. They will tell you that these images and fetishes are but forms and stepping stones through which they can rise to the true God. A Roman Catholic who mumbles her rosary and counts her beads and looks up to the saints and images on her altar, and the Buddhist who talks about Nirvana, alike claim that they are doing it unto the Lord. They have a sense that there is a God, and they desire to meet Him. But this does not make their practices any more acceptable. The motive does not make the act right.

Similarly, in our religious ceremonialism, we may have much piety in building our chapels, in erecting our altars, in contributing to the costly machinery of our splendid rituals and in keeping our fasts and our Lenten services, but it is idolatry all the same. It will be a sad day for many "devoted worshipers" when they find that God has accepted none of their foolish sacrifices, and that all their expenditure of money, time and bodily exercise has been as vain as the grossest idolatry of heathenism and the licentious orgies of Baal worship.

Notice, though, in this woman's consecration, how she betrayed herself by an act of insincerity in the midst of her pretended sacrifice. "I solemnly consecrate my silver to the LORD," she said. Yet when it came to actually giving up the money, she only took out 200 shekels and kept the rest for herself. She was the grandmother of Ananias and Sapphira. She was not even honest in the little religion she had.

We see the same spirit in many religions today. The Buddhist will try to cheat his god as openly as the Christian worshiper who puts a bad penny in the plate if he can do it unnoticed. It is the custom of some ancestor worshipers to offer clothing and articles of furniture at the graves of their ancestors. They are made of tissue paper and set on fire, that they may go up in smoke and reach the dead for their habiliments in the land of spirits. But I noticed one Chinese man who made only half a garment—one side of a pair of pants or jacket. The reason given was the gods would not notice it and he would save the other half.

How natural it is to let self come into our devotions. We need to heed the admonition of Paul: "Now finish the work, so that your eager willingness to do it may be matched by your completion of it, according to your means" (2 Corinthians 8:11).

RITUALISM

We see too a picture of ritualism. Micah made the image and set it up in his idol temple, where he performed a whole ritual of idolatrous worship. He "had a shrine, and he made an ephod and some idols and installed one of his sons as his priest" (Judges 17:5). It is all a piece of man-made religion.

Now here is where the emphasis lies. Micah's religion was all manufactured according to his own patterns—not God's. And this is the essential defect of all forms of false religion—they are man-made. It matters not whether they are the grossest idolatries of pagan nations, with their common fetishisms and priestly idols, or the licentious forms of gross idolatry, which but expresses the passions of the human heart, or the more artistic and ideal religious systems of more refined ages, with their Confucian morality, their Buddhist philosophy, or their ancient Vedas and Shastras. Whether they are the dreams and pretended revelations of Mohammed and Joseph Smith, whether they are the imposing ceremonials of the papacy or whether they are the elaborate rituals of the modern Church, they are all the thousand man-made forms of so-called worship. Their basic fault is that they are human, that they are based upon the traditions or inventions of man and not upon the revealed Word and authoritative commandment of Jehovah.

God's command to Moses was that he should do all that was told him according to the patterns shown him on the mountain. Christ's command to His disciples asserted the same notion: "Therefore go . . . and teach them to obey everything I have commanded you" (Matthew 28:19–20). But Satan has tried to institute into the Church a whole system of theological teaching and ceremonial worship that God never revealed or commanded and to change the whole divine system of the Church into a piece of human machinery that he could manipulate at will.

How much of our religious work today is entirely human? Our revivals are gotten up by careful organization and artificial mechanism. Our worship is sustained at an enormous cost by trained performers who belong to the world, the flesh and the devil on six days, and for a consideration give a few hours to the Lord on the Sabbath. And much of our so-called religion is what Scripture describes as "teachings . . . taught by men" (15:9) and as things that "are all destined to perish with use, because they are based on human commands and teachings" (Colossians 2:22).

After Micah had set up his "temple," he felt as if something was lacking. He wanted God to recognize his man-made church to give it a touch of authority and sacredness. One day a young man from Bethlehem came by Micah's house and stayed with him a few days. Micah, discovering that he was a Levite, asked him to come live with him and be his priest and take charge of the temple and service that he had recently fitted up. He offered him a salary of 10 shekels a year, his clothing and his room and board.

The young man accepted and was installed as the hired preacher in Micah's church. Micah had just enough of God in his man-made church to justify his calling it a religious institution. He said with delightful self-complacency, "Now I know that the LORD will be good to me, since this Levite has become my priest" (Judges 17:13).

In the same way men and women today are making up their various religious programs, wanting only to get ecclesiastical recognition, to get some Levite with real apostolic succession to countenance the thing. It does not matter whether God approves or disapproves.

Alas, it is only too easy to get ecclesiastical recognition for any form of doctrine or medley of so-called worship. I have seen men with liberal minds and attractive personal qualities go forth as teachers, winning the confidence and acclaim of many Christians. Their creeds are so tactfully phrased that they are accepted by Unitarians, Jews, Spiritualists—as well as Christians. These men, if they are tactful enough in pointing their phrases and prudent enough in guarding their expressions, could stand as representatives of the most conservative of the churches and be recognized as true Levites.

And I have seen men who, with the wild license of modern theological thought and the passion for freedom and originality, have literally excised every supernatural thing from the Bible. These men can laugh away the Pentateuch and the books of Isaiah and Daniel and yet somehow these same individuals manage to secure the highest places in our theological seminaries. They are recognized as star lecturers at our Christian conventions. And no one seems to challenge their positions.

I know, too, of churches that use their sanctuaries—the temples of God—as places for religious entertainments and exhibitions, some of which would not even be considered decent on Broadway. Their schedules include the weekly dance as well as the weekly prayer meeting. And somehow, they are able to justify it all as scriptural. The members and officers of this man-made medley fold their arms in self-complacency, like Micah, and say, "It is all right. We have a 'man of God' as our pastor."

THE EVILS OF COMPROMISE

Finally, we see a picture of the sad fruits of religious compromise. The sequel of the story of Micah is ironic and most tragic.

> The tribe of the Danites was seeking a place of their own where they might settle, because they had not yet come into an inheritance among the tribes of Israel. So the Danites sent five warriors from Zorah and Eshtaol to spy out the land and explore it. (Judges 18:1–2)

This band came to the house of Micah and spent the night. They recognized Micah's young priest, and after finding out what he was doing there, they asked him to inquire of God about whether their mission would be successful. The priest told them, "Go in peace. Your journey has the LORD's approval" (18:6).

They continued on their journey, and finding a prosperous land, they returned home and urged their people to arm for battle. The army set out, stopping first at Micah's house. There they stole his priest and his gods.

When Micah found out what had happened, he and his clan went after the Danites. "As they shouted after them, the Danites turned and said to Micah, 'What's the matter with you that you called out your men to fight?' " (18:23). Seeing that he was overmatched, Micah turned around and went back home. The Danites marched on with their booty and invaded the city of Laish, utterly destroying this peaceful people. They then set up their own idolatrous shrine and seat of worship, which became in succeeding years the most corrupting influence in the religious life of the entire nation.

Thus we see Micah's sin and folly bearing fruit. First, in his own suffering and loss, and the ruin of all his cherished hopes and plans, and the very loss even of his religion. Second, in the cruelty and wrong which swept away a whole defenseless community. Third, in the long-continued and baneful influences which it started and kept in operation throughout all the centuries of Israel's history.

These are the effects of religious compromise and the sin of Micah in every age. First, they lead to the bitter disappointment of the worshiper. The day will surely come when the devil will steal the worthless religion that he gave his wretched follower and leave him nothing but scorn and despair. Secondly, superstition leads, and always will lead, to cruelty and crime. False religion becomes a persecutor and a destroyer of the rights and liberties of men. The two most cruel and destructive influences of medieval and modern history have been Islam and Roman Catholicism. They are both forms of false religion, very similar in their history and religious principles to Micah's hybrid religion. The early conquerors of South America took possession of the land in the name of God. Even the very geographical names of the country today bear witness to their pretensions of piety. But the degradation which still rests upon the land today bears witness to their cruelty, rapacity and wickedness. Thirdly, the leaven of false religion becomes a corrupting principle in all the future history of a people. Micah not only corrupted his own family, but he laid the foundation of evils that lasted to the latest age of their history and corrupted the whole nation, leading eventually to the captivity of the race and the sins and sorrows of threescore generations.

When we defile the streams of divine truth and life, we poison a whole generation. When we plant weeds with the wheat, we leave behind seeds of thorns and thistles for the eternal burning. We may think it is a very innocent thing to play with "higher criticism" and toy with ritualism, but doing so will undermine the faith of our children and our children's children. We are kindling the fire that will burn up our altars and homes. And we are pioneering the awful procession of anarchy, socialism, immorality, crime and the horrors of lawlessness and wrong that will usher in the days of Antichrist and the catastrophe of the world.

CHAPTER 10

OUR KINSMAN-REDEEMER—LESSONS FROM THE BOOK OF RUTH

For your Maker is your husband—
the LORD Almighty is his name—
the Holy One of Israel is your Redeemer;
he is called the God of all the earth.
(Isaiah 54:5)

The book of Ruth can be considered as a part of Judges. It is a vignette inserted on the background of that mingled picture of the dark ages of the Old Testament. As such, it is a companion picture to the story of Micah. Both are incidents gathered out of the same period of Hebrew history, and they illustrate the life of the people—the one the dark side, the other the bright.

But before we look at Ruth, we should briefly consider the shocking series of incidents recorded in the last three chapters of Judges—all of which grew out of a single unholy relationship. These chapters tell the story of a licentious woman destroyed by the wickedness she pursued, and of a sinful man who allowed her to draw him into her wicked life, and who, through her influence, became unfaithful to his high calling as a priest of the Lord. Out of their relationship grew a crime that involved all the tribes of Israel in a destructive civil war—a war that destroyed three armies and nearly one whole tribe.

We see from this that even the smallest sin can produce the most disastrous results. How solemn and true is the verse in James: "Then, after desire has conceived, it gives birth to sin; and sin, when it is full-grown, gives birth to death" (James 1:15).

THE STORY OF RUTH

Now we come to the story of Ruth. It is like an oasis in the desert. The

German poet Goethe has called it the finest poem in human language, and yet how few of us really understand its beautiful meaning and teaching. It is said that a literary man once read it in an English drawing-room to a select company of cultivated people. He slightly changed the principle names and the style of the story, but read it substantially as it is given in the Bible. His audience was delighted with this new and wonderful literary production and eagerly questioned him about its authorship and origin. They retired, with significant silence, when they learned that it was one of the books of their neglected Bible.

We need only to recall briefly the incidents of the story: the famine in Bethlehem and the emigrant family, Elimelech and his wife Naomi, with their two boys, Mahlon and Kilion. Then came the death of the father and the marriage of the two sons to two women of Moab, Ruth and Orpah. Next, the two sons died, and the three widows were left alone in a foreign land.

Naomi decided to return to her home in Judah, but she tried to dissuade her daughters-in-law from following her on a journey that promised so little for them. Orpah, the more demonstrative of the two, expressed great affection, and went home. But Ruth clung to Naomi, and expressed those ever memorable and noble words, which have been inscribed with the point of a diamond as the loftiest expression of loyal affection and devotion:

> Don't urge me to leave you or to turn back from you. Where you go I will go, and where you stay I will stay. Your people will be my people and your God my God. Where you die I will die, and there I will be buried. May the LORD deal with me, be it ever so severely, if anything but death separates you and me. (Ruth 1:16–17)

So the two lone widows went back to Bethlehem and began to seek a livelihood in the humblest way. Ruth took upon herself, as a loving daughter, the support of Naomi and went out like other Jewish young women to glean in the wheat and barley fields. It was there that she met Boaz, the rich farmer, who had heard of her kindness to her mother-in-law. He became attracted to her, showing her special kindness without sacrificing her independence.

Naomi, meanwhile, watched the unfolding situation with motherly intuition, looking constantly to God, under whose wings they had come to trust. Soon Naomi recognized that Boaz, being her close relative, was their "kinsman-redeemer." It was his duty to redeem her husband's inheritance and take his widow to be his wife. Naomi advised Ruth to take the step by which she could claim her rights.

The sequel, we all know. Boaz recognized the claim, but kindly told her that there was another who was before him. If, however, this man would refuse to do the kinsman's part, Boaz would follow through. The other kinsman declined to do his part, and Boaz kept his word. He redeemed the inheritance of Elimelech and took Ruth as his bride. Out of this union came the birth of Obed, the father of Jesse, the father of David. And thus Ruth, a Moabite, became the great-grandmother of David, and the ancestress of Jesus Christ, the Son of man, and the King of kings!

DOMESTIC VIRTUE

The first thing we notice in this story are the fine examples of virtuous character. How fine is the picture of Naomi, one of the much-abused class of mothers-in-law, who was, indeed, a true mother. She considered Ruth as her own child and sought her best interests, thereby gaining her confidence and love.

Perhaps the sorest need of society today is true mothers. The guilt of many a lost girl lies heavily on the soul of selfish, ignorant and unholy motherhood.

In Ruth we see a genuine love toward her mother-in-law. But we also see a woman of true modesty. What a perfect combination! Modesty is a woman's finest jewel. It is her most attractive quality in the eyes of every true man. This was what drew Boaz to Ruth. She did not chase after the younger men, but stayed with Naomi and worked in the fields.

The social freedom of our day is bound to bear its fruit in social corruption. "If she is a wall," says Solomon, "we will build towers of silver on her./ If she is a door,/ we will enclose her with panels of cedar" (Song of Songs 8:9).

We see too that Ruth was an industrious woman. She was not afraid of hard work. It is not a bad suggestion for idle and pleasure-loving girls to know that it was in the harvest field that Boaz fell in love with Ruth. Even when he did desire her, he let her stay in the harvest field, only making her work a little easier, not for a moment wanting to destroy her independence by offering to provide for her without her own honest labor. Luther has well said, "The devil tempts men, but the idle man tempts the devil." This is just as true of women as of men.

But above all is the piety of Ruth. It was not only the love of Naomi that made her true, but it was the love of Naomi's God. Very finely Boaz alludes to it when he said, "May you be richly rewarded by the LORD, the God of Israel, under whose wings you have come to take refuge" (Ruth 2:12).

Boaz exhibits some outstanding character attributes also. He was wealthy and influential, but he worked his fields alongside his men. Even in this, Boaz maintained his dignity and reserve, and held his position without pride on the one hand or undue freedom on the other. How fine was his chivalrous spirit and manly respect for Ruth! He recognized Ruth's situation and acted in kindness toward her. He did just enough to encourage her, but not enough to damage her self-respect.

And he acted justly in his relation to Naomi. Boaz was ready to carry through with his obligation as her kinsman-redeemer, yet at the same time he knew that another man had first rights. Boaz gave this man the chance to claim these rights, even though his own heart was interested in Ruth.

DIVINE PROVIDENCE

The next thing we see in this story is a beautiful illustration of divine providence. We see God working in human affairs to carry out His divine purpose. We see Him overruling the sorrow of former days to bring about a greater blessing. We see Him leading this daughter of a Gentile race and making her a partner in the hopes of His people. We see Him fitting the times and seasons of our lives in bringing these wanderers back to Bethlehem just at the right time, the harvest season. We see His loving care for His children expressed in the beautiful figure of Boaz—"the wings of the Almighty." The God of the widow and fatherless is not dead. Under His sheltering wings His children still lie. And through each perplexing path of life, He will guide their footsteps, providing for their need and safely leading them home. He that watched over the lone widows of Bethlehem will some day wipe our tears away and make us even thank Him for the trials that now we cannot understand.

We see too a type of redemption. In the helpless condition of Ruth, we see our lost condition. Ruth was born of a Gentile race, the Moabites, a race that was under a curse. Moab literally means "son of his father," and we know that the tribe was descended from the union of Lot and his daughter. As such, Ruth well represents the sinful state of God's redeemed people under the curse of a fallen race.

Not only was Ruth a Gentile and a stranger, but she was a widow. Her natural protector was gone, and her nearest kinsman, who had the right to redeem her, refused. How well she represents our helpless condition. Not only lost, but with none to help. And even the law, which came, as it seemed, to save, was unwilling and helpless to save the sinful soul.

But in beautiful contrast to all this, how fine the picture of redemption unfolds in this book. Under Mosaic law, there is a statute providing for what are called Levirate marriages, under which provision is made so a family name was not allowed to perish from the tribe. When a man died, his brother was to take his wife, have children by her and redeem his inheritance. Now, under this provision, Elimelech and his sons having died, it was the right and duty of the nearest kin to step in and save the inheritance and family name, and through the widow raise up seed unto the dead husband. This, of course, involved the forfeiture of the kinsman's own family name and marred his own inheritance. But it was recognized as a patriotic and social duty, overriding personal considerations.

This is what Boaz did for Ruth and what the nearer kinsman refused to do. Boaz merged his own personality and family into Ruth's family, making a real sacrifice, and thus he became her kinsman-redeemer, and then, also her husband.

And this is what our Kinsman-Redeemer, Jesus Christ, did for us! He sacrificed His own divine rights:

> Who, being in very nature God,
>   did not consider equality with God
>   something to be grasped,
> but made himself nothing,
>   taking the very nature of a servant,
>   being made in human likeness.
> And being found in appearance as a man,
>   he humbled himself
>   and became obedient to death—
>   even death on a cross!
>   (Philippians 2:6–8)

Christ gave up a place of dignity and position in heaven, where He was known as God and God alone. And now, He is forever known as man, still divine, yet not exclusively divine, but united to the person, flesh and form of a created being. His whole inheritance is merged in ours. He laid down His rights and honors and took up our wrongs and reproaches, our liabilities and disabilities, and henceforth He has nothing but His people.

He is the merchant man seeking pearls, who, having found one pearl of great price, sold all that He had and bought that pearl. The Church, His Bride, is all He owns. He has invested everything in us. The Lord's portion is His people. Therefore, let us make up to Him what He has laid down. Let us understand His sacrifice and love. And let Him find in us His sufficient and everlasting recompense.

The redeemer not only sacrificed his own inheritance, but he bought back the forfeited inheritance of the dead husband. Likewise, our Kinsman-Redeemer has brought back for us all that we lost in Adam and has added to it infinitely more—all the fullness of His grace, all the riches of His glory, all that the ages to come are yet to unfold in His mighty plan, victory over death, the restoration of the divine image, sonship with God, triumph over Satan, a world restored to more than Eden's blessedness and beauty, the crowns and thrones of the kingdom and all the exceeding riches of His grace and kindness. All this and more is the purchase of His redemption.

> In whom the tribes of Adam boast
> More blessings than our father lost.

But the best of all the blessings brought by our Kinsman-Redeemer is Himself. Not only does He redeem the inheritance, but He purchases the bride and He becomes her Bridegroom. When Boaz bought the inheritance of Elimelech, he took Ruth also, and she became his bride. And so our Kinsman-Redeemer is also our Husband. Not only does He come down into our nature in the incarnation, but He takes us up into His person in the relationship that is to reach its consummation in the marriage supper of the Lamb.

THE COURAGE OF FAITH

We see in Ruth's example the pattern of faith that dares to claim and enter into all the possibilities of its inheritance. It was a bold move on Ruth's part to claim her rights under the Levirate law. They would not have come to her as the snowflakes fall, but they had to be recognized and definitely claimed. And so her mother-in-law told her all about it, and showed her that it was not an unwomanly or immodest thing to put herself at the feet of Boaz, in the place to which she was entitled. It left upon him the responsibility of accepting or refusing her.

Still it cost her many a struggle and many a tear before she robed herself in her wedding garments and, stealing through the night, lay down at the threshing floor of Boaz, putting herself and all that was dear to a woman's honor at his mercy.

Her act was the abandonment of faith. But faith must always abandon itself before it can claim its blessing. We see the same type of faith in Mary, the mother of Jesus. She risked her reputation on the angel's message and believed for the blessing that was to bring the world its Redeemer. "I am the Lord's servant. . . . May it be to me as you have said" (Luke 1:38). And the answer came back, "Blessed is she who has believed that what the Lord has said to her will be accomplished!" (1:45).

Likewise, faith must always claim its promised rights. Every victory costs a venture, and the blessing is in proportion to the cost. Faith must still see its inheritance under the promise and then step boldly forward and take what God has given. Salvation is not now bestowed as mercy to a pauper, but is claimed in Jesus' name by a trusting child who inherits under his brother's will.

That is how we take His forgiveness and how we must take every blessing and answer to our prayer all along the way. God has given us the right to take this place of boldness. We are not presuming, but we are honoring His Word. We are not entering beyond our rights, but we are showing our confidence in our Father's truth and love by daring to take all He has dared to give. Let us have boldness to enter into the holiest by the blood of Jesus.

> And to its utmost fullness prove
> The power of Jesus' name.

THE RECOMPENSE OF FAITH

Finally, we see that the fruit of Boaz and Ruth's marriage was the dynasty of David and the birth of Jesus Christ, the Son of man, the King of kings and the Lord of lords. Ruth's faith brought her into a family of princes and a kingdom of glory. And so for us, too, redemption means a crown and a throne at the Master's glorious coming.

But behind the throne and the crown lies the story of redemption and the bold appropriation of faith. We must learn to know the Bridegroom now, if we would sit with Him upon His throne then and share the glory of His millennial reign. Shall we take Him as our Redeemer, our Husband and our coming Lord, and have Him say to us,

> For your Maker is your husband—
>   the LORD Almighty is his name—
> the Holy One of Israel is your Redeemer;
>   he is called the God of all the earth.
>   (Isaiah 54:5)

CHAPTER 11

SAMUEL, THE GREAT REFORMER

Speak LORD, for your servant is listening. (1 Samuel 3:9)

The LORD was with Samuel as he grew up, and he let none of his words fall to the ground. (3:19)

The life of Samuel marks a transition period in the history of Israel from the time of the judges to the kingdom of Saul and David. His was an epoch life like Abraham's, Joshua's and Luther's.

THE GREAT REFORMER

He stands out as the great reformer of his time, lifting his people out of the dark ages of the Old Testament and leading them into the golden age of David's kingdom and Israel's preeminence among the nations. More than any other character of the ages he resembled Martin Luther, the great reformer of the Christian dispensation, who lifted the Church of God out of the corruption of bondage and superstition and gave us the Reformation, the Bible, the doctrines of grace and the light and liberty of Protestantism.

THE FOUNDER OF THE PROPHETICAL ORDER

Samuel also enjoyed the distinguished honor of being the founder of the school of the prophets and the first in that glorious succession of holy men who spoke as they were moved by the Holy Spirit, and who formed the unbroken line of truth and righteousness in the history of God's ancient people.

There were three representative official classes in the Old Testament—prophets, priests and kings. Among the priests were many honored names—Aaron, Phinehas and Ezekiel—but the priesthood often became corrupt and allowed the very sanctuary of God to be defiled by the abominations of heathenism. The kings were also nobly represented by such names as David, Jehoshaphat, Hezekiah and Josiah.

But the prophets formed an unbroken line of faithful witnesses and glorious examples. Amid all the declensions of the nation and the apostasies of their priests and kings, they not only stood true in their testimony to the will of God, but lived out in their lives the principles of integrity and uprightness. From the days of Samuel they formed a distinct class and had a regular school of training, corresponding somewhat to our theological seminaries and training institutes. Samuel had the preeminence of being the founder of these prophetic schools. Later in his life he went about the country as a pastor and overseer, visiting the towns and villages, holding conventions from place to place and instructing the people in the law of God and the schools of the prophets in the principles of the kingdom.

HIS SPOTLESS LIFE

But, above all his public ministries and even his national influence, Samuel was himself a beautiful and spotless character. In an age of almost universal corruption, he lived a life of blameless piety. And at a later period, when bidding farewell to the nation as their judge, he could truly call upon them to witness to his uprightness and integrity. " 'Now,' " he said, " '. . . I am old and gray, . . . I have been your leader from my youth until this day. Here I stand. Testify against me in the presence of the LORD and his anointed. Whose ox have I taken? Whose donkey have I taken? Whom have I cheated? Whom have I oppressed? From whose hand have I accepted a bribe to make me shut my eyes? If I have done any of these, I will make it right.' 'You have not cheated or oppressed us,' they replied. 'You have not taken anything from anyone's hand' " (1 Samuel 12:2–4).

Samuel stands with Joseph, Joshua and Daniel, one of the blameless lives of sacred history. He was no doubt human in his infirmities, but no fault has been recorded against him and his personal character is the most eloquent testimony of all his history.

HIS MOTHER

But we are permitted to trace this beautiful life to its source. Some characters, like Elijah suddenly burst upon our vision and we know them only in the public and closing chapters of their history. Some, however, are like a beautiful river that you can trace to its crystal fountain and follow through all its winding channels until, like our own Mississippi, it pours its volume into the sea and flows long after as a Gulf Stream through the mighty ocean.

We are permitted to stand by Samuel's cradle and even to know something of his prophetic future before his very birth. We enter into the joys and sorrows and the believing prayers of the holy mother, who was the real fountain, not only of his natural life, but also of his piety and holy power. And we walk side by side with him through his childhood and his youth until, at last, we meet him in the busy activities of his manhood and follow him until he lays down his ministry and passes to his honored rest.

HIS TIMES

We do not need to go farther than his own family to understand the social condition of the age. Samuel's own mother, poor Hannah, was the victim of the curse of polygamy—ever a sign of a low condition of social morality. Then, when we turn to the priesthood, as illustrated in the family of Eli, we see a shocking exhibition of low sensuality, licentiousness and cupidity that would disgrace even the grossest heathenism. Eli himself, while a just and holy man in his own private character, was weak and inefficient as a judge and priest and utterly failed to restrain his ungodly family or exercise any just administration of public affairs.

The whole nation was, therefore, in a most pitiable condition, at the mercy of its foreign oppressors and so enfeebled that at a period a few years later we find that there was not a sword in Israel, and they had even to go to the grindstones of the Philistines in order to grind their plow coulters for the ordinary operation of husbandry. It was at such a time as this that God called Samuel to be the deliverer of his country.

We need never say that the adverse circumstances of our life forbid the possibility of living to purpose and living for God. The blacker the cloud the brighter may be the rainbow. The harder our situation the more can our life become a protest against it. The lighthouse needs the midnight darkness and the stormbeaten shore to bring out its value and its purpose. There is no situation so trying and difficult but God can sustain us in it, and when we have learned our lesson, enable us to triumph over it.

We, too, like Samuel, are called to live in degenerate times. We are approaching the closing age of the dispensation, and the apostasy and tribulation which are to precede the coming of the Lord. It is not for us to excuse ourselves by prevailing wickedness, but to make our lives a protest against it and to shine as lights in the world, holding forth the word of truth in the midst of a crooked and perverse generation (Philippians 2:15–16), a savor of life unto life if possible, but, if not, at least a savor of death unto death (2 Corinthians 2:15–16).

HIS BIRTH

He was the child of faith and prayer, and his very name means "asked of God."

God loves to have every glorious thing born of someone's faith. Moses could not come until there was a Jochebed to believe for his deliverance and then to train him for the marvelous events of his history. Before even the Son of God could appear, Mary of Bethlehem had to be taught by the Holy

Spirit to believe for His birth and to lay down her womanly pride in the most costly sacrifice she could have been called to make at her Lord's command. And so Samuel is but the outcome of Hannah's piety, consecration and faith.

Back of that faith there lies a broken heart, a woman's tears, a life of bitterness, disappointment and humiliation. Poor Hannah was the second wife in a polygamous system whose fruit must ever be jealousy and sorrow. But out of her crushed heart came at last the believing prayer that brought her victory and consolation. All other sources of comfort had failed her, and at last she went to God, and at the tabernacle in Shiloh she poured out her prayer in sobs and tears until old Eli, the priest, thought her drunk and reproved her for her conduct. But she told him her story, and he sent her away with blessing and encouragement, and God whispered to her heart that her prayer was granted and her days of mourning ended.

And she did not forget when the blessing came that it was not hers, but God's, and lovingly and faithfully she gave it back to Him from whom it came. As soon as her little son was able to be left without a mother's watchful care she took him to the tabernacle and gave him to Eli to be brought up as a child of the sanctuary. "So now I give him to the LORD," she said. "For his whole life he will be given over to the LORD" (1 Samuel 1:28).

Not for a few days or weeks did she give him up, but she gave him wholly and with a sacrifice that only a mother could understand. She consented that the little feet for whose pattering she had longed should be heard no more in her cottage, that the prattle for whose music her lonely heart had waited a lifetime should sound no more in her ears; but that she should live on till the end alone, glad to know that he was all the Lord's and she was giving back to God the blessing which He had brought to her. This is love and this is the difference between the love of earth and the love of heaven. Earthly love loves for the pleasure it can find in loving. Heavenly love loves for the blessing it can give to the loved one. Hannah knew that her sacrifice was best for Samuel, and that in giving him to God she was getting more for him than a mother's selfish fondness could ever have bestowed.

And yet there was still the sweet thought behind it all that he was hers. She was not losing him but lending him, and God counted her sacrifice a real service and some day would restore the loan with infinite and eternal additions.

If only every father and mother today could understand the privilege of giving their child to God and getting him back some day with God's compound interest. You will give your daughter to a worthless man, but how slow you are to give her to Him who gave His life for you.

SAMUEL'S CHILDHOOD

There are some lives whose glory it is to have been saved from the depths of sin. But there is even a higher beauty in having been so fully saved that our very childhood has been kept from the blight of corruption and depravity. This was Samuel's high privilege. He was always a holy child. He never knew the defiling breath of wickedness. This may be the privilege of your child, Christian mother. God help you to protect your innocent child from the foul breath of sin's contamination and always to shelter that trusting life under the protecting wings of God. This may be your privilege. Pray that God will have your child's earliest years, and may he never know the mystery of iniquity and the memories of sin and shame which, though they may be forgiven, yet come back to defile and distress the heart.

DIVINE GRACE

But Samuel was not holy and good by natural birth or disposition. He was not called because he was good by natural temperament, but he was saved and sanctified as we and our children still must be only by the grace of God. Samuel, like every child of Adam, had to be born from above and receive the divine touch and the divine grace, and be brought into fellowship with the same supernatural power that saves us all.

We have the story of Samuel's first touch of God, and it gives us the keynote not only of his life, but of every holy and heavenly life. The whole story is told in a single word—Samuel became acquainted with God. God revealed Himself to Samuel and Samuel hearkened, listened and henceforth, forever, always implicitly obeyed.

HIS HEARKENING

The keynote of Samuel's life and of every saintly life is, "Speak, for your servant is listening" (1 Samuel 3:10). Samuel's task was not a hard one, and yet how rarely it is repeated. He had simply to attend to God, and say and do just what He told him.

This is the difference between the earthly and the heavenly life. The one is merely human, the other is divine. The crisis moment comes in every life when God speaks to us, and we hearken to Him and begin to walk in His holy fellowship and His perfect will. The very peculiarities of Samuel's call linger in his later life in his message to Saul, "To obey is better than sacrifice,/ and to heed is better than the fat of rams" (1 Samuel 15:22).

All his blessings had come to him by hearkening and obeying, and all Saul's calamities had come to him because he willfully took his own way and refused to listen to God.

At first even he made some mistakes and misunderstood the voice that spoke to him so gently in his little chamber. Three times it called to him in vain, and he thought it was the old priest's message. But even when he did not understand he still responded and sprang to his feet, ready instantly to obey. And so God will give us time to understand His voice and learn His will. What He asks of us is the obedient spirit, and the readiness to hear and understand. He will call again and yet again if necessary, and teach us to know all that He would have us to do. Let us listen so attentively and respond so quickly that we will not need the stroke of His hand or the bit or bridle of His discipline to make us comprehend His will. He can guide us with His eye and flash into our inmost being the instinctive intuition of His holy will. Oh, the sweetness and the rest! Oh, the safety and the strength of the life that walks with God in this inner fellowship and knows no will but His!

HIS OBEDIENCE

But Samuel had to obey as well as hearken, and it was no easy task to go to Eli and tell him all that God had spoken against his house. It was the hard test which often came again in his later ministry as the messenger of God to sinful men. Again and again did he have to go to those he loved and say to them the thing which nearly broke his heart. A faithful minister cannot always say smooth things. Often must we speak the words of God where we know that they will wither and break and perhaps alienate the dearest friendships of our lives. But Samuel obeyed so perfectly this time that he never was tempted to disobey again, and he learned the lesson well, which in later years was so often repeated in the history of Israel and the story of Saul.

HIS LIFE AND WORK

We have a picture of Samuel's life and work. Henceforth, "the LORD was with Samuel," we are told, ". . . and he let none of his words fall to the ground. And all Israel from Dan to Beersheba recognized that Samuel was attested as a prophet of the LORD" (1 Samuel 3:19–20).

What a picture of a successful life, where every word counts and the Lord lets nothing fail or have to be undone or taken back. How many of our words fall to the ground! How vain our efforts and our prayers and how often we have to traverse over again the paths of vanity!

How can we have an established life whose every step is fixed in God and led in the way everlasting? Only by doing as Samuel did, ever hearkening to God and speaking and acting only and always in Him. Then we will not need to advertise ourselves. Men will find us out. Sad and empty lives will come to us for help, and our work will be its own witness that God is with us. God help us to live such lives!

OUR EPOCH AGE

We, too, are in an epoch age. God help us to be epoch men—men for the times on which the end of the age has come. Samuel was called to act in the beginning of the Hebrew history. We are permitted to see the close of our dispensation. Never before did the world so need the highest types of men and the noblest, truest kinds of ministry—lives that understand God, souls that hearken, ears sensitive to His lightest whisper and wills adamant to obey implicitly His every word. These are the men that God is looking for to mold the history of the world's last generation, and to usher in the kingdom of David's greater Son, as much as He needed a Samuel in the darkest days of Old Testament history and for the inauguration of David's reign.

CHAPTER 12

THE REFORMATION UNDER SAMUEL

And Samuel said to the whole house of Israel, "If you are returning to the LORD with all your hearts, then rid yourselves of the foreign gods and the Ashtoreths and commit yourselves to the LORD and serve him only, and he will deliver you out of the hand of the Philistines." (1 Samuel 7:3)

W e have looked at the great reformer; let us now look at the reformation.

FAILURE

It began in the complete failure of the people themselves and the demonstration of their utter inability to lift themselves out of their helpless condition. God has to let us come to the end of ourselves before He can interpose for our deliverance.

A mother stood on the deck of a ship, hardly restrained from throwing herself into the sea to save her drowning boy, while men stood by and waited as he sank again and again. At last, as he rose for the third time, a brave seaman leaped in and caught the sinking lad and held him safely while both were drawn to the deck. "Why didn't you save him sooner?" cried the frantic mother, as her boy slowly came back to consciousness. "Because," said the sailor, "I had to wait until his strength was gone, or he would have drowned both himself and me." And so God has to wait until our strength is gone before he can save or sanctify or heal us.

This was Israel's state when Samuel came to the front as the leader of the new reformation. Politically, the country was under the power of the Philistines. Morally and socially the people were corrupt, and the fearful example of Hophni and Phinehas, the very priests of God who turned the sanctuary at Shiloh and the very services of Jehovah's worship into an orgy of license, could not fail to have a fatal influence upon the manners and the morals of all the people. Even Eli himself, who was still recognized as the ecclesiastical and judicial head of the nation, while honest and sincere in his purpose, was a helpless tool in the hands of his family. And so the very fountains of justice and religion were utterly corrupted and all that was lacking was the crisis hour when this system of iniquity should fall to pieces by its own weight, as it really did at last. The critical moment came when the Philistines once more invaded the land, and in a moment of presumptuous despair leaders of Israel's forlorn hope brought out the ark of Jehovah. The Philistines realized at once their danger and their opportunity. They were fighting now not only Israel, but Israel's God. So with redoubled valor the captains roused the host to do their best, and by one victorious blow not only to crush their enemies but secure for themselves the supernatural secret of their victorious power.

ELI'S DEATH

As old Eli sat by the tabernacle court at Shiloh that evening a cloud of dust appeared upon the distant horizon, and a swift runner rapidly dashed along until he stood breathless before the aged judge. As he rushed along, the people had already caught from his manner and his looks the fearful tidings, and a great cry arose throughout the city. Eli heard the tumult and called the messenger to his side. The aged patriarch of 98 was too blind to see his form, and could but dimly hear his words; but he eagerly asked him for tidings from the field, and as those fearful words fell upon his ear, "Israel fled before the Philistines, and the army has suffered heavy losses. Also your two sons, Hophni and Phinehas, are dead, and the ark of God has been captured" (1 Samuel 4:17). That last word broke the old man's heart, and he sank back in a swoon and fell heavily to the ground. As they picked him up his neck was broken and his life was gone. Among the tragedies of that terrible day was the dying anguish of the wife of Phinehas and the significant name she left with her parting sigh of agony to the poor little orphan child which came that moment into life as the memorial of his country's shame— Ichabod, "the glory has departed" (4:21). Yes, it was the deepest, darkest hour of the nation's woe; but it was the darkness just before the dawn and deliverance was near.

REVELATION OF GOD

The next stage in the preparation of the coming reformation was the revelation and vindication of God as Himself the nation's hope. The one great design of Israel's history as a nation was to be the witness and the revealer of God. All the supernatural manifestations of their glorious past were intended not to show the greatness of their leaders, but the glory and all-sufficiency of their divine Lord and Leader. Sometimes, therefore, God had to let the human instruments utterly fail so that He Himself might be the more gloriously vindicated in His own all-sufficiency and power.

And so we find in the later history of the nation that there came a time when the kings and the prophets and priests of Judah and Israel completely failed to glorify Jehovah among the nations or to accomplish His purpose for the world, and yet this became the most illustrious day of His own manifestation. He had to let the very kingdom of Judah and Israel pass away in ignominious defeat, and even the temple itself become a heap of smoldering ashes before the victorious power of Nebuchadnezzar. And yet, in that very hour, He called four humble Hebrew youths in Babylon to stand for Him in the furnace of fire and the lions' den, and so to vindicate His own glory and supremacy that in the hour of his pride Nebuchadnezzar, the mightiest king and conqueror of the earth, was compelled to acknowledge that Jehovah was the only true God, and to issue a decree calling upon his subjects to worship the God of Daniel as the true God and the Sovereign Ruler of the universe. And a little later he compelled Cyrus, Artaxerxes and even Xerxes, the proud despots of Persia, to recognize His supremacy, to protect His people and even to send back the captives from Babylon to rebuild the city and the temple at Jerusalem.

GOD VINDICATED

And so here we find in this period of Israel's history that, while the nation failed and the priesthood failed and the very ark of God seemed to fail, God Himself became the more gloriously vindicated even in the midst of His enemies. No sooner had the ark of God been taken by the Philistines than a long train of desolation followed in its path wherever it went. They set it up in the temple of Dagon among their gods, and in the morning Dagon was fallen on his face before the ark of God. They set him up again, and the next morning he was not only fallen down, but shattered to pieces before the awful presence of the God of the ark. The most humiliating and distressing plagues began to fall upon the people. They begged that it should be sent away from Ashdod, but no sooner had they taken it to Gath than there they begged that it be removed. And so they took it to Ekron, but the people of Ekron protested, saying, "They have brought the ark of the god of Israel around to us to kill us and our people" (5:10). And so at last they called a council and determined to send it back to Israel once more.

So, preparing a costly present and choosing two cows, they put it on a cart and committed it to the God whom it represented in some superstitious way to their terrified minds. But it needed no human hand to guide the holy symbol of Jehovah's presence. Contrary to their own instincts, those Hebrew cows went steadily forward at a divine command which they could neither understand nor disobey, lowing as they went, because their hearts carried them backwards to their calves. Yet on they went at the bidding of a power that drove them in the opposite direction until they reached Beth Shemesh, where the Levites met the sacred ark and took the cattle that bore it and offered them up in sacrifice unto the Lord and presented the costly offerings before the Lord. Thus God showed that He could vindicate His own glory and lead His own way without the help or wisdom of man.

And even a more solemn lesson still had to be learned, for as the men of Beth Shemesh presumed to approach the holy symbol of the presence of God with forbidden familiarity they were smitten with death and, as nearly as we can understand from the doubtful readings of the passage (1 Samuel 6:19), 70 men (not 50,070, as the Revised Version states) perished for their presumption.

This is the lesson that we all need to learn before we are prepared to truly represent God: God does not need us or our strength, but we need to understand Him and know that He is all-sufficient for His own work. And what He requires of us is that we know Him, bear witness to Him and truly represent Him. He is able to take care of His own cause if we only give Him right of way. "But I, when I am lifted up from the earth, will draw all men to myself" (John 12:32).

The best way to glorify God is to hold Him up to men and He will glorify Himself. As we go forth to meet the tests and conflicts of these last days we need to understand our God, and to know that One is in our midst and on our side who, standing between heaven and earth, has already said, "All authority in heaven and on earth has been given to me. . . . And surely I am with you always, to the very end of the age" (Matthew 28:18–20).

We have plenty of people today who know the culture and wisdom of the ages and even the theology of the Bible. But what we want are people that know their God and can stand alone and trust Him in the hour of trial, in the face of difficulties, in the midst of enemies, in the lands of the heathen and in situations where there is no hope or help but God and God alone.

REPENTANCE

The next step in Israel's reformation was national repentance and the turning of the people with their whole heart from all idolatry and sin unto the Lord. And so Samuel calls them together at Mizpah to a great day of national humiliation, and addresses to them the language of First Samuel 7:3, which is the watchword of every true reformation and revival.

The essential conditions of God's acceptance and blessing always must be deep sincerity, penitence and absolute rightness with God. No matter how long or how far you may have wandered, no matter how great your sin, or how deep your sinfulness, the honest, earnest heart will always and instantly find the heart of God. If you have not found Him, it is because there is some reservation, some insincerity, some idol to which you cling, some disingenuousness of heart or cherished crookedness of life. God has fixed the instant when every soul will find Him, and that is "when you seek me with all your heart" (Jeremiah 29:13).

And so they came together, not only with fasting and with the symbolic pouring out of the waters of cleansing before the Lord, but the best of all is that "Samuel judged the children of Israel at Mizpah" (1 Samuel 7:6, KJV). It is this judging of ourselves that puts us right with God. It is not emotional feeling nor fountains of tears, but simple calling things by their right names and putting them in their true places. Therefore the promise is, "If we confess our sins, he is faithful and just and will forgive us our sins and purify us from all unrighteousness" (1 John 1:9).

He does not say anything about great sorrow or deep feeling, but simple, straightforward confessing. What He wants is to have us see things aright, diagnose the disease, recognize the fault, and then we shall be saved from future deception and disobedience. This is the emphatic meaning of that remarkable passage in First Corinthians 11:31: "If we judged ourselves, we would not come under judgment." That is, if we would discern ourselves and put everything in its right place in our lives, we should not need God's heavier blow to wake us out of our deception and hold us back from evil.

THE BLOOD

The next stage in Israel's reformation was the precious atoning blood. How beautifully that sacrificial scene is described: "Then Samuel took a suckling lamb and offered it up as a whole burnt offering to the LORD. He cried out to the LORD on Israel's behalf, and the LORD answered him" (1 Samuel 7:9).

This was the difference between the present reformation and many of those that had gone before. There was at this time a thorough recognition of that atoning blood. Without this there can be no radical and lasting change in the life of an individual or people. The disposition to ignore the sacrificial meaning of Christ's death and to reduce His vicarious offering to a mere object lesson is the most alarming condition of our Christian life and the real secret of the declension of practical righteousness and holiness.

The deepest meaning of the blood, too, many of us fail to understand. It means not cleansing, but crucifixion; not blotting out, but burying. It is not merely that the blood wipes out the sin, but it wipes out the sinner, too. The real significance of the death of Christ is that the man who committed the sin is judged, condemned and crucified with Christ, that he is not the same man that lives now, that he has been repudiated and forever put aside, and that a new man, born of Christ and descending out of heaven, has come in his place so truly that we can say in the literal language of the great apostle, "I have been crucified with Christ and I no longer live, but Christ lives in me. The life I live in the body, I live by faith in the Son of God, who loved me and gave himself for me" (Galatians 2:20).

This is the reason men hate the cross, because it is not only Christ's cross, but it is bound to be their cross, too. It means not only a dead Savior, but a dead sinner. But this is the only way that the sin can ever cease and the cleansing ever be permanent and complete.

THE ENEMY

Next comes the test of faith and the attack of the foe. Just as the deliverance is about to come, the enemy musters in double force, and all Israel's fears seem about to be realized. How emphatic is the time of this attack. "While Samuel was sacrificing the burnt offering, the Philistines drew near to engage Israel in battle" (1 Samuel 7:10), and the trembling people stood unarmed, defenseless and dismayed. "Do not stop," they cried to Samuel, "crying out to the LORD our God for us, that he may rescue us from the hand of the Philistines" (7:8).

And as that smoking sacrifice ascended silently to the heavens, along the sky there burst the artillery of heaven, and a terrific thunderstorm poured down upon the embattled foe, doubtless with quivering lightning stroke and mighty hailstones. As in the day of Gideon's battle, the enemy fled in confusion, pursued by their triumphant foes until they were scattered and dispersed. So signal was the victory that we are told in the next verse they "did not invade Israelite territory again. Throughout Samuel's lifetime the hand of the LORD was against the Philistines. The towns from Ekron to Gath that the Philistines had captured from Israel were restored to her, and Israel delivered the neighboring territory from the power of the Philistines" (7:13–14). The victory was complete and permanent, and the reformation had become a restoration.

EBENEZER

The last chapter was a doxology of praise. "Then Samuel took a stone and set it up between Mizpah and Shen. He named it Ebenezer, saying, 'Thus far has the LORD helped us' " (7:12). This is ever the consummation of penitence and believing prayer. The sorrow is turned into joy and the prayer is translated into praise. This is the true way to show that we really do believe God. Not until we cease our pleading and begin to thank Him that the blessing is given shall we really have cause for thanksgiving. In the City of Salvation all the gates are praise, and the reason many fail to enter in is because they try to creep through the tunnels rather than enter through the open gates of thankfulness and praise. This is the secret of victory forevermore, to take what He gives and thank Him for it in advance.

This is also the secret of defeat and failure—a spirit of gloom, depression, moroseness and murmuring. The moment you begin to grumble God will give you something to grumble about; and the moment you begin to praise He will give you cause for love and praise. The dreary pathway that missed the Land of Promise and for 40 years trod the lonely desert all began in the murmuring at Taberah (Number 11:1). On the other hand, the glorious renaissance which led through Samuel's reformation to David's throne and Solomon's glory, all began in the stone of Ebenezer, and the praise of a trustful, thankful people.

Let us set up today over against every place of failure, over against every sorrow, over against every sin as we cover it with the cleansing blood, not a banner merely, nor even a song, but a stone of Ebenezer, and write upon it, "Thus far has the LORD helped us" (1 Samuel 7:12).

CHAPTER 13

SAUL, OR SELF-LIFE LEADING TO DESTRUCTION

1 Samuel 8–15

The place of Saul in Old Testament history is significant and, I believe, typical of great spiritual truths. It is conceded that Israel's redemption from Egypt foreshadowed human redemption through the cross of Calvary. It is also beyond question that the triumph of Joshua and the conquest of Canaan pointed forward to the Pentecostal baptism, the blessing of the apostolic church and the deeper rest into which the Holy Spirit brings the individual Christian.

We have already seen that the dark period of declension recorded in Judges and the earlier chapters of Samuel typify the dark ages of Christianity. The reformation under Samuel could be compared to our Protestant Reformation and the revival of the Church from the bondage of medieval darkness and superstition. A little further on we will find that the kingdoms of David and Solomon are representative of Christ's millennial throne.

THE COUNTERFEIT KING

But what was the meaning of the strange parenthesis of Saul's life? I believe it represents the counterfeit kingdom that Satan is seeking to set upon the throne of human selfishness and worldly pride—the rule of the antichrist. Unfortunately, we have too many evidences in the compromising and worldly ecclesiasticism of our day, and in the Laodicean picture given in Revelation of the church that is to be rejected at the coming of the Lord.

But while this is the dispensational meaning of Saul's life, it has a still more solemn personal application for every Christian. It is God's fearful object lesson of the power and peril of the self-life and the need of its utter crucifixion before we can enter into the true kingdom of spiritual victory and power.

THEIR MOTIVES

We see the spirit of self in the motive that prompted the kingdom of Saul. Samuel recognized it for what it was—a rejection of God as the supreme King of Israel and a vainglorious desire to be independent of divine control and to be like the surrounding nations of the world. "Now appoint a king to lead us," they said, "such as all the other nations have" (1 Samuel 8:5). No wonder Samuel was deeply displeased. When he prayed to God, God answered, "Listen to all that the people are saying to you; it is not you they have rejected, but they have rejected me as their king" (8:7).

Nevertheless, Samuel still protested and solemnly warned the Israelites of the burdens and the exactions which a king would bring upon them and the trouble they were bringing upon themselves. "When that day comes, you will cry out for relief from the king you have chosen, and the LORD will not answer you in that day" (8:18). But Samuel's warnings were to no avail. The people had set their hearts on having a king: "We want a king over us. Then we will be like all the other nations, with a king to lead us and to go out before us and fight our battles" (8:19–20).

This is like the spirit of the prodigal son when he told his father to give him his share of the inheritance. It is the desire of independence which is the root of human sin, and it is the spirit of conformity in the Church today. We are conscious of it in our own natural hearts. It is the large, self-asserting and dominant "I" that makes a man a god unto himself and refuses to surrender his will to Christ, or yield the direction of his life to the will of God and the government of the Holy Spirit.

The first step, then, in the new life is surrender. The essential condition of the baptism of the Holy Spirit is to yield everything to God, even the things that in themselves may be harmless. Why? For no other reason than to prove our will is wholly laid down and that God is all in all.

SAUL, THE FLESHLY MAN

We see the spirit of self in the character of Saul, in the qualifications that made him the choice and the idol of the people. Saul represented all that was strong, chivalrous, attractive and promising in human nature. He was of splendid physique, a head taller than all the people, a magnificent specimen of physical manhood—"every inch a king."

He possessed the intellectual, moral and social qualities that constitute a leader. He was brave, heroic, enthusiastic and generous, and the early years of his reign were adorned with stirring examples of heroic deeds. He was all that the human heart would choose. He represented the best possibilities of human nature. As the people looked at his splendid figure, they shouted again and again that patriotic cry which has so often re-echoed since, and which has so seldom been fulfilled as a prayer to heaven, "God save the king!"

But God had to let Saul stand before the ages to show that man at his best is only man, and that human self-sufficiency must end in failure and sorrow. This is the lesson that God is still trying to teach His children. How few of them have found it out so fully that they can say, "I know that nothing good lives in me, that is, in my sinful nature" (Romans 7:18). The sentence of death has been passed on the flesh, and there is only one thing that we can do with it—nail it to the cross of Jesus Christ, reckon it dead and keep it forever in His bottomless grave.

ALL THE RIGHT QUALITIES

The spirit of self in Saul was combined with much that was good and attractive, both naturally and spiritually. Naturally, we have seen that he was not only a man of princely bearing, but one of many noble and heroic qualities. He also had a fine family. His son Jonathan is one of the most attractive figures in the long gallery of Bible characters.

When Saul came to Samuel and was first called to the kingdom, he seemed to have many elements of sterling virtue and genuine humilty. Like a dutiful son, he went to search for his father's donkeys, and then he went to the prophet Samuel to ask counsel about finding them. When he came to Samuel and was told the extraordinary message and anointed to be king, there was no unbecoming self-consciousness about him. He kept his secret with discretion and modesty. Even in telling his uncle about the words of Samuel he said nothing to him about the greater message concerning the kingdom.

When he left Samuel he did just what he was told to do. When he met the company of prophets, he joined them and received a baptism of the Spirit and prophesied among them with genuine religious enthusiasm. And even when Samuel told his relatives to bring him forward so that he could present Saul to the people, Saul was hiding among the baggage. He seemed a paragon of modesty and unobtrusiveness.

But as we well know, Saul let the dark shadow of self blight his life and ruin his kingdom and his family. How self-deceptive is the human spirit! How pride itself will hide away in the very guise of deepest humility! Later, speaking of Saul's earlier life, Samuel pays a tribute to Saul's former humility: "Although you were once small in your own eyes, did you not become the head of the tribes of Israel? The LORD anointed you king over Israel" (1 Samuel 15:17).

We cannot doubt that Samuel was sincere in giving Saul credit for a measure of genuine humility. What then was the defect? May it have been this? It is one thing to be little in our own eyes, but it is quite another thing to be out of our own sight altogether. True humility is not thinking little of ourselves; it is not thinking of ourselves at all. What we need is not so much self-denial but self-crucifixion and complete self-forgetfulness. The perfect child is just as unconscious in the highest place as in the lowest. The true spirit of Christ in us recognizes ourselves as no longer ourselves, but so completely one with the Lord Jesus that we may truly say: "I no longer live, but Christ lives in me" (Galatians 2:20).

But what are we to learn from this combination of so many excellencies in one life and its ultimate failure and ruin? That Satan's cleverest ploy is to mix the good with the bad—to cover his poison as a sugar-coated pill. He knows we would never accept it in its uncovered form. Satan's choicest agents are those who are attractive and naturally lovely. Esau was more appealing than Jacob, but Jacob was the chosen one.

A person can be beautiful, wise, cultured, moral, useful, noble and generous but living for himself or herself, and in the end be self-destroyed like Saul. Satan does not want our souls outright; he only wants a mortgage on them. He is content to take a lien for $1,000 if he cannot get one for $100,000. He can wait for the day of foreclosure. All he wants is to have his hand in it. It is these mixed lives that are doing the mischief.

But God says,

> "Therefore come out from them
>   and be separate,
>   says the Lord.
> Touch no unclean thing,
>   and I will receive you."
> "I will be a Father to you,
>   and you will be my sons and daughters,
>   says the Lord Almighty."
>   (2 Corinthians 6:17–18)

SAUL'S FIRST TEST

The first test came to Saul in an hour of severe trial when, beleaguered by his enemies and deserted by almost all of his soldiers, he seemed to be facing destruction. Waiting seven days for Samuel to come and begin the battle by the usual sacrificial offering, Saul at last grew discouraged and impatient. Then he presumed to take upon himself the priestly functions which belonged only to Samuel, and to offer up the sacrifice without waiting for the prophet. As he was offering it, Samuel arrived and questioned the king.

"What have you done?" asked Samuel.

> Saul replied, "When I saw that the men were scattering, and that you did not come at the set time, and that the Philistines were assembling at Micmash, . . . I felt compelled to offer the burnt offering."
>
> "You acted foolishly," Samuel said. "You have not kept the command the LORD your God gave you; if you had, he would have established your kingdom over Israel for all time. But now your kingdom will not endure; the LORD has sought out a man after his own heart and appointed him leader of his people, because you have not kept the LORD's command." (13:11–14)

Many of us live successful lives while things are going well. But in the hour of trial self always shows through. Saul was a splendid king until that first trial, and then he became discouraged, distrustful, self-asserting and presumptuous, daring to take in his own hands the things that belonged only to God. He usurped the throne of God Himself and showed his true nature. He was a man of his own heart and not of God's heart. Therefore, God sought out a man after God's own heart who would do God's will and not his own, thereby being a true representative of Israel's true King.

Because of Saul's actions, God showed him how little He needed his strength and wisdom—He used Jonathan and his armorbearer and one sword to defeat the Philistines and show Saul how all-sufficient God is to those who truly trust Him. But Saul missed all this, nearly wrecking the victory God brought by his unthinking interference (1 Samuel 13:23–14:45). After this it became apparent that Saul could not be trusted with God's work, and that his persistent self-will would always hinder the will of God.

Saul's crisis did not come immediately; God let the spirit of self work out into its full development. It was now evident that Saul's life would fail, and that Samuel's prophecy was all too true.

THE SECOND TEST

God gave Saul another opportunity and a second test. He sent him on an important expedition to destroy Amalek, the race of Esau that had tried to hinder Israel in their passage through the wilderness.

There is a deep spiritual meaning back of this story: Amalek is a type of the flesh, and it is an illustration of the principle represented by Saul's life. Saul's failure to destroy Amalek shows how deeply rooted the self-principle was in his own life. The man who spared Agag was the man who spared the principle of self in his heart. And the two pictures blend with an awful significance for us.

Saul successfully accomplished the invasion and returned smugly victorious. He even seems to have been so possessed with the spirit of self-complacency that he failed to realize his own true character until Samuel uttered his fearful words of doom. Upon seeing Samuel he said, "The LORD bless you! I have carried out the LORD's instructions" (1 Samuel 15:13). But the prophet's words answered him back: "What then is this bleating of sheep in my ears? What is this lowing of cattle that I hear? . . . Why did you not obey the LORD? Why did you pounce on the plunder and do evil in the eyes of the LORD?" (15:14, 19).

"But I did obey the LORD" (15:20), Saul maintained, saying that he saved the best of the plunder to sacrifice to God. But Samuel replied,

> Does the LORD delight in burnt offerings and sacrifices
>   as much as in obeying the voice of the LORD?
> To obey is better than sacrifice,
>   and to heed is better than the fat of rams.
> For rebellion is like the sin of divination,
>   and arrogance like the evil of idolatry.
> Because you have rejected the word of the LORD,
>   he has rejected you as king. (15:22–23)

It is doubtful if even then Saul fully realized the nature of his sin. So subtle and self-deceiving is the spirit of self that all he seemed to feel was the fear of being humiliated before the people. He begged the petty bauble of Samuel's public recognition and honor, and this bit of vainglory was the solace and the comfort of his spirit when the sentence of death and ruin was thundering in his ears.

What a spectacle of self-complacency and self-deception! We see the snare of a religious motive, keeping the spoil to sacrifice to the Lord. And we see the fear of man, in the unwillingness of this weak man to displease the people when they begged him to save the precious booty of Amalek.

COMPROMISE

One word above all others seems to crystallize the very element of Saul's stupendous folly—compromise. Saul obeyed but with a compromise. He did much good, but he compromised with evil. God's commands are uncompromising, inexorable and unqualified, and our obedience must be inflexible, absolute and complete. The faintest reservation is really the spirit of disobedience. And the failure to hearken to the full meaning of God indicates a spirit of unwilling obedience.

Saul stands before us in this picture as the incarnation of self-will and as such, the enemy of God, even the rival of God upon His throne. Could there be any other issue? "You have rejected the word of the LORD, and the LORD has rejected you as king over Israel" (15:26).

GOD'S PATIENCE

Not immediately did the judgment culminate. Slowly still the coil of self unwinds until all its hidden sinuosities have been revealed. Saul accomplished much good work after this; he fought a number of battles—fought them well—reigned over Israel and established a powerful kingdom. But it was Saul's kingdom, not God's.

All his remaining years were ones of self-activity and self-vindication. For nine of those years he pursued his rival David with ferocious hate. The Spirit of God left him, and an evil spirit—by God's permission—possessed him. And as the years went on, the beginning and the end of his existence was Saul and not Jehovah. It was self incarnate, with all its miserable works and fruits.

THE SAD CULMINATION

At last the culmination came. Eaten out by the canker of self, his heart became the dwelling place for Satan. The devil took entire possession of him. In one dreadful hour Saul gave himself up to spiritism and, rejected of the Lord, sought the counsel of a medium, whom he had formerly persecuted and banished from the kingdom. It was his last fatal step. Self had driven God from the throne and had given it to Satan, and the next chapter of the self-life was self-destruction.

Trembling and prostrated by the fearful vision which his own presumption had brought up from the depths of hell, Saul rushed with reckless despair into the last battle of his life. The next day the tragedy was complete—the flower of Israel's youth was lying on the slopes of Gilboa. The army of Saul was annihilated, the Philistines were victorious on every side and the kingdom Saul had built up for a quarter of a century for himself was broken to pieces and scattered to the winds. Even Saul's sons had been killed, and in the end Saul killed himself.

The scorpion self had stung others, and now, at last, it stung itself to death. The revelation of human selfishness was complete.

Before this sad and fearful spectacle we may well stand in awe and humbly, earnestly and fervently pray:

> Oh, to be saved from myself, dear Lord,
>   Oh, to be lost in Thee!
> Oh, that it might be no more I,
>   But Christ that lives in me.

CHAPTER 14

JONATHAN, OR THE FRIEND THAT STICKS CLOSER THAN A BROTHER

There is a friend who sticks closer than a brother. (Proverbs 18:24)

God has made the human heart to be an alphabet of higher things. The material world was made to be a type of the higher spiritual realm, and all the objects of nature are but living characters by which God has written His name upon His works. God has given us the filial heart that we might understand the love we ought to feel for our Father in heaven. He has made the love of father, mother and brother that we might in some measure realize God's divine paternity—the Holy Spirit's motherhood and the heart of that "friend who sticks closer than a brother."

The best of human friendships is but a bit of broken glass reflecting something higher in the heavens above us. As in the little fragment of a shattered mirror you can see the sun reflected from above, so in our poor, imperfect hearts and our broken earthly ties we have a revelation of the heart of God.

The story of Jonathan stands out in vivid relief against the dark background of his father's life, and is one of the finest examples of human character and holy friendship. Beautiful in itself and reflecting the highest nobility in the subject himself, it is a still higher object lesson of divine love, and unfolds, as no other sacred picture, the friendship of Christ, the "friend who sticks closer than a brother." There are several aspects in which we may look at this beautiful picture.

HEROIC FAITH

It is an example of high character and heroic faith. True love must rest on a basis deeper and stronger than mere sentiment or passion. The pretty face, the charm of manner, the thousand little things which become like fetishes to attract the fancy or even the idolatry of the superficial and the selfish world, will soon be forgotten, and instead of the rose will be the thorn of bitter disappointment and hopeless heartbreak.

The only true foundation of a lasting friendship is high and noble character. Love is the magnetic attraction of two kindred lives to each other, meeting like two drops of water because they are akin. Respect and esteem must ever lie back of affection, and the more intimately we know each other the more perfectly ought we to be able to respect each other's character, or else our love must become one-sided and transient.

Jonathan and David were both lofty natures, who recognized in each other the nobility of highest manhood. Their souls were knit together by an esteem that was as perfect as their affection was intense. Jonathan well deserved the regard of his friend. He was a born hero and his heroism was not a romantic sentiment, but a deep and settled principle of faith in God.

One startling example shines out, and stands no doubt for many an unrecorded act behind (1 Samuel 13:1–14:14). The Philistines had gathered in overwhelming force, and the little army of Saul was wearing away until only about 600 remained around the royal standard. In the Philistine host there were 6,000 cavalry, 3,000 chariots of iron and hundreds of thousands of infantry—a mighty and apparently irresistible foe.

Saul had waited for Samuel to come and inaugurate the campaign by the sacrificial rites, and then despairing of his arrival had rashly presumed to assume the priestly functions and offer the sacrifice himself. The result was the divine displeasure, the rebuke of Samuel and the withdrawal of divine favor.

It was the darkest hour that could possibly have come to the nation and the cause. But dark hours are always the hours when character reveals its sterling qualities. The stars shine out at night as they cannot in the day, and this was the hour when Jonathan's true character was made plain.

Accompanied by his solitary armor-bearer, he looked across the valley to the Philistines' stronghold in the clefts of the naked rocks, and he suggested to his armor-bearer that they should go up against them. "Perhaps," he added, in the language of true faith, "the LORD will act in our behalf. Nothing can hinder the LORD from saving, whether by many or by few" (14:6). He was not looking at numbers, but at God. Happily, he had in his armor-bearer a kindred spirit. There were two heroes that day, and it is just as noble to help a noble nature and to stand out of sight but in full accord as it is to lead the front-line troops in some glorious advance. Noble natures find out noble natures, and it is a glorious thing to have on our side in the hour of trial and in the hour of lofty daring some kindred heart to, like the armor-bearer, say to us, "Do all that you have in mind, . . . I am with you heart and soul" (14:7).

WISE LEADERSHIP

We see in Jonathan not only a daring adventurer, but also a wise and prudent leader who has learned not only to initiate a great movement but to carry it through in wise caution and unceasing dependence upon the strong arm of God. Many a movement is well begun but disastrously ended because we let human impulse take the place of humble faith and, holding the bit in our own teeth, we dash ahead of God and sometimes are hurled headlong over the precipice of presumption.

Jonathan waited for God to make every step plain, and so they agreed that God should give them a further sign whether they were to make the advance as proposed. The sign was that the Philistine garrison was to invite them up for a parley on that rocky height. That was all he wanted; and now bold impulse and humble dependence upon God were changed into instant and effectual action, and they quickly scaled the height and threw themselves upon their unsuspecting enemies until 20 had fallen at their feet.

Suddenly a panic seized the host, and God seconded the bold attack by a startling earthquake, which shook the ground. A dreadful fear fell upon the foe, so that, thinking there was some mighty host behind them, they turned and fled, pressing one another down as they were swept away before the avalanche, until Saul's watchmen saw from the distant heights of Gibeah that host of myriad men in full retreat. Then Saul and his soldiers took up the pursuit and, once again, his presumption, folly and willfulness almost ruined the victory that God had wrought. If it had not been for the intervention of the people, who rescued Jonathan out of his hands, the noble hero, who had been the instrument of all the blessing of that day, would have been the victim of his father's willfulness and haste. This illustration is sufficient to show us the background of strength in the character of Jonathan and the qualities which, had he lived and reigned, would have made him, doubtless, as illustrious as the friend for whose sake he gave up his opportunities and honors and even sacrificed his life at last.

It should be your aim and mine, not so much to win the love of others as to be worthy of it; not so much to be esteemed as to be deserving of esteem; not so much to bind to ourselves the hearts of men as to stand so high and glorious that we will draw them to us as the magnet draws the steel. It is better to be than to seem; and true character, like precious gems, cannot remain always undiscovered, but will find its place and reach its full appreciation and glorious coronation.

You, who are setting your affections on all the capricious fancies of your mind and becoming attached to those you lightly meet, are weaving for yourselves a future of intolerable bondage and a shroud of agony and death. You are letting your hearts become bound by a spell that even you cannot break, to persons and things that will drag you down and make your life a disappointment if not a disaster. Remember that it is a sign of a noble character to love the noble. Do not link your lives with the unholy and the earthly, but let your associations be regulated by holy principle and your friendships fastened to the skies.

HOLY FRIENDSHIP

We see the picture of a holy friendship. The attachment of David and Jonathan is spoken of in the highest terms. "Jonathan became one in spirit with David, and he loved him as himself" (1 Samuel 18:1). In the pledge of his affection he made a covenant with his friend and stripped himself of his princely robe and tunic, bearing, no doubt, the monogram of his royal name. He gave even the very sword, which was to a warrior the badge of his highest honor, and his bow and his very belt, which was the most sacred article of personal apparel in an Oriental wardrobe, for it was his purse and the repository of all his secrets and sacred treasures. All these Jonathan gave to David as the expression of his unreserved oneness with the friend of his inmost heart.

Speaking of his affection afterwards, David uses in his exquisite dirge over his fallen friend this extreme and almost extravagant language, "I grieve for you, Jonathan my brother;/ you were very dear to me./ Your love for me was wonderful,/ more wonderful than that of women" (2 Samuel 1:26). Perhaps there is no human affection so intense as a pure woman's whole-hearted love when she yields her whole being to the one she utterly trusts. But even this was surpassed by the noble and wonderful devotion of this lofty heart.

Jonathan proved it well. Not only did he give these pledges of his confidence to his friend in the first emotion of his early love, but he stood true to him through all the perils of the succeeding years. There is no higher proof of love than loyalty to a friend in the midst of foes.

A noble nature cannot be disloyal. A double-faced friend is worse than an enemy. You may always distrust a traitor. The man that can receive the confidence and kindness of another and then go and speak against him or let others speak against him, is not only a false friend but a worthless character in every other relation of life.

You may safely distrust the man or woman who comes to you with evil tales of a former friend. Some day they will be the bearer of worse tales respecting you. Such people deserve to be rebuked wherever we find them, and taught the lesson of their ignominy and meanness.

Jonathan was no such friend. When he found his father's jealousy against David becoming dangerous he tried to check it, and for a while succeeded in overcoming it and bringing about a reconciliation. But as time wore on, and his father's bitterness grew more malignant, and Jonathan knew that nothing would satisfy it but David's life, he even risked his life to vindicate his friend. And, then, when he found it was hopeless to make a further attempt, he was true enough to sacrifice his own pleasure in David's companionship and warn him that he must flee. And so at last the two friends parted, probably to meet no more, parted with many an embrace and many a tear, one to wait for his kingdom and the other to lay down his life and know that he was yielding his kingly prospects, his very crown, to the friend he loved.

It was to Jonathan's interest even more than Saul's that David should die, because David's survival meant that he should succeed to the throne of Saul. Jonathan knew this and, knowing it, accepted it, acquiesced in it, rejoiced in it, and gladly gave place to the one he loved, and at last laid down his very life, glad, perhaps, to know that the way was made clear for David's future throne.

UNSELFISH LOVE

The deepest principle of true friendship and, indeed, the greatest thing in the universe, is unselfish love. Satan delights to pervert the best things, and the way he perverts love is by inverting it and turning it into selfishness. The saddest thing in the world is that which ought to be the noblest but is the meanest, when even love itself becomes corrupted into its own opposite by terminating on itself. Whenever we love because of the pleasure it ministers to us we cease to love and it becomes self-love. True love always looks outward to the object and finds its pleasure in the pleasure it communicates and the blessing it gives. Love inverted and perverted becomes lust, which is the vilest blot and curse of human character and human history.

Do you know the secret of a holy friendship and a happy love? Learn to forget yourself, and live for others and to let your fondest affections and friendships minister blessing to those you love. The reflex action, without your seeking it, will be your own highest happiness.

God is love in this sublime sense. His constant occupation is to bless and, therefore, God is blessed, too, and His bosom is the source and the sum of all true joy.

THE HEAVENLY FRIEND

Jonathan was a type of the Friend who sticks closer than a brother. The friendship of David and Jonathan leads us up to the higher love of the Lord Jesus Christ for us, and the divine friendship which He permits us to claim with Him. If Jonathan's love was wonderful, passing the love of women, Christ's love is more wonderful, surpassing all human friendship and transcending all examples and tests of love.

Jonathan's heart was knit unto David and he loved him as his own soul, but Christ is not only knit unto us, but He is one with us. He has partaken of our very nature, our blood flows through His veins and He has loved us better than His own soul, for He poured out His soul unto death and laid down his life without a reservation, because He loved us and gave Himself for us.

Jonathan gave David his outer robe, and even his tunic, but Christ has given to us the robes of His glory and His kingly dignity, and the very raiment of His righteousness and His personal character and life.

Jonathan gave to David his sword, the very symbol of his power, and Christ has armed us with His own strength and given to us His own victory.

Jonathan gave David his bow as well as his sword, and Christ has not only armed us for the foes that are immediately around us, but He has given to us the weapons by which we can reach the very heights of heaven and the uttermost parts of the earth. By the bow of faith and the arrows of prayer, we can reach the omnipotence of God, and our influence can extend to the farthest reaches and the lowest depths of human sin and sorrow.

And Jonathan gave to David his belt. In one sense the belt binds all the raiment together, and might well represent the whole person and apparel. Christ gives us everything He has and is. The belt was especially the symbol of strength for service. The girded soldier was ready for battle, the girded servant ready for work. Christ girds us with His own power and enables us for the service which He claims from us.

And if the belt contains the more sacred treasures, containing his wallet, papers, money, jewels and the things he most prized, so Christ has given to us also the very treasures of His love and the very secrets of His confidence. He has held nothing back from us, but He takes us into His inmost heart and says to us, "I no longer call you servants, . . . I have called you friends, for everything that I learned from my Father I have made known to you" (John 15:15).

Most touching of all, however, is the fact that Christ, like Jonathan, has died for us that we might inherit His very throne and enjoy the rich bequests of His will. He has given us the New Testament as His last will, bequeathing to us our glorious inheritance, and He has risen again to secure it to us from every adversary or failure.

> Oh, what a wonderful place
>   Jesus has given to me!
> Saved by His glorious grace,
>   I may be even as He.
> All that He has shall be mine;
>   All that He is I shall be.
> Robed in his glory divine
>   I shall be even as He.

CHAPTER 15

AGAG, OR THE SUBTLETIES OF THE SELF-LIFE

Then Samuel said, "Bring me Agag king of the Amalekites."
Agag came to him confidently, thinking, "Surely the bitterness of
death is past."
But Samuel said,

> *"As your sword has made women childless,*
> *so will your mother be childless among women."*

And Samuel put Agag to death before the LORD at Gilgal.
(1 Samuel 15:32–33)

We have already referred to Samuel 15 as an illustration of Saul's character. But there is still a deeper type of the subtleties of the self-life in the picture of Agag, which the Holy Spirit has framed into the narrative of this solemn history. Both Saul's and Agag's lives teach the same lesson—offer the same warning—of the peril of a self-centered life. But they teach it in different ways, and the story of Agag is worthy of our prayerful and heart-searching consideration.

AMALEK OR THE FLESH

Agag belonged to the race of Amalek and the family of Esau, who represent through their entire genealogy the life of the flesh. From the beginning of the human race, God has drawn the line of demarcation between two races—the fleshly man and the spiritual man. Just outside the gate of Eden the division began. The family of Seth called themselves by the name of the Lord, while the race of Cain went off and built their city of culture and pride and became the pioneers of worldliness and wickedness, refined and ameliorated by all the grace of human culture and all the attractions of earthly delight.

257

The separation, though, soon began to disappear, and by the time of Noah the two races had mingled and intermarried. The result was progeny so degenerate and depraved that God turned with loathing from the whole race and pronounced the awful sentence, "I will wipe mankind, whom I have created, from the face of the earth" (Genesis 6:7).

After the flood God chose a separate family, the line of Abraham, and again endeavored to keep His chosen people separate. Down that family tree we see off-shoots separating from the central trunk and going out into the world. The first of these was Ishmael, a type of the spirit of bondage and sin. The next of these was Esau, the progenitor of a whole race who inherited the earthly spirit of their father—Isaac's son who sold his birthright for a morsel of meat and afterward married the daughters of Canaan, becoming as corrupt and polluted as they were. In the same line were the descendants of Lot's unnatural daughters, the Moabites and the Ammonites.

Above all this, the race of Esau and subsequently the Amalekites were the representatives of the spirit of the flesh and the world. This was the reason why God pronounced the decree of their extermination. We find that when the Israelites left Egypt and started on their journey to the Land of Promise, Amalek was the first to attack them. It is not difficult to see in this the foreshadowing of the fact that the first adversary we have to contend with when we leave our sinful past of bondage and iniquity is the carnal nature in our own hearts. It soon asserts itself and tries to force us back into that life of bitterness and captivity to sin (Acts 8:23). This is what Agag represents, and this is what each of us has found to be real in the experience of the Christian life.

THE SPIRIT OF PRIDE

The name of Agag is significant. It is from the root word *hak*, which is a generic term denoting, like Pharaoh, "a ruler." It represents the spirit of self-will, self-assertion and self-dependence. Its prototype is Lucifer, the prince of light and glory, who, being lifted up with pride and refusing to be controlled, turned from being an angel to a fiend and has become the desperate leader of the rebellious hosts of hell.

We see it next in the supreme temptation of the Fall: "You will be like God" (Genesis 3:5)—the desire for supremacy. We see it in the spirit of human ambition, in the despot, in the world conqueror, in high society and in politics. All belong to the same family—the race of Amalek and the house of Agag. Their cry is like the prodigal's: "give me my share of the estate" (Luke 15:12) and let me be free from parental control to do as I please.

There is no country where it is so rampant as our own United States. It appears to us as young mannishness and womannishness and calls itself liberty. But its end is lawlessness and that lawless one who is yet to embody the combined elements of human wickedness and pride, and end the present dispensation by defying God and man, and perishing, like his father, the devil, in his presumptuous pride.

This spirit is found in every human heart. It may be disguised in many insidious forms, and it may call itself by illustrious names and ape the highest ambitions and the noblest pretensions, but it is Agag and Satan every time. The thing in you that wants to rule, wants to have its own way, to be independent, to refuse control, to despise reproof, is wrong in its very nature. The first thing you need in order to be of any use anywhere is to be thoroughly broken, completely subjected and utterly crucified in the core and center of your will. Then you will accept discipline and learn to yield and obey in matters in themselves right, and your will will be so merged in His that He can use you as a flexible and perfectly adjusted instrument. Henceforth you will only do what God wills and choose only what God chooses.

This is the real battleground of human salvation; this is the Waterloo of every soul; this is the test question of every redeemed life. This was the point where Saul lost his kingdom and Agag lost his life, and where eternal destinies are lost or won as we learn the lesson or refuse to be led in triumph by our conquering Lord.

Let us mark it well. Let us not miss the warning. Let us remember forever that no man can rule others until he himself is absolutely led of God, that no man can conquer foes until he first is conquered, that no man can lead in triumph the hosts of evil or the hearts of men until he himself is led in triumph as the willing captive of the Savior's love and the Master's will.

THE FLESH MUST DIE

God has determined that the race of Amalek and the house of Agag should be utterly exterminated. They were not to be spared, but to be destroyed. It was a case of no compromise. There was nothing good in them. The last element of Agagism was destructive; and the whole community, with all their goods and belongings, must be put out of existence, just as in history when the effects of a household where some have died of contagious disease were wholly given to the flames.

This is God's decree against the flesh in us. It cannot be cleansed. It cannot be improved. It cannot be cultivated. It cannot be educated into ideals and principles. It must be exterminated.

What is the flesh? Is it the bad principle in man? Is it some outward or inward evil that can be cut away like a tumor by a surgical operation? "The sinful mind is hostile to God. It does not submit to God's law, nor can it do so. Those controlled by the sinful nature cannot please God" (Romans 8:7–8). There is the uncompromising decree of the total depravity and the hopeless condition of the flesh.

"You, however, are controlled not by the sinful nature but by the Spirit, if the Spirit of God lives in you" (8:9). There is the distinction clear as a ray of celestial light. Every man who does not have the Spirit of God is in the flesh. And everything outside the Spirit of God is flesh. Therefore, the flesh is not simply the sinful part of human nature, but the whole of human nature. It is the Adam race. It is the natural man. It is the whole creature, and the whole thing is corrupted and polluted. The tree is so crooked that it cannot be straightened without cutting it in two. The tumor is so interwoven with the flesh that you cannot cut it out without killing the man.

There is no remedy. There is no hope. The old life must be laid down and the new creation, wholly born of heaven and baptized with the Spirit of God, must take its place as a resurrected life, as a new creation, as an experience so supernatural and divine that its possessor can truly say, "I have been crucified with Christ and I no longer live, but Christ lives in me" (Galatians 2:20).

Do not try to sanctify the flesh. Slay it! Don't attempt to evolutionize the kingdom of heaven out of the kingdom of hell. It is not evolution; it is creation. It is not morals or manners; it is a miracle of grace and power. Take no risks with the old man. He will fail you every time. You may think your trained hawk is a dove, but in an unsuspecting moment its beak will be buried in your flesh. Your little wolf may have all the manners of a lamb, but in an evil hour it will destroy all your lambs and perhaps rend you limb from limb.

The flesh is hopelessly, eternally corrupt. It cannot please God, and it must be completely dethroned, renounced and crucified with Christ.

COMPROMISE WITH THE FLESH

We see next in this account the attempt of man to compromise with the flesh and to disregard God's decree for complete extermination. Saul spared Agag so that he might use him to build up his triumph before the people. He kept the best of the spoil that he might sacrifice them to the Lord.

He obeyed God's command to a certain extent. In a sense he defeated Amalek and destroyed the nation. Saul did all God told him to do as far as it was agreeable to him. But he took his own way when it served his self-interest. His obedience, therefore, was not really obedience to God but obedience to self. He retained just enough of the flesh to destroy the whole service.

The very essence of the command was extermination, and the very essence of the disobedience was compromise. The worst thing about it was that he tried to put the evil to good use. It was an insult in the face of heaven to bring the forbidden thing and offer it to the God he had defied. This is the spirit of modern religious culture: "Don't go too far. Don't be extreme. Don't be puritanical. Go easy. Be liberal. Meet the world halfway. Marry that scoundrel to save him. Take the bar owner into church membership because you can make good use of his money. Put that brazen-faced woman up in the choir because she will draw her theatrical set to hear her sing. Go to the theater and the play with your husband to get him to go to church with you on Sunday."

Nonsense! The devil will always get the best of you in such an unequal contest, and instead of being saved the husband will drag the wife to his level. Or the operatic singer, instead of bringing her friends under the influence of religion, will bring the church to the level of her set and turn it into a clubhouse and a concert hall. The bar owner's money will moderate the tone of the preaching so that it will be a comfort to Sodom, and vice and sin will sit unchecked and even count themselves the buttress and pillar of the cause of Christ.

Do you think God will accept such service? Will He who owns the treasures of the universe, He who could create a mountain of gold in a moment, He who could send a thousand angels to sing in His sanctuaries, accept the money that is stained with the blood of souls and polluted with the filth of dethroned purity and honor? Will He accept the meretricious service that is sold for sordid gain? Will He go begging to the devil's shrine, asking his permission to let go his captives that they may be saved? Absolutely not! Shame on our unfaithfulness and our compromise! Oh that we had the sword of Samuel to hew in pieces the compromises that are an offense to heaven and a disgrace to the bride of the Lamb!

INDULGENCE MASKED IN HUMILITY

We see the fawning pleading of the flesh for indulgence. Agag came forth, walking delicately, mincing like a silly, coquettish girl, smiling, seeking by his blandishments to disarm opposition, to win favor—looking like an incarnation of gentleness and innocence. Indeed, he was the perfect gentleman! Surely, he could not harm a child! Surely, no one could dream of doing him harm!

But that is the old flesh pleading for its life, pointing out its refinement, its culture, its graces, the good that it is doing and wants to do, its claim upon our consideration and regard. It will decorate our churches with the finest taste; it will sing in our choirs with all the harmonies of classical music and attract crowds; it will bring society to our churches; and it will give us a bright and liberal theology. It is full of humanitarian plans for the relief of the suffering and the uplifting of degradation, and it offers us a Pullman palace car prepaid to the gates of heaven.

Surely, such a beautiful, gentle creature should not be rudely slain. But behind its disguises and fawnings, the Holy Spirit will show you, if you will let Him, the serpent's coil, the dragon's voice and the festering corpse of the charnel house.

Death is not always repulsive at first sight. The daughter of Jairus was beautiful in her shroud and a flush of life still lingering on her cheek, but she was as dead as Lazarus festering in his tomb. And so that sweet-faced girl with her fawning charms, that brilliant minister with his intellectual sophistries, that voice that sings like an angel in the choir, is as corrupt and polluted as that poor creature that lies in the hospital dropping to pieces in the last stages of corruption, or that red-handed assassin reeking with the blood of his victim. They are both flesh, only at different stages of their moral putrefaction.

COUNTERFEITED CROSSES

We see in Agag the flesh feigning death. "Surely," said Agag, "the bitterness of death is past" (1 Samuel 15:32). Similarly we find plenty of people in pulpits and pews, on platforms and in obscure corners, who would make us believe that they are dead. Yet we are reminded, when we get a good look at them, of corpses walking around in their grave clothes. They are so conscious of their deadness that we know they are alive. They are so proud of their humility that we would rather they were proud than humble. And they are so constantly in their own shadow that they try us by their religious egotism.

Surely, people who are really dead do not know it, do not think about it, are unostentatious, unobtrusive, modest, simple, natural, free and, like good water, without taste, color or consciousness. Oh for this blessed simplicity and this place of self-forgetting rest! Oh for this fulfillment of the prayer, "Lord, let me die so dead that I will not know it!"

There is no danger so great, especially among Christians somewhat advanced, as that of counting ourselves in a place where we really do not live. There is nothing so hardening to the heart as to take the place of self-surrender and then live a life of self-indulgence, self-will and adding to it the greater fault of self-complacency—calling things holy that are not, bringing the heavenly standard down to our own experience and filling ourselves with a self-complacent dream. Truly, we are to reckon ourselves as dead, but we are not to reckon that we are reckoned dead. We are to reckon on a reality and to insist upon it and take nothing less from God or from ourselves. Oh that we would dare to call things by their right names and have no counterfeit, even from ourselves!

GOD'S SWORD

Finally, we see self exposed and slain. Agag could not deceive Samuel. The old prophet pierces him through with one glance of the Holy Spirit, and looking at his mincing, fawning figure, we can imagine him saying, "You cannot fool me. You are a murderer and a selfish, cruel tyrant. Your sword has made many a mother childless, and many an innocent victim has been crushed beneath your tyranny. Behind all your smiles is a skeleton and a serpent's sting." And then with that sharp sword, Samuel cut through his blandishments and hewed him to pieces before the Lord.

A notorious woman, who was once the star of the vaudeville stage, had in her role a hideous song in which one verse may be translated, "Go bring thy mother's heart to feed my dog." It is a true picture of that diabolical selfishness that seeks to hold the very soul of her idolatrous admirer in her power, that can even make him rend his loving mother's heart to please his devilish mistress. That is the skeleton back of the society queen. That is the serpent coiled around the heart of beauty and pride.

"But that is the darkest and worst picture," you say. Ah, but sin never stops until it reaches its worst. Here, God shows us the extent to which the smallest seed of selfishness can ripen.

Let us ask God to expose it in our hearts. Let us open our being to the sword of Samuel, the sword of the Holy Spirit. That sword is described in the solemn words of Hebrews: "For the word of God is living and active. Sharper than any double-edged sword, it penetrates even to dividing soul and spirit, joints and marrow; it judges the thoughts and attitudes of the heart" (4:12).

All that we need to be delivered from self and sin is to be willing to see it, to recognize it, to call it by its right name, to throw off its disguise, to brand it with its true character, to pass sentence of death upon it, to give God the right to slay it and to stand upon the sentence without compromise. Then there is power enough in the sword of the Spirit, in the blood of Calvary, in the faithfulness, love and grace of God to make us dead indeed to sin, but alive to God through Jesus Christ our Lord!

SAMUEL, KINGS AND CHRONICLES

INTRODUCTION

The eye of spiritual discernment loves to trace in the story of the Old Testament the type and foreshadowing of the New. The deliverance of Israel from Egypt's bondage looked forward to the grander story of human redemption. The victories of Joshua prefigured the apostolic age and the early triumphs of Christianity. The dreadful declension under the judges foreshadowed the dark ages of Christian history. The reformation under Samuel pointed toward the great Reformation of the 16th century. The reign of Saul was the counterfeit of the true kingdom; and so there is a worldly Church and even a false ecclesiasticism before the manifestation of Christ and the revelation of the Bride of the Lamb. At last David comes, God's true king. And the story of his rejection, exile and final triumph vividly foreshadows the conflicts and victories that are to usher in the reign of our Lord, and "make Jesus King." Finally the reign of Solomon, in all his glory, sets forth the great consummation, the millennial age, and the glorious reign of the King of kings and Lord of lords. This is the lofty theme which the following chapters and discourses attempt to trace. May they prove, through the blessing of the Holy Spirit, a divine incentive to make us "of one heart to make Jesus King."

CHAPTER 1

DAVID, THE MAN AFTER GOD'S OWN HEART

I have found David son of Jesse a man after my own heart; he will do everything I want him to do. (Acts 13:22)

David is the antithesis of Saul, and as the latter foreshadowed the counterfeit kingdom which Satan is trying to palm off on the world, so David represents the true kingdom and the true spirit of His kingdom. Let us look for the present at David's call and consecration to his high office as God's anointed.

SECTION I—*God's Seeking*

In First Samuel 13:14 the prophet is represented as saying to Saul, "The LORD has sought out a man after his own heart and appointed him leader of his own people." God was seeking a true man to represent Him in the government of His people. It is peculiar to notice how this language is used by the prophet of Judah's declining kingdom, "I looked for a man among them . . . but I found none" (Ezekiel 22:30). God is represented as seeking for a man who can understand His thoughts and represent His will. Even David afterwards failed to meet His expectation. And it was not until the Lord Jesus at length stood on Jordan's banks, the first spotless man since Adam failed, that God at length could say, "This is my Son, whom I love; with him I am well pleased" (Matthew 3:17).

GOD'S MAN

Saul had utterly failed and God was seeking for a man to take his place. But a little later the language changes and He exclaims, "I have found David my servant;/ with my sacred oil I have anointed him" (Psalm 89:20). God has discovered a true man, or, as the inspired Scriptures expresses it, "a man after my own heart; he will do everything I want him to do" (Acts 13:22).

269

What God wanted was a man after His heart. Saul was a man after his own heart and after the world's heart. He represented man's ideals of manhood and he aimed to gratify his own ambitions and work out his own plans. God, the true theocratic King of Israel, wanted a man that would simply represent Him, that would catch His thought and reproduce it and work it out in his life. The same testimony is borne to David elsewhere, when it is said, "David had served God's purpose in his own generation" (Acts 13:36). The aim of David's life was to do the will of God.

But there is a third passage in this chain of references which completes the story of David's call. It is First Samuel 16:1: "Fill your horn with oil and be on your way; I am sending you to Jesse of Bethlehem. I have chosen one of his sons to be king." God had been seeking a man and He had found him at last, and here the secret is told: "I have chosen one of his sons to be king." The reason he met God's expectations was because God had provided him. The people provided Saul. He was their choice; but God provided David contrary to the expectations of man and all outward appearances or probabilities. God never will find things that will satisfy Him until He first provides them. The secret of pleasing God is to possess God, and let Him possess you; for He gives what He commands and enables for that which He requires.

THE CONTRAST

As we look at these two men—Saul and David—it is not strange if we should sometimes be perplexed in reference to God's strong preference of the one and unqualified rejection of the other, for there was much in Saul to commend, and there was much in David to condemn. Saul was naturally noble, generous and brave. The very act of the character of Jonathan, his son, implies that there must have been something naturally good in the character of his father, so far as any fallen man can have any good in him. Then the early life of Saul has many attractive features. He seems to have been a dutiful son, seeking industriously for his father's lost asses, and when he failed to find them he quickly responds to the suggestion to go to the prophet and ask counsel of God.

There were some elements of piety apparent in his conduct; and when Samuel gave him his extraordinary commission, he behaved himself with singular propriety. He kept his secret well. He opened his heart to receive the Holy Spirit, who came upon him in a peculiar power. He joined a band of prophets and sang and ministered like them. If we except excessive humility in connection with his inauguration—in his hiding among the stuff—he seemed unobtrusive and becoming in his deportment.

His first exploits as commander and king of Israel's hosts were marked; and still later in his life attachment to David breaks out in the midst of his wild and passionate vindictiveness, and he breaks down and cries like a baby when he discovers the generosity of the man whose life he had been seeking.

Then, on the other hand, David had most glaring faults, notwithstanding all the beautiful traits of his personal character and his deep and genuine piety.

God's Word does not excuse the unbridled lust and the cool deliberate cruelty with which he could, as Nathan expresses it, snatch the one ewe lamb from the bosom of his faithful servant and soldier, Uriah, and then calmly and cunningly send that brave and loyal man, in the very ardor of his devotion to his king, right into the jaws of death, on purpose to get rid of his interference with his royal master's shameful selfishness. The worst of all is the torpor and paralysis of David's conscience, which for two whole years was utterly insensible to the double-dyed crime until God's strong reproof and chastening at length brought him to his senses, and struck a flash of light into his deadened moral sensibilities. God's faithful Word always tells the worst about the subjects of His grace. How then can we explain this strong language of preference in which God speaks of David and the une-quivocal censure which condemned and rejected Saul?

SELF-WILL AND GOD'S WILL

1. Saul represented self-will; David represents God's will. Saul's great object was to carry out his own ambition. David's chief desire was to understand and accomplish the divine purpose concerning him. When he erred he did it blindly, but the moment he recognized and realized his disobedience, he broke down like a penitent child. There was no self-will, no obstinacy, no rebellion in his spirit. There was error, terrible error. There was impulse, there was earthly passion; but his will was true to God when he really understood the will of God.

THE NATURAL AND SPIRITUAL MAN

2. Saul represented the natural man, and David the spiritual man. Saul was the embodiment of what was best in human nature. All that David had that was commendable was due to the grace of God, and speaking of his own life afterwards he could say with the deepest humility: "But who am I, and who are my people, that we should be able to give as generously as this? Everything comes from you, and we have given you only what comes from your hand" (1 Chronicles 29:14).

David was a monument of divine grace. Saul was the embodiment of human nature, self, selfishness and pride. God hates our pride and wants our weakness, self-renunciation, nothingness and dependence. David had learned the lesson of divine grace, and therefore God allowed him to be one of the princes in that kingdom of grace where our highest hope is the mercy of our God.

This is the kingdom to which we belong, and its watchword forever shall be, "Not to us, O LORD, not to us/ but to your name be the glory" (Psalm 115:1). It was because David had learned this watchword that God could choose him and use him notwithstanding even his gravest faults.

SORROW HARDENING OR SANCTIFYING

3. The sorrow and sins of Saul drove him further from God, while David's brought him nearer. This is one of the most certain tests of our spiritual condition: how are we affected by our trials? Do they discourage us, or do they drive us to the bosom of our heavenly Friend? Still more searching is the question: how are we affected by our faults, our failures and our sins, when we discover them? Do we try to cover them, to excuse them, or, failing in this, do we give up in discouragement and despair, and say, "There is no use trying; everything is against me"? Poor Saul went from bad to worse, and at last turned from God and sought counsel from Satan when the heavenly Source on which he had depended failed him at last. His trust never was quite true, or he would have clung to it most closely in the hour of darkness and seeming despair. David came out of his worse faults a better man, and God could teach him, even by his temptations and sins, to die to self and rise to loftier heights of the grace of God.

THE 51ST PSALM

There is nothing more perfectly instructive and more supremely strong than the trial of David's heart unfolded to us in the 51st Psalm, which gives us the inner history of his soul after his greatest sin. There is no notion of trifling, there is no excuse or palliation of anything. He paints his crime in the darkest colors. He talks of blood guiltiness. No, he goes deeper than his crime, to his own personal character, and he says, "I was sinful at birth,/ sinful from the time my mother conceived me" (51:5). He sees nothing good in himself. Every prop is gone, every hope is gone, as far as the human is concerned. After a life of blessed communion with God he stands self-convicted of inexcusable weakness and total depravity. Could a human soul ever be placed in a more terrible situation? But for the grace of God it would drive any man to despair and self-destruction.

But we see this man looking straight up into the clear blue sky of heaven and claiming with unshaken confidence the infinite mercy of his God, and the higher spiritual blessing that he had not before. "Wash me," he cries, "and I will be whiter than snow" (51:7). According to the days wherein he has seen evil so he dares to claim that God will bless him with the days of heaven. His profound penitence is only surpassed by his boundless faith. He sinks to the uttermost depth, and then he rises to the very heights of heavenly grace. This was, doubtless, the crisis of David's life. Out of this he came, not only a saved, but a sanctified man, crucified to self and to sin, and knowing, even as we know, in some measure at least, the indwelling of the Holy Spirit.

DAVID AND PETER

One cannot help being reminded of the parallel between this Old Testament story and the New Testament picture of Judas and Peter. Like poor Saul, Judas was driven by his sin to desperation and suicide. Like David, Peter sinned as deeply, but he received the unspeakable grace of repentance, and there was something in his heart which led him in his darkest sorrow to the mercy of Jesus. Judas "went away and hanged himself" (Matthew 27:5). Peter "went outside and wept bitterly" (Matthew 26:75), and when Jesus was risen from the dead and stood at length upon the Galilean shore, Peter did not slink away from His presence abashed and guilty, but he leaped into the sea and was the first to swim ashore, and there he is at the blessed feet of Him whom he had once dishonored. God give us all the spirit of grace, which even in our darkest sorrows and deepest sins will turn heavenward for mercy that will pardon, and grace that waits to help in time of need (Hebrews 4:16).

SECTION II—*David's Anointing*

David is anointed to his high calling. God has called His servant, now He sets him apart. Let us notice:

THE DEATH OF SELF

1. David's anointing immediately followed after the death of Agag. It is not until self dies that Christ can be enthroned as King in our hearts and lives. David cannot come in till Agag goes.

GOD'S THOUGHTS NOT AS OURS

2. David's anointing as the choice of God among all his brethren was contrary to every human appearance and expectation. Even Samuel expected that one of the other sons would have been chosen, but neither Abinadab's appearance nor Shammah's attractive person could meet the divine conditions. They were all passed by until the whole seven had been rejected, and they had to send for the youngest born, the lad of the family, whose extreme youth had made him kind of errand boy for all the rest and left him entirely out of sight on this occasion.

It was not accidental that David was the eighth of Jesse's sons, for the numbers seven and eight are especially significant and symbolic in the Scriptures. Seven represents the perfection of the old dispensation and the natural creation. It is the first week. Eight is the first day of the second seven, and thus it represents the new creation and divine order. Therefore, circumcision was on the eighth day representing the death of the old life and the beginning of a new life. Therefore was Christ's resurrection on the first day, which is also the eighth day, the beginning of the second week. The seven sons of Jesse represent the perfection and the completeness of the earthly; David, the eighth, represents the new generation and the new dispensation, the supernatural and the divine. It is not based on the conditions and qualifications which appear in the natural; therefore the stronger, the wiser, and the attractive, are passed by, and little David is chosen, instead of Eliab and Shammah; because "God chose the foolish things of the world to shame the wise; God chose the weak things of the world to shame the strong. . . . and the things that are not—to nullify the things that are, so that no one may boast before him" (1 Corinthians 1:27–29).

THE HOLY SPIRIT

3. David's anointing was more than an outward symbol. It was accompanied by a special impartation of the Holy Spirit, who came upon him from that day forward and enabled him for all his trials, duties and difficulties. David's life henceforth was supernatural and divine. The Holy Spirit was his counselor and his strength, empowering his arm for battle and instructing his brain for the demonstration of his great trust, and the vessel of the Holy Spirit and the instrument of the power of God. In like manner the Holy Spirit is our divine enduement for every need of our Christian life and work, and the direct source of complete supply and the equipment for every situation in which God can place us. He will give us wisdom and counsel. He will give us courage and faith. He will give us patience and love. He will work for us in the providences and circumstances of life. He will influence for us hands and hearts of men, and He will carry through our plans and purposes which are according to the will of God to success and blessing; and it is our privilege to count upon Him for all needed supplies, for every trust that is committed to our hands.

THE DIVINE SEAL

4. The supernatural anointing and enabling for this great trust is confirmed by God's manifest seal upon his life, that all men were made to know by his actual life and character that he was God's chosen and anointed one. God not only calls us, but He puts His credentials upon us and forces men to see that we are His chosen servants and representatives. And so we read in First Samuel, chapters 16 and 18 this extraordinary testimony that one of Saul's servants brought to the palace of the king, "I have seen a son of Jesse of Bethlehem who knows how to play the harp. He is a brave man and a

warrior. He speaks well and is a fine-looking man. And the LORD is with him" (16:18). What a testimony! Personally attractive, wise, judicious, with cultivated tastes, and a brave, valiant soldier; and, above all, a man of God. Beloved, God wants the world to see this in us also and to bear witness to it so manifestly that we shall not need letters of commendation, but our lives shall be living epistles known and read of all men (2 Corinthians 3:2).

First, God opened the way for his going to the court of Saul in the most natural and providential manner, as his companion and armor bearer, to cheer his nervous and distracted moments by his wonderful harp and gift of song, and to become acquainted with the life of the court which he was afterwards to fill so prominently. And so God will open our way if we are God's men. No combination of circumstances can shut you out. If you are right with heaven, every circumstance and providence will conspire to bring you the occupation, the opening, the work, the friends, for which you and God have need. You do not need to plead the wiles of human diplomacy and selfish influence to ingratiate yourself. David was not seeking the kingdom, the kingdom was seeking him. Beloved, wherever God has a David, a Daniel or a Joseph, He has a place prepared for him, and all the powers of earth and hell shall be unable to keep him out of it.

THE TEST

5. It was necessary once more that David should be proved; and so the situation came at last. The mighty Goliath had defied the armies of Israel and the God of heaven for days together, and no man had dared to answer his challenge. But one day David came to the camp to visit his brethren, and as he heard his defiant boast he modestly and simply answered, "Let no one lose heart on account of this Philistine; your servant will go and fight him" (1 Samuel 17:32). It did not even occur to him that he was doing anything unusual. It was so natural for him to be noble that he was unconscious of his own nobility. We need not dwell upon the stirring scene, the unobtrusive modesty and the fearless trust of the brave young warrior and the utter simplicity with which he committed the whole issue to the God of heaven— how could his trust be disappointed?

There was but a minute of suspense, as the giant stalked forth in his defiant pride, and the shepherd lad with his loaded sling ran down the valley to meet his foe, and hurling that stone with heaven-directed aim, saw the giant fall, his skull crushed in and his life crushed out, while all the Philistine hosts were flying in dismay, and Israel knew that God's choice was vindicated before earth and heaven.

The ordination that every true worker must have is not the placing of human hands upon our heads, but the living power of the living God, and the actual works of Christ wrought out in our lives. These are the credentials that man can understand and that no criticism can silence or neutralize. Oh, may the Holy Spirit thus choose, thus call, thus qualify and thus seal our lives and ministries.

CHAPTER 2

THE TRIALS AND TRIUMPHS OF DAVID'S FAITH

I am still confident of this:
I will see the goodness of the LORD
in the land of the living.
(Psalm 27:13)

And the God of all grace, who called you to his eternal glory in
Christ, after you have suffered a little while, will himself restore you
and make you strong, firm and steadfast. (1 Peter 5:10)

T hese two passages express the supreme lesson of the nine years of David's life that immediately followed his anointing as God's appointed king. It is the law of faith for God to give us the promise of blessing, and then put us to the test to see if we will hold our faith and prove worthy of our high calling. No life has ever been more severely tested than David's, and everything in his life, the record of his personal trials and triumphs, is given in such fullness of detail that we can walk by his side as we read the story; and we can even feel the beatings of his inmost heart as we follow the wondrous Psalms, in which he has given us the deeper portrait of his inmost heart and his spiritual experience.

SECTION I—*His Trials*

BITTERLY HATED

1. The first of these was Saul's jealous hate. The favor with which he met him at first and welcomed him to his palace and his court as his trusted minstrel and honored armor-bearer, and even as the captain of his guard, was soon turned into mistrust and jealousy as he saw that he had already won the hearts of the people. He began to feel that David was the dreaded rival of whom Samuel had already given him a solemn intimation. The first open

outbreak occurred when the maidens of Israel shouted the praises of Saul and David, and ascribed to Saul his thousands, and to David his 10 thousands, of trophies of victory. Saul "eyed" David, we are told, from that day forward and was very wroth. There is nothing more painful than to be the victim of keen-eyed jealousy, which watches all our movements and imputes wrong to the most innocent action. It injects a sting into every pleasure, and destroys the frankness and confidence of every friendship.

DECEIVED

2. Next, we find Saul intriguing for the destruction of David, and using even the affection of Michal, his own daughter, who loved the noble young Bethlehemite, and whose love her father played with. Saul wanted to inveigle David into a fatal snare and sacrifice his life while nobly striving to win the 200 Philistine lives which Saul demanded as the dowry of David's chosen bride. But God carried him safely through, and Saul had the mortification of having to give his daughter to the man he hated and placing him in the powerful position of the king's son-in-law.

ATTACKED

3. Next, we find Saul cherishing no longer a mere sentiment of jealousy, but a deep, determined purpose of destruction. Twice Saul hurled the javelin at David's breast as he played in his presence. When David was forced to flee Saul sent his officers to pursue David to his own home, where he was saved only by the strategy of his loving wife, who let him down through a window that he might flee from his pursuers.

PURSUED

4. Next, Saul pursued him even to Ramah, where he fled to the protection of Samuel the prophet; but as Saul and his soldiers came to the prophet's precinct, the old spirit of inspiration came upon him and his soldiers, and they were compelled to prophesy like the rest, and returned baffled by the interposition of God. But it now became too evident that Saul's purpose was unchanged, and that Samuel's protection could not save David from his murderous hands.

INNOCENT BLOOD

5. Next, he fled to Nob, the priestly city, where Ahimelech, the high priest, and the priestly colony dwelt, and there he obtained refreshment and also the direction of God through the priestly ephod, and took away with him the sword of Goliath. But, alas! he had soon the deep sorrow, far more distressing to him than his own danger, of learning that for this kind and hospitable act Ahimelech and the whole priestly family had been cruelly

slain by the order of Saul, through the mean and treacherous tale-bearing of Doeg, the Edomite, who had been the witness of Ahimelech's kindness and had quickly gone to Saul to tell the tale.

It was in vain that Ahimelech pleaded that he only meant to honor Saul in honoring his son-in-law and knew nothing of the trouble between them. His life was ruthlessly torn from him, and when even Saul's soldiers refused to touch the Lord's anointed priest the low and despicable Doeg was only too glad to do the work. With his own hand he slew in cold blood 85 of the priests of the Lord. And not only so, but the very city of Nob was razed to the ground and every living creature in it was ruthlessly murdered. David learned from Abiathar, the only survivor of this tragedy, the fearful story, and his heart must have been crushed with the deepest of all griefs—that of being the innocent occasion of bringing ruin upon others because of their attachment to him.

SEPARATED

6. The next great sorrow that came to David was the loss of his own dearest friends. Michal, his wife, was cruelly taken from him, and given to a neighboring chief with the hope that he would become the murderer of David through jealous rivalry. Jonathan, his dearest friend, became separated from him, and after one more parting they never met again. Samuel, his aged and venerated father in the Lord, was separated from him for the remainder of his life, and when the old prophet died and was buried with high honor in Israel, David was not permitted to stand by his bier to pay the last tribute of affection to the man who would have appreciated his presence more than all the others. Even his own father and mother became separated from him, for with loving consideration for their safety he early took measures to remove them from Bethlehem where they were sure to be the objects of Saul's unkindness, and to send them away over to the land of Moab to a remote kinsman of his, through Ruth, his ancestress, until his own plans should be settled. Henceforth he was alone and friendless, a fugitive among the mountains, with no friend to comfort him but God alone.

AMONG STRANGERS

7. Next, he fled to Achish, the king of Gath. Here he found himself in even greater danger, for Achish and the Philistines remembered but too well his victory over Goliath, their champion, and he had to find means to escape with his life from the Philistine court. It must have been a peculiar trial to the simple, frank nature of David to have to resort to artifice for self-protection.

A FUGITIVE

8. His next refuge was the cave of Adullam in one of the valleys of

southern Judea, and there his camp became the resort of all the outlaws, criminals and discontented persons in the land, who fled to his standard because of a certain community of distress and helplessness. So the man who had been accustomed to the sweetest of associations and the most congenial friendships found himself the chief of a band of freebooters, a sort of Rob Roy, at the head of a lot of vagabonds whom he had to accept as his comrades and friends.

Oh, you who complain of uncongenial associations, learn a lesson from the life of David. He did not complain about his associates, but he set himself to lift them up to his own level. Before he got through every man of them was a nobleman, and they were trained to be the future princes of Israel. This is what Christ did when He came down from heaven to be the companion of rude and ignorant men of earth. This is the honor of the missionary who goes among the heathen, and, overlooking all their degradation and misery, finds it his chief honor and glory to lift them up to the loftiest and noblest lives, and, like Christ, who has thus lifted us, found his joy in realizing the glorious transformation. If God has associated you with those who are beneath you, lift them, inspire them, and let the wilderness and the solitary place of your life rejoice and blossom as the rose.

TREACHERY

9. Next, he has the bitterness of treachery. While a fugitive in the mountains he found that the Philistines had invaded the land and attacked the city of Keilah, and he personally marched to its rescue and saved it from its enemies. But, in turn, instead of gratefully remembering his kindness, the men of Keilah plotted to betray him into the hands of Saul, and, but for God's forewarning through the oracle of the priest, he would have perished through this cruel conspiracy. There are few trials harder than to have our kindness met by base ingratitude, and to have those we have befriended and even saved become our cruelest foes. Was there any cup of sorrow that David did not drink?

HUNTED

10. Next, we find him pursued by Saul even into the wilderness with a troop of 3,000 soldiers, until he had to fly from place to place and find new refuges among the barren mountains and the precipitous fields of Maon, En Gedi and the desolate region around the Dead Sea. But all through this God protected him, and enabled him on two occasions to have the opportunity of taking the life of Saul had he so wished, and of proving his magnanimity in the very sight of the king. Day by day for weeks and months he was hunted like a partridge in the mountains. His life was continually in his hand, and the strong language of many of the psalms can only be under-

stood as we realize his imminent and instant peril and his marvelous escapes from destruction. Are you in a position of danger? Is your life assailed? Are you surrounded by enemies on every side? The God of David still lives to deliver those who trust Him and sends His angels to encamp around their dwelling.

NABAL THE CHURL

11. One of the meanest trials of his wilderness life was the churlish and niggardly Nabal, a shepherd of Carmel, who, after David had protected his herdsmen and his flocks for several months in the mountains, turned back his messengers with coarse insult and sent to David the rude taunt that he was probably a runaway slave from his master, and why should he give him his flesh or his bread. For once David was provoked to wreak sudden vengeance on this miserable cur, but was saved from the crime by the tact of Abigail, Nabal's beautiful wife. There are times when the bite of a mosquito is more trying than the roaring of a lion. There are little imps in life that worry us more than the larger foes that assail us, and we need more grace to keep our sweetness amid the thousand petty and harassing worries than in the roar of the torrent and the crash of the tempest. David knew this, and Christ knew it well. The last and bitterest trials of the cross were the taunts and the jeers and insults of the crowd whom He could have withered by a glance had He allowed Himself for a moment to lose the victory of His love.

AN EXILE

12. The crowning trial came at last when, in a moment of utter discouragement, he said, "One of these days I will be destroyed by the hand of Saul. The best thing I can do is to escape to the land of the Philistines" (1 Samuel 27:1). So, in an hour of unbelief, he left the land where God had told him to stay, and went down and accepted a home at Ziklag, which he made his headquarters for nearly a year and a half. Thence he went out on marauding expeditions against the Philistines, carefully concealing his movements lest they should drive him from the country, working all the while with loyalty toward his own land.

DISASTER

But at last the crowning disaster came, when he returned one day with his soldiers to find Ziklag a heap of smoldering ashes and all their wives and property carried away by a horde of Amalekites. For a while they could only lift up their voices and weep, and we are told that they wept until they had no more power to weep. It was an hour of hopeless despair, and at last David's very companions turned upon him, and even threatened to stone him as the occasion of all their sorrow. But just then shines out the triumph of his faith, and it is added: "But David found strength in the LORD his God" (30:6). Quickly he sent for Abiathar, the priest, and asked counsel of God, and by divine direction he pursued and overtook the raiders. Striking them with sudden surprise, David scattered them and recovered all the spoil, their wives and children and their property unharmed. Indeed, so vast was the booty that he was able to send a portion of the spoil to all his friends in Judah as a kind of foretaste of the kingdom which he was soon to bring them.

Such were some of the tests and trials of David's early life. God gave him the promise of the kingdom, and then He put him to the test for nine bitter years until he was disciplined and trained for his high calling.

SECTION II—*His Triumphs*

Notice the spirit in which he endured these trials:

PRUDENCE

1. It was with the spirit of prudence. He was not reckless and he did not bring needless trials upon himself, as we often do. Many of our afflictions are simply the results of our imprudence or foolishness; but we are told expressly that "[David] had great success" (18:14), and gave no occasion to his enemies to reproach him or to take advantage of him. It is a great thing in the hour of sorrow to maintain a good conscience, and, looking up into the face of God and man, to be able to say, "My conscience is clear" (1 Corinthians 4:4).

SWEETNESS

2. He kept his sweetness and his love through all the bitter provocation. Again and again the enemy tried to make him meet hate with hate and wrong with wrong, but he triumphed in the end in the spirit of generosity and love, and in spite of the injustice of Saul, he made even that wicked man acknowledge his own righteousness and magnanimity when he might have taken his life, and nobly spared him notwithstanding the demands of his own soldiers that he should slay him when God gave him the opportunity. Next to a good conscience is a sweet spirit in standing through tests and trials. Love can endure all things, but even faith will break down if we lose our gentleness and become irritable and vindictive.

FAITH

3. He overcame by faith. It was this that Satan assailed as he ever does. It is the trial of our faith which is much more precious than gold that perishes. It is thus that he assailed the Master in the wilderness. God had told Jesus

that He was His beloved Son, and then suddenly He plunged Him into circumstances of deepest distress, and Satan pointed to the barren desert and
the naked rocks and Christ's own physical hunger, and he whispered with a
horrid sneer, "If you are the Son of God" (Matthew 4:3, 6). But Christ
believed in His Father's love and waited for His Father's deliverance. And so
Satan comes to us and points to our distress, tries to make us doubt our
promise; but let us never let go our confidence, but hold it fast, for it has
great recompense of reward. God is just waiting to see if we will trust Him
to the end.

JOYFULNESS

4. David not only believed, but he rejoiced. More even than faith and the
very blossom and fruit of faith is the spirit of joy and praise. All through
those days of darkness, David kept his joy and his song. He not only trusted
but he rejoiced. He not only stood, but he stood singing, triumphing and
rejoicing, and out of these dark hours have come to us the sweetest of his
psalms and the noblest notes of victorious praise that are found in this
wonderful Psalter with its unequalled notes of joy and triumph.

PSALMS OF LIFE

Space will not permit us to go over all the psalms which are described with
some prefix connecting them with these days. There is the 59th, written
when they were watching his house to slay him. There is the 11th, sung
when he was like a bird driven to its mountain and hunted as a partridge
among the hills. There is the 57th, composed when he was in the cave; and
the 52nd, when he heard of Doeg's despicable crime against the priests of
Nob; and the 54th, when the Zithites are treacherously trying to sell his life
to Saul. But out of them all there are no grander songs than four that we will
specially name:

One of these is the 27th, a psalm of triumph, which was written just after
he parted from his father and mother in the land of Moab, and was left
alone in the desert. Oh, what a new meaning it gives to the words literally
translated, "Though my father and mother forsake me,/ the LORD will
receive me" (27:10). Oh, what a lofty elevation it adds to the shout, "The
LORD is my light and my salvation—/ whom shall I fear?/ The LORD is the
stronghold of my life—/ of whom shall I be afraid?" (27:1). "I am still confident of this:/ I will see the goodness of the LORD/ in the land of the living"
(27:13).

The next of these psalms of praise is the 34th, perhaps the richest of all the
psalms of David in the spirit of triumphant praise. But we may have often
failed to notice that this psalm was written when David was driven from the
presence of Achish, the king of Gath, and was supposed to be out of his

mind. People still think us out of our mind when we use his language, but he was anything but crazy when, amid his desolation and helplessness, he could look up and say, "I will extol the LORD at all times;/ his praise will always be on my lips" (34:1). "A righteous man may have many troubles,/ but the LORD delivers him from them all" (34:19). And thus looking over all his foes, he could add, "The angel of the LORD encamps around those who fear him,/ and he delivers them" (34:7).

There is another of these memorial psalms, written just after God had delivered him from the hand of all his enemies and from the hand of Saul. It is, perhaps, the most elegant in imagery of all his compositions. How vividly he speaks of his sorrows: "The cords of death entangled me;/ the torrents of destruction overwhelmed me./ The cords of the grave coiled around me;/ the snares of death confronted me" (18:4–5). How sublimely he describes the interposition of God for his deliverance (18:10, 16–19). How eloquently he describes the glory of his divine Friend (18:29–35). How tenderly, as a soft undertone, there sings through all the magnificent oratorio of his praise that little soft, sweet chord that tells at once the story of David and of God, "You stoop down to make me great" (18:35).

There is yet one more psalm which, while written later in David's life, doubtless refers all through to the story of David and of Saul. It is the 37th Psalm. Back of these wonderful beatitudes there are two figures that we can clearly trace. One of them is the man of hate who seeks to slay the righteous. The other is the man of meekness who frets not because of evil doers, who trusts in the Lord, who commits his way unto the Lord, who rests in the Lord and waits patiently for Him. The culmination is, "I have seen a wicked and ruthless man/ flourishing like a green tree in its native soil,/ but he soon passed away and was no more;/ though I looked for him, he could not be found" (37:35–36). And then, "Consider the blameless, observe the upright;/ there is a future for the man of peace" (37:37). "The meek will inherit the land/ and enjoy great peace" (37:11).

Truly out of David's sorrow came David's songs. What is God getting out of our trials? What are we getting out of them? Are we meeting them with wisdom, with love, with faith and with praise? After 3,000 years are we yet so far behind the man who not only sang, but who lived the song of faith and praise in life's darkest hour? Do we wonder that he was "a man after [God's] own heart" (1 Samuel 13:14)? God help us to be more like him, too!

CHAPTER 3

MAKING JESUS KING

You are those who have stood by me in my trials. And I confer on you a kingdom, just as my Father conferred one on me. (Luke 22:28–29)

David left Gath and escaped to the cave of Adullam. When his brothers and all his father's household heard about it, they went down to him there. All those who were in distress or in debt or discontented gathered around him, and he became their leader. About four hundred men were with him. (1 Samuel 22:1–2)

All the rest of the Israelites were also of one mind to make David king. (1 Chronicles 12:38)

We have looked at David as a fugitive. We are now to behold him crowned a king. Nine years of bitter persecution are exchanged for 40 years of glorious triumph. In his kingdom we behold a type of the kingdom of his greater Son and the crowning of Jesus Christ as earth's millennial Sovereign. In the loyal fellow-sufferers and soldiers who so nobly fought to win for David the high crown of Israel, we behold the picture of men and women that God is summoning today to follow our rejected and crucified Master outside the camp, in reproach and suffering, to win for Him the crown of all the world and then to sit down with Him on His throne even as He has sat down with His Father upon His throne.

It is said of the proud Napoleon that he refused to be crowned by human hands, but with his own arrogant fingers he placed upon his brow the crown of what he designed as the world's last empire, and stood before the world a self-made monarch. Our blessed Lord and Savior, while He might well conquer His own kingdom without the help of any of His followers, chooses to take it from our loving hands and to permit us to share with Him at once His sufferings and His glory.

THREE STAGES

In the followers of David and in the successive stages of his triumph and coronation we see the most vivid foreshadowings of the age to come, upon which we are about to enter. There were three stages in David's kingdom.

1. The Wilderness

The first was his trial, when he was a fugitive from Saul, and his court was the cave of Adullam, and his followers the outcasts of Israel. In like manner our blessed Lord is also as yet a King without His crown, still driven outside the camp, rejected by the world and followed by a faithful few to whom He is still saying, "You are those who have stood by me in my trials" (Luke 22:28).

2. Crowned at Hebron

The second stage of David's kingdom was his coronation at Hebron, where for seven and a half years he reigned over the tribe of Judah alone, while Abner maintained for Ish-Bosheth, the son of Saul, at Mahanaim, a temporary crown and kingdom over the other tribes of Israel. So, in like manner, our Lord Jesus Christ is to have at His coming the first fruits of the gospel, the called-out ones of the first resurrection, and He shall form with them the government and the rulers of the millennial age; for God is not now calling to Himself the subjects of His future kingdom, but He is calling out its rulers, and preparing the men and women who are to form His cabinet and sit with Him on His throne in the age to come.

3. The Throne of Israel

There was a third stage in the kingdom of David when, more than seven years later, he became the king of Israel, and the whole land recognized its sovereign. His scepter extended over the surrounding nations until he was the ruler of an important and more mighty kingdom than any of his time, reaching from the Mediterranean Sea to the Euphrates, and from the Persian Gulf to Damascus and Lebanon. And so there will be a heavenly stage in the kingdom of Christ when, in the millennial years, He shall reign from sea to sea, and all the nations shall be subject to Him, and earth's millions shall, without exception, own His peaceful sway.

Now we are called to take part in the first two stages, to be true to Him in His exile, and to reign with Him in His first coming, and then to sit at His side and rule over the universal empire which He is then to bring.

Let us look at the men that helped to make David king, and let us emulate them and be "of one mind to make Jesus King."

SINFUL MEN

1. They were sinful men; they were outcast men; they were men without a character or a reputation; they were men in debt and deep discredit, men under a cloud and without a hope, whom the instinct of a common sorrow drove to David's side in the caves and mountains of Judah. David accepted them, not because they were bad men, but because they were true to him, and he trained them and lifted them up to his own level and afterwards made them his princes and commanders in the kingdom of Judah and Israel. And so our Leader and Lord is calling to His side and choosing for His kingdom not the mighty and the noble of the earth nor always the good, but He hath chosen the "weak things" and the "foolish things" and the "despised things" and "the things that are not" (1 Corinthians 1:27–28). Yes, He has even chosen the most worthless, hopeless and sinful of our race to be the special objects of His mercy and the prized jewels of His crown.

It is the noblest nature that Satan seeks to devour and destroy. When a man is at his worst, you may be sure that he might have been at his best under different influences. God takes such men and turns them back to their true center, and there is power in the blood of Christ and in the Spirit of God not only to blot out the past but to transform the character, and out of the thistle and the thorn to create the fir tree and the myrtle for the paradise of God. Don't let your sinfulness keep you back. Don't let your misery discourage you. Don't let your failure crush you. Others have failed you. You have failed yourself. Hope is gone. All is lost. There is One that will receive you still. One drop of His blood will make you pure. One touch of His hand will make you noble, and in one moment you may pass from the kingdom of darkness into the kingdom of God's dear Son and the aristocracy of the new Jerusalem.

TRUE MEN

2. They were true men. The one redeeming quality of their lives was that they loved David and were loyal to him. When they first came to him, David had good cause to suspect their motives, and he frankly looked them in the face, and said: "If you come to me in peace, to help me, I am ready to have you unite with me. But if you have come to betray me to my enemies when my hands are free from violence, may the God of our fathers see it and judge you" (1 Chronicles 12:17). Then came the frank reply, "We are yours, O David!/ We are with you, O son of Jesse!/ Success, success to you,/ and success to those who help you,/ for your God will help you" (12:18).

No matter how lost a man may be there is one thing that may always become a link of hope and a bond of contact with God, and that is the simple, single, rare and indispensable quality of true sincerity. If the worst of men can look up into your face with an honest look and an earnest heart and say, "God knows, and you know, that I mean to be true," there is hope, there is salvation for him, and all the resources of God's grace and strength are on his side. But a traitor, a double-hearted man, a man with a reservation, a man, who, back of all his pretenses and services, is seeking his own interest and ready to barter all else for it in the supreme moment, that man is base to the core, a man of whom we may well be afraid in every true work. He is bound to betray himself at last. He is the most unfortunate creature on earth. The very object which he is seeking will yet fail him, and detected by all men, rejected by God and execrated by himself, he will go down to the damnation of a hypocrite and a traitor.

BRAVE MEN

3. These men were brave as well as true. They were not afraid of danger. Their faces were as the face of lions, and even Jordan's swelling floods could not dismay them. They did not wait for propitious circumstances or favorable seasons, but they made circumstances subservient to their high purpose and turned difficulties into stepping-stones of victory. They came up to Jordan in the first month, when all its waves had overflowed, and they found on both banks of the river a strong force of armed foes; but they met their enemies on the eastern shore and scattered them. Then they plunged into the swollen floods and swam and forded the raging Jordan, and when they landed on the western bank, another army was confronting them. But again they charged their foes and scattered them, and came to David victorious over flood and foe.

And so the men that would make Jesus King must not wait for favorable circumstances nor be intimidated by the devil's growl. The best evidence that you are in God's will will often be some sudden difficulty, some fierce assault of the foe, some bitter trial of your faith. When Paul began his great campaign to give the gospel to Europe, the first place he found himself was in the Philippian jail with bleeding limbs and feet fettered in stocks. But this did not dismay him. Rather he accepted it as a pledge of the devil's hate and the Father's love and he went forward undismayed until all Europe had received the gospel, and victory had been wrung from the defiance of the foe.

God is preparing men today for days of conflict, danger and the utmost trial, before the Lord shall come. Let us not shrink from the higher classes in the University of God and the School of Sorrow. There all great souls have graduated, and there all high character must be proved. God give us courage, and make us brave enough to believe all that this Book declares, to testify to all we believe, to live all that we testify, to do what others only dream about and glory in what others dare to do.

ALL-ROUND MEN

4. They were all-round men. "They were armed with bows and were able to shoot arrows or to sling stones right-handed or left-handed" (1 Chronicles 12:2). So many Christians have only one hand for service; the other is so busy grasping for the world that they cannot be whole-hearted for God, or free-handed for work. So many men can work when things suit them, but cannot adjust themselves to unfavorable circumstances and unusual methods. God wants ready men, and all-round men, who can meet the devil, who can adjust themselves to all the necessities of the Master's work.

MEN OF FAITH

5. They were men of faith. They "could handle shield and buckler" (1 Chronicles 12:8, KJV). The shield is the type of faith. The buckler is the type of a kind of faith that we do not have to keep, for it keeps us. It is what Paul calls "the faith of God" (Romans 3:3, KJV). It is a divine trust wrought within us by the Holy Spirit and fixed, like the buckler, which was fastened on the arm, and still remained even though the shield might fall and every other defense be lost. The work of hastening our Master's kingdom needs men of mighty faith, with a divine trust which rests not even on their own best feelings, but is nothing less than the faith of the Son of God who lives within (Galatians 2:20).

SELF-SACRIFICE

6. They were men of self-sacrifice. They shrank from no peril or pain when their leader needed their service or their sacrifice.

A noble example is given of three of these heroic men who one day, when David longed for a drink from the well of Bethlehem by his father's gate, dashed through the ranks of the Philistines, who filled the valley between, and while their enemies scattered on either side, or looked on with amazement, they brought back a helmet full of crystal water and handed it to their king. But David would not drink of that which was the blood of men who had jeopardized their lives for him.

The richest quality of love is sacrifice, and the noblest credential of any work is the spirit on the part of the members which has laid every selfish interest down at Jesus' feet, and counts all things loss for Christ (Philippians 3:7); which holds its money, its friendships, its life, all subservient to the Master's claim, and, living a dying life, at last gives life itself as a willing offering to Him who gave His life for us. In this selfish and luxurious age, it is the rarest quality found, but it is the most needed, and as the end approaches and the last tribulation draws near the age of martyrdom will reach the climax, and the tears of sorrow and the blood of sacrifice be transformed into the jewels of the coronation day. It needs a greater sacrifice sometimes to live than to die, and the men who will be found some day ready to die for Christ are those whose lives are now laid down in 10,000 little tests that come to us all from day to day.

WISE MEN

7. They were wise men. They "understood the times and knew what Israel should do" (1 Chronicles 12:32). Christ needs more than blind devotion. He wants intelligent partnership in service. He still needs men that have understanding of the times, not wasting their lives on ideas that are obsolete and for work that is needless, but grasping the Master's thought and working out His plan for the age in which we live. "David served his own generation by the will of God" (Acts 13:36, KJV).

It is a great thing to understand the will of God for our own generation and fulfill it. Millions of dollars are thrown away today in building costly cathedrals and ambitious universities for the display of man's ecclesiastical and intellectual pride, none of which helps forward in the faintest degree the kingdom of God or the coming of Christ. Many a well-meant offer is wasted for lack of sympathy with the Master's thought. Millions are giving and working today to get the world converted instead of working intelligently with Christ to gather out a people for His name, and to hasten His return and the inauguration of that day which will accomplish more for the conversion of the world than all the centuries of our ignorance and failure.

DISCIPLINE

8. They were disciplined men. They "were fighting men who volunteered to serve in the ranks" (1 Chronicles 12:38). They were working together. They were working in unity, in order, and in wise organization. Many a brave man throws his life away in isolation and independent efforts, and they fail because of no wise cooperation. The great work of missions requires fellowship of service, and intelligent organization by which workers on the field can stay in touch with those at home, and all together move as an army in wise and intelligent cooperation. Christ wants men who are able to subordinate their own strong opinions and work in subjection to one another in the fear of God. No man is fit to lead until he has long learned to follow. No man is a good commander who has not proved a perfect soldier. No lesson needs more to be learned by young missionaries than the lesson of humility and mutual subjection in Christian service. It has been wisely said that there is no trouble in getting along with a fully consecrated Christian, but a half consecrated one is always in trouble and always getting others into trouble.

PATRIOTIC

9. They were men of one patriotic purpose: to make David king. They had a sublime ambition and a single aim, and to this all else was subordinate. They were there to make David king. This suggests the real purpose of Christian consecration and service in our day. Our business is to make Christ King. It is not to achieve for ourselves a high position. It is not even to save a great multitude of souls. It is not even to build up a cherished cause, but it is so to sacrifice and witness that we will hasten the return of our blessed Lord.

It may be hastened. God's times are not wholly regulated by the progress of centuries and the lapse of years, but by spiritual conditions. One generation may live as much as 10 that preceded it; and by wise and patriotic energy, we may hasten the coming of the Lord in our own lifetime by working for the preparation of His bride and the immediate evangelization of the world. Often in the last few years it has seemed as if the providential conditions of His advent were just about to be fulfilled, and the great political events of the world were converging to the crisis. But something seems to hold, and that one thing is the spiritual preparation and the sanctification of Christ's own people, and the calling out from among the Gentiles of the remnant of His bride.

Let this be our object, and thus let us be of one mind to make Jesus King. That is what our world needs. All other plans must fail, all other governments disappoint, all humanitarian, moral, social or political movements end in confusion. The only remedy for all earth's wrongs is Jesus. The only campaign that will never disappoint its self-denying leaders and martyr followers is the noble campaign of true hearts bound in one ambition to make Jesus King.

FUTURE KINGS

And let us not forget that the men who made David king were the men that reigned with him when the kingdom came. The fugitives of the wilderness became the nobles of Israel. The outcasts of Adullam became the aristocracy of Jerusalem. Christ is, as we said at the beginning, calling out not the subjects of His future kingdom but the rulers. The millennium will bring earth's millions to His feet, but these days of testing and of conflict are bringing to Him the tried and the faithful ones who are to sit with Him on His throne and share with Him the government of the millennial age.

CHAPTER 4

CAPTURING THE STRONGHOLDS

But thanks be to God, who always leads us in triumphal procession
in Christ. (2 Corinthians 2:14; compare with 2 Samuel 5:6–10)

The remarkable passage which is found above is susceptible of two translations: "Thanks be to God who always *leads* us in triumph," and "Thanks be to God who always *causes* us to triumph." Together, they express a profound truth, namely, this: that the conqueror must first be himself subjected, and that it is when we have been led in triumph by our Lord and all our being laid in subjection at His feet, that we go forth in turn to be "more than conquerors through him who loved us" (Romans 8:37).

JEBUS

This great truth is illustrated in the story of the capture of Jerusalem and the establishment of David's throne in the ancient stronghold of the Jebusites. Its former name was Jebus, the down-trodden. Its permanent name was Jerusalem, the city of peace. Its story is remarkable.

Naturally impregnable by its situation and its defenses, this ancient citadel had defied the conquests of Joshua, the Judges and even Saul. David himself had reigned for seven and a half years at Hebron, and still Jebus was in the hands of the enemy. It was held by a little tribe, many of whom were helpless cripples, but they dwelt so secure in their lofty fastness that they defied their more powerful adversaries. And so centuries had passed, the Land of Promise had been won, the throne of David had been established, and yet the most beautiful and the most important spot in all the land was held by the enemy.

As soon as David, however, was put in possession of the throne of Israel he decided with great wisdom and force to change his capital from Hebron to Jerusalem—the natural center and metropolis of the land. He offered a splendid bribe to the man who should take it, and Joab was quick to answer the challenge. But so confident were the Jebusites of their absolute security that they laughed to scorn David's peaceful proposition to them to surrender, and they added insult and defiance to their refusal by suggesting to him that the blind and the lame were all the defenders that they needed. With skillful strategy and heroic bravery, Joab had his men scale the lofty citadel by way of the aqueducts, it would seem, and soon planted the standard of David on the heights of Zion. David's promise to Joab was redeemed, and he became henceforth the commander-in-chief of the armies of Israel. Moreover, the new citadel was immediately changed into a national capital. The loftiest height of Zion became the very stronghold of the city and the site of David's splendid palace, and a few years later the neighboring hills were covered with splendid buildings, and before long the height of Moriah, a little further to the east, was crowned with the Temple of Solomon, the architectural wonder of the ages.

The story of Jebus is full of spiritual lessons, and they are lessons of the deepest solemnity and lessons for the children of God at the most advanced stages of their Christian experiences.

SECTION I—*The Stronghold of the Enemy*

We see in Jebus the picture of the Christian life where, notwithstanding many a spiritual blessing and many a real experience, some secret place, some place of pre-eminent importance, is still under the control of self, or sin, or Satan. The land may be subjected, but one critical point is still held by the enemy.

A FEEBLE FOE

1. It was a feeble enemy. The Jebusites constituted but a little tribe, and they might easily have been expelled had their individual strength been the only thing considered. Their very smallness led them to be perhaps overlooked and despised. They seem to have had a great many cripples among them, for the walls were garrisoned by the blind and the lame. They were rather a contemptible few, and yet they held the strongest position in all the Land of Promise, and they held it for centuries. Beloved, there are little foes that are working more harm in our Christian life than more formidable adversaries. There are little borers that perforate the vessel's hull unseen, and in an unsuspected moment the ship founders in mid-ocean. There are little insects whose touch is almost impalpable, but whose sting is death. There are little ingredients, one drop of whose corrosive poison will destroy life itself in a moment. There are little foxes that only destroy the little buds, but with the buds they destroy the fruit and ruin the vines. There are little indulgences and little irritations, and little secret habits, and little dark corners in the heart, where Satan has just hold enough to have a partnership in our life.

Like the petty Hindu landowner, who held one small lot in a splendid town and refused to sell it to a wealthy millionaire, who had built a place nearby and wanted to own the whole estate. But the little fellow held on to his corner in spite of the most splendid offers, and one day when he met his wealthy neighbor he looked in his face with an inexpressible glance of vindictive triumph and hissed in his ears the words, "Don't forget, please, you and I own this town." All the devil wants is to have his finger in it, and be a partner in the concern with God and you. It gives him a respectability that the world could not confer. He would rather wear a white necktie than an epaulet. He would rather have a pulpit than a politician's seat. He would rather teach theology in a religious seminary than write the biggest novel of the age. He will let you put 99 parts in the pill and coat it with the finest sugar; only let him insert one grain of arsenic and he is satisfied. Look out for the little Jebusites, and be sure you don't despise the lame ones. There is nothing you so need to fear as the harmless habits, as you call them, which you think you could easily overcome and which you toy with sometimes until they destroy you.

AN ANCIENT FOE

2. These Jebusites were the descendants of Lot and his degraded daughter. They were born in Sodom, and they retained the awful odor of the slime pits. They represent the natural carnal heart, the things that are born in us, and that come to us by that awful law of heredity which enters so truly into every human life. There are men and women who come into this world under the power of a transmitted curse. It is a frightful thing to be a frivolous, selfish and godless mother, and to transmit your heartlessness and selfishness and deep depravity to the helpless child born of your selfish passion. It is a fearful thing to be an intemperate and brutal father and pass on to another life the frightful disposition which had made you a blot and a bane to every life which you have touched. Surely, it ought to be enough to live your worthless life without repeating the tragic story in some other existence which cannot help the misfortune of being born with your transmitted wickedness burning like an unquenchable fire in the very veins. It is a sad and bitter thing to inherit from a drunken father the love of alcohol, and to drink in from a mother's breast the duplicity, intrigue and heartlessness of a worldling's life and find yourself with a thousand foes within you to strive for your will and your self-restraint until you are often forced to cry, like one of old, "Old Adam is too strong for young Melancthon."

God knows this fight to be true and this principle to be a real moral power, and He has the deepest sympathy for those who come into existence with a birthright of terrible temptation. It is vain and presumptuous for you to think that you can overcome such adversaries. You cannot without the omnipotent grace of God, and even this will mean a battle as strenuous and as stern as life and death. Recognize at its full weight the power of your adversary and take God alone for the victory. You have not only an aggravating foe around you, but you have an inveterate enemy within you coiled around your very heartstrings and interwoven with the fibers of your being. It is the race of the Amorite. It is the carnal mind which "is hostile to God. It does not submit to God's law, nor can it do so" (Romans 8:7).

A PERSISTENT FOE

3. This tribe of Jebus had stuck to its stronghold for more than 500 years. Joshua's army had marched about, but the Jebusite still remained. Caleb's heroic followers had captured Hebron, but still the enemy held Jerusalem. The sun stood still on Gibeon and the moon o'er the valley of Aijalon, but the lofty heights of Zion were still securely held by the Amorites. Gideon's hosts swept on in victorious battle, Jephthah's legions drove out the vaster hordes of the neighboring nations, Samson went to and fro with gigantic strides, Jonathan and his armor-bearer smote the Philistines, Saul passed with his victorious armies from stronghold to stronghold and blotted out the whole tribe of Amalek, and even David was crowned king and had reigned for seven and a half years at Hebron—the type of Christ's victorious reign—and yet there was Jebus with its defiant defenders laughing at them. Oh, how it speaks of some enemy that has hidden away in your heart through years of blessing and victories of grace!

You have been converted, but still it has remained. You have seen yourself and your sin and yielded in sincere consecration and surrender up to all the light you had, and still that hidden foe was undisturbed. You have received the baptism of the Holy Spirit, and Christ has come to reign in the Hebron of your heart, and made it a place for His heavenly fellowship and love; yet, in the depths of your being there is a place where self and Satan still have enough control to assert themselves when they choose. Perhaps it is a little bit of the world still cherished. Perhaps it is a secret bitterness if not a forbidden love. Perhaps it is a friendship that God does not control. Perhaps it is a secret indulgence that you think as trifling as the blind and the lame of Jebus. Perhaps it is a habit that you have justified or ignored. Perhaps it is your cigar or your snuff-box, or your novel, or your love of music, art or the theater. Perhaps it is your sickness, which you finely cherish as an angel of light, and put the blind and lame on your fortifications as the defenders of your sanctification, and tell how much these things do to keep you humble and holy. Perhaps it is a little cherished misery or morbidness, just the faint right to pity yourself and feel bad sometimes; a little Jebusite just big enough for Satan to say, "Now, mind that you and I own this citadel."

A DANGEROUS FOE

4. They were an important and dangerous foe. The worst of all is that this subtle foe is usually enthroned in the most important center of our life. The Jebusites held the best position in the land. It was the very spot that God wanted for his capital. And so the thing which Satan seizes is always the best thing; and the place where self sits down is always the very throne of the heart. The devil does not want the offscourings of society. It is the noble, the beautiful, the gifted, the highborn, the men and women that should have been the very princes of the kingdom of heaven, that he selects as the instruments of his destructive sway, and the part of your being that he seeks to control is always the strategic point. It is your heart that he is aiming for; it is the singleness of your purpose toward God. It is your very spirituality that he will seek. And as an angel of light if he can sit down in the very secret of your being and make you serve him while you think you are doing God's very will, he is satisfied. It is Jerusalem that he uses for his reign. God help us to understand him, to expose him, to expel him, and, like David, to make his seat the very throne of heaven and the very glory of our after life!

Do not say, "I am not saved." "I am not sanctified, because I have discovered this thing still within my heart." I have been saved, I am utterly surrendered, but I have not known all the depths of Satan and the disguises of sin, but as I enter into the deeper light and larger opportunities I will have all "God's . . . good, pleasing and perfect will" (Romans 12:2).

SECTION II—*The Victory*

THE COURAGE OF FAITH

1. It takes a brave, victorious struggle. It was not an easy conflict. The height of Zion stands 300 feet above the valley of Hinnom, and up that cliff they had to climb and scale those rocks before they could drive out the enemy. And it is not easy for us to fight the good fight of faith, and refuse the insinuating wiles of self and Satan. Many a bitter tear, many a night of agony may have to intervene, and he who is not brave enough to suffer and to say "No" to himself can never enter into the heights of Zion and sit on the throne of David. "Better . . . a man who controls his temper/ than one who takes a city" (Proverbs 16:32). God help us to be brave enough to conquer self and to sit down with Christ upon His throne!

THE STRATEGY OF FAITH

2. It needs more than courage to win this conflict; it takes wisdom. We have the evidence of the deepest strategy as well as courage in the assault of Joab. David himself suggested the plan of the attack. It was to be by way of

the "water shaft." These water shafts seem to mean the water-courses or the aqueducts by which the city was supplied across the valley of the south, from the fountains on the heights of Bethlehem. But through these water-courses Joab's men seem somehow to have waded or climbed, and then entered the unsuspecting city, carrying all before them. This suggests, too, not unnaturally, that we, too, must win our fight by holy wisdom. We are not strong enough to overcome our spiritual foes, but there is a way by which we, too, may climb through the water-courses and accomplish by divine power what we ourselves are unequal to. Water is always the symbol of the Holy Spirit, and it is the Spirit who lifts up the standard when the enemy comes in like a flood. There is a heavenly stream into which we may plunge, and it will bear us through the difficulties and over the obstacles that we never can surmount.

A traveler tells a little incident which perhaps is in keeping with this thought and may illustrate this lesson. A little party descending one of the glaciers above the valley Chamouni, in Switzerland, suddenly found that the pass was closed by a heavy accumulation of ice and snow, and they could go no farther down. It was too late to go back, for the night was on, and it seemed at first that they must perish. But the guide looked carefully and noticed that the little stream, which they had been following, cut a channel in the ice, and he could hear it thundering on the other side of the mountain as it fell into the valley below. In a moment his resolution was made, and, bidding his companion follow him, plunged into the current and was followed by his dazed but obedient fellow-traveler. There was a sudden shock, a rush of waters, a moment of darkness, a strange terror and then a blaze of light, and they were thrown out on the other side of the mountain on the green, smooth bank of the little river in the valley of Chamouni. They had trusted themselves to the water-course and it had carried them through all their obstacles and difficulties.

Beloved, there are times when we fight in vain against our barriers and against our foes. There is a better way. Turn from self and Satan and everything inward and turn upward to Him. Receive the Holy Spirit, commit your way to God, wait on Him, be filled with the Spirit, plunge into the water-course, the current of God's mighty life and love, and you will forget your foes, you will forget yourself, and you will find yourself filled with God and lifted high above all your enemies and all your trials. Plunge into the water-course and let God make you "more than conquerors" (Romans 8:37).

SECTION III—*The Glorious Recompense*

THE CAPTAIN

1. There were two splendid results that followed this victory: the first was Joab's leadership over the armies of Israel, and all the victories that afterward

followed. And so when we win the complete victory over ourselves, we shall henceforth become conquerors, too, and a life of triumph shall surely follow. Led in triumph we shall always triumph. Oh, beloved, the reason you are always failing is because you have not allowed God to overcome in the supreme test of your life.

THE CAPITAL

2. The second result was the establishment of the city of Jerusalem as the throne of David, and later, the throne of God; for this is God's chosen city. It is not only the capital of Israel, but it is the city of the great King; and in the coming days it is to be the center of the earth, and perhaps in the same sense, the metropolis of the universe. And so when we let God overcome and win for us the victory of our lives in the hardest place, God chooses that place and sets His heart upon it, and loves it and honors it and uses it. And so the men and women that have dared to be true, and that, in the supreme test of their lives, have yielded and died to self and become God's bondslaves, God's conquered ones and God's conquering ones.

Beloved, what is the lesson for your life? Is there still some hidden thing, some unconquered place, some refuge of the enemy tolerated in the kingdom of your heart? God help you to see it, and to meet the issue as David did of old.

And so it comes to pass that we sometimes see a life that has seemed to be right and even eminently useful, at length go down like some noble ship at sea, and many have wondered and stood in awe. Ah, it was because there was a Jebus that had been left in the hands of the enemy, and in an unguarded hour the hidden foe arose and overcame the heart that had dwelt at ease.

TRANSFORMATIONS

3. And so, on the other hand, it comes to pass that we see a life that has gone on in comparative failure, and with little promise of strength or nobility, suddenly rise to the loftiest heights of heroism and spiritual power and become the glory and inspiration of some great movement; and we wonder. But when the secret is disclosed it will be found that it is the old story of Jebus, that the heart had found its secret foe, had risen as David rose against the Jebusites, had expelled the lingering enemy and had turned the place of subjection into the place of triumph.

Oh, shall someone who reads these lines awake to righteousness today, and from this moment rise to be a conquered one and then a conqueror through Him that loved us—a conqueror, yes—and "more than conquerors through him who loved us" (Romans 8:37)?

CHAPTER 5

GUIDANCE AND VICTORY

Put on the full armor of God so that you can take your stand against the devil's schemes. . . . Therefore put on the full armor of God, so that when the day of evil comes, you may be able to stand your ground. (Ephesians 6:11, 13; compare with 2 Samuel 5:17–25)

There is an old couplet full of deep instruction and suggestiveness which runs as follows:

> If conquered, for tomorrow's fight prepare;
> If conqueror, of tomorrow's fight beware.

This is finely illustrated by a significant and striking incident in the life of David. He had just achieved the most splendid victory of his life. Secure in the fastness of Zion, he might well defy, if any ever might, the threatenings of his foes, and might indeed be tempted to imagine that his protracted conflicts were over. But this superb victory was immediately followed by some of the severest tests. As we look at the picture, we are reminded for ourselves that the very time to expect temptation is in the hour of triumph, and that there are many deep lessons to be learned every step of our pathway if we would escape the wiles of the devil and stand at last, having done all.

TEMPTATION

1. We see an example of temptation after victory. "When the Philistines heard that David had been anointed king over Israel, they went up in full force to search for him" (2 Samuel 5:17). It was when they heard that he was crowned that they came to take him. It is when God has signally blessed us and sealed us by His Holy Spirit's power that the adversary always seeks to assail us. He feels it is a crisis hour and he must challenge our high position and drive us back from this advance ground or his control over our lives will

be lost. Therefore it happens that after we enter upon the highest blessing we are always exposed to the fiercest conflict. The new convert expecting to find a life of delightful freedom from the things that have assailed his life, is plunged into the severest testings. The newly consecrated life, glowing with high hope and holy purpose, finds itself confronted by the most subtle forms of strange temptation, and the first impulse is to become discouraged and to feel a touch of bitter disappointment. The real truth is we never feel temptation until we resist it. The man who is following his natural bent is unconscious of any opposing current, and his life is one of passive peace; but when we meet with the fires of evil within us and the adversary beside us, then we understand a little of what the apostle means when he speaks of withstanding in the evil day. It seems at such times as if all the Philistines had come up against us, and there was not a temptation in the category of evil which had not tried its hand upon our encompassed spirit. Let us not think it strange concerning the fiery trial which is to try us as though some strange thing happened unto us (1 Peter 4:12); but let us remember Him who, after the baptism at the Jordan, was immediately led into the wilderness to be tempted of the devil, and let us rejoice inasmuch as we are partakers of the sufferings of Christ that when His glory shall be revealed we may be glad also with exceeding joy.

VIGILANCE

2. We see an example of prudence in meeting temptation. When David heard that the Philistines had come up against him, we read that he went down into the stronghold of Zion, which may have been at a little lower level on the height than his palace and his headquarters. He immediately took refuge in the fort. He did not rashly and impulsively dash into battle without divine direction, but he took refuge in the hiding place that God had afforded him. He went down to a lower level of humility and safety, and he waited for divine instruction.

When the enemy comes the truly wise and brave spiritual soldier will always go down into the hold. He will humble himself at the Master's feet. He will take refuge behind the defenses which God has provided him, and he will wait for orders from on high. There is no real courage in making light of danger, and the wise soldier of the cross knows that he is no match for Satan. God will not suffer us to be tempted above what we are able to bear, but let us not forget what is added: He will also, along with the temptation, make a way to escape (1 Corinthians 10:13). It is often a way of escape rather than a way of attack, and when God has given us our defenses let us quickly hide behind them and find refuge for our helplessness, like the little conies in the shelter of the rock.

GUIDANCE

3. Next we have an example of implicit dependence upon divine guidance. David inquired of the Lord. He was a trained soldier and a skilled strategist, but he did not trust his skill or strength, but went like a little child to his God and asked immediate counsel. It is very remarkable to notice the form in which he asked counsel. He did not first ask if He should be successful, but he first asked what the Lord wanted him to do. His primary desire was to please God; his second request, to know what God was going to do for him. This is very beautiful and very important. It is much more natural for us to say, "Lord, will you bless me in this?" and then if He promises us prosperity we are disposed to accept His direction and go forward in it. David's attitude was far more single and sincere. With him the supreme question was, "Lord what will you have me to do?" and quite subordinate to that was the other, "Lord, what will you do with me?" There are instances where God bids us go forward when it is to face suffering, self-denial and, it may be, even death. It was there that the spirit of the Hebrew witnesses came out so clearly in ancient Babylon, "If we are thrown into the blazing furnace, the God we serve is able to save us from it, . . . But even if he does not, we want you to know, O king, that we will not serve your gods or worship the image of gold you have set up" (Daniel 3:17–18). Let us only be sure of the path of duty, and then we can confidently ask the Lord to take care of us. And so God gave David both assurances. First, He told him what to do and then He promised him absolute and certain victory. Oh, how safe it is to go forward with God's assurance! Nothing can daunt us, nothing defeat us.

PRAISE

4. We see an example of modest and becoming acknowledgement of God as the source of victory. When the Philistines were defeated and scattered before the power of God and the onset of David, he did not, like Saul, set up a pillar of personal celebration, but he commemorated the praise and honor of God alone and gave Him all the glory. "As waters break out," he said, "God has broken out against my enemies by my hand" (1 Chronicles 14:11). We are not told anything about the spoil that he took, but we are very distinctly told that he destroyed the images of the Philistines. It was a holy war, and David was much more concerned to destroy the enemies of God than to secure his own trophies of victory.

A NEW TEST

5. We see an example of repeated temptation on the very same lines. It was not very long before the Philistines came up again into the same valley.

This time, no doubt, they came with greatly augmented forces, and determined that they should avenge themselves upon their enemy and recover their lost prestige.

The spiritual lesson here is very important. God sometimes suffers us to be tempted over again on exactly the same lines, even where we have had complete victory before. It may be the devil wants to surprise us through our very security, as we are less likely to expect him to repeat his attack. It may be that God wants to teach us, as in the present instance, some new lesson. It often is because we have not quite triumphed on this line before, and God is good enough to give us a second opportunity. Let us never be too sure of the subjugation of our Philistine foes, but let us ever watch and be ready.

A NEW WAY

6. We see the same temptation met in an entirely different way. This was the great lesson that God was seeking to teach David and us also. Our danger is, when a similar experience comes, to go on by the forces of habit on the same lines, and thus really be trusting unconsciously in our own experience and wisdom. David was graciously delivered from this. It would have been perfectly natural for him to say, "I have defeated these Philistines here before, and I have only to do as I did then and I shall defeat them again." But David, with great wisdom and simplicity, went straight to God, as though he had had no experience and possessed no wisdom of his own, and he was rewarded by receiving an entirely different direction. "Do not go straight up," said the oracle, "but circle around behind them and attack them in front of the balsam trees" (2 Samuel 5:23). God had an entirely different lesson this time, and David was wise enough to be open to receive it. There are times when we are not to face the foe but to seem to retreat from the foe and let God fight our battle for us. A retreat is often a flank movement and a more certain victory. There are people who attack us that we can better answer by leaving alone. There are things that are said against us that can most strongly be met by silence. There are inward conflicts which, the more we think about, the more we provoke, and the best way is to turn from the conflict and be occupied with God.

But the great lesson is that of listening, hearkening and obeying. We may often begin a good thing with God and end with ourselves, and there is failure. And so David clung close to God all the way through, and waited every moment for His direction in the minutest details.

THE SOUND OF MARCHING

7. We have an example of God's manifest interposition in the trials and conflicts of His children. There is a very sublime picture given in this incident of the unseen forces that are in alliance with God's faithful and

obedient children. The Hebrew language, in which the march of these heavenly hosts is described, is exceedingly sublime. "As soon as you hear the sound of marching in the tops of the balsam trees, move quickly, because that will mean the LORD has gone out in front of you to strike the Philistine army" (2 Samuel 5:24). In the original the style is dramatic and majestic, and it suggests the march of mighty armies in the air. The rustling of those leaves was caused by no passing breeze, but David knew that myriads of angels and chariots of fire were sweeping down the fields of air, and that his little army was just following in the train of the legions of the sky. All he had to do was to wait for the signal to advance. But he must wait. A premature step would have been an error, and perhaps a fatal blunder.

During the battle of Waterloo, Wellington posted a brave detachment of British troops on a salient point of the field, and their orders were to stand firm and hold the point at all hazards. Again and again through that awful battle they had opportunity to charge upon the foe, and again and again their leader sent an orderly to the headquarters of Wellington to ask permission to charge, but again and again he sent back the answer, "Stand firm." One by one the little band slowly fell without being permitted to make that charge for which they were so eager, and at last the messenger left the Duke of Wellington with the words, "You will find us all there." When the battle was over they lay in a heap slain, but they had proved a living wall against the foe. That point was the key to the situation. The secret of victory was to wait and obey orders.

WAIT

8. And so our heavenly Master bids us wait as well as go. "But stay in the city until you have been clothed with power from on high" (Luke 24:48) is essential to all true success when we do go forward. We are to wait for "the sound of marching" (1 Chronicles 14:15), not on earth, but in the air—the moving of the breath of the Holy Spirit. It is hard to explain to any dull spirit what this means. There are lives that, like the dull-eyed ox, never catch a gleam of the light from the heavens, but see only the pasture field and fodder trough. There are others that are open to the voices that not all can hear and visions which many never see. We do not mean the trance vision of the fanatic, but the deep spiritual impulses and elevations which God still gives to sensitive hearts and quickened ears and eyes. They come to us when the Holy Spirit is pressing down upon our hearts with the baptism of power. They come to us when we have gone through the hour of trial, and our heart is bursting for some message from our Father to comfort and inspire. They come to us in the crisis time of life, when everything around is dark and difficult. They come to us in the providences of God when strange things lie in life's pathway and the heart instinctively responds, "It is the

Lord." They are coming to us in these signs of our times, in the wonderful movements of our day, in the providences of God among the nations, in the shaking of the kingdoms of the earth and the harbingers of the coming of Christ. Oh, surely, there is a "sound of marching" in the earth and air and sky. God give us eyes to see and ears to hear and an understanding of our times!

WORKERS WITH GOD

9. There is one more lesson of supreme importance, namely, the necessity of our cooperation with God when He begins to move. There was something for David to do as well as God, and that was to bestir himself when he heard the sound of marching. God's work did not displace David's, but it only led up to it; and it required that David should be the more alert and prompt to follow it up with intense activity and holy courage. There is a time to tarry, but there is a time to go out, and the men that have best learned to tarry know best how to go. Christian life is no dream, no listless, sentimental waiting for something to happen. It is the posture of hearkening until we hear His voice, and then it is the attitude of intense obedience, alacrity and holy activity in fulfilling our great commission and making the most of the divine opportunity and the command. There is the sound of marching in the tops of the balsam trees. Let us bestir ourselves. It is a time of marvelous opportunity in Christian life and Christian work and the world's evangelization. God teach us to tarry in Jerusalem until we are endued with power from on high. God enable us then to go in the power of the Spirit and disciple all nations, and so haste the coming of the Lord.

CHAPTER 6

THE ARK IN ZION

Arise, O LORD, and come to your resting place,
you and the ark of your might.
(Psalm 132:8; compare with 2 Samuel 6:1–23)

After the capture of Jebus and the establishment of the national capital at Jerusalem, David's next great public act was to remove the ark of the covenant from its resting place in the house of Abinadab to its permanent abode in Zion. This was an act of great significance, expressing in the most emphatic manner the covenant of God, of whose presence the ark was the special symbol, as the Sovereign of His theocratic people.

REMOVAL OF THE ARK

Its removal was accompanied by the most stately ceremonies. The king himself, with his courtiers and ecclesiastical officers, went down to Gibeah and accompanied the ark on its journey.

They seem to have overlooked the special command of God in the Levitical law, that the ark should be carried only by the Levites. Instead they put it upon a cart borne by oxen, and on the way the oxen shook it so that Uzzah, one of the sons of Abinadab, in attempting to steady it touched it with his hands, and was suddenly stricken down by the hand of God for his presumption.

This so appalled the king and his attendants that they left the ark for a time in the house of Obed-Edom, but three months later, learning that God, instead of letting it be a curse, had made it a blessing to Obed-Edom and his house, David renewed the attempt, and, with imposing ceremonies, the ark was finally transferred to Jerusalem.

David participated in the dances with unreserved joy and ecstasy in the public procession, disgusting his wife, Michal, and bringing upon himself her scorn and rebuke.

PSALMS OF COMMEMORATION

Some of the finest Psalms were composed in connection with this event, and sung in the responsive service connected with the ascension of the ark. One of these is the 24th Psalm, where the two choirs of priests sing in response:

> Lift up your heads, O you gates;
>   be lifted up, you ancient doors,
>   that the King of glory may come in.
> Who is this King of glory?
>   The LORD strong and mighty,
>   the LORD mighty in battle.
> Lift up your heads, O you gates;
>   lift them up, you ancient doors,
>   that the King of glory may come in.
> Who is he, this King of glory?
>   The LORD Almighty—
>   he is the King of glory.
>   (24:7–10)

Another of the ascension Psalms is the 15th. "LORD, who may dwell in your sanctuary?/ Who may live on your holy hill?" (15:1). Still another is the 132nd, expressing in the sublimest poetry the joy of David's heart when he is permitted to "find a place for the LORD,/ a dwelling for the Mighty One of Jacob" (132:5). As they ascend the heights of Zion they sing, "Let us go to his dwelling place;/ let us worship at his footstool" (132:7), and the chorus resounds, "arise, O LORD, and come to your resting place,/ you and the ark of your might./ May your priests be clothed with righteousness;/ may your saints sing for joy" (132:8–9). And then from a responsive choir comes the answer, "This is my resting place for ever and ever;/ here I will sit enthroned, for I have desired it—/ I will bless her with abundant provisions;/ her poor will I satisfy with food./ I will clothe her priests with salvation,/ and her saints will ever sing for joy" (132:14–16).

The 68th Psalm is also connected with this occasion. It commences with the old glorious shout of the wilderness which they used to sing when the ark began to move, "May God arise, may his enemies be scattered" (68:1), and it rises with the ascending ark to the elevated prophetic height of Christ's ascension until the seer beholds in the distance the chariots of the angels that attended the ascent from Mount Olivet to heaven. "When you ascended on high,/ you led captives in your train;/ you received gifts from men,/ even from the rebellious—/ that you, O LORD God, might dwell there" (68:18).

But let us pass from the historical circumstances to the spiritual significance of this scene.

SECTION I—*The Significance of the Ark Itself*

It was the most significant of all the symbols of the Jewish ceremonial system.

RECONCILIATION

1. It expressed as no other object in all the Mosaic ritual the first principle of the blood—reconciliation to God through the atoning blood. It was a little chest of precious wood covered with gold, and contained the tables of the law and some sacred memorials from the wilderness. Its lid or cover of solid gold was called the mercy seat or propitiation, and was the especial symbol of the atonement. It was always covered with blood, and was peculiarly fitted to suggest the idea of the covering of human guilt by the vicarious sufferings of Christ. Underneath that cover of gold lay the broken law in the ark, that broken law, the witness of the mercy seat, and the sprinkled blood; and God saw not the iniquities of His people, but the sacrifice of His beloved Son. This is the idea of propitiation. It is expressed in the 32nd Psalm, "Blessed is he . . . whose sins are covered" (32:1). It was finely expressed in the prayer of the penitent, "God be," not merciful, but "God be the propitiation for me, the sinner." It is expressed more perfectly still by the Apostle John in the simple evangelical statement, "He is the atoning sacrifice for our sins, and not only for ours but also for the sins of the whole world" (1 John 2:2).

SANCTIFICATION

2. The ark expressed the idea of sanctification. That ark was the type of Jesus Christ, and it was the sacred depository of the law of God. The first time the law was given at Sinai and the tables were committed to the hands of Moses, as we read in the narrative, he let them fall upon the rocks as he descended from the mount, and they were broken. This was no mere accident, but it was the sad symbol of the broken law which man had already shattered by his transgressions. The second time that law was given by God on Mount Horeb and written on new tablets of stone, but this time He did not commit them to Moses to keep, but He commanded them to be put in the ark and there preserved. The ark, therefore, was the repository of the law. In this it is a perfect type of Christ, our Sanctifier. God gave us His law the first time and we broke it. He does not now in our sanctification trust us with it, for we should break it again; but Jesus keeps it for us, and keeps it in us. We receive Him into our hearts as an indwelling Presence, as our holy Ark, and in His

heart that law is hidden and kept; and He, keeping it in us as once He kept it for us, becomes our sanctification. And so it becomes true, "For what the law was powerless to do in that it was weakened by the sinful nature, God did by sending his own Son in the likeness of sinful man to be a sin offering. And so he condemned sin in sinful man, in order that the righteous requirements of the law might be fully met in us, who do not live according to the sinful nature but according to the Spirit" (Romans 8:3–4).

INDWELLING

3. The ark also signifies God's dwelling in the midst of Israel. It represents not merely the blessings of salvation and sanctification, but the supreme blessing of God Himself, the glory and strength of Israel and of His people. It means that we have God in His personal Presence and in His infinite all-sufficiency to be our all in all. There were several occasions in the history of Israel when the ark came signally to the front. One of these was when Moses had invited Hobab to be their guide through the wilderness, adding: "You can be our eyes" (Numbers 10:31). In the very first place we are told that the ark of the covenant removed and went before them to seek out a dwelling-place for them. God was thus emphatically teaching them that He was to be their God, and that no man could be the eyes to the people, to whom He says, "I will counsel you and watch over you" (Psalm 32:8).

Again, when they crossed the Jordan the ark went before them, and as the feet of the priests that bore it touched the waters they rolled aside and made a pathway for the people to go over. But when they came to the middle of the stream, to the deepest and most dangerous place, then the ark paused in midstream and waited in the depths of the Jordan until all the host had clean passed over. This beautifully sets forth the precious truth that Christ not only goes before us, but holds for us the hardest place and sees us through in the darkest and most dangerous crisis.

SECTION II—*The Removal of the Ark*

The removal of the ark to the very citadel of the nation and the throne of Israel was an act of great significance.

JEHOVAH, THEIR KING

1. It recognized the fact that God Himself was King over Israel. They were seeking out a habitation for the mighty God of Jacob. They were installing their theocratic King on His own throne. It was the inauguration of theocracy on a public and permanent basis, and the handing over of the scepter to their heavenly King in the most solemn and impressive manner.

CHRIST'S ASCENSION

2. It was a type of Christ's ascension to the right hand of God, and, therefore, in the 68th Psalm, the thought of the prophet sweeps forward to the glorious hour when He led captivity captive and ascended on high, taking possession in behalf of His people, not only of the throne of earth, but of the throne of the universe.

THE ENTHRONED CHRIST

3. It represented the enthronement of Christ in the human heart. It is rather striking that this did not take place until after Jebus was taken from the hands of the Canaanites and the last relic of the ancient foe was cast out. And so the full enthronement of the Lord Jesus Christ in the human soul must be preceded by a surrender of the last remnant of the life of self and sin. Not only so, there had to be a time of testing. The Philistines came up against David even after the fall of Jebus, and they were driven back and David proved that God was Israel's Almighty King. And so the full government of Christ in the human heart comes after seasons of testing and proving. The baptism of the Spirit came to Jesus on the banks of the Jordan, but it had to be followed by the 40 days in the wilderness before the fullness of the power was manifested. We receive the Holy Spirit at the moment of surrender, but we do not realize the fullness of His power until we have been fully tested and have stood triumphant with Him in the conflict with evil. There are stages in the manifestation of God's presence and power in the human soul long after the crisis of a spiritual life is passed, and the wise and watchful disciple will be ever pressing on from strength to strength, proving not only that good and acceptable but also the perfect will of God (Romans 12:2).

SECTION III—*The Blessing and the Curse Brought by the Ark*

A BLESSING OR A CURSE

We read in this chapter of both a blessing and a curse. It was a blessing to the house of Obed-Edom, and the presence of Christ is the supreme blessing of a nation, a church, a home and a human life.

But there was a curse as well as a blessing. It is in this chapter we read of the folly and fault of man and the judgment of God. The first was the presumption of Uzzah, for which he was stricken with death, because he tried to steady the ark of God. The next was the blight that fell upon Michal, the wife of David, because she looked with scorn upon the full and holy joy of the king, and felt no sympathy with the enthusiasm of this glorious hour. She was smitten with a withering curse that left her a barren and fruitless branch in the house of Israel. Both of them are fitted to teach us solemn and profitable lessons.

HANDS OFF!

The story of Uzzah leaves one brief and epigrammatic message to all the ages: "Hands off!" It tells us there are some things that we must not attempt to do, even with the best of motives and the most earnest, honest purpose. Uzzah, no doubt, felt that the ark was in danger, and that it was right for him to steady it; but it was none of his business. It was an interference with God's work for which others were appointed, and his best service was to do nothing but the simple task that had been committed to him—to drive the oxen, and let God take care of His own ark. We, too, must keep our hands off God's cause when it is not our business to interfere.

There are many people who spend their lives trying to keep things straight, and they often get killed, like Uzzah, for their interference. Perhaps God does not always want things straight according to our standards of straightness. God has not only made straight sunbeams, but He has made zigzag lightnings. God has not only Moses and Aaron to prophesy in regular form, but an Eldad and Medad to speak out of time and out of season. God often in His work raises up special geniuses and irregular methods, and in trying to steady them we may destroy the work of God. Very wise was the counsel of Gamaliel, "For if their purpose or activity is of human origin, it will fail. But if it is from God, you will not be able to stop these men; you will only find yourselves fighting against God" (Acts 5:38–39).

We must keep our hands off other people. We must simply let our brother alone, and remember that "to his own master he stands or falls" (Romans 14:4). Miriam, in trying to regulate matrimonial affairs for Moses, God struck with leprosy. And likewise many a man or woman has been withered for life spiritually because of interference, unkindly criticism, personal animosity, jealousy and bitterness.

There are many things in life we must keep our hands off—cares and worries. Nine tenths of our troubles are troubles that never come. We get into all our hard temptations by touching things that we had better leave alone. A wise Christian will spend much of his life like a good, well-pitched roof, shedding things and letting them roll into the gutter and go into the sewer. Others spend their lives as gutters and sewers, catching all the devil's rain and all the dirty water that his emissaries are so ready to throw out, and passing it on until their own lives become rusted, defiled and polluted.

There are really very few things in the course of a day that we need to think about, and if we should confine ourselves to the actual realities of life we should find it possible to live well and to accomplish all life's real work. There are innumerable worries, annoyances, anxieties, cares, troubles and fears that we can simply let alone. Refuse to think about them. Leave them to God. Hands off!

A Christian woman who had been living a very unhappy life, and was always overwhelmed with burdens and with cares of the future, came downstairs one morning telling her family that she had had a beautiful dream, and that through it God had delivered her from all her fears and worries. She said she had seen a great crowd of people passing along a broad way, and weighed down by innumerable burdens they were carrying. To and fro in the crowd a lot of imps were passing, throwing these burdens all around, and getting people to pick them up and carry them. Among others she was carrying several of these loads of lead, and was almost worn to death. Suddenly, in the crowd she saw the face of the Lord coming toward her, and she eagerly beckoned for Him to come and help her carry her burden. He looked sternly at her and refused to touch it. He said: "I have no strength for that. I have no grace for loads like this. It is one of the devil's bundles, and all you have got to do is to drop it and you will have plenty of strength for the loads that I bid you carry." It was a revelation to her. She simply dropped the little black bundles, and instantly it seemed that she was winged with strength and gladness, while the Master looked in her face with inexpressible love and said: "Do not be anxious about anything, . . . And the peace of God, which transcends all understanding, will guard your hearts and your minds in Christ Jesus" (Philippians 4:6–7).

THE SIN OF WORRY

Once more, when we commit our way to God we must keep our hands off. We must let the Lord lead and work. Even though we may not understand His way, we must still believe that all will be well. We must learn the lesson that David has inscribed in the 37th Psalm, "Commit your way to the LORD;/ trust in him and he will do this" (37:5), and then we must add, "Be still before the LORD and wait patiently for him" (37:7). Anxiety is as much forbidden as stealing. Worry is as wicked as worldliness. In the same breath in which He says, "You cannot serve both God and Money" (Matthew 6:24), the Lord Jesus also says, "Therefore I tell you, do not worry about your life" (6:25).

Now these sins are greatly aggravated in a life of consecration and dedication to God. It is not so strange that the world should worry, that people who know not their God should be continually struggling for themselves and fighting their own weary battles, but it is a dreadful thing for the child of God to commit his way to his heavenly Father, to confess his confidence in His power and love, and then to worry and fret and act as worldlings do. It is a shameful dishonor to Christ, and it is an aggravated sin by the very fact of our having received the Holy Spirit. It would have done little harm for Uzzah to have steadied his cart had the oxen been bearing a load to market, but it was a very awful thing for him to do so when the living God was in the midst of the burden that he was bearing. It is a very dreadful thing for one in whose bosom the Son of God is enthroned to be fretting and flurrying like the people who know not God. There is a fine story told of an old auntie in the South, who saw a young disciple who had just received the Holy Spirit, acting in some foolish and inconsistent way. "Go softly, honey," she said, "go softly; mind, you are carrying the Holy Child in your arms." Let us go softly, because we bear the mark of God, and in our bosom is enthroned that awful Presence before whom angels bow and veil their faces with their wings.

CHAPTER 7

MEPHIBOSHETH, OR MERCY MEETING MISERY

When we were still powerless, Christ died for the ungodly. . . . For if, when we were God's enemies, we were reconciled to him through the death of his Son, how much more, having been reconciled, shall we be saved through his life! (Romans 5:6, 10)

David asked, "Is there anyone still left of the house of Saul to whom I can show kindness for Jonathan's sake?" (2 Samuel 9:1)

David had now become established upon the throne, and had extended his empire far and wide by numerous conquests, until his kingdom reached from the Mediterranean to the Euphrates, and covered all the region that God had promised in His covenant with Abraham as the inheritance of Israel. Not only so, he had recognized his Jehovah as the true Sovereign of Israel, and installed the sacred ark in the tabernacle in Zion as a symbol of Jehovah's presence and sovereignty over all the kingdom. Israel was a true theocracy, and David was only a vice-regent of a greater King. His business, therefore, was to represent Jehovah in all his works and in all his ways. This gave a high and holy dignity to his person, and a lofty incentive and inspiration to his life. As the representative of Jehovah, and as the great type of the coming Messiah, it became him to walk with a perfect heart, and to show forth in his life the attributes and character of the God he represented.

This is indeed the true motive of Christian living. It is only as we stand in the name and stead of Christ, and endeavor to live as those who are called to show forth the character of our great Example and Head, that we shall be lifted above the selfishness and sinfulness of fallen humanity and enabled to walk worthy of our high calling.

DAVID'S KINDNESS
David, instead of setting an example of royal arrogance and selfishness, felt

315

it incumbent upon him to be a pattern of lowliness, righteousness and mercy. And so, as soon as his throne was established, he began to look about him for objects upon whom he could bestow his kindness. He did not wait for the need to present itself, but he was seeking for an object upon which to pour out his own beneficence and love. It is one thing for us to respond to the appeal of charity when it comes to us, and it is quite another thing for us to be looking about for objects for our beneficence. This is godlike. God did not wait until man came supplicating at His feet, but the Father sought the wandering prodigal. Before Adam ever asked for mercy, we hear the pleading of God's voice amid the trees of the garden, calling, "Where are you?" (Genesis 3:9). And so we find David asking with beautiful benignity, "Is there anyone still left of the house of Saul to whom I can show kindness for Jonathan's sake?" (2 Samuel 9:1).

In this, David was an example of loftier kindness—even the mercy of that heavenly Father who is ever seeking as well as saving the lost and waiting to be gracious. We have a beautiful example in this incident, of the mercy of God and the abundant grace which, for Jesus' sake, He vouchsafes to the most hapless and miserable of sinful men.

SECTION I—*The Picture of the Sinner's Condition*

UNDER THE CURSE

1. Mephibosheth was a true illustration of the sinner's curse. He was under the shadow of the house of Saul. He was born of a family whose head had left an inheritance of sorrow to all his seed. Saul's sins had ruined his house, and slain all his children but this poor cripple, in consequence of his follies and crimes. And poor Mephibosheth had been spared only because he wasn't worth killing. This is our lost condition by nature. We are born in the world with an inherited curse. We may argue and criticize as we please the doctrine of the fall, but the stern fact remains today patent to every observer that men still inherit in the present life the sins of their ancestors. The pagan father bequeaths his blindness, superstition and degradation to his children. A drunken parent transmits to his posterity a heritage of woe, and all the fine-spun arguments of the critic do not prevent the bitter blight of this hereditary curse. Heredity is a fact in the human life today, and how do we know but that it will be a fact in the eternal tomorrow? God's Book tells us it will be. And so poor Mephibosheth inherited the curse of Saul, and the sinner inherits the curse of fallen humanity. "Like the rest, we were by nature objects of wrath" (Ephesians 2:3). It is not that God delights in inflicting hereditary suffering, but it is one of God's own laws, and the only way He can prevent its operation is through the intervention of His mercy, which is now offered to every child of fallen Adam.

HELPLESS

2. Mephibosheth was helpless. He was lame in both his feet. He was unable to move without assistance, and he is a vivid type of the helplessness as well as the guilt of our human race. People idly talk about the injustice and cruelty of teaching that the heathen must be lost without the gospel. And they lightly tell us that God is bound in justice to save all men, irrespective of Christ's atonement, if they do right and live up to the light they have. We are perfectly willing to concede that a just and righteous God will always accept a righteous man, and that if there is a heathen on the face of the earth who has obeyed the light of his conscience he will receive divine approval. But here the question ends in a pure theory, for the fact remains that there is not a human being on the face of the earth that is able to live up to the light of his conscience without supernatural assistance.

The very essence of man's fall is helplessness. Like Mephibosheth, he is lame in both his feet, and the cry of the wisest and noblest sages in every age has been, "When I want to do good, evil is right there with me" (Romans 7:21). I know better, but I do not do it. I see the right and hate the wrong, but something attracts me into it all the same. I condemn myself, and yet I do the things which I condemn. Man's supreme need is not only mercy to forgive his past sins, but also power to take away his sinful nature and make him fit for God's heaven. The only remedy, therefore, for fallen humanity is the gospel of Jesus Christ, and the power of the Holy Spirit to impart a new nature and to give supernatural assistance to enable us to do the will of God.

WORTHLESS

3. Mephibosheth was a type of the sinner's worthlessness. As he described his own condition he was but a "dead dog," utterly unworthy of David's generosity. God loves not because we deserve it, but because He cannot help it. There is something in Him that draws Him to us, not something in us that claims His approval. "I want you to know that I am not doing this for your sake, declares the Sovereign LORD. Be ashamed and disgraced for your conduct, O house of Israel!" (Ezekiel 36:32). Salvation is an act of unmerited mercy, and God is able to love, to pity and to choose the things that are despised, and to place a sovereign value all His own on souls which might be called even the devil's castaways.

SEPARATED FROM GOD

4. Mephibosheth represented the sinner's separation from God. He was living away across Jordan somewhere in the land of Gilead, far from Jerusalem, among strangers, a type of the poor sinner—"excluded from citizenship in Israel and foreigners to the covenants of the promise, without

hope and without God in the world. But now in Christ Jesus, you who once were far away have been brought near through the blood of Christ" (Ephesians 2:12–13).

SECTION II—*The Father's Mercy*

GOD'S MERCY

The question of David, "Is there anyone still left of the house of Saul to whom I can show kindness?" (2 Samuel 9:1) is just a revealing of the heart of God and His great mercy to poor, lost, sinful men. But it was not unconditional mercy. It was all "for Jonathan's sake."

There are people today who love to make light of the old gospel of Christ's atonement and the mercy of God through a Mediator. They tell us that the Father can forgive at His own pleasure and they need no intercessor by whom to approach Him, but can go as the prodigal came to the father, without any reference to the blood of Calvary or the name of Jesus. These people forget that the parable of the prodigal son is only the last of three parables in the 15th chapter of Luke, and that there are two that go before without which the third would be impossible. It is true that the father was waiting to be gracious to his returning son, but we must not forget that before that story could be written it was necessary that the Good Shepherd should go far out into the dark mountains and the cruel night, and suffer bitterly before He could find the lost sheep; and it was necessary that the woman should sweep the house, and seek diligently until she found the treasure. These two parables express the part of the Lord Jesus Christ and the Holy Spirit in our salvation, and open the way for the Father's part in welcoming back the returning son. The Good Shepherd is the Son of man going all the way to Calvary to find and save us. The seeking woman is the Holy Spirit sweeping our house and illuminating our dark soul to find the lost treasure. When the Son and the Spirit have done their part, then the Father's heart is open, and the Father's way is clear to receive us and bless us. "Salvation is found in no one else, for there is no other name under heaven given to men by which we must be saved" (Acts 4:12).

You may come and plead for mercy in heaven if you only do it for Jesus' sake. After all the cost of Calvary, God will never dishonor nor ignore the dying agony and the precious blood of Jesus Christ, our crucified Redeemer.

SECTION III—*God's Royal Bounty to the Returning Sinner*

RESTORATION

1. David gave back to Mephibosheth all the lands of Saul, restoring his lost inheritance in full. And so God gives us back all that we have forfeited

through sin, and it is indeed true

> In Him the tribes of Adam boast
> More blessings than their father lost.

SONSHIP

2. But this is not all. God also gives us His own royal bounty. Mephibosheth not only received his forfeited inheritance back, but he was accepted as the child of the king and henceforth ate at the king's table, and was shown all the hospitality of the royal palace. And so God takes us into His heart and home, and makes us His very sons and daughters, and shares with us all the fullness of His love, grace and glory, saying to us, "My son, . . . you are always with me, and everything I have is yours" (Luke 15:31).

How rich our inheritance as the children of the King! How infinite our resources! How glorious our prospects! How we should dwell on high, above all low and groveling things, and bear the dignity of princes of heaven, so that men looking upon us shall say once more, "Each of them looked like the children of the king." How unworthy to be living a life of discontent, strife and misery. "All things are yours" (1 Corinthians 3:21). Let us live as if we meant it, and had translated the old psalm into our shining faces and victorious lives, "The LORD is my Shepherd, I shall not be in want./ . . . /You anoint my head with oil;/ my cup overflows" (Psalm 23:1, 5).

SECTION IV—*The Grateful Return*

Mephibosheth was not unmindful or unworthy of David's generosity.

HUMBLE GRATITUDE

1. He sets us a beautiful example of humility. He calls himself a "dead dog" (2 Samuel 9:8), and he really meant it. He expressed what is just as true of every sinner. The only trouble is that we don't quite believe it. There is nothing more useless and contemptible than a dead dog. Other animals are of some use when dead, but a dog is worse than worthless. Well for some of us if we were truly dead dogs. There is a good deal of a live dog about many professing Christians, with all the snarl and strife of savage brutes. What we need and what Christ expects is that we should take the place of the dead dog and die out forevermore to all our rights and all our pretensions, and get forever out of the way, that Christ may come in with a new life and be forever the Substitute of our worthless, wretched self. The only secret of a sanctified life is to pass sentence of death on all that belongs to you in your natural and former state and never recall it.

Once there lived another man within me,
Child of earth, of self, of Satan he,
But I've nailed him to the cross of Jesus,
And that man is nothing now to me.

That is the only place of rest, the only place of holiness, the only way to find the all-sufficiency of Christ.

Now it is the grace of Christ that brings us there. It is His mercy that slays us. It is when we receive His generous love that we loathe ourselves and want to pass forever out of view. Oh, let us let Him love us to death!

LOYALTY

2. Mephibosheth was loyal as well as lowly. True, his loyalty was questioned, and he was greatly slandered by Ziba, his unfaithful servant, who complained to David that Mephibosheth was false. But this made no difference to him. He was not loyal as long as David believed in his loyalty. He was not loyal for the sake of being considered loyal, but he was loyal on principle, loyal for David's sake and his own. It was in him to be loyal, and he could not be disloyal. So loyal indeed was he, that when David came back months later, after his own sad exile, he found that Mephibosheth had been fasting in sackcloth and sorrow all the days of his absence, and nothing could make him happy until the king came back unto his own again.

And when he found that Ziba had ingratiated himself into the favor of David and cheated him out of his inheritance, he manifested a sublime indifference and answered nobly, "Let him take everything, now that my lord the king has arrived home safely" (19:30). Beautiful spirit of disinterested fidelity and noble unselfishness! Unable to enjoy the world until our King has received His inheritance and been requited for His shame and cruel death. Oh, if the followers of Christ were only as true! Oh, if He could but see some of us waiting and watching in grief and sorrow because of His dishonor and his absence! Oh, if we were but as indifferent to the end, and would obey fully, and say, like Mephibosheth, when men take advantage of us, when fortune fails and earthly things go by, "Let them go. Let them take all, but give me Jesus and my blessed hope and inheritance with Him!" Oh, to have such a hope of His coming, such a realization of His kingdom, such a stake in His future reign, such an inheritance laid up with Him, that the world has dropped away from us by the superior attraction of the world to come! This is true loyalty, and this alone is worthy of His grace and the glory in store for us at His return.

CHAPTER 8

SINS AND SORROW OF DAVID'S REIGN

You are the man! (2 Samuel 12:7)

We have been dwelling on the virtues of David's character and the glories of his reign. But suddenly the sky is clouded, and the chain of blessing rudely broken by a series of sins and sorrow that would crush us with discouragement and despair were it not for the infinite grace that shines out in contrast with man's unworthiness.

The Bible makes no attempt to hide the faults and crimes of its favorite characters. It is not given to reveal the virtues of humanity, but the grace of God, and therefore presents a frank and unbiased picture of man at his best. And then on the dark background of human infirmity and sin it spans the rainbow of heavenly mercy and infinite grace. There are lessons which we can only learn through the sad experience of deepest self-revealing, and David had to go down into the depths of failure in order to rise to the heights of grace.

It is needless to dwell on the familiar details of the sad story of David's fall. Let us also learn its lessons.

SECTION I—*The Causes of His Failure*

IN THE WRONG PLACE

1. The first of these causes was that he was out of his true place. We read in the previous chapter that "at the time when kings go off to war, David sent Joab out with the king's men and the whole Israelite army. They destroyed the Ammonites and besieged Rabbah. But David remained in Jerusalem" (2 Samuel 11:1). This was his first mistake. He was out of place. He should have been at the front with his brave soldiers. We are always in danger if we are out of God's order. It matters not where we are; even the house of God, even the quiet chamber of rest, is the place of peril, if God has sent us somewhere else.

IDLENESS

2. Idleness was the next cause of David's fall. He was unemployed. He was loitering, dallying, driveling. Luther says that "while the devil tempts other men, the idle man tempts the devil." Satan always furnishes occupation for the unemployed. He is a busy, restless spirit, and he lets no man rest. If labor be the curse of Eden, surely God has transformed it into a blessing by laying upon fallen man the blessed influence of preoccupation as a necessity of his existence. The idle, dallying throng are bound to become vicious. There is no greater curse that you can bequeath to your children than to train them up in luxurious idleness, and there is no greater blessing you can give them than to inure them to habits of industry and toil, and teach them to love work. The silly and sinful novel, the game of cards, the convivial debauch, all these are but inventions to pass the time away, to occupy idle hours, and they breed inevitable sin and sorrow.

SINFUL GLANCES

3. But the direct cause of David's sin was an unholy look. John Bunyan told us that we must guard our eye-gate and ear-gate, or the adversary will soon capture the citadel of our heart. "Turn my eyes away from worthless things" (Psalm 119:37) is the wise prayer of this man, who had found out to his bitter cost the wretched consequences of a sinful glance. And his wiser son has crystallized the same lesson into one of his immortal proverbs when he says,

> Above all else, guard your heart,
>   for it is the wellspring of life.
> Put away perversity from your mouth;
>   keep corrupt talk far from your lips.
> Let your eyes look straight ahead,
>   fix your gaze directly before you.
> Make level paths for your feet
>   and take only ways that are firm.
> Do not swerve to the right or the left;
>   keep your foot from evil.
>   (Proverbs 4:23–27)

Sin does not come to us full born. It is nursed by foolish words, worldly scenes, suggestive pictures and unholy glances. The daily Broadway parade is the nursery of thousands of ruined lives. The shop window is a prolific garden of unholy weeds. The prurient literature of the book stores, the pink page pictures of vice and debauchery and the abominable theatrical posters that defile the fences of every vacant lot stamp our cities as modern Gomorrahs—these are the roots of lust and licentiousness—these are the soft-winged moths that breed the worms that destroy the robe of virtue.

THE CURSE OF PROSPERITY

4. Doubtless there are still deeper causes. David's prosperity had doubtless induced a condition of pride and unwatchfulness, and David's inner life had not kept pace with the extraordinary blessings which God had showered upon his outward circumstances. And so it became necessary that he should be rudely awakened to understand his true spiritual state, and then lifted into a higher, better place.

SECTION II—*The Gradations of David's Sin*

The apostle has given us the genesis of evil in a very vivid pedigree. "Then, after desire has conceived, it gives birth to sin; and sin, when it is full-grown, gives birth to death" (James 1:15). David's sin was true to this pedigree.

PASSION

1. It began with an unholy passion. The sin of impurity has been so dangerously gilded with the false light of poetry and romance that the world is in danger of forgetting its sordid beastliness and utter degradation. It is the most debasing of all forms of evil, and most surely and swiftly obliterates all moral principle and religious sensibility from the human soul, deadening and hardening the heart until "having lost all sensitivity, they have given themselves over to sensuality so as to indulge in every kind of impurity, with a continual lust for more" (Ephesians 4:19). And yet it is today undermining the family life, the social life and the morals of all civilized communities, and reaches its most fearful maturity in nations that are under the influence of culture and prosperity.

We have only to read the shocking columns of our daily press to understand how truly our social life is being demoralized by the sins of Sodom and Gomorrah. Let us never lower the standard of social purity or lightly esteem the fearful sin which brought upon David and his kingdom the dark shadows that clouded all his future. Passion meets us with a crimson rose and tempting perfume, but behind it is the sting of a thousand thorns and the fetid breath of the pit.

DECEPTION

2. The next element in David's sin was falsehood, duplicity and deceit. This form of sin almost always leads to deception, evasion and a double life, until the conscience becomes utterly calloused and men and women are

living a lie. One would scarcely think that the simple-hearted shepherd of Bethlehem was capable of the deep duplicity that first tried to snare Uriah into hiding the crime of the royal usurper of his home, and, failing in this, by the most cunning contrivance using Joab as a tool to push him into the place of peril and cause his cruel death while, at the same time, palming it all off as an accident of war.

David's heart must have been stung to the quick by the letter he got back from the crafty Joab, who had deeply divined the secret of the king, and sent him this word which sounds like the hiss of a serpent: "The kings's anger may flare up, and he may ask you, 'Why did you get so close to the city to fight?' Then say to him, 'Also, your servant Uriah the Hittite is dead' " (2 Samuel 11:20–21). How utterly hypocritical and devilish was the answer that David sent back to his twin hypocrite, Joab: "Say this to Joab: 'Don't let this upset you; the sword devours one as well as another. Press the attack against the city and destroy it.' Say this to encourage Joab" (11:25). To such steps of duplicity may the soul step when once it begins the downward slide of the slimy track of licentiousness and sin.

BLOOD GUILTINESS

3. But the dark crime of murder was also added to the sin of David. Bitterly and truly might he cry afterwards, "Save me from bloodguilt, O God!" (Psalm 51:14). Little did it avail him to plead an excuse that it was not his hand that struck Uriah down. Truly and terribly might Nathan answer in the name of the Lord, "You struck down Uriah the Hittite with the sword and took his wife to be your own. You killed him with the sword of the Ammonites" (2 Samuel 12:9). It was the sword of Ammon that slew him, but it was David that slew him all the same.

These two sins of uncleanness and bloodshed so terribly linked in the fall of David are the two sins that are specially held up in the prophetic word as the signs of the last days. "It was the same in the days of Lot" (Luke 17:28). This gives us a picture of lust. "Just as it was in the days of Noah" (17:26). This is the vision of violence and blood. "It will be just like this" in both respects, "on the day the Son of Man is revealed" (17:30). And surely these are the two forms of open iniquity that in our day are becoming most flagrant and most frequent. Look at the columns of our morning papers steeped in filth and blood, with their stories of divorce, intrigue and murder, increasing from year to year far in advance of the increase of our population and far in excess of any other nation. Indeed, these two sins usually go together. The love that fawns today will flame tomorrow as a devouring fire. And indeed it is true, in the most literal sense, that "after desire has conceived, it gives birth to sin; and sin, when it is full-grown, gives birth to death" (James 1:15).

SPIRITUAL DEATH

4. But there is another sense in which death came to David as the fruition of his crime. It was the death of his conscience and the entire suspension of his moral sensibility. It is frightful to see how speedily and how utterly the sensitive, spiritual nature of this man of God was paralyzed and petrified by one brief hour of sin. For two long years he seems to have been utterly unconscious of having done wrong, and to have enjoyed the fruits of his shameful conspiracy with absolute impunity, not even shedding a tear over Uriah's noble sacrifice, but immediately sending for the wife of the man that he had wronged, and establishing her openly and shamelessly as his wife. Indeed, when Nathan told him the story of the ewe lamb, he was quick to condemn the cruel conduct of the oppressor in the parable, and it never even occurred to him that he was condemning himself. Surely this is death. Surely the saddest thing that can come to a noble nature is to sink into the depths of iniquity, and become reconciled to the most revolting associations and vices, and even forget what it once was like to be holy and pure. It is certain that David did not write any psalms during the two years of his profound spiritual catalepsy.

SECTION III—*The Aggravation of David's Sin*

HIS AGGRAVATED SIN

1. It was aggravated by the person who sinned. Sin is always sin; but sin is more heinous when it is committed by one of whom we might expect better things. David occupied a pre-eminent position. He had received every kindness from the hand of God. Jehovah might well say to him: "I anointed you king over Israel, and I delivered you from the hand of Saul. I gave your master's house to you, and your master's wives into your arms. I gave you the house of Israel and Judah. And if all this had been too little, I would have given you even more. Why did you despise the word of the LORD by doing what is evil in his eyes?" (2 Samuel 12:7–9). And so it is true of us. "From everyone who has been given much, much will be demanded" (Luke 12:48). When God has dealt kindly by us and trusted us with a high calling and a glorious work, it is a very fearful thing for us to drag His honor in the dust, and to degrade ourselves and our sacred trust by disobedience or unfaithfulness.

AGAINST HIS FRIEND

2. It was aggravated by the one against whom he sinned. It was against a true and noble man, a man who had done him no wrong, a man who trusted in his royal generosity, a man who left his wife's honor in his keep-

ing, a man who refused even the most innocent indulgence because his king and country were in danger, a man who nobly sacrificed his beloved wife and his happy home that he might hasten forth again to the battlefield, who, even when treacherously slain by his king, gladly gave up his life, believing it to be a worthy sacrifice for his sovereign and his country. Against such a man the sin of David was inhuman, monstrous and utterly inexcusable. Well is it portrayed in the simple-worded parable of the poor man with the one ewe lamb, robbed and wronged by a rich oppressor who had all he needed beside and might well have spared that one treasure. And so our sin is aggravated by the person against whom we sin. It is a very dreadful thing to sin against innocence, purity, goodness, loyalty and holiness. It is a very dreadful thing to harm the children of God, for God is their avenger. It is a more dreadful thing to speak or act an injury against the Lord's anointed. There is many a wrecked life today, many an unhallowed grave, and perhaps many a raving maniac because of words hastily spoken and wrongs willfully done against the servants of the Lord.

AGAINST GOD

3. It was aggravated by the scandal and blasphemy it brought against the name of the Lord. "But . . . by doing this you have made the enemies of the LORD show utter contempt" (2 Samuel 12:14). This was the severe aggravation of David's crime, and this always makes the sin of a Christian peculiarly offensive to God. It dishonors Christ and makes Him seem false to a scorning world. God help us to walk humbly and watchfully because we carry about with us the honor of our King!

AGAINST HIMSELF

4. There were the consequences of David's sin. God graciously forgave him the moment he acknowledged his transgression, but at the same time He put him under a course of severest discipline and chastisement, which lasted for years and covered the remainder of his reign with many a shadow and many a sorrow. We must understand this principle of God's government.

It is not judgment in fierce anger, but it is a wise and loving chastening intended to teach great moral lessons, and lead the subject into a deeper and better place. There are great laws of moral and spiritual cause and effect which make sorrow inevitably follow hard in the tracks of sin. Grace does not abolish these laws, but grace gives us strength to stand the discipline; but we bring the discipline upon ourselves all the same when we sin, and we oft make life much harder than it need have been had we walked more closely with our God. It is like the decree which Xerxes made against the Jews at the instigation of Haman. Afterwards when Esther pleaded, the decree was not annulled, but instead, the Jews were given power to defend themselves against it. And so when we turn to God there are things which meet us in our lives hard and strange, which God does not always put aside, but He gives us grace and strength to go through the ordeal in victory. He gave this to David; but, oh, how much David might have escaped if he had stood true to God to the end!

Seven great troubles entered into his cup of sorrow. The first was the death of the child born of this unholy passion. The second was the ruin of Tamar, his beautiful daughter, by the crime of Amnon, her half brother. Next was the murder of Amnon by Absalom. Then came the rebellion of Absalom and his cruel death, which broke David's heart. And then came the curse of Shimei, and a terrible pestilence that almost blotted out Jerusalem. Last of all came the rebellion of Adonijah, and even the complicity of Joab with him. What a catalogue of sorrows—all the brood of that single sin! "Do not be deceived: God cannot be mocked. A man reaps what he sows" (Galatians 6:7).

SECTION IV—*Mercy Triumphing over Judgment*

Out of all this and above all this comes the "clear shining after the rain" (2 Samuel 23:4, KJV), and the marvelous grace of God in the later history of David.

LED TO DEEPER LIFE

1. There was the deeper life it brought to his soul. It was a life through death. It was in this that he learned, as he tells us in the 23rd Psalm, to "walk through the valley of the shadow of death" (23:4), and to come out on the other side with a newer, higher life. It was in this experience that he learned the secrets that he has evolved in the 51st Psalm, where he can look down into the full depths of his iniquity and say, "My sin is always before me" (51: 3), and from there can look up through the blood into the unclouded light of the throne, and say with profound confidence, "Wash me, and I will be whiter than snow" (51:7). Marvelous paradox of faith! The deepest sin, the brightest glory. The darkest stain, the whitest robe. Crimson and scarlet stains, but whiter than the snow, and spotless as wool cleansed to its finest fiber. It was in this that he learned in advance of his times the indwelling of the Holy Spirit, and could sing, in the penitential Psalm, that wondrous song and prayer: "Renew a steadfast spirit within me./ Do not . . ./ take your Holy Spirit from me./ . . . grant me a willing spirit, to sustain me" (51:10–12). Henceforth he lived the resurrection life, and he knew the baptism of the Holy Spirit.

THE TRANSFORMATION OF LOVE

2. Not only so, God transformed the outward circumstances so that the

curse at last became a blessing, and the second son of this same Bathsheba was chosen by the Lord to be the heir to his throne. And we read about him this wonderful testimony: "They named him Solomon. The LORD loved him; and because the LORD loved him, he sent word through Nathan the prophet to name him Jedidiah" (2 Samuel 12:24–25).

The lesson it teaches us is this: if we deeply and thoroughly repent, if we pass judgment unreservedly upon our sinful self, and accept the mercy of God in its fullness and freeness, we will not only be forgiven but restored. Some day in yonder world of glory, of which Solomon was the type, we shall find the curse transformed into a blessing, and "instead of the thorn bush will grow the pine tree,/ and instead of briers the myrtle will grow./ This will be for the LORD's renown,/ for an everlasting sign,/ which will not be destroyed" (Isaiah 55:13).

CHAPTER 9

ABSALOM

Is the young man Absalom safe? (2 Samuel 18:32)

How could he be safe! How could any young man be safe with such a character and life as his! Vainglorious, worldly minded, disobedient and disloyal to his loving father, passionate, vindictive, self-indulgent and shameless in his profligacy, full of duplicity and deceit and utterly destitute of moral principle or real godliness—how could even a father's love save such a boy from inevitable ruin! The only good that such a life can do is to be a beacon upon the shores of danger, warning other men from his terrible mistakes and fearful destruction.

A SAD PICTURE

A king and father sat in the gates of Mahanaim, waiting for tidings from the neighboring battlefield. All day long the fight had raged in the woods of Ephraim, while on one side Amasa led the hosts of Absalom, the army of the rebellion and on the other hand Joab commanded the trained veterans of David as they fought for their king and their country against the treacherous legions who gathered to the standard of the usurper. Fierce and long the battle waged, but as the sun began to wane the veterans of David's army prevailed, and the hosts of Absalom began to melt away in retreat and terrible slaughter. Pressing hard in close pursuit Absalom himself was overtaken in the forest. He was found by one of Joab's followers hanging from an oak by his splendid tresses of flowing hair, which had caught in the thicket and suspended him while he was still alive, so that he was helpless to extricate himself. Joab needed no further notice to strike the fatal blow which removed at once the head and cause of the rebellion. With three darts flung by his own hand he pierced the heart of the wretched man and then left him to his soldiers to cut to pieces and bury under a heap of stones in the wilderness.

When they found that Absalom was dead the pursuit was recalled and the

329

battle ceased. Then Joab sent a swift courier to bear the tidings to the king. They had with difficulty restrained him from taking part in the battle. Well they knew that his fondness for his foolish boy would probably risk the victory to save his son, and they persuaded him that his life was worth 10,000 and must not be rashly ventured. But he gave them the tenderest charges for the security of Absalom and waited eagerly to hear the earliest tidings from the field.

As the sun was sinking in the west, he looked across the country, and lo, in the distance a cloud of dust betokened a swift runner. Sweeping forward to the gate of the city came Ahimaaz, the son of Zadok, David's friend, and throwing himself upon his face upon the ground he quickly told the story of the victory of David's army. But the king was as though he heard not, and with eager heart he cried, "Is the young man Absalom safe?" (2 Samuel 18:29). Ahimaaz's heart was too tender to tell the truth, and so he gently avoided the question. Meanwhile another runner was described swiftly following the first, and as he came near him shouted out the story of the triumph, too. But again the king with bursting heart asked the tender question, "Is the young man Absalom safe?" (18:32). Cushi, who was not as thoughtful as the other, but whose only idea was to tell the message in all its meaning, let out the dreadful secret as he answered, "May the enemies of my lord the king and all who rise up to harm you be like that young man" (18:32). That answer broke the father's heart. Hurrying to his chamber he burst out in bitter wailing: "Oh my son Absalom! My son, my son Absalom! If only I had died instead of you—O Absalom, my son, my son!" (18:33). His grief was inconsolable, and at last even Joab had to go and remonstrate with him about the dreadful shadow he was throwing upon the hearts of the brave men that had risked their lives to save his life and kingdom. "Today you have humiliated all your men, who have just saved your life and the lives of your sons and daughters and the lives of your wives and concubines. You love those who hate you and hate those who love you. You have made it clear today that the commanders and their men mean nothing to you. I see that you would be pleased if Absalom were alive today and all of us were dead" (19:5–6). This was sufficient to arouse the king from his stupor of agony, and he came back to his palace and rallied the scattering forces who had already begun to steal away. But that weight of sorrow never left his heart. Well might he groan for the foolish boy whose life had gone out that day in darkness and despair, which none better knew in all its meaning than the godly king, who understood better than Absalom the meaning of eternal retribution, whose own hands had written the solemn words, "The ransom for a life is costly,/ no payment is ever enough" (Psalm 49:8). Let us pause while still we may receive and profit by the warning of this ruined life, and look at the secrets of his failure and the lessons of his terrible example.

THE FALL OF PRIDE

1. The first and most predominant feature in Absalom's character was his vanity and self-conceit. His personal appearance was strikingly beautiful. He was the handsomest man in Israel, and from the crown of his head to the soles of his feet there was no blemish in him. This, instead of a blessing, became, as it often does, a bane, and led him to center his life in himself, and he became conceited, vainglorious and utterly selfish. Personal vanity is weak and sad even in a woman, but in a man it is contemptible. Beauty loses its charm when the possessor becomes conscious of it. Personal appearance ceases to attract us when the possessor is manifestly aware of it. To spend one's life in making a good appearance, in studying the latest fashions in garments, neckties and society manners, is an occupation too small for an immortal being created to resemble God and to live for high eternal things. Even the Greek language, in the name it chose for man, "*anthropos,*" expresses the idea of a being looking upward, and yet how very far from this idea is the character and manhood of men of today!

Personal conceit, however, is not only silly, but it is dangerous. It is the handmaid of sinful companionship, extravagance, worldliness and godlessness in all its forms. It led Absalom to ruin, and it is weaving a silken snare for thousands of young lives today.

Absalom's vanity displayed itself in his equipage and style of living. He got himself chariots and runners to run before him and announce that Absalom was coming. He posed as the foremost prince in all the land, and showed his princeliness by his pompous display. This, too, is one of the perils of modern society, to belong to the smartest set, to have the finest equipage, to make the greatest social impression, to give the finest entertainments, balls and receptions, to have the most showy and expensive mansion and style of living, to have the acquaintanceship of the most notable people, to be the guest or host of kings or queens or princes—all this is the goal to which multitudes to whom God has entrusted beauty, position and wealth, are pressing forward in the silly strife at which angels must blush and smile as they look ahead to the crumbling castles of human pride, to the corruption and the worm that is so soon to take the place of all the splendid pageant of what men call society. How very sad that on a single ball in our metropolis every winter enough money is often spent to send a thousand missionaries to the field and stud the crown of Christ with 10,000 immortal jewels in the form of redeemed souls.

But still more sad and terrible, Absalom's vanity did not even stop short of the grave itself, for one of the brightest ambitions of his life was to build a splendid monument in the beautiful valley of the Kedron, known as the King's Valley. And there between Mount Olive and Mount Moriah he reared a beautiful structure, which is known to this day as Absalom's Tomb. But true to the irony of fate he never slept in his beautiful sepulcher. His bones were buried in the woods of Ephraim, and his monument remains to this day as a derision and scorn at which every Jew, as he passes by, pitches a stone as an expression of his contempt and abhorrence. And even this is still repeated among the extravagances and follies of the selfish world. All around us men are spending fortunes on piles of stones that will not make their selfish dust sleep more easily, while the poor and hungry are crying for bread and the heathen are dying without the gospel.

HIS SELFISHNESS

2. Absalom was the slave of selfish and worldly ambition. His supreme object was to make for himself a splendid position and attain the very highest place, even the throne itself. For this he unscrupulously risked everything, and at last lost honor and life. He had become intoxicated with the cup of pride. He had become fascinated with the dream of fame. He had set out in the race, which multitudes are running still, for earthly power and greatness. It is a very sad and usually hopeless struggle. Even when the prize is won it is not worth its cost. What did Bonaparte get for all his victories but a disappointed ambition, a lonely exile and a death without a single ray of hope? What could be more sad than the dying words of Gambetta, the hero of the French Revolution, who, dying in the highest place that the country could give him, left these sad words, "There is no use denying it, everything is lost." How few of the men that have struggled in our own lifetime for political preeminence have got anything out of it to pay them for the cost. The men that triumphed for a time as political bosses were turned out at last by successful rivals, and their very names are soon forgotten. The man who enters the White House at the beginning of a term amid praise and honor steals out of it at the end with none to do him reverence, having disappointed his political friends and won the derision of his enemies, and even failed perhaps to please himself. These are the apparently successful ones, but what of the myriads who fall in the struggle and lose not only the object of their pursuit but everything else as well as the prize?

God save our young men from the demoralizing and disappointing struggle for political preeminence and worldly honor. With all its perils and risks, even the strife for wealth is less degrading. No man can be safe in such a contest. He is bound to compromise with evil. He is sure to be associated with ungodly men. He must trample under his feet God's holy day as he holds himself at the bidding of political caucuses and the calls of politicians. Honor, principle and godliness must often be sacrificed, and it will be a great miracle of grace if he shall not miss winning the whole world and at the same time lose his own soul. There is a better ambition. There is a safer hope. There is a nobler aspiration. There are crowns and kingdoms to be won by the sacrifice of self and sin. Let us nobly enter these high contests and let the world go by.

HIS UNBRIDLED PASSION

3. Absalom was a man of passion. His passion was of two kinds, as it usually is. It manifested itself first in the form of vindictiveness and retaliation, and afterward in a shameless disregard of morality and purity in the sight of all the land. The first outbreak of his over-strained nature was the murder of Amnon, his own half-brother, because of the cruel wrong he had done to Absalom's sister, Tamar. There was something natural and perhaps chivalrous in the indignation of Absalom at this abominable crime, but there was a better way to deal with it. Absalom's course was bloody and treacherous. Let us not forget that the blood we shed will come back to us and demand our own. "Whoever sheds the blood of man,/ by man shall his blood be shed" (Genesis 9:6). "For all who draw the sword will die by the sword" (Matthew 26:52). Violence and self-avenging are altogether wrong, and the high-spirited young men of our day who delight in these things will find in the end that there is a nemesis of retribution that follows surely the bloody track of the murderer to the bitter end.

But Absalom stooped to deeper depths of indulgence and crime when he openly debauched the very household of his vulnerable father, and in the sight of all the city and in the very light of the sun dishonored both himself and his father's name by the most shameful of open excesses. It may be said that he did this thing as an act of policy, and did it at the advice of his crafty counselor. He did it in order to be detested by David's friends and to alienate them more fully from him. This only makes vice the more abominable when it is used as the handmaid of policy. The saddest thing about the vice of our times is that it has become shameless, too. There are thousands of well-bred and well-educated young men who betray no blush of shame when exposed in the most disgusting orgies of licentiousness. There is a little passing talk, and a slight sensation in the channel of public opinion and a decent protest against it by a portion of the press, perhaps a threatened suit at law. But then it all quietly passes over and the same men are received into society without a blush and claim the hands of pure and gentle girls who would be driven from every social circle if their names were even distantly suspected in similar connections. And yet there are men who, in the popular literature of our times, are trying to excuse the license which is permeating our society as justifiable, and are telling us that God has endowed men with these passions and how can He blame them for acting according to the nature He has given them. There is no doubt but that the greatest peril to young men today lies in the direction of social immorality and license. How can such young men be safe?

The same law that follows the murderer to his doom will pursue the adulterer, not only to his grave, but to the horrors of an eternal retribution. There are great laws in the human soul which bring their own punishment. You may conceal from the public eye your wrongdoing, you may hide your shame from man, but there is a phonograph which God has put within your breast which has recorded the story of your crime, and will tell it over again, if not to other ears, to your conscience and memory forever. There is an hour and there is a place where faces will look into yours and the cursing maledictions of ruined lives will be your tormentors. You will need no bitterer hell than for God to send you away with the companions of your vices and say to you, "Son, remember" (Luke 16:25). Sometimes these things overtake men in this life, and the iniquity of their heels compasses them about until life becomes intolerable and the world is the only door of escape from the horrors of an accusing conscience and a tormented life. Young men, be warned and beware. "Her house is a highway to the grave,/ leading down to the chambers of death" (Proverbs 7:27).

A DISLOYAL SON

4. Absalom was a disobedient and disloyal son. He cared not for his father's love. No, he plotted against David's very life as well as his throne. With cold and heartless indifference he schemed with his evil counselors for the surest way to secure his life and to ignominiously destroy his kingdom. He was unnatural, ungrateful, unfilial and utterly unfaithful. How could such a young man be safe? God has written the law of the fifth commandment in human nature, and the sons and daughters that dishonor their parents will find themselves pursued to the end of life with a certain retribution. It is said that perhaps the reason that the Chinese nation today has outlived all others is that above all other people they honor parental relation. Be kind and gentle to your father and mother even if they are wrong and treat you wrongly. Meet them in the spirit of filial respect and tenderness. Of course there is a limit. We dare not let them control our conscience in the things of God. Even there you can do it so gently that your example will speak to them more loudly than your words, and God at last will give you the blessing of the fifth commandment, "Honor your father and your mother, so that you may live long in the land the LORD your God is giving you" (Exodus 20:12).

A TRAITOR

5. Absalom was deceitful, false and treacherous. His course was one of deep artifice and studied duplicity. He secured his recall from banishment by the deepest cunning. When he returned he set himself by the arts of flattery to captivate the hearts of the people and to undermine the influence of his

father. He sat in the gates of Jerusalem meeting all that were in trouble, listening to their grievances and telling them how he would treat them if he was king, until gradually their hearts went after him and he had laid the foundation for his rebellion. How could such a young man be safe? The deceiver sinning against the nature of things. Truth is just reality, just a law of God's order, and the man who sins against it sins against the very law of nature. It must react against him with fatal rebound and destroy him. Truth is essential to morality, and falsehood in every form must end in disappointment, exposure and defeat. Young man, be true. It is not necessary that commercial business should be based upon a tissue of falsehood and misrepresentation.

UNSCRUPULOUS

Finally, Absalom was unscrupulous, unprincipled and ungodly, and in his own character lay the secret of his ruin. And so, on the other hand, the secret of character is godliness. It is not by natural endowments that we can be true and pure. It is only possible by union with God through the Lord Jesus Christ and by receiving into our hearts that blessed Man who is pre-eminently the pattern for young men and the ideal life for them to live. Not only had He once lived and walked before us as our pattern, but He comes to live again in every true heart that will receive Him, and to lift us up to His own ideal of holy, eternal manhood. Jesus Christ is forever a young man, and He wants to lead young manhood up to the high place where He has risen, our Leader and Head. Oh, let us receive and follow Him!

The contrasted picture of our text presents not only the folly and failure of Absalom, but the beautiful example of David's life. It is the love of the father's heart who gladly would have died for his ruined son. It is also the picture of a more loving heart, even that heavenly Friend, who not only would have died for us, but has died for every man who will accept His blessed sacrifice. He is pleading with you, young man, and saying, "Why should you die? Why should you be lost? Even if you have sinned and grieved Him and ruined yourself like Absalom, I have died for you, and I will teach you how to live and lift you up from that self-inflicted misery and make you to be even as I." Oh, receive Him, and never let Him have to weep over you in heaven as He once wept over Jerusalem, saying, "I have longed to gather [you] . . . but you were not willing" (Luke 13:34). Never let Him have to say for you, my brother, "Oh, Absalom, my son, why have you let me die for you in vain?"

"Is the young man Absalom, safe?" Brother, send back the answer, as you close this page, "Yes; he is safe because he is saved through a Savior's dying love."

CHAPTER 10

THE IDEAL KING

"When one rules over men in righteousness,
  when he rules in the fear of God,
he is like the light of morning at sunrise
  on a cloudless morning,
like the brightness after rain
  that brings the grass from the earth."

Although my house be not so with God; (KJV)
  Has he not made with me an everlasting covenant,
  arranged and secured in every part?
Will he not bring to fruition my salvation
  and grant me my every desire?
But evil men are all to be cast aside like thorns,
  which are not gathered with the hand.
Whoever touches thorns
  uses a tool of iron or the shaft of a spear;
  they are burned up where they lie.
    (2 Samuel 23:3–7)

These are the last words of David, the backward look at the story of a life. How different life looks in the retrospect and prospect. How the exaggerating hazes and the rose tints disappear in the clear, cold light of life's sterner reality and we see things a little as we shall see them when we look back upon the record from the heights of judgment and in the light of eternity. David had no exaggerated estimate of his own life. Whatever his failures may have been he seems to have seen them in their true light and significance. Yet he had that God-given faith, which could look over his own failures to the bright and blessed hope of that greater King, of whom he was but the type and the distant foreshadowing. And so, while in one sense it is true that this passage is the discouraging review of an imperfect reign, on the other hand it is just as true that it is the King, who would fulfill more perfectly the ideal that David saw and in whose coming glory David could forget the faults of his imperfect reign and even the sins of his oft-erring life.

DAVID'S IDEAL OF A TRUE KING

David at least has learned this much of what a king ought to be, and he wisely describes the picture of an ideal ruler.

1. He should be just, free and right in all his relationships with his fellow-man and with his subject.

2. He should be godly, ruling "in the fear of God" (23:3). He should recognize himself as the representative of the divine King and work in all things under His direction and in His stead. This is the only true impulse of righteousness. It must spring out of heaven and be inspired by the fear and love of God.

3. Beneficence must be a part of his reign. What a beautiful picture of a reign of peace, prosperity and blessedness, as the light of the morning, the rising sun, a cloudless sky and the light and warmth of the heavenly sunshine, more bright and beautiful because it comes after the storm; as the "clear shining after rain" (23:4), while on the disappearing clouds the rainbow spans the heavens and every leaf and flower is flashing like crystal jewels from the myriad drops in their reflected light.

DAVID'S FAILURE TO FILL THIS IDEAL

"Although my house be not so with God" (23:5, KJV). This little sentence tells us how honestly he realizes his failure to measure up to his own conception of what a king should be. He was the best of Israel's kings and all through the coming generations "his father, David," is held up to each of his successors as a model of a true reign. And yet he felt how far short he had come of God's highest purpose for his theocratic people. His life was overshadowed by many an infirmity, sin and bitter sorrow.

If David was a failure, what an awful failure human government must be considered. How fearfully the kings of earth have failed to represent the beneficent government of the heavenly reign. What were the long dynasties of Egypt, Babylon, Assyria, Medo-Persia, Greece and Rome, but menageries of wild beasts, whom Daniel well might represent in his prophetic vision as ferocious beasts devouring and destroying in their fierce career of selfishness and violence. How little better the governments of today are, may be witnessed by the testimony of our own times in the ferocious cruelties tolerated by civilized nations against weak and defenseless natives.

What else may we look for to take the place of earthly despotisms? How much better is a republic? Shall we entrust our popular democracy with the scepter of government? Alas, the money kings of earth today are monopolizing the world's wealth, and the masses and the classes are getting ready for a relentless war of which we constantly hear the mutterings. There is no despotism so heartless and cruel as that of avarice and gold.

Or shall we enthrone culture and crown her with a scepter of government? Alas, the golden age of art and literature is often the gross age of vice and license as gross as the days of the Borgias in Italy, or the Caesars in Rome and Pompeii. Culture without Christianity gives people only greater power for wickedness. Our criminals today are no longer the unlettered classes, but the graduates of universities. Our teachers of irreligion and vice, the men that would legalize suicide, prostitution and intemperance and burn up the Bible, are among the most brilliant wits, poets and orators of our time. No, earth needs a stronger, holier king, and she must go from worse to worse until He shall "make it a ruin," and at last shall He come "to whom it rightfully belongs" (Ezekiel 21:27). And He shall "defend the afflicted among the people/ and save the children of the needy;/ he will crush the oppressor./ . . . / In his days the righteous will flourish;/ prosperity will abound till the moon is no more" (Psalm 72:4, 7).

David looked forward from his failures and the failures which he foresaw in prophetic vision in the lives of his successors and in the distant future he beheld a King who "will reign in righteousness" (Isaiah 32:1) and a Man who should be "like a shelter from the wind/ and a refuge from the storm,/ like streams of water in the desert/ and the shadow of a great rock in a thirsty land" (32:2).

CHRIST THE TRUE KING

1. He was true to David's ideal.

He is just, and ruling in the fear of God, and all the exquisite imagery of this beautiful picture is fulfilled in Him. He is as the light of the morning. He is the Author of truth and light. He brings morning to the dark world. It is "a cloudless morning" (2 Samuel 23:4). Its sun shall no more go down. He shall be to us an everlasting light. And yet it is a light and sunrise that follow the night of darkness and sorrow. It is the "brightness after rain" (23:4), and it is all the clearer and brighter because of the rain that went before.

Oh, how sweet it is to have Him enter our hearts and bring the peace of his benignant sway after the long night of our despair, the "clear shining after rain"! Oh, how sweet it will be some day to receive back from the grave our lost ones and to have Him bring light out of our darkness, joy out of our sorrow and crowns out of our crosses! Heaven will be all the sweeter and the brighter because of the grave and the gloom from which we have emerged, even as the "brightness after rain." Oh, how beautiful it will be for earth to awake to her millennial morning after the night of the tempest which will precede it and the Armageddon battle which will be just before.

His coming will be as the morning after the midnight and the "brightness after rain."

The figure also speaks of fruitfulness, "that brings the grass from the earth" (23:4). Oh, the fruits which His kingdom brings to us out of trial: the fir tree that comes instead of the thorn; the myrtle that grows out of the briar; the curse turned unto a blessing, "a harvest of righteousness and peace for those who have been trained" (Hebrews 12:11) by the chastening of our God.

2. This coming King is the antitype of David.

David was His type, and He fulfills many characteristics of Israel's first true king. David was born in Bethlehem. So was He. David was despised and rejected of men. So was He. David was anointed of the Lord. So is He, the anointed One. David was persecuted and pursued by his enemies, and for years a king in exile. So He was persecuted and murdered by hostile men, and even today He is still an exiled King awaiting His throne. David was surrounded by a multitude of wretched, outcast and sinful men, attracted to him by the tie of common misery, but true to him in their sorrow and afterwards honored by him as the princes of his realm. So Jesus today is gathering His princes from the ranks of sinners and outcasts. And some day they will be the nobility of heaven, washed in the blood of the Lamb, and sitting by His side upon His millennial throne. Then David received his kingdom in sections, first Hebron and then Jerusalem over all Israel. And so our coming King is first to be crowned by the little flock He shall bring with Him, and then He is to sit down upon the throne of all the world and reign from pole to pole and shore to shore.

3. He was David's Savior.

"This," he says, "is my salvation" (2 Samuel 23:5). David understood that his Seed and his Offspring was to be his Redeemer, and from the sins of a lifetime he found peace and hope in trusting in the coming Deliverer and accepting Him as his personal Savior.

4. David had entered into a covenant with the coming King.

"Has he not made with me an everlasting covenant,/ arranged and secured in every part" (23:5). He had got the ear of his Successor and had secured in advance his place and his inheritance in the coming kingdom. It was a personal covenant. His own name was written there and all his rights and hopes secured beyond the possibility of disappointment of failure, "arranged and secured in every part."

Beloved, have we this covenant made and secured with the coming King? Have we had an audience with Him in the days of His retirement and settled all the questions of our future in advance? There is a day coming when myriads of angels will surround His throne and it will not be possible to reach His presence and bring your request to His feet, but you shall go to "where [you] belong" (Acts 1:25) and reap the results of your earthly life.

Before the installment of our president, his friends visited him in his retirement, and their various requests were presented at leisure in his presence. It would be no easy task now to press through the formalities of even his modest court and claim his costly leisure for any personal need. This is the time to secure our covenant with our King. Let us not rest until our names are written down upon His hands and His heart and upon the seat prepared for us, and the high calling and an immortal service to which He bids us aspire.

5. David's whole heart was in the coming King and kingdom.

"Will he not," David asks, "bring to fruition my salvation/ and grant me my every desire?" (2 Samuel 23:5). He had invested his being there, and all his hopes were passing upward and onward to the age to come. Life for him was over now. Its praises and its penalties were past. Alas for him if this were all. But no, his fortune was laid up on high, his inheritance was insured beyond the grave. All his being was reaching forward to that glorious day when his illustrious Son should sit upon His greater throne and David should lay his crown at His feet and hail Him as "the Root and the Offspring of David, and the bright Morning Star" (Revelation 22:16).

Beloved, is our heart in the hope of Christ's return? Are our affections clustered there? Are our ambitions in the skies? Are our investments, our plans, our pursuits all tending to that imminent event? David looked forward to it but knew it was far in the distance. Daniel went to his grave with the words, "As for you, go your way till the end. You will rest, and then at the end of your days you will rise to receive your allotted inheritance" (Daniel 12:13). We are living on the very threshold of its dawn. Oh, how much more it should mean to us! How we should watch and pray, and work, bending every energy, concentrating every plan and making all our lives subsidiary to this one great and supreme aim, to hasten the coming of our Lord and Savior Jesus Christ!

David knew he had been an unfaithful and sinful man. He could honestly say, "Although my house be not so with God; (KJV)/ Has he not made with me an everlasting covenant" (2 Samuel 23:5). He had accepted the infinite mercy and saving grace of Jesus Christ. He had come as a sinner without merit or claim, and he had generously accepted all that God's mercy had so freely to bestow. Oh, there may be some of us today who can say, "My house is not right with God, my life has been a failure, my work has been disastrous, I am all wrong and I have nothing to bring but shame"; beloved, come all the same. It is the door of mercy that you are entering. If you deserve it you could only take an angel's place, but because you do not deserve it you can take, through the infinite grace of God and the gift of Jesus Christ, a place as high as that of Jesus Himself. Come although you have to come, saying,

The mistakes of my life have been many,
The sins of my life have been more,
And I scarce can see for weeping,
But I'll knock at the open door.
My mistakes His free grace will cover,
My sins He will wash away,
And the feet that tremble and falter
Shall walk through the gates of day.

THE OTHER PICTURE

On the other hand, how dark the picture of the wicked with which the scene closes! "But evil men are all to be cast aside like thorns,/ which are not gathered by the hand./ . . . /they are burned up where they lie" (23:6–7). Live for the world if you will, pursue its ambitions if you choose, be a thorn and bramble if you prefer, but there is a law of spiritual gravitation that leads all at last to "where [they] belong" (Acts 1:25). And if you belong to another world, there will you tend. The thorns are for flames and are useless for anything else. The soul born of God mounts to God and can be kept nowhere else. It is the law of the fitness of things, it is the law of nature, it is the law of eternity. "Let him who does wrong continue to do wrong; let him who is vile continue to be vile; let him who does right continue to do right; and let him who is holy continue to be holy. Behold, I am coming soon! My reward is with me, and I will give to everyone according to what he has done" (Revelation 22:11–12).

"Amen. Come, Lord Jesus." (22:20). Amen.

CHAPTER 11

SHIMEI'S CURSE

A man from the same clan as Saul's family came out from there. His name was Shimei son of Gera, and he cursed as he came out. . . .

Then Abishai son of Zeruiah said to the king, "Why should this dead dog curse my lord the king? Let me go over and cut off his head."

But the king said, "What do you and I have in common, you sons of Zeruiah? If he is cursing because the LORD said to him, 'Curse David,' who can ask, 'Why do you do this?' "

David then said to Abishai and all his officials, "My son, who is of my own flesh, is trying to take my life. How much more, then, this Benjamite! Leave him alone; let him curse for the LORD has told him to. It may be that the LORD will see my distress and repay me with good for the cursing I am receiving today." (2 Samuel 16:5, 9–12)

There are flowers that bloom only in the glaciers of the Alps and the wild sirocco of the Sahara desert. And so there are virtues and graces that only appear in the wintry atmosphere of obloquy, calamity and sorrow. No man can be sure that he knows himself or is proved and tried until he has passed through the experiences of cruel misunderstanding and shameful wrong. The Son of man was made perfect through sufferings, and in the perfecting of the Christian character, patience is the last of the graces. Even charity, the queen of all graces, reaches her maturity in the school of sorrow. The first feature in her portrait is, she is "patient," and the last, she "always perseveres" (1 Corinthians 13:4, 17).

And so we see the highest qualities of David in the hour of his keenest trials and in the face of the most humiliating experiences. It is one thing to bear the cool treachery of such a son as Absalom. It is another thing, and in some respects a little harder, to endure the taunts and scoffs of a creature like Shimei. There is a sense in which the bite of a sandfly is more annoying than the artillery of a battalion. And so the present subject speaks to our own life in a place which many have found to be intensely irritating and often intensely hard.

THE CURSE OF THE WICKED

Primarily it is the curse of the devil.

1. This is his peculiar business. His very name means "accuser" (Revelation 12:10). It is natural for him to throw stones, hurl epithets and utter curses. This alone should arm us against his blows. When we know they come from him, we need not greatly mind them since they are almost certain to be found unjust and in the end harmless. The spirit of fault-finding, sarcasm, criticism and calumny are all satanic, and every one who indulges in them is voluntarily wearing the devil's livery.

2. But the devil has some human voices to repeat his curses—the critic, the calumniator, the backbiter, the passionate and profane. These are all of the race of Shimei, and the business is not by any means wound up. No man or woman can pass through life without having to face the detractor and feel the keen wound of the slanderer.

3. It is a comfort to know as Solomon has so well expressed it, "An undeserved curse does not come to rest" (Proverbs 26:2). Unjust accusations and false calumniators can never harm us in the end.

4. The curse of the wicked almost always comes in the hour of our calamity. It made it doubly hard for David because Shimei took advantage of the darkest hour of his life. It was mean and cowardly. If ever there was a time when common humanity would have looked in respectful silence upon so great a sorrow as his, it was the hour when his own child was seeking his father's life. But this was the time when the cowardly Shimei chose to strike his defenseless king, and add sharpness to the wound which was already stinging him to death.

5. It was made still harder by David's own sensitive conscience, and the sense of his own sin for which God was doubtless chastening him. At such a time it is so easy for the great adversary to inject into our hearts his most cruel poison, and to make our own errors seem darker and more malignant. It is a very dark hour in human life when, with circumstances arrayed against us and calamity overwhelming us with its angry billows on every side, our own heart turns against us, and the devil tries to make us seem worse than we are and to undermine even our confidence in the mercy of God and our very right to call Him our Father. At such a time the curse of the wicked seems to the sensitive and morbid conscience like the very voice of divine judgment, and the great accuser loves to play the part of a divine messenger, and torture us with his reproaches and forebodings.

THE SPIRIT IN WHICH DAVID ENDURED THIS TRIAL

1. He saw God in it above the devil and the devil's miserable instrument. "Let him curse," he said, "for the LORD has told him to" (2 Samuel 16:11). This is the highest ground that faith can take in the most trying hour. This was the way Joseph was able to look back over his distressing experience. "It was not you who sent me here," he could say, "but God" (Genesis 45:8), "because it was to save lives that God sent me ahead of you" (45:5). When we can look over the devil's head and see our blessed Master ruling and over-ruling, we can endure anything that He may permit. God does allow the wicked to assail us and the devil to tempt us. Sometimes it is to make manifest their wickedness and allow them to fill their cup of judgment. Sometimes it is to glorify Christ by our example of patience and gentleness.

2. David overlooked the petty trial of Shimei's cursing in the light of the greater trial of Absalom's crime. "My own son," he said, "is seeking my life; why should I be unduly tried by this trifling nettle that seeks to sting my hand?" Nearly all our troubles would become trifling and seem unworthy of our notice if we looked above them to the greater issues of life. At the very time that we are fretting over some petty wrong, there is a graver issue pending that needs our whole attention—perhaps some child or friend in great temptation, danger or sin, perhaps some great peril threatening our life and work, perhaps some duty that we are neglecting in the pursuit of this miserable side issue, perhaps the very crown of our eternal future is being risked while we let the devil preoccupy us about our reputation, our rights, or the punishment of some petty slanderer whom we might better leave to God. I have known a minister of the gospel to spend years of his life in hunting down petty adversaries and following up contemptible assaults upon his character while his work suffered continued distraction and finally destruction and he came out in the end as a man always comes out who goes in to fight all the dogs in the street. He may succeed in defeating the dogs but he will bear away scratches to last him for a lifetime and find he has lost his time in the bargain.

That was wise advice that Abraham Lincoln gave to his son. "My boy," he said, "men tell you to be slow to quarrel, but when you do quarrel make your quarrel so strong that you will not need to quarrel again, for your enemy will respect you for life. My boy, do not take their advice. My counsel is, never quarrel. Even if you succeed in your contest you make an enemy and you lose more than you gain." Let us be so preoccupied with the great issues of life that we shall pass by all these trifling things, and with a wide estimate of life's real values shut our eyes to the devil's side shows and treat him and his emissaries with that which he least can stand, silent contempt.

3. David refused to avenge himself. He would not allow Abishai to cut off

Shimei's head as he easily might have done, but he left his cause unvindicated, and he committed his case to the hands of his faithful Creator as we are commanded likewise to do (1 Peter 4:19).

4. Better still, he even took Shimei's curses as the promise of blessings and said with deep ingenuity and lofty faith, "It may be that the LORD will see my distress and repay me with good for the cursing I am receiving today" (2 Samuel 16:12). That is a fine view to take of the devil's unkindness, to ask the Lord to enter a credit in our account and balance the books with a blessing for us in consideration of his curse.

God does requite His children for the devil's cruel blows. He gives them grace and strength through the trial, and He makes up to them for every blow by His loving kindness and His faithful providences. A dear friend once remarked to me respecting a child of God who had met with a terrible affliction and borne it with heavenly patience. "It seemed to me that ever afterward her God was trying to make up to her by His goodness for the sorrow that she had borne."

And so God does make up to us now. "As a mother comforts her child,/ so will I comfort you" (Isaiah 66:13). And by and by we shall find in the reversion yonder a chain of gold for every chain of iron Satan forged; a crown of glory for every curse, teardrops transformed into diamonds and thorns and thistles blooming as myrtles in the Paradise of God. So when the devil rages, scolds, strikes and blasphemes, let us calmly look up and say, "Lord, remember his wrong and give me judgment against my adversary."

THE ISSUE OF SHIMEI'S CURSE AND DAVID'S TRUST

1. David was vindicated. His trial at length passed away, the sunshine came again, the rebellion was suppressed, the king was restored and the millions of Israel came to pay their homage at his feet. Shimei found himself in the cold minority, an object of contempt and helplessness, obliged even to plead for his own worthless life.

2. The punishment that he so well deserved came at last upon him through his own folly and recklessness. David never lifted his hand to touch him, but when Solomon came to the throne, he called Shimei to account for his former wickedness. Solomon gave Shimei perfect immunity while he remained in his own house in Jerusalem, but Shimei broke his parole. Disregarding his solemn covenant, one day on a trifling pretext Shimei left his home and returned to find himself condemned by his own folly to the execution that had waited so long for his wicked old head. So if we leave our enemies in the hands of God they will bring upon themselves the judgment of that we would avert from them if we could. Could we only see the sorrow and ruin that await many of those who have often wronged and tried us we would weep with compassion and we would kneel at their feet and implore

them to save themselves from retribution and ruin. There are laws of inexorable consequence by which the bitter word which we send forth against
another, and the unjust act by which we strike an innocent head, after
describing their parabolic course through our mingled lives, come back in
the end and strike our own head with all the accumulated force they have
gathered on their way. These things can afford to wait, but the issue is as
certain as the eternal laws of God. "As you have done, it will be done to
you" (Obadiah 1:15), is the principle that has been inscribed on every page
of human history and stands emblazoned on the records of God's providences and pillars of the judgment throne.

3. David also got his blessing as well as Shimei his curse. The best of it
was, not the deliverance of David from the calamities that Shimei
prophesied, but the fact that this little chapter could be written with its
beautiful story of meekness, Christlikeness and heavenly patience. It gave
David an opportunity to be a truer type of Christ and to leave a portrait in
the galleries of eternity for which it would have been worthwhile to live.
This, after all, is the greatest meaning of life. Our situations come to us not
so much that we may get out of them or get into them, but that they may
furnish occasions for our exemplifying the Christian spirit. Like the dum-
mies in the shop windows that are there to hold the various wares and robes
that are exposed for exhibition and sale, so we are called to show forth the
excellencies of Christ before a careless world. Our various circumstances
come to us in the providences of God as opportunity for us to exhibit the
life of our Master to a world that can see Him only through us. When circumstances smile upon us, we are to exhibit the spirit of humble gratitude
and unselfish joy. When sorrow comes we are to show a spirit of patience
and trust. When others revile and wrong us, we are to exhibit the character
which David displayed under the circumstances of our text. Everything is to
be looked upon as an occasion for testimony and service for our Master.
"This will result in your being witnesses to them" (Luke 21:13) was the
master's intimation to His disciples as they went forth to witness for Him
and to be imprisoned and persecuted by their fellowmen. He did not say,
"You shall be delivered, you shall be protected," but He said rather, "You
shall find the prison a pulpit and the judgment hall an auditorium where
you can preach My gospel and set forth My character before sinful men."

Thus we are making our eternal records. By and by we will find that God
has kept the record correctly and completely, and that, while we have been
endeavoring to represent Him, He has been standing for us weaving our sorrows into chaplets and crowns of eternal recompense.

The little pearl oyster receiving accidentally into its shell a rough fragment
of rock or sand tries in vain to expel the intruding and irritant substance. It
only suffers in the struggle until rasped and bleeding it gives up in agony and

helplessness. Then a new force comes into play. From its peculiar physiological system, the little mollusk sends forth a crystal fluid which covers and coats the rough piece of rock with a soft crystalline cushion. As this grows and hardens, it becomes a beautiful pearl. It ceases to irritate and soothes and rests the wounded side of the little creature until the curse has become a blessing, and some days later the pearl fisher discovers the hidden treasure, opens the shell and takes forth a gem of purest luster and boundless value which is worn in the coronets of kings and adorns the highest rank and grandest occasions. So some day our sorrows, irritations and wrongs, having first been sweetened by the Holy Spirit into heavenly virtues, will become the jewels of an immortal crown and will shine in the diadem of Jesus and adorn our brow forever.

Don't let us be turned aside by sandflies, barking dogs and biting thorns from the glorious possibilities of a life of sweetness, righteousness and victory, and "the crown of glory that will never fade away" (1 Peter 5:4).

CHAPTER 12

THE LAW OF SACRIFICE

"I will not sacrifice to the LORD my God burnt offerings that cost me nothing."

So David bought the threshing floor and the oxen and paid fifty shekels of silver for them. David built an altar to the LORD there and sacrificed burnt offerings and fellowship offerings. Then the LORD answered prayer in behalf of the land, and the plague on Israel was stopped. (2 Samuel 24:24–25)

T hree great thoughts are vividly presented and illustrated in the story of this chapter.

SIN

We have an account of the last great sin of David's life. It was quite different from his former transgression and represented more subtle elements of temptation and disobedience. In the account given in the parallel passage in First Chronicles, it is represented as a masterpiece of Satanic subtlety. It was the devil who suggested and instigated it that he might lead David to provoke God and bring upon himself and his kingdom divine judgment.

It was a sin which to the ordinary mind might seem comparatively trifling or, at least, difficult to weigh in the same balance with the foul crime committed against Uriah. And yet it provoked God's severer judgment. It was the simple act of numbering the people, taking a census of the whole population of his kingdom, especially of the men able to bear arms.

The peculiar element of sin in this act was the spirit of vainglory and self-conscious pride which prompted it. It was really the treacherous departure on David's part from his humble and supreme reliance on Jehovah as the theocratic King and supreme Sovereign and support of the Hebrew monarchy, and a turning to the arm of flesh as well as the spirit of self-complacent pride in his own greatness and glory. It was the same spirit which afterwards manifested itself in the proud boast of Nebuchadnezzar: "Is not this the great Babylon I have built . . . for the glory of my majesty?" (Daniel 4:30), and which brought upon him a swift and terrible blow that sent him for seven years to grovel in insanity among the beasts of the field.

This is one of the gilded sins of human nature whose enormity escapes the self-conceited thought of human ambition and pride. But it is the source of all sin and the very cause of Satan's downfall. Pride is the "devil's trap" (1 Timothy 3:7). And it seems the idea of Holy Scripture as well as the highest human genius, that when Satan looked into the mirror and saw his own beauty and brightness he became intoxicated with holy ambition and pride, and, assuming the place of a god, he sank from the heights of heaven to the depths of hell, and has ever since been dragging down all the spirits that he could control by the same subtle temptation.

This was the eventual result which he made upon the innocency of Eve when he appealed to her spiritual pride and said, "You will be like God, knowing good and evil" (Genesis 3:5). Ever since that eventful morning her sons and daughters have been infested with a spirit of a false ambition and a delusive vainglory which has strewn the world with wrecks of ambition, vanity and pride.

This was the subtle snare which Satan prepared for David's latest days. It was the unconscious desire to display the greatness of his kingdom and the strength of his military resources.

Joab, his shrewd commander-in-chief, while a man of no moral or religious principle whatever, was wise enough to know that David's proposal was wrong, and he earnestly tried to dissuade him from it without success, and then reluctantly proceeded to carry out his master's instructions. The census proceeded for nearly 10 months, including the whole kingdom except the tribes of Levi and Benjamin, and showed an available military force of more than a million and a quarter men.

But the moment the result was announced to David, he felt in his inmost soul that he had erred and sinned; and with that deep intuition of a true and tender conscience which was so beautiful a feature of his character, when he really saw his fault he humbled himself before God and said, "I have sinned greatly by doing this. Now, I beg you, take away the guilt of your servant. I have done a very foolish thing" (1 Chronicles 21:8). God was pleased to accept his penitence. But, nevertheless, He proceeded to teach him the important lesson rightly imparted to him and to the ages for whom he was living as a great object lesson. Happy for us if we could learn that lesson without having to go through the same sad discipline!

This sin of vanity, self-consciousness and pride is one of the most alarming signs of our public, social and religious life of today. We see it in the proud despots of great nations. We see it in the spirit of bragging both in our own and in other lands. We see it in the disgusting and extravagant social display so characteristic of our time. We see it in ecclesiastical and religious ambition. And its subtle snare attends every stage of our religious experience and makes it so easy to seem rather than to do, and to turn even our holiest blessings into a dramatic exhibition or a self-conscious display of our own graces or victories or Christian work.

Whenever we become occupied unduly with even the best religious experience, or think or speak in the spirit of pride of the most useful Christian work, we at once obscure it with its own shadow and defile it with the foul odor of carnal pride. Lowliness, whether it be physical, intellectual or spiritual, loses all its charm when it becomes conscious of its own attraction; and modesty is a heavenly veil which covers with divine beauty even the homeliest face and the simplest action. Let us take care as we come near the holiest to veil our faces with our wings and to be so absorbed with God that we shall not know that our faces shine. Let us never forget, as He blesses our work, to hide both it and ourselves under the shadow of His hand, and laying every crown at His blessed feet, to say, "Not to us, O LORD, not to us/ but to your name be the glory" (Psalm 115:1).

David's great sin was marked by God with the severest chastening. It was chastening mingled with mercy because David had already seen his fault and knew that God was dealing with him, not in judgment but in paternal discipline. It is very sweet to recognize our Father's hand in our sorest trials. It would be terrible to find ourselves in the hands of an angry God. God's disciplinary dealings with His children are always merciful and the tenderest proof of the Father's love. "You only have I chosen," He says, "of all the families of the earth;/ therefore I will punish you/ for all your sins" (Amos 3:2).

We see, in the manner in which David received God's dealings with his sin, a beautiful example of penitence and submission of a believing soul. God gave David his choice of three judgments, either of a destructive famine, defeat in war or three days of pestilence. David's answer is very instructive. "Let us fall," he says, "into the hands of the LORD, for his mercy is great; but do not let me fall into the hands of men" (2 Samuel 24:14). Here lies the difference between the natural heart and the erring child of God. The former wants to get away from God, and the latter wants to fall into His hands and be dealt with by His wisdom and mercy. Here Peter and Judas part. The latter went out from the presence of Christ to despair by his conscience. The former lingered to catch his Master's look, and was the first to swim to the Galilean shore when Jesus met His disciples after His resurrection.

The hardest part of David's chastening was the suffering it brought upon others, the innocent "sheep" (24:17), as he called them, who had done no wrong, and yet who suffered the most terrible effects from his transgression. There is no form of trial so severe as that which comes to our innocent and loved ones in consequence of our own disobedience to God. Many a parent whose heart would not be reached by a personal affliction is often broken into penitence and humility by the dying anguish of a beloved child who acts as a messenger of discipline to that parent's heart.

> Smitten friends
> Are angels sent on errands full of love.
> For us they languish and for us they die.
> And shall they languish, shall they die in vain?
> Shall we tread under foot their agonizing groans,
> Frustrate their anguish and make void their death?

You may say, if you like, that this is unjust on God's part, but its reason lies in the very nature of things. As well might you say that it was unjust for the branch to wither when the root of the tree is cut. God has interwoven us all together so that one involves many in mutual suffering. A father's intemperance bequeaths a curse upon his innocent babes. A pastor's fall wrecks the eternal hopes of many who leaned upon his faith and are undermined by his unfaithfulness. Every one of us carries with us the fate of precious souls as surely as the captain carries the lives of his passengers in his hand. David found this out when he saw 70,000 of Israel's innocent men, women and children laying black with plague and convulsed with agony because of his rash, presumptuous act.

Oh, is God thus dealing with you through another's sorrow? God forbid that your hearts should be so hard as to "let them languish, let them die in vain." Listen to the voice that speaks to you from their pallid brow and expiring breath, and turn to God whose hands have smitten, and He will again make you whole. David's heart was crushed by this terrible calamity, and at last unable to endure it longer he cried out in truly magnanimous spirit as the angel lifted his sword above Jerusalem to destroy it, "I am the one who has sinned and done wrong. These are but sheep. What have they done? Let your hand fall upon me and my family" (24:17).

ATONEMENT AND EXPIATION

But David's self-sacrifice could not atone for his great sin. He and his father's house, had they all perished, could not have made right the wrong which he had done.

And so God taught him and taught the world through him that greatest lesson of divine revelation which had been enacted so often on the Jewish altars, and which was yet to be accomplished in its reality by the world's Redeemer, that nothing less than the blood of God's own appointed sacrifice could expiate the sins of men. And so the command was given,

"'Go up and build an altar to the LORD on the threshing floor of Araunah the Jebusite.' . . . David built an altar to the LORD there and sacrificed burnt offerings and fellowship offerings. Then the LORD answered prayer in behalf of the land, and the plague on Israel was stopped" (24:18, 25).

Here, on the very site where Abraham offered up his Isaac ages before as the type of the world's greater sacrifice, and near where Jesus afterwards died, David reared by divine command a sacrificial altar and offered up victims which were but figures of the Lamb of God who, ages later, laid down His own life for the sins of men, and thus laid the foundation by which God can be just and the justifier of him that believeth in Jesus. This is the greatest truth of divine revelation, and this was the highest lesson which David could learn or teach.

But what his own grief and penitence and sorrow and even his very death could not have done, the blessed Substitute whom God had for ages been preparing was at last to accomplish, and thus make an end of sin and bring in everlasting righteousness through His atoning sacrifice and His precious blood. This is the supreme truth which the folly of the world's wisdom is setting aside, making the blood of the covenant a common thing. But this is the only foundation for the sinner's hope and the loftiest themes of the sons of ransomed souls on earth and in the heavens. "To him who loves us and has freed us from our sins by his blood . . . to him be glory and power for ever and ever" (Revelation 1:5, 6). Never can this story grow old as long as the human conscience needs that precious blood to efface its sense of sin and dread of judgment.

Every little while we see some illustration of the deep conviction in the human heart that blood must go for blood, and that the man who has outraged, wronged and murdered human virtue and innocence must receive in kind the wrong that he has done. Back of this lies a true instinct that is part of the nature of things, that sin must be expiated, and that the sin which has had grosser aggravations needs a corresponding satisfaction. Talking lately with one who had greatly sinned, the remark was made, "How can I expect to be so easily forgiven when my fault was so aggravated and shameful?" As I looked up for an answer, God gave me such a view of the judgment hall and the cross as I have never seen, and I answered, "Jesus Christ not only suffered death for sinners, but He suffered all the shame and horror, all the insult and ignominy and aggravated sufferings which every form of sin could deserve. He was insulted, abused, outraged and degraded before brutal men because He was standing for those that had outraged, insulted and fiendishly wronged the innocent and helpless, so that these vilest sinners might look back to His sufferings and see in them a substitution for what they deserved." And so Christ is a qualified and complete Savior for every sort and degree of sin.

This was the vision which God no doubt gave David in that day, and through which David found peace for his great transgression, and had a dying vision of Calvary and Christ such as he had left on record in some of his Messianic Psalms, where we can behold the dying agony and hear the cries of the Lamb of God as distinctly as if we ourselves were standing under the very shadow of His cross. Oh, beloved, have you had that vision? Has it lifted your burden, quenched your guilt, healed your conscience and given eternal peace and eternal gratitude to your redeemed soul?

SELF-SACRIFICE

But the sacrifice of Calvary demands from us another sacrifice, not by way of expiation, but by way of grateful love. What right have we to take that precious life as our substitute unless we are willing to give our consecrated lives in loving return. Therefore that sacrificial scene on Mount Moriah has a companion picture in the spirit of self-sacrifice which we see exemplified there, both in Araunah, the princely Jebusite, and in David. As David came to buy the site for the altar, Araunah with princely liberality offered to give both the site and all the accompaniments, oxen, ploughs, implements and everything. "Here are oxen for the burnt offering, and here are threshing sledges and ox yokes for the wood. O king, Araunah gives all this to the king" (2 Samuel 24:22–23). He met the occasion with kingly nobility of spirit, and God paused a moment to pay tribute in the narrative to his nobleness of character.

But David was not to be outdone by Araunah. "No," he replied, "I insist on paying you for it" (24:24). There was no petty bickering to get the best of the bargain, but the two men were contending who would be the nobler, and David insisted on giving him his price, uttering as he did this epigram of sacrifice and service, "I will not sacrifice to the LORD my God burnt offerings that cost me nothing" (24:24). This is always the spirit produced by the true vision of Calvary. "Because we are convinced," says the apostle, "that one died for all, and therefore all died. And he died for all, that those who live should no longer live for themselves but for him who died for them and was raised again" (2 Corinthians 5:14–15). The blood of Calvary is fruitful seed in consecrated hearts and lives and reproduces itself in a similar spirit of self-renunciation.

This was really why God chose this spot for David's sacrifice. It was dear to Him because it had been the scene of an earlier sacrifice, where Abraham, as the type of God the Father, gave up his only son in willing sacrifice representing the greater sacrifice of Calvary.

These are things that will live and shine when earth's palaces and thrones have passed away. This is the light of heaven, the light of the coming judgment when the brightest rewards will be given, not so much for what was done as for what was sacrificed.

Beloved, are you giving God that which costs you nothing? Is there real blood in your consecration? Have you ever shed a tear for Christ, or let go a pleasure that some soul might be saved or some cause might be helped for His dear sake?

God lets these opportunities come to us in life to give us a chance of being like Christ, to help us to crucify our natural life and to lift us into His own likeness. If you have not yet learned this law of sacrifice it is because you have not yet gone out of self into Christ. It is one thing to have the blood of Christ on us. It is another to have the heart of Christ in us. The spirit of sacrifice is too hard for the human heart. It is possible only for Him who has already died for us, and is willing to live in us and teach us how to die with Him and live for Him. The blood of Christ upon your soul will save you from wrath and admit you to heaven; but unless you learn the law of sacrifice, and know Him in this deeper death and life through His own indwelling, you never can join the inner circle of His crowned ones, or know "the power of his resurrection and the fellowship of sharing in his sufferings" and "the resurrection from the dead" (Philippians 3:10–11).

CHAPTER 13

GOD'S COMPENSATIONS

I had it in my heart to build a house as a place of rest for the ark of the covenant of the LORD, for the footstool of our God, and I made plans to build it. But God said to me, "You are not to build a house for my Name, because you are a warrior and have shed blood." . . . *He said to me: "Solomon your son is the one who will build my house and my courts, for I have chosen him to be my son, and I will be his father." (1 Chronicles 28:2–3, 6; compare with 2 Samuel 7:1–29)*

There could be no stronger evidence of David's perfect loyalty to Jehovah as the theocratic king of Israel and of his true conception of his high calling as the representative of a divine sovereignty than the fact that as soon as he was established upon his throne his very first thought was to prepare for the removal of the ark to Jerusalem, and a little later for the erection of a splendid house for this sacred memorial of Jehovah's presence and covenant. Feeling quite ashamed of his own palatial residence while the ark of God remained under the shelter of curtain and tent poles, he sent for Nathan, the prophet, and announced to him his high purpose to build a temple for Jehovah, a house for the ark of the covenant.

Nathan's first impulse was to encourage the king in his lofty intention, and he quickly answered without having consulted God, "Whatever you have in mind, go ahead and do it, for the LORD is with you" (2 Samuel 7:3). But a little later, when he had time to listen to Jehovah's counsel, the message was entirely changed and he was sent to David with instructions to say to him that he could not be permitted to build the temple which he had proposed, because his reign had been one of conflict and bloodshed. God accepted the will for the deed and announced to him that his favorite son, Solomon, whose name and reign were to be significant of peace, should be chosen for this high service, and that God would give to David, in compensation for the rejection of his proffered service, a covenant of blessing for the ages to come, and would build him a house and make him the ancestor of a greater Son, who should inherit his throne and become at once his offspring and his Lord. At the same time David was to be permitted to cooperate in this great enterprise and work with all his heart to provide the means and resources for its successful accomplishment afterwards by Solomon, his son.

All this is finely illustrative of several important principles in God's dealings with His people and several striking features in the character of David, and the whole incident is fraught with most important and spiritual lessons for us in our Christian life and service.

A HIGH AND HOLY PURPOSE

"Here I am," exclaims David, "living in a palace of cedar, while the ark of God remains in a tent" (7:2). How much this reveals of the deepest heart of the man of God.

How natural it is for us to think of our own houses and dwell either upon their lack or upon their luxury. But David felt quite ashamed to be so comfortably situated while the cause of his Lord seemed exposed to humiliation and reproach, and he longed to do something for the honor of God and for the extension of His kingdom.

God did not lay this upon David by an express command. He loves to have us think about His cause and plan for His glory and honor. How often do we think as David did? What proportion do our personal and family expenses bear to our sacrifices to the cause of our Redeemer? Could we but realize, as we sit surrounded by comforts and luxuries, the condition of the famishing millions for whom Christ poured out His richest blood and for whom our affluence and extravagance would purchase eternal salvation! How much ought we to realize the injustice and selfishness of our conduct and the light in which some day we will look upon our misspent lives? What must heaven think of the spectacle of this one city in a Christian land spending more in a single summer for pleasure yachts than all the missionary societies in the world will spend in two years to evangelize the heathen!

The surplus and waste which professing Christians are expending in absolutely needless indulgence, in extra buttons on their gloves, extra furniture in their homes, extra splendor in their equipage, extra houses for their residence in town and country, extra decorations on their churches, extra music in their choirs, these useless, wasteful things alone would be sufficient, if given to God, to evangelize the entire world in a decade of years.

This single question which David asked himself if pressed home to a hundred thousand consciences in Christian America would revolutionize our social life and our aggressive work for the salvation of men. It was the same question that Haggai asked the people of a later age,

> Is it a time for you yourselves to be living in your paneled houses, while this house remains a ruin?
>
> Now this is what the LORD Almighty says: "Give careful thought to your ways. . . . You expected much, but see, it turned out to be little. What you brought home, I blew away. Why?" declares the LORD Almighty. "Because of my house, which remains a ruin, while each of you is busy with his own house." (Haggai 1:4–5, 9)

May not this be as truly said today as in the days of Haggai because of our financial panics and commercial depression, but when God does bless His people they spend it for themselves and care not for His suffering cause and the trust which He has committed to their hands to give the gospel to all mankind? Is God first in all our expenditures and all our thoughts? You may have many debts, but is your first debt always paid and are you careful to see that God gets His part no matter what else may fail? This is the test of loyalty, and this is the secret of prosperity and blessing.

A KEEN DISAPPOINTMENT

God declined David's proffered service. Lovingly and unreservedly was it offered, but God could not accept it, and He sent His servant Nathan to say, "Are you the one to build me a house to dwell in?" (2 Samuel 7:5). He said it very tenderly and with many promises of blessing and assurances of appreciation, but David had to relinquish his purpose and give up the task on which he had set his loving heart.

And so God sometimes declines our service and refuses the gift which we have proffered. Perhaps you offered your life for missionary service and He has not opened your way. Perhaps you have laid your child upon the altar of the Lord and He has not accepted your gift. Perhaps you have thought of some great project of beneficence or religion and God has held you back. Perhaps you planned some mighty work and threw all the strength of your being into it and God has not prospered it. Your plans have failed, your efforts have come to naught and you can see that it was not of God.

This is a very keen and painful experience, but it is an experience that is essential for the disciple of Christ to thoroughly learn. It is not enough that we are willing and eager to work for God, but the work itself must be of God. It must be God's man, in God's way, at God's time and according to God's plan. This is one of the deepest deaths that Christians are often called to die. Indeed, our work is unacceptable to God and useless to ourselves and others until it first has been bathed in the blood of Calvary and touched with the sign of crucifixion. It must cease to be our work and thus become His and His alone. We must learn to acquiesce in God's refusals and to believe where we cannot see that He has something better for us than the work we chose. To do this without losing time and becoming discouraged and morbid requires the very highest manifestation of the grace of God and the Spirit of Christ. To learn to wait without fretting, without petulance, without haste, is the perfection of discipline and the best preparation for effectual work. The order of service is first tarry, then do.

A GRACIOUS COMPENSATION

While God declined David's service, He gave him the grandest compensation. "You will not build Me a house, but the LORD will build you a house." He turned the tables upon him effectually by saying, "You thought to do something for Me, but, instead, you must consent that I shall do something greater for you. I am the Sovereign of all worlds and the Lord of all resources. I need not your gifts, but I need those who can accept My gifts and receive My blessings in the magnanimous spirit in which I bestow."

And so God proceeded to give to David a series of covenant promises covering all the future and reaching down to the very throne of His glorious Seed—the great Messiah, who was to be the Son of David, the King of Israel. The most critical examination of this prophetic chapter (2 Samuel 7) leaves no doubt that while immediately it refers to Solomon yet ultimately it reaches forward to the Lord Jesus Christ Himself. "He is the one who will build a house for my Name, and I will establish the throne of his kingdom forever. I will be his father and he will be my son" (7:13–14). This cannot refer to Solomon primarily because his kingdom was not established forever, but ended in failure. In Hebrews 1:5 it is directly quoted as a Messianic prophecy relating to the Lord Jesus Christ exclusively.

But how can the words in Second Samuel 7:14 be consistently applied to Christ? "When he does wrong, I will punish him with the rod of men, with floggings inflicted by men. But my love will never be taken away from him" (7:14–15). A critical study of this passage has furnished the answer and shown that it may be correctly translated, "If iniquity be imputed to him," and we know that iniquity was imputed to the Lord Jesus Christ, for "God made him who had no sin to be sin for us" (2 Corinthians 5:21), and when so imputed to Him He was "punish[ed] with the rod of men and with floggings inflicted by men," for "it was the LORD's will to crush him" (Isaiah 53:10), "and by his wounds we are healed" (53:5). Still later in the story we reach even a higher point of Messianic fulfillment. In responding to this great promise of the Coming One, David answers, "Who am I, O LORD God, and what is my family, that you have brought me this far? And if this were not enough in your sight, O God, you have spoken about the future of the house of your servant. You have looked on me as though I were the most exalted of men, O LORD God" (1 Chronicles 17:16–17), "and of a Man of great estate," as the last clause of this verse may be more correctly interpreted. This "Man of great estate" of whom God has spoken was no other than the Lord Jesus Christ.

And so we see for our comfort and instruction that, when God refuses our proffered service or our earnest prayer, He has for us a compensation as precious as that which He gave to David.

In the first place it is a compensation through Christ. It is something in Him which He gives us. It is some deeper revelation, some fuller experience of His grace and love, which is worth all that we could ask or the world could give. Did He keep you back from some cherished plan or take from you some treasure of your affection? Beloved, it was that He might give you Jesus through it in some deeper way, and make up to you with heavenly solace for the loss of earthly blessing.

Then, as in David's case, He gives you something "about the future" (1 Chronicles 17:17). He may refuse you some present gratification, but He lays up in store for you some eternal heritage of glory. Oh, if we could extend our vision and take in the far perspective, we might be laying up every day some "treasures in heaven, where moth and rust do not destroy" (Matthew 6:20), and out of life's disappointments we might be forging eternal gains. Do men wrong us? Let us look up and say, "Lord, lay up for me some word of commendation at the throne." Do earthly fortunes fail us? Let us by the wand of faith transform the curse into a blessing, and take instead the mansions and the thrones which He has promised us by and by.

Sometimes I have seen His children fail to receive even their believing prayers just now, but I have felt that God had answered these very prayers in some substantial form which was to meet them on the other side.

God's bonds are long-time ones, and they all accumulate compound interest, and when the day of maturity comes we shall weep with wonder to see the meaning of His hundredfold.

A WISE SUBSTITUTION

While God refused the service that David proffered, He appointed his son, Solomon, to perform the task. At the same time He gave a reason for this substitution which is deeply significant. He told David it was not fit for him to build the temple because his reign was associated with conflict and blood, and that the temple was a symbol of the condition of peace and triumph where the battle was already fought and the throne of peace established forever. The symbol of David's reign was the shifting tabernacle of the wilderness, suggestive of change, conflict and trial. The temple, however, was significant of that future age when Christ shall reign in His millennial glory, and sway the scepter of a peaceful empire for a thousand years. Now, Solomon was a true type of all this, and therefore it was his part to build that temple. This will explain why God often refuses to accept some of our services or to bless some of our plans. We are trying to build a temple here and accomplish a work which belongs only to the millennium.

When we set out to have a perfect church and an ideal society, when we expect to close all the saloons, convert all the heathen, put down all the wickedness and have some utopia of perfect blessedness, we are anticipating the age, we are ahead of the times, we are trying to translate a season of conflict, sin and temptation into a millennium that has not yet dawned. And God will not bless these plans. Many of us have tried them and failed and come back to the realization that we are not building temples here or accomplishing any form of perfect work. We are simply quarrying stones out in the mountains and hewing timbers for a building that will be erected by and by when Christ Himself shall come and rear a temple for the millennial age. Let us be content to work at the rough materials, to see our ambitions dissolved and fail, and look forward to the "future" (1 Chronicles 17:17) which David saw, when all our hopes will be fulfilled and we shall dwell in a "city with foundations, whose architect and builder is God" (Hebrews 11:10).

There was another reason suggested for God's refusal of David's proffered service. He intimated that He did not care very much about temples anyhow, and had been perfectly content to wander through the wilderness in shifting tents. What God wants is not splendid architectural palaces, but living temples of holy hearts in which He can dwell and rule. I do not believe a song would cease in heaven if all the splendid gothic cathedrals in the world would be shaken to pieces by an earthquake tomorrow. God would let them all go rather than have a single saint defile the living temple of the Holy Spirit.

BEAUTIFUL ACQUIESCENCE AND COOPERATION IN GOD'S PLAN

David not only acquiesced in the divine message, but went to work with all his might to help to accomplish it, and labored as unselfishly for the temple that Solomon should build as if he himself had been entrusted with the entire task. During the remaining years of his reign he collected the prodigious sum of $3 billion in money and materials, and gave himself, of his own personal wealth, the magnificent contribution of over $80 million for this work.

Further, he devoted himself to prepare a service and ritual for the house of God that should be built with 24 corps of ministering priests, 288 leaders of song, a choir of 4,000 voices, 4,000 porters and 24,000 Levites for the other offices of the service of the Lord. All this he left in perfect order for Solomon's administration, and he himself lent his splendid genius and inspired gift of poetry and music, leading sometimes the choral service with his own harp and voice with divine enthusiasm.

Beloved, have we learned to take as much delight in God's work through the hand of another as when it bears the impress of our own personality? The only way to do this is by seeing no man in it, but recognizing it wholly as the work of God, remembering that the workers are His instruments subject to His authority, summoned and prepared at His sovereign will. No man is ready to say, "Here am I. Send me" (Isaiah 6:8) until he has first learned to say, "Lord, send who you want to send."

Finally, let us learn from the spirit of David the spirit of large-heartedness and magnanimity in the work of God. What a splendid spectacle! A king and a whole kingdom laying themselves out with all their resources to honor God and build a monument for His glory may well put to shame our pretensions of being a loyal Christian nation or even an honest church of Christ, while we are putting our billions into the enterprises of commerce and the armaments of war, and our paltry pennies are deemed sufficient to supply the resources for the evangelization of the world and the bringing in of the kingdom of the Lord Jesus Christ. Oh, how small, how shameful, how unworthy the spirit of modern Christianity!

God forgive us and lift up some voice that can penetrate to the selfish ear of trade and strike some blow that will shatter the coffers of religious selfishness and consecrate their treasures to build, not a temple of material masonry, but a house of spiritual stones of saved and sanctified men and women, a work which will fulfill the loving purpose for which He died, and give the knowledge of salvation to all the world that so He Himself may come and build that greater temple of the new Jerusalem of which Solomon's splendid edifice was only a transient type.

CHAPTER 14

THE LAND OF CABUL

And [Hiram] called them the Land of Cabul. (1 Kings 9:13)

This is a little chapter from the story of Solomon and Hiram; it is also a chapter from the story of many a Christian life. Solomon had given to his friend 20 cities in the land of Galilee in recognition of his kindness in supplying timber and other material for the magnificent temple which had just been erected; but when Hiram went to view the cities he was displeased with them and bitterly disappointed with the gift of his friend, so he called them Cabul, which means displeasing.

There are a good many people still who live in the Land of Cabul—the country of discontent—the clime where the sun rarely shines and the birds never sing. Let us look a little at this inhospitable land, so that we can learn some lessons which will lead us to emigrate from it and live rather in the Land of Beulah, where the sun no more goes down and the days of our mourning are ended.

THE GEOGRAPHY OF THIS LAND

There were 20 cities in this country of Cabul. We are not told what their names were, but it will not be hard to guess.

The first of these cities was called Discontent, and the people who lived in it were never pleased with anything they had. They were always comparing it with the pleasures of others and wishing they had something they did not possess.

Nearby was the city of Envy, which was located sufficiently high to be able to look over the surrounding country, and the point of view was such as to make every other city look as if it lay in the sunshine, which never came to the dwellers of Envy. Everyone else seemed to be better off than they, and as they contemplated the pleasures around them they only made themselves the more miserable.

Another city in the same direction was Covetousness. Its inhabitants were always thinking of the pleasures they did not have and wishing for the blessings of others without trying legitimately to secure them.

One of the largest towns in the Land of Cabul was Unthankfulness. Its inhabitants seemed to think that they were entitled to all that they possessed and never thought of looking to a higher Power and acknowledging His goodness for all they had.

Worry was another town of Cabul. Its people seemed to be always talking about tomorrow, and were constantly making plans against the trials of the future, fortifying themselves against foes which never came and fearing because of the clouds that might come and the obstacles that might intervene. Their fears made their imaginary troubles so real that they were constantly suffering from the troubles that did not come and the worry of others which were never realized.

Despondency was another of these 20 cities. The people who lived in it never smiled, the birds were all ravens and owls, the flowers had no sweet odors and the air was malarial and unpleasant.

There was another city called the Croaking City, situated in a swamp where the frogs could be heard day and night, making the air dismal with their gloomy notes, and the people seemed to talk in a similar tone. Everything was always wrong. The times were always bad, the weather wretched, they themselves were miserable and the prospects were darker still.

On a somewhat elevated plane on this land there was a city called Stoicism, where the people seemed to have a somewhat better feeling and had made up their minds to endure their miseries and make the best of the bad situation, in other words, to grin and bear it. Among the inhabitants there was a general feeling to endure anything, but there was no life or spring of joy or hope.

It is needless to say that the people of this country of Cabul had the worst kind of health, and therefore nothing exhilarated them. The other blessings that came to them were poisoned by the miasmas that rose from their dismal swamps and were hidden by the clouds that hung over their murky skies. The rivers all ran the wrong way instead of running out and bearing their foul tides away. Everything about this wretched country spoke of selfishness, and the waters of the rivers, borne by the sluggish tide, were left upon the unhealthy shores to breed poison and death. A heavy mist was always hanging over the country, so that the people could not see the sun that was shining right above them, nor the bright and beautiful forests and hills of the happy countries immediately adjacent. Indeed, when they did get a glimpse of these brighter prospects, the air had a peculiar property of discoloring and distorting everything that made it impossible to see anything in its true colors. It seemed, indeed, a very wretched place to live in. One greatly wonders that it was so thickly populated and why its foolish inhabitants were so slow to fly from its uncongenial shores to the happy regions of peace and gladness, where heavenly messengers were constantly inviting them in vain.

THE GEOLOGY OF THIS COUNTRY

If we examined the structure of its strata to see how such a wretched country was ever cast up, some interesting things we would find.

1. We see the bedrock of selfishness. Immediately below the surface we would find the soil very hard and impervious. As we examined the rock very carefully we would find that it contained a solid mass of selfishness and understand why the people of Cabul were so unhappy; they were always thinking about themselves; they were always looking at things as they affected their own interest. It is a law of the spiritual world that everything we do for ourselves directly will disappoint us, but everything that we do for others will come back to us again in blessings. This is the very law of God's own being, the law of His love, and arises from the fact that He is always blessing others and living for others. This is the very law of the universe, and whenever we disobey it by selfishness we defeat our very object and destroy our very happiness. As long as we are looking at our end of things, they will seem to be all wrong, and we shall have a sad and disappointing time. When we rise out of self altogether and live to bless God and man we shall dwell in the joy of the Lord, "and sorrow and sighing will flee away" (Isaiah 35:10).

2. Next was the stratum of worldliness, right under the bedrock of selfishness. The people of Cabul were looking at things from an earthly standpoint and depended for their happiness on the things of life rather than on those holy sources which are above all circumstances and things. God has made us for a higher world, and if we seek to feed our spiritual and moral nature on "the pods that the pigs were eating" (Luke 15:16), we shall certainly die of spiritual dyspepsia. The great apostle could say, "Having nothing, and yet possessing everything" (2 Corinthians 6:10). And the Master Himself once said, "A man's life does not consist in the abundance of his possessions" (Luke 12:15). Our true life finds its satisfaction in the heart of God and the things unseen.

When General Gordon met the despot of the Nile, who threatened to kill him, Gordon calmly looked into his face and said, "You cannot hurt me or take away my life, for, indeed, you could not do me a greater favor than to shoot me down, as you threatened to do, for then I would be the more quickly introduced into the presence of my Savior and my Lord." The Arab was dumfounded. He had never met a man who would defy his worst and could laugh at his most terrible threats, because he did not know anything of God. If you would get out of your misery, get out of your earthliness and selfishness and learn to know your heavenly calling and your Savior's joy.

3. Next we come to the substratum, Pride, on which the Land of Cabul rests, and we find that the misery of its people arose largely from an undue estimate on their part of their rights and desserts at the hand of God. They seemed to think that they had not gotten what belonged to them and that what they had already was theirs by right, and to forget that they were wretched creatures, deserving only to die, who had been saved only by divine mercy from destruction and ought to realize that the smallest blessing from His hands was a favor far exceeding their desserts, and for which they ought to be profoundly grateful. If we could only see our blessings in the light of our sins, we would be grateful for anything. If we could only see that the smallest blessing that we enjoyed had to be purchased for us by the precious blood of our Redeemer, we would lead a life of praise.

4. Unbelief is another mass of subterranean rock in this land. Could we regard God in all the circumstances of our life, trust Him through everything, believing in His love no matter what may come, we should look over these things and know that it is His love that sends these trials to test us and prepare us for a higher plane of strength and service. If we could see our Master watching from on high until we overcome in a trying place, and smiling with unspeakable delight when we triumph, and turning away with shame when we give up, we would never doubt or fear.

5. Another cause of depression is found in a wrong way of looking at others. There are two ways of seeing people in the trials of our life. There is the misjudging method, which attributes to everything the worst motives; and there is the loving way that always finds some better motive to which to attribute all actions, and a more charitable way of looking at them, thus excusing them and saving us that sense of wrong which hurts us so severely.

6. Wrong motives in our work for God are at the bottom of many of our troubles. Hiram seems to have expected to get a larger recompense than he got. Had he been doing this work for God he would have been paid by the fact of having the privilege and opportunity to do it. When people do their work for the sake of a salary or for the smiles and applause of men or women, their work will turn to wormwood and their joy to bitterness. Love of God will bring its own reward.

7. The secret of all unhappiness and the foundation of all joy is to be found in this one thing—the presence or absence of Christ in our heart. The one joy that is incorruptible and eternal is the joy of the Lord Himself, dwelling within ourselves, and to abide with Him face to face. This is joy; this is the Land of Beulah and the country of Hephzibah, the land where the sun shall no more go down and the days of our mourning shall be ended.

THE THEOLOGY OF THIS SUBJECT

What is the practical lesson of this theme?

1. The spirit of gloom keeps us out of Canaan. The beginning of Israel's failure to reach the Land of Promise was their falling into the sin of murmuring. It was the first backward step and was speedily followed by others which brought on them at last God's tremendous curse, and left the bones of a whole generation to whiten on the Arabian sands. A spirit of murmuring, discontent and despondency will surely keep us back from a life of communion with God and the power of the Holy Spirit. The first thing in consecration is a complete acquiescence and delight in the will of God, and this is wholly inconsistent with a spirit of discontent, depression and unhappiness.

2. A spirit of unhappiness and discontent will rob us of God's blessing. He loves to bless the happy and thankful heart, and the soul that nurses its wrongs and feeds upon its grievances shall always have sorrow to grieve over.

3. A spirit of cheerfulness and content is our reward. It fills the heart and life with joy and renders existence a continual delight, while a heavy heart, an anxious mind and a gloomy disposition are harder to bear than are the misfortunes, calamities and ills that could befall the most unhappy life. For our own sakes, if for nothing else, let us dwell in the land of gladness and keep free from the dreary shores of Cabul.

4. A spirit of joy is a spirit of power. It attracts others to us. It becomes a bond of sympathy and influence with other lives. "I am as happy as an angel since I became a Christian," was the testimony of the Countess of Huntingdon, and that testimony led two of the peeresses of England to give their hearts to God, for they said they had found no such happiness in the world. We are to be examples to mankind of the beauty and the glory of a consecrated life, and as they see us they too will say, "Let us go with you, because we have heard that God is with you" (Zechariah 8:23).

May the Holy Spirit baptize us with the power of a holy gladness and save us from sorrow as well as sin.

> So let our lips and lives express
> The holy gospel we profess.
> So let our words and actions shine
> To prove the doctrine all divine.

CHAPTER 15

SOLOMON'S CHOICE

But seek first his kingdom and his righteousness, and all these things will be given to you as well. (Matthew 6:33)

At Gibeon the LORD appeared to Solomon during the night in a dream, and God said, "Ask for whatever you want me to give you."

Solomon answered, "You have shown great kindness to your servant, my father David, because he was faithful to you and righteous and upright in heart. You have continued this great kindness to him and have given him a son to sit on his throne this very day.

Now, O LORD my God, you have made your servant king in place of my father David. But I am only a little child and do not know how to carry out my duties. Your servant is here among the people you have chosen, a great people, too numerous to count or number. So give your servant a discerning heart to govern your people and to distinguish between right and wrong. For who is able to govern this great people of yours?"

The LORD was pleased that Solomon had asked for this. So God said to him, "Since you have asked for this and not for long life or wealth for yourself, nor have asked for the death of your enemies but for discernment in administering justice, I will do what you have asked. I will give you a wise and discerning heart, so that there will never have been anyone like you, nor will there ever be. Moreover, I will give what you have not asked for—both riches and honor—so that in your lifetime you will have no equal among kings. And if you walk in my ways and obey my statutes and commands as David your father did, I will give you a long life." (1 Kings 3:5–14)

This passage gives the first keynote of Solomon's inner life. The sacred historian has already given us a picture of his inauguration and the splendors of his throne, but here we get a glimpse of his heart and see the true man who was greater than the kingdom.

RECOGNITION OF GOD IN THE VERY BEGINNING OF HIS REIGN

His first important act was to go to Gibeon, the seat of the ancient tabernacle and, up to this time, the public place of worship, to offer sacrifice and wait upon God for His message and commission. The journey was made with splendid display, as was usual with Solomon in all he did, and the sacrifices were marked by great magnificence, no less than a thousand victims being offered upon the altar during the days of this great feast. It was intended as an act of public acknowledgement of Jehovah as the true king whom he, like David, his father, only represented. And God was pleased to accept this act of homage and recognition and to bless the king and his kingdom.

RECOGNITION OF GOD'S GOODNESS TO DAVID AND TO SOLOMON

We see, in the language which he uses in respect to his father, David, a recognition of God's goodness to his father, David, and to himself, as the son and successor, and especially of the principles of righteousness and uprightness which God required in the administration of the king. He speaks of God's goodness to him as a great mercy and refers to the fact that this mercy was extended to David as he walked in truth and righteousness and uprightness of heart. These are the true principles which form the foundation of all right government, and Solomon wisely recognized them as the elements of David's prosperity and strength, and as those which must enter into his administration also.

No government deserves to be prospered or can expect permanency of blessing which is founded upon injustice or any kind of wrong. We talk about our hard times and our national troubles as the results of political errors and the outworking of financial theories and principles. These things are God's judicial chastenings for the selfishness of His people. It is because we do not use the blessing He bestows and the means He supplies for the real object which alone is dear to Him, of building up His kingdom and blessing mankind with the gospel and the truth, that He takes them away from us and sends distress of nations with perplexity. Solomon himself crystallized this principle into an eternal epigram when he said, "Righteousness exalts a nation,/ but sin is a disgrace to any people" (Proverbs 14:34). Solomon recognized therefore the necessity of righteousness and uprightness and he traced his throne and the blessing that had brought him to it not to any merit of his own but to the sovereign goodness of the King of kings, his father's God and his.

RECOGNITION OF HIS OWN INSUFFICIENCY AND NOTHINGNESS

"But I," he says, "am only a little child and do not know how to carry out my duties" (1 Kings 3:7). This is the language of true modesty, and modesty is always a sign of true worth. Alas, it is rare that we hear such language on the part of young men. Youth is usually self-conscious and full of assurance of its own strength and sufficiency, and it has to go through the discipline of suffering and failure before it learns to take the true place of humility which brings greatness and blessing.

Happily Solomon had learned this lesson. All God's most honored servants have learned it, too. Moses, in the confidence of his early enthusiasm, when he sprang to the front unbidden and slew the Egyptian that oppressed his brother, was not fit for this task. But Moses, shrinking back and saying, "O Lord, I have never been eloquent, . . . send someone else to do it" (Exodus 4:10, 13), was the man that God wanted for this high commission. Jeremiah, the last of Israel's prophets, repeated almost the very words of Solomon as he cried, "Ah, Soverign LORD, . . . I am only a child," (Jeremiah 1:6), and Jeremiah became the greatest of the prophets of his country and was recognized as the patron spirit of Jerusalem in her darkest days of sorrow. Paul himself, the leader of the great missionary host, took his name of Paul just because it means "little." And as he grew riper and richer in his high and heavenly life and work he grew downward until he called himself, first, "not even [deserving] to be called an apostle" (1 Corinthians 15:9), next "less than the least of all God's people" (Ephesians 3:8), and, at last, the "worst of sinners" (1 Timothy 1:16). Humility is not self-degradation. It is self-forgetfulness, not counting upon ourselves at all, but looking only unto Jesus as our Strength, our Wisdom, and our All in All.

SIMPLICITY AND SINGLENESS OF HIS PRAYER

There was but one thing that he asked. He might have asked much more. He might have asked anything he would, for God had given him a mighty option and said, "Ask for whatever you want" (1 Kings 3:5). And so He comes to us sometimes and tests us through our very prayers. Should He come to you just now with that splendid offer and say, "Ask for whatever you want," what would your answer be? What was the first thing you asked this morning? The last thing you breathed in prayer last night? What is the desire that would spring to your lips if God met you with this unlimited proffer, "Ask for whatever you want"? Solomon's answer was ready. He had but one desire, one prayer, namely, that he might have from God the grace, the strength, the power, the wisdom, to meet the situation in which God had placed him, to be equal to his post, to be God's best in the great trust which had been committed to his hands. He did not ask anything for himself, but all for his high calling and great work. What he wanted was the power to meet God's will and satisfy God's expectation concerning his life.

Surely this is the spirit of a single-hearted life, a life that has been rightly poised in perfect conformity with the will of God. The wisdom which Solomon asked just means the power to use the right means to bring about the right end. It needs much wisdom to get the right end and aim in life, and then it needs much more to attain it. This is what Solomon asked, that he might rightly understand the great purpose of his being, and then that he might know how to accomplish it. Surely this includes all that is worth living for. Surely this is the burden of Solomon's deepest teachings in the volume that afterwards came from his pen in the collection of his wisest sayings—the burden that runs through it all:

The fear of the LORD is the beginning of wisdom.
    (Proverbs 9:10)

The fear of the LORD is to hate evil. (8:13)

Blessed is the man who finds wisdom,
    the man who gains understanding,
for she is more profitable than silver
    and yields better returns than gold.
She is more precious than rubies;
    nothing you desire can compare with her.
Long life is in her right hand;
    in her left hand are riches and honor.
Her ways are pleasant ways,
    and all her paths are peace.
She is a tree of life to those who embrace her;
    those who lay hold of her will be blessed.
    (3:13–18)

God has left to us a greater promise. He has given us as the Wisdom of God nothing less than the very person of his own dear Son, the Lord Jesus Christ, "who has become for us wisdom from God" (1 Corinthians 1:30), and who comes to live in us and work out in our lives the very thought of God for us in all its fullness, blessedness and strength. It is not our wisdom that He gives us. It is not even the abstract quality of a higher sense, but it is a living personal mind, the very mind and thought and heart of Christ within us to lead us and guide us in all His will and work out for us and in us, all His plan. This is the wisdom we may have if we but truly seek Him, and the life thus guided and thus blessed can never fail of reaching God's highest thought and life's highest possibilities. It is this high purpose that saves us from a thousand distractions and complications. It is because we want so many other things that we miss them and the chief thing, too. The greatest blessing that can come to a soul is to desire only God and God's will and glory. It was this that brought Solomon's answer so swiftly to him from heaven. God saw his heart was true and He could afford to bless him not only with what he asked, but with much more besides.

GOD'S ANSWER

1. He gave to Solomon the thing he asked—wisdom—such as none ever before or none afterward possessed. And it was not long until He vindicated this wisdom by putting Solomon into situations where it was sorely tested and where it was fully vindicated. Before another sun had set there came to him two women with a question which was surely enough to try the heart of the wisest judge. Both were disputing the ownership of their alleged child, and both seemed to the outward eye to love it with equal fondness. Instinctively did the true test come to the wise king. Commanding a sword to be brought he offered to divide the child in two and give to each a half. It was then that the mother heart shone out in all its strength. "Please," she cried, "my lord, give her the living baby! Don't kill him!" (1 Kings 3:26), and in that surrender she showed herself the mother and won what she had yielded. And so God will bring to you many a test in answer to your prayers. You ask Him for patience and He will immediately put you in a position where you will need great patience. And if you allow Him He will give it to you. You ask Him for joy and He will put you in a place where all earthly joy will fail you and you shall be thrown upon Him for comfort, peace and victory. You ask Him for love and He will probably test you by the most unloving things on the part of others and then He will give you His love to triumph over unkindness and wrong. You ask him for wisdom and He will bring you up to a situation so full of perplexities and difficulties as to appall you. But this is just where His wisdom will shine out and you will go through in victory while you cry, "But thanks be to God, who always leads us in triumphal procession in Christ and through us spreads everywhere the fragrance of the knowledge of him" (2 Corinthians 2:14).

2. But God not only answered Solomon's request, but expressed His peculiar approval of Solomon's spirit and Solomon's prayer. He was delighted with it because of what Solomon had not asked. There is quite as much in what we do not say as what we do say. The silences of our prayers are more eloquent than their words. How God must grow tired of our petulant and peevish repetitions of worry and anxious care and the thousand things we reiterate in His ears about which He knows already and has long

ago provided. This is what the Psalmist meant in that beautiful sentence in Psalm 37:7, "Be still before the LORD and wait patiently for him." In the margin it is "Be silent unto the LORD." Hold your peace, stop your pleading, teasing, feeble complaints and prayers. Your heavenly Father knows that you need all these things (Matthew 6:32), and if you will only think for Him, you will find Him thinking much more for you.

But, further, God gave Solomon the very things he had not asked. He said unto him, "I will give what you have not asked for—both riches and honor—so that in your lifetime you will have no equal among kings" (1 Kings 3:13). So when we cease to think about the temporal needs of this earthly life, God gives them to us with an abundance that we never can know as long as we are anxious and worried concerning them. Indeed, when we cry too much for them, we are better without them; but when we care supremely for Him and His kingdom, then they lie lightly in our hands and do not become a snare but only a means of greater blessing, and He is pleased to add them to us. This is the very essence of the Master's perfect and lofty teaching in the Sermon on the Mount all summed up in our text, "Seek first his kingdom and his righteousness" (Matthew 6:33), or, as it is better expressed by the other evangelists, "But rather seek ye the kingdom of God" (Luke 12:31, KJV). It is the only thing to seek; and "all these things shall be added unto you" (Matthew 6:33, KJV). It is to be noted that the word "added" is used. This looks as though in many cases they might not be given until later in our history, namely, in that millennial day when the earthly shall be added to the heavenly, and the material shall crown the spiritual inheritance of the saints. This would be true to the type, for Solomon, who was so richly endowed with these outward blessings, was the special type of the millennial age when we shall receive the glory and the hundredfold for every sacrifice and deprivation here.

In conclusion, the story of Solomon's choice speaks to each of us as we stand today in the same place of difficult perplexity or high and holy trust. Each of us, like him, has a kingdom for which we are unequal and insufficient of ourselves. Perhaps it is the kingdom of your own soul, and you feel that you are not wise enough or strong enough to sway the scepter over your thoughts and passions and will. Bring it to Him, as Solomon did. Ask Him for but one thing: to make you equal to your post, to glorify Himself in you and enable you as a helpless little child to please Him and accomplish the real purpose of your being and trust Him for all besides. Then you will surely find the blessing that Solomon found and the addition which so enriched his life.

Perhaps it is the kingdom of your home. Perhaps you are an anxious and troubled mother with many an encompassing difficulty, uncongenial surroundings, poverty, toil, lack of sympathy and help and a thousand temptations surrounding the path of those you love, until your heart sinks and shrinks, and you cry, "Lord, I know not how to go out or come in. I am but a little child. Oh, give me wisdom. Whatever else you withhold help me to be my best," and God will hear you and bless you and make you a blessing to your household and help to save your loved ones and lead them up to Him. Perhaps you are a Christian worker in some place of difficult responsibility, feeling that you are unequal to the obligations that rest upon you and the expectations of those that look to you. Go to Gibeon. Bring a simple, single heart. Ask for but one thing, that you may please and glorify God and be enabled to do His perfect will, and He that answered Solomon will enable you for all His perfect will, will bless you and make you a blessing, and will add unto you all things. Or, perhaps, you are a young man or woman setting out in life with some new position opening to you, some place of important influence or service, some influential situation, some place of public trust. Oh, do not try to be the architect of your fortune. Like Solomon, begin with God. Hand over your life and all its possibilities to Him. He will take pride in being your Patron, and seeing you through and some day rejoicing with you amid the raptures of the glory, because through His grace you have not run in vain (Galatians 2:2) nor labored in vain (1 Corinthians 15:58).

CHAPTER 16

GOD'S TEMPLES

Don't you know that you yourselves are God's temple and that God's Spirit lives in you? (1 Corinthians 3:16)

These poles were so long that their ends could be seen from the Holy Place in front of the inner sanctuary, but not from outside the Holy Place; and they are still there today. There was nothing in the ark except the two stone tablets that Moses had placed in it at Horeb, where the LORD made a covenant with the Israelites after they came out of Egypt.

When the priests withdrew from the Holy Place, the cloud filled the temple of the LORD. And the priests could not perform their service because of the cloud, for the glory of the LORD filled his temple. (1 Kings 8:8–11)

In building the temple, only blocks dressed at the quarry were used, and no hammer, chisel or any other iron tool was heard at the temple site while it was being built. (6:7)

The first great work of Solomon after the establishment of his throne was to carry out the great commission that had been entrusted to him by David—the erection of the temple. He entered upon this work in the third year of his reign and completed it in the 11th, so that it occupied between seven and eight years up to the day of its dedication, which was delayed a few months in order to make it coincide with the Feast of Tabernacles. It was the most stupendous work of his reign and his grandest monument. As a work of unequalled magnificence it might well challenge the wonder of the world, and as an object lesson of spiritual truth it is full of instruction for the Christian's heart. Let us look at it briefly in the first aspect and then more fully in the second.

MATERIALS AND WORKMEN

Some idea of its vast expense and elaborate workmanship may be formed from the fact that it cost in silver and gold alone $4 billion, while the other materials—brass, wood, iron and labor—would aggregate at least half as much more. If we were to combine all the ecclesiastical buildings in this country in one huge cathedral pile they would not cost nearly as much as the single Temple of Solomon.

Eighty thousand workmen were employed in the mountains as hewers of wood, 70,000 more as carriers, while 3,300 were overseers, and, in addition to this, we read of another levy of 30,000 men who went by monthly courses. This vast army of nearly 200,000 men were employed for years in this stupendous undertaking.

The stone for its foundation was quarried from beneath the hills on which Jerusalem is built. It was cut in vast masses of rock, some of them nearly 40 feet in length and as much as three to four, and even six feet in breadth, so that it is difficult to understand how these ponderous stones could have been removed and placed in the foundation walls. They were cut so exactly and fitted so perfectly that no mortar or cement was used in the masonry, but they absolutely supported their own weight and the immense structure above them.

The wood employed in the building was cut in the forests of Lebanon. It was cedar, fir, olive and other costly woods, and in some cases sandal wood was imported from India for portions of the building.

The decorations were simple but most costly, and consisted of rich embroideries, figure work in silver and in gold, and gold lining for all the woodwork and all the chambers in the sanctuary. The artistic work was under the direction of Hiram of Tyre, namesake of the illustrious king of Tyre, who entered into a treaty with Solomon and gave him such invaluable aid with so free a heart and hand.

THE SITE

The temple was erected on Mount Moriah, the sacred spot where Abraham offered up Isaac, and where Araunah so generously offered his threshing floor, his oxen and his implements, to sacrifice to the Lord. As a place of loving sacrifice it was especially dear to Jehovah and became the monument of His presence and glory. The naked rock of the summit was selected as the spot for the Holy of Holies (Most Holy Place, NIV) and the ark of the covenant to rest. The slope below was leveled for the site of the Holy Place and the declivity of the hill was leveled up by costly masonry along the east and south side of the mountain, rising in sheer walls several hundred feet high. And the space enclosed in the foundation walls filled up with innumerable arches of stone and interlacing walls to support the super-structure. In addition, vast reservoirs were built here and connected by aqueducts with springs in Bethlehem, by which enormous supplies of water were brought to the city for the temple service and the use of the king and his household.

A large surrounding space of about 500 by 550 feet was enclosed with a wall of stone and planted with trees as the temple area, and within this on a higher plane the temple itself rose in costly splendor, a shining mass of marble and gold.

FORM AND FURNITURE

The structure built on this costly site and at such vast expense would not have compared for a moment in imposing proportions with the splendid and colossal temples of Egypt or Babylon. It was not even as large as an ordinary church in one of our modern cities. Its extreme length was 90 feet—less than a city lot—and its breadth was only 30 feet, also about the size of a single town lot or ordinary dwelling. Its height was 45 feet. The interior was divided into two chambers, one 60 by 30 feet and the other 30 feet square; the first, the Holy Place, and the second, the Holy of Holies. The building was approached by a magnificent porch, 30 by 15 feet, and said by Josephus to have been very high, much higher than the temple. Two splendid pillars, called Jachin and Boaz, 18 feet in circumference and 30 feet in height, and molded in the form of a lily, supported the porch.

The temple itself was furnished somewhat as the tabernacle. In the innermost shrine, the ark stood alone in the Holy of Holies under the outstretched wings of cherubim, which were vast symbolic figures of pure gold 15 feet high, and their wings spanned seven and a half feet horizontally. The Holy Place had the golden table for the bread of the Presence, the altar of incense, and, instead of the seven golden lampstands, 10 lamps of splendid workmanship. The court in front had an altar as in the tabernacle, and a laver of brass; on the altar was an immense erection 15 feet high and 30 feet square, where the sacrifices were constantly ascending before the Lord, and the laver was a great brazen sea, no less than 15 feet in diameter and shining like a polished mirror externally, while the crystal water filled its basin and flowed from the faucets at its foot.

The chambers of the priests were built around the outer walls, but slightly detached from them. All the contents of the temple were similar to the tabernacle, and the order of worship the same, it all being designed to typify Christ and the great principles of redemption.

ERECTION OF THE TEMPLE

The materials were all prepared completely before they were brought to the site. Every stone was squared and beveled and fitted for its place. Every piece of timber was hewed, polished and, doubtless, marked and numbered for its precise position in the framework. The timber was floated down the mountain streams to the Mediterranean and then floated in rafts to Joppa and forwarded to Jerusalem. The stones in like manner were quarried in the excavations under the hill and brought to their place ready for erection. The brass work was cast in the Jordan valley north of Jerusalem.

Finally, when the building was ready for erection, it was simply put together according to the plan already prepared and the materials fitted to hand, as we see in the beautiful striking description in First Kings 6:7, "In building the temple, only blocks dressed at the quarry were used, and no hammer, chisel or any other iron tool was heard at the temple site while it was being built." Silently as a great tree would grow in a forest this mighty edifice arose as if by invisible hands, without the din and roar of the hammer and the workman's tool, and all was simply and silently beautiful as God's great handiwork of creation, as the winter bursts into the summer and the vegetation rises from the ground. The beautiful spiritual teaching of this we shall afterwards see, but the very conception is thrilling, and is finely described in Bishop Heber's familiar lines,

No sound was heard, no ponderous axe was swung.
Like some tall palm the stately fabric sprung.

THE DEDICATION

Finally the house was ready and the work was done. There was no undue haste in its dedication, but they calmly waited until the proper season, the Feast of Tabernacles. Then all Israel gathered—from the regions of the tribes, from the vast new empire, from the maritime colonies, from land and sea. They gathered at Jerusalem for the most magnificent event in their national history. When the appointed day had come Solomon himself, clothed in robes of spotless white and assuming for the time the office of the priest as well as the king, took charge of the inauguration ceremonies accompanied by a great company of priests and vast choirs of singers. With the princes and the people of Israel on every side he stood upon the platform. The opening chorus of praise was about to begin the service, when suddenly it was perceived that God Himself had already descended and taken possession of the building, for all the house was filled with a cloud of deepest darkness, and with a thrill of awe and unutterable joy all recognized the awful but glorious symbol of Jehovah's immediate presence. God had come to dedicate His own temple. As soon as Solomon recovered from the deep prostration of this glorious manifestation he proceeded to utter the wonderful prayer of dedication, which seemed inspired of the Holy Spirit and which covered all the future of his people. This was followed by the sacrifice on an enormous scale of no less than 22,000 oxen and 120,000 sheep, until the altar became too small and the whole court was transformed into a place of sacrifice. Then the fire of God came down from heaven and consumed the sacrifices, and the glory of the Lord filled the house, and as the people witnessed the manifest presence and power of God they fell upon their faces and worshiped the Lord, saying, "For he is good,/ his love endures forever" (2 Chronicles 7:3).

The solemn service closed with a personal revelation of God to Solomon, as He had appeared before to him at Gibeon, in which God was pleased to accept his prayer and the house that he had built and to renew His covenant with him and the promise of His blessing so long as he should walk in heavenly obedience.

Henceforth, this building became the center of Israel's national life and worship, and we find the Psalms breathing the most ardent devotion and longing for the house of God in such expressions as this, "One thing I ask of the LORD,/ this is what I seek:/ that I may dwell in the house of the LORD/ all the days of my life,/ to gaze upon the beauty of the LORD/ and to seek him in his temple" (27:4). To them it was the center of their religious affections, associations and hopes. We are permitted to know God more directly; but that was the steppingstone by which they reached His throne and the mirror through which they saw the reflection of His glory, although, alas, at length they lost the thought of Him in the outward form, and even the very temple had to perish because it stood between them and the Lord Himself.

SPIRITUAL SIGNIFICANCE AND PRACTICAL LESSONS

1. It expressed the presence of God with Israel as their covenant God.

2. It was intended to foreshadow the Church, the spiritual house of the future, in which God now dwells through the Holy Spirit.

3. It represented the individual believer as the temple of the Holy Spirit, the house which God values most and in which He loves to dwell, for "don't you know that you yourselves are God's temple and that God's Spirit lives in you?" (1 Corinthians 3:16).

4. It was intended to represent the glorified Church. The tabernacle represented the earthly Church amid the trials and vicissitudes of this wilderness life. The temple represented the triumphant Church, the new Jerusalem above, when the trial and change shall all be passed and Christ in more than Solomon's glory shall come to share with His people the sovereignty of a regenerated world.

For us as individuals, however, the chief lesson is the third. And we may, through the indwelling of Christ in our hearts, anticipate the fourth, and enter even here into something of the fullness of the heavenly state, for we are recognized in the Scriptures as having passed within the veil and are dwelling even now in the heavenlies seated with our risen Lord upon the throne.

There are several touching lessons for us as individuals in the inspired reference to Solomon's temple.

(a) There is much suggestive teaching in the beautiful fact that the temple was built without the noise of materials already brought to hand. This is a perfect type of the processes of grace by which we are built up in Christ to be habitations of God through the Spirit. We do not have to frame and forge our spiritual graces by the blacksmith's hammer and carpenter's tool of struggling effort. All these things are ready-made for us in Christ and brought to us by the Holy Spirit for us to put on moment by moment and day by day as we take Him in all His fullness and make real in our experience such precious verses as these:

> Rather, clothe yourselves with the Lord Jesus Christ, and do not think about how to gratify the desires of the sinful nature. (Romans 13:14)

> Christ Jesus, who has become for us wisdom from God—that is our righteousness, holiness and redemption. (1 Corinthians 1:30)

> For we are God's workmanship, created in Christ Jesus to do good works, which God prepared in advance for us to do. (Ephesians 2:10)

> From the fullness of his grace we have all received one blessing after another. (John 1:16)

> His divine power has given us everything we need for life and godliness through our knowledge of him who called us by his own glory and goodness. (2 Peter 1:3)

> For this very reason, make every effort to add to your faith goodness; and to goodness, knowledge, . . . [etc.] (1:5–7)

The teaching of all these passages and many more is most clear and simple, namely, that Christ Himself has provided and laid up for us the grace, the wisdom, the faith, the love, the strength and the courage that we need in each new situation of life, and we have simply to take and use that which is ours by faith for taking, and thus put together the stones which He has made and grow up into the immeasurable stature of the fullness of Christ.

(b) Again, there is much beautiful teaching in the fact that when the ark was moved into its resting place in the temple, the staves by which it was carried through the wilderness were taken out and were no longer visible to the eyes of the worshipers. The ark had ceased its journeyings and was forever at rest. And so the psalm triumphantly exclaims, "This is my resting place for ever and ever;/ here I will sit enthroned" (132:14). Oh, reader, it tells you that you may reach that place where Christ shall fix His dwelling in your heart to leave no more, where the staves of your wandering life shall be withdrawn and He in you and you in Him shall be at home forever.

(c) There was nothing in the ark but the tables of the covenant. Even the pot of manna that had been there before, as a memorial of the wilderness life, was gone. Even the budding rod of Aaron, which was the reminder of their temptations in the wilderness and, perhaps, also, which was suggestive of the stage of budding and blossoming faith, but not a complete fulfillment, was gone, too. There was nothing there but the white tablets with God's will inscribed upon them, which only spoke of one thing, a heart wholly consecrated and having only one desire, and that to glorify God and do His will.

Is not this the place to which at least we want to come: where we are not seeking any blessing, where even the pot of manna and the thought of our wilderness needs shall be forgotten, and even Aaron's rod of prayer shall be changed to praise and rest, and our one object shall be, as our Master's only and ever was, to do the Father's will? We cannot even imagine Christ having any anxious care about Himself in any regard. He had but one business and that was to bless God and bless others. Oh, when we get there we shall be saved from all our sorrows, from all our cares, from all our conflicts, and the one deep consciousness of our whole being shall be, "I desire to do your will, O my God;/ your law is within my heart" (40:8).

(d) We read once more that when the glory of the Lord filled the house the priests could not stand to minister because the cloud of the "glory of the LORD filled his temple" (1 Kings 8:11). This is the secret of getting rid of self. Get filled with God and then there will be no room for you. Do not try to turn yourself out but take Him in, and sin and self will go in the blessedness and glory of a divine preoccupation.

CHAPTER 17

THE QUEEN OF SHEBA

They came to Philip, who was from Bethsaida in Galilee, with a request. "Sir," they said, "we would like to see Jesus." (John 12:21)

When the queen of Sheba heard about the fame of Solomon and his relation to the name of the LORD, she came to test him with hard questions. Arriving at Jerusalem with a very great caravan— with camels carrying spices, large quantities of gold, and precious stones—she came to Solomon and talked with him about all that she had on her mind. Solomon answered all her questions; nothing was too hard for the king to explain to her. When the queen of Sheba saw all the wisdom of Solomon and the palace he had built, the food on his table, the seating of his officials, the attending servants in their robes, his cupbearers, and the burnt offerings he made at the temple of the LORD, she was overwhelmed.

She said to the king, "The report I heard in my own country about your achievements and your wisdom is true. But I did not believe these things until I came and saw with my own eyes. Indeed, not even half was told me; in wisdom and wealth you have far exceeded the report I heard. How happy your men must be! How happy your officials, who continually stand before you and hear your wisdom! Praise be to the LORD your God, who has delighted in you and placed you on the throne of Israel. Because of the LORD's eternal love for Israel, he has made you king, to maintain justice and righteousness.

And she gave the king 120 talents of gold, large quantities of spices, and precious stones. Never again were so many spices brought in as those the queen of Sheba gave to King Solomon. (1 Kings 10:1–10)

The story of the Queen of Sheba is authenticated by our Lord's direct allusion to it in the New Testament (Matthew 12:42), and in the same passage He clearly intimates that Solomon in this incident of his life was a type of a Greater than he. This is also brought out very clearly in a single phrase in the first verse of the narrative in the 10th chapter of First Kings, where it is said that "When the queen of Sheba heard about the fame of Solomon and his relation to the name of the LORD, she came to test him with hard questions." That phrase, "his relation to the name of the LORD," identifies Solomon with the Lord in her conception, and makes it evident that she thought of him not so much as a wonderful man and a glorious king but rather the representative of Jehovah, the true theocratic King of Israel. We are to look at this passage, therefore, as typical of the Lord Jesus Christ, both in His present relation to the world, which He has redeemed, and more especially in His future relation, when He shall come again in a glory grander than Solomon ever knew.

This remarkable woman, evidently a princess of enormous wealth in some portion of Arabia, had heard of Solomon's wisdom as well as the splendor of his kingdom, and came with a vast caravan and costly treasure to visit him at Jerusalem and commune with him of all that was in her heart. The gifts that she brought him aggregated more than $3 million in value, and the spices were superior to anything which ever again was known in Israel. She was royally welcomed and received into Solomon's most intimate confidence and fellowship and sent back with a heart fully satisfied and her own gifts all returned, while the king added much more of his own royal bounty.

This picture represents the cry of the nations after God. Her longing to meet this wonderful man was just the expression of her deep desire to find someone that could meet the needs of her heart and satisfy the doubts and perplexities of her troubled and burdened mind. The world's cry is, like the Greeks of old, "We would like to see Jesus" (John 12:21). It does not know that this is its cry, but it is all the same. In the blind idolatries and stupid superstitions of the heathen world, we see many groping after God according to the best light and truest conception they know. It is not true that the heathen are ready to welcome the gospel of Jesus Christ, but it is true that their hearts are earnestly seeking for something which Christ alone can satisfy. Let us send the true light and it will awaken a response in every true heart.

Again, she represented the individual seeking God and coming to Him with his hard questions and consecrated offerings. Doubtless, also, she represents that grander scene which the millennial ages are to unfold when her people and all the nations of the earth shall come as she came to Jerusalem to visit not Solomon but the greater King, to lay their tribute at the feet of the King of kings and the Lord of lords. This was the vision that Isaiah saw down the distant future, and of which he wrote so often in glowing characters, "Some [will come] from the north, some from the west,/ some from the region of Aswan" (49:12). "Your sons come from afar,/ and your daughters are carried on the arm" (60:4). "Herds of camels will cover your land,/ young camels of Midian and Ephah./ And all from Sheba will come,/ bearing gold and incense/ and proclaiming the praise of the LORD" (60:6).

WHAT SHE BROUGHT

She did not come empty-handed, but she brought an offering to the great king (1 Kings 10:2, 10). She brought the best she had. Her costly treasures of gold and more precious spices express the finer figures of the heart's devotion and love. It may seem strange that she should bring such a costly gift to one who did not need it, for he was richer far than she. But that is just the reason God asks our gifts. He does not go begging for help for His cause because He is in distress, but He tells us that all the fowls of the mountain are His, the cattle upon a thousand hills (Psalms 50:10–11) and all the gold of earth's mines, and that He asks our offerings not for His sake, but for ours, that we may be kingly, too, and like Him in our largeness of heart and fellowship of service. He gives us the privilege of taking part with Him in the work of these momentous days. Some day we shall understand what a privilege and honor it was. We are to bring Him our gifts as the recognition of His sovereignty and our trust and love, and He, like Solomon, will show His character by giving back to us more than we brought. You may talk of sentimental piety and keep your money to yourself, but the truth is, God knows and you know, also, that you mean it just to the extent to which you are willing to pay for it and sacrifice for it. The test of love forever must be action and sacrifice. Jesus asks something of us, nay, He asks everything of us as a guarantee that we mean it with all our hearts and then He treats us on the same principle and gives us all that He has. When the woman of Samaria met the Lord, He asked something of her before He blessed and saved her. He required her to give Him a draught of water and He gave her in return an ocean of living water. The highest spiritual experience is not to receive merely, but it is to give. "My lover is mine" is not so deep a place of holy blessing as to be able to add, "My lover is mine and I am his" (Song of Songs 2:16). The very height of rapture is the single utterance of entire surrender, "I belong to my lover" (7:10).

WHAT SHE SOUGHT

1. She sought light upon her hard questions (1 Kings 10:1). There were many things that she longed to know. Doubtless she asked him about that great God whose name was written upon the spangled skies of her southern home but whose nature was unknown to her. Doubtless she asked him about herself and her strangely confused condition, the perplexities of her struggling soul, how to satisfy her accusing conscience, how to resist her fierce temptations, how to be right, how to be happy, and, doubtless, she asked him about

the great future, the destiny of the soul and the hopes and fears that look out upon the eternal future; all this which has perplexed the ages, no doubt, was brought to him for the searching light of truth and wisdom from above. We, too, have our hard questions to bring to Christ. We need keep nothing back, for He has said that we may tell Him of all our cares, perplexities and sorrows, and that He will never send us away unblessed.

2. She sought Solomon's own personal acquaintance and fellowship (10:2). It was not merely truth that she wanted to know, but she wanted to meet a living heart that had made all this truth real and proved all these hard questions in the ordeal of life. And so it is not so much knowledge and light we need as it is Jesus Himself. The heart is reaching out for a Person, One strong enough and wise enough for us to lean all our weight upon and One tender and true enough for us to feel we may come to and open our heart with all its wounds and even with all its sin. This she found in Solomon and this we find in Jesus Christ.

WHAT SHE SAW

1. She saw Solomon's wonderful wisdom and personal work and glory (10:4–5). It was Solomon himself that impressed her most. The marginal reading gives a fine sense to her tribute. "Behold," she says, "thou hast added wisdom and goodness to the fame which I heard" (10:7, KJV marginal reading). It was his wisdom and goodness that impressed her most. To her he represented the character of God and helped her to understand that greater Being in whose bosom the heart finds its resting place.

2. She was struck with the house that he had built (10:4). The temple was finished, and with its massive columns, its splendid marbles, its glittering pinnacles of burnished gold and its priceless treasures of interior adornment, it was the most wonderful building in the world. But, doubtless, Solomon explained to her in all its minuteness of detail the higher meaning of the interior, the deep significance of that altar of burnt offering, that laver of cleansing, that lamp of celestial light, that table significant of the Living Bread, that sweet incense that spoke of the very breath of heaven, and that innermost shrine where God looked out from the Shekinah flame with His loving eye from between the cherubim. As all this had opened upon her spiritual vision and had lifted her up to God, that wonderful house became the symbol of all sacred truth and the type of that glorious spiritual edifice, the Church of the living God, the company of all the holy, the body and bride of the Lamb, the next most wonderful thing in the universe after God Himself, namely, God's people. Some day we shall be part of it and then we shall not wonder that Christ died for this glorious Church.

3. The food on his table next impressed her (10:5). The ample and immense provision which Solomon provided for the food of his household—

20 oxen and 120 sheep every day, besides innumerable other sources of supplies, made up the larder of his palace. But it may have spoken to her, and certainly it speaks to us, of that heavenly table where our God provides the richer supplies of His grace for His household, living Bread hewn from the rock, refreshing wine, the very life and love of Jesus, who gives us His flesh to eat and His heart to nourish our spiritual and physical need and make us partakers of His glorious life and members of His body, His flesh and His bone.

4. The "sitting of his servants" (10:5, KJV) impressed her. The first thing she noticed about them was that they were sitting. They were resting and waiting for orders. How it speaks to us of the true posture, where service must begin. Sitting at the feet of Jesus to hear His word and to be filled with the Spirit, to be commissioned for His service and to be broken into yieldedness and nothingness that He may use us and we may not hinder.

5. The standing of his servants was the next thing she noticed (10:5). It is not only necessary for us to sit at the feet of Jesus but to stand waiting to do the commands of Jesus. This expresses the attitude of readiness with girded loins and attentive ear to catch the first whisper of His will.

6. She also noticed his cupbearers (10:5). These represented a still higher service. They are the men who waited on the king himself, and they suggest the sort of service which is not for men, but for God, which is not what the world would call usefulness, but which is the direct, personal ministry of the Lord Jesus Himself which He requires at our hand. He has a right to exclusive love. He has needs which His people's hearts alone can fill. There are prayers and songs which should be poured into His ears, not to bring back the supply of some selfish want, but to manifest to Him some sweet sense of His children's love, some cup of wine from the chalice of an overflowing heart.

7. The ascent by which he went up to the house of the Lord (10:5, marginal reading) was one of the things she saw. To her it spoke of that higher life which was the real glory of Solomon's character and reign. It is to tell us of the resurrection and ascension of our glorious Lord and of our partnership with Him in the throne life where He sits at the Father's side in our name and as our Head. Perhaps she did not understand all these things as we do, but she saw something of their deeper meaning and she felt more. Her heart was lifted up to a new world of peace and hope and joy and henceforth life had an upper passage to her by which she, too, could ascend to the house of the Lord and live in the higher planes of heavenly communion and eternal hope.

WHAT SHE GOT

1. She got the answer to all her hard questions (10:3). She got the light she needed. She got the direction which made her pathway plain. She got

the rest which quieted her troubled heart and led her forth into the ways of peace. So will you receive at His blessed feet the light, the truth and the peace that you so sorely need, and you shall go forth singing:

> I came to Jesus as I was,
> Weary and worn and sad.
> I found in Him a resting place
> And He has made me glad.
> I came to Jesus and I found
> In Him my shield, my sun,
> And in that light of life I'll walk
> Till traveling days are done.

2. She got back all that she gave to Solomon (2 Chronicles 9:12). He returned all her costly gifts, not in such a way as to hurt her sensitiveness, fully appreciating the love that prompted it, but in the generosity of his heart he refused to let her lose what she had so lovingly given. This is the way God loves to test us, first to take all that we have and then give back in some better way what we so willingly resigned.

3. She got, besides all this, Solomon's own royal bounty (1 Kings 10:13). He gave her a present from his kingly treasures, which was certainly not less than the one she brought up, as much as she esteemed him greater than herself. And so she went back partaker of the king's riches as well as the possessor of her own. Thus we gain by giving. Thus we possess twice over by letting go. Thus we slowly learn the folly of driving a close bargain with our God and the blessing of being whole-hearted, especially with our consecration.

We must remember in order to fully understand the typical lesson that Christ has not yet fulfilled all the meaning of the Solomonic type. It reaches forward into the age to come. It is then that we shall have the added things in all their fullness and understand the hundredfold which He has promised and all the glory of our inheritance in full partnership with Him as our exalted King and blessed Bridegroom.

WHAT SHE SAID

Her testimony was beautiful and simple.

1. She bore testimony to the word which she had heard and said it was true (10:6). So should our lives witness to God's Word.

2. She bore testimony that it was less than the truth. "Not even half" (10:7), she said, was told. So should our lives not only fill out, but amplify, adorn and expand God's Word. His Word is the skeleton and we are to fill it out with real flesh and blood until it becomes an attraction and an inspiration to the world, which sees its interpretation in our lives.

3. She bore witness to Solomon's servants and attendants (10:8). She had as many good words to say about them as she had about Solomon. And so our testimony should be as bright and as cheerful about the people of God as it is about Christ. And yet how much we hear of the faults of Christians. If the world were to judge God's people by what you say about them, it is very doubtful that they would want to be in such company. Beloved, are you talking about Christ's servants as you talk about Christ? What kind of a testimony are you giving? What kind of an impression are you reflecting upon the world? Are you leading them to say, "Let us go with you, because we have heard that God is with you" (Zechariah 8:23)?

4. She bore testimony to Solomon (1 Kings 10:6, 7), and this high testimony, that he himself was more than his surroundings. This is the greatest thought in connection with Christian life and testimony and in connection with their Christian character—the man should be greater than his work and his surroundings. This was true of Solomon. As splendid as his surroundings were, his own personal qualities transcended all his greatness, and his surroundings were but a fit setting for the jewel of his personal character.

When the late Queen of England stood in the center of a pageant assembled from all the world to pay honor to her on the 60th anniversary of her coronation, the highest testimony on that occasion, and the testimony that was repeated in all languages and by representatives of all nations, was this: that the woman was greater than the queen and that her personal worth was the truest glory of her reign.

This is true of our blessed King, the Lord Jesus Christ. It is not His gifts, but it is His heart that makes Him the love and pride of heaven. And this should be the aim of the child of God. It is not the place you want but the personality that will claim the highest place. It is not things you need, but personal qualities that will lift you above all things and bring all things to pay tribute to you. *God, lead us to Christ Himself, who is the center of Christianity. And with Him incarnate in our lives, let us be living embodiments of the Christianity we profess, and commendations of the gospel which we preach.*

CHAPTER 18

SOLOMON'S FALL AND ITS LESSONS

The LORD became angry with Solomon because his heart had turned away from the LORD, the God of Israel, who had appeared to him twice. Although he had forbidden Solomon to follow other gods, Solomon did not keep the LORD's command. (1 Kings 11:9–10)

Like some splendid ruin reminding us of the stately temple that once stood there, like some glorious sunrise ending in lurid tempests, like some noble ship sailing away amid waving pennants and cheering multitudes and then disappearing in mid-ocean and leaving no trace behind, so Solomon's career became darkened with the deepest shadows as it neared its close, and ended at last in awful mystery. No man, perhaps, would dare to say that Solomon was lost; but no man may affirm that Solomon was saved. Like a ship that founders in mid-ocean, he sank out of sight in the impenetrable darkness of apostasy and divine judgment.

All through the ages God has been looking for someone to meet His expectation and satisfy His ideal of a true man, but the race has always failed him. Adam stepped upon the scene encompassed with every proof of God's goodness, love and care, but e'er the sun had fairly risen the light went out in the dark eclipse of sin and ruin for the race. Abraham was chosen to be the peculiar type of faith, but Abraham failed in the place where he should have been strongest and left the old human blot upon his imperfect record. Moses led forth a new election of redeemed and chosen people from bondage to freedom, and was honored to stand in the innermost presence of Jehovah face to face; but Moses failed in the very quality for which he was most remarkable and broke his own law, and so failed to win his inheritance in the Land of Promise. David, the man after God's own heart, the very type of Jesus Christ, the anointed King, stooped to the depths of a double crime and covered the closing years of his reign with clouds of domestic and national calamity.

And now Solomon, the glorious, the man who seemed above all other men to have reached the climax of human character and success—good and wise, successful and prosperous, enjoying the smile of heaven and the honor and admiration of the whole world—Solomon at last became the most stupendous failure of the human race. He closed his career in a mystery of sin, sorrow and utter failure, and left the heritage of strife, misfortune and judgment to the nation he had governed. In the lapse of centuries nine-tenths of that nation were exterminated, and the remaining tribes were driven from their land and left in sad humiliating captivity, the temple that he had reared became a heap of smoldering ashes and the city that he had glorified a derision and was condemned in the hands of his heathen foes. He was allowed to be the true type of the Son of man, earth's true King. Then the picture was shivered into fragments and thrown away that we might know that it was only a transient picture, and that the best of men were only men, and the only ideal that can ever satisfy God or meet the needs of man is the divine Man, the blessed One, of whom all these were but broken images and imperfect types. What are some of the lessons that this sad story is fitted to teach?

FAILURE OF WISDOM

It teaches the insufficiency of human wisdom and culture to save the race. Solomon was the wisest man, and one of the best of men; but Solomon failed, and the wisest and best will fail. The world is purchasing culture today but the golden age of art and literature has usually been an age of moral corruption and shameless sin. The worst elements in the heathen nations today are those who have had a touch of our civilization without the power of divine grace. The more you educate men, the more power you give them for mischief. It is not culture the world needs, but Christ. It is not even character the world needs, not even moral training, good examples, rigid discipline, self-improvement and higher standards of our virtue. All these will fail. There never was a higher standard than that of God's ancient law. There never was a stricter discipline than that of the Old Testament and God's rigid dealings with his chosen people. But they all failed. The only hope for the race is a new and heaven-born life; nay, more, the indwelling of the divine Person in the human nature, the union of Christ with our fallen life and the reliving His life in us by the power of the Holy Spirit. Looking out upon the wreck of his race with a broken heart, Ezekiel saw the picture of the past, and his one hope for the future was this: "I will give you a new heart and put a new spirit in you; I will remove from you your heart of stone and give you a heart of flesh" (Ezekiel 36:26). But even that was not enough, for he adds: "And I will put my Spirit in you and move you to follow my decrees and be careful to keep my laws" (36:27). If ever wisdom and personal worth could save mankind, the experiment was truly tried in Solomon, and the lesson ended in their desperate failure.

THE CURSE OF PRIDE

One of the deepest sources of Solomon's failure was the spirit of pride and the love of display which were strongly marked in his life and formed the predominant tendency of his nature. His life was one constant pageant. His ambition was to surround his throne with unparalleled magnificence. His every movement was a triumphal procession. Robed in garments of white, superbly decorated and magnificently equipped with a stud of thousands of horses, splendid chariots and horsemen, and in all the display of oriental magnificence, he went from place to place in a blaze of glory. He lived in an atmosphere of luxury. Every vessel in his household was of purest gold. He was surrounded with the dazzling beauty of a thousand queens, and innumerable courtiers waited upon him and them and brought the homage of all nations to his feet.

Alas, we see the same spirit today in the love of luxury and social preeminence which is abroad among our people. The competitions of society for ascendancy and lavish display in entertainment, equipage and palatial residences are even vying with the magnificence and extravagance of Europe and striving to outshine them. It is a sad and shameful picture. It brought to Solomon only vanity and vexation of spirit; and its end in our age will be financial distress, social corruption, national wickedness, spiritual ruin, a shadow as deep and dark as that in which Solomon passed from the resplendent stage of his fatal career.

FAILURE OF WEALTH

The love and pursuit of wealth was another of Solomon's snares. He was the richest man of his age. His commercial enterprises were stupendous and successful. His income from them brought him millions every year. If money could make a life happy and successful, he had all that it could claim. Alas, he was one of the many whom God has entrusted with great riches to show how little He values them. The other day a multimillionaire of London and Cape Town leaped into the sea in despair to escape the toils and torments of a hundred millions. Today millions of souls are lost through the snares and temptations that come to them through boundless wealth. Money will be a blessing if we hold it as a trust; but it will sink us in the depths of ruin if we ever allow ourselves to own it or prize it. If we give it to Him and only for Him, He may trust us with it in boundless measure; but once it gets its heartless grip upon our souls, it will drag us down to the grave as dark as Solomon's. How solemn is the warning of the faithful apostle, "The love of money is a root of all kinds of evil. Some people, eager for money, have wandered from the faith and pierced themselves with many griefs" (1 Timothy 6:10). That is the certain result of coveting after money, hankering for it, and setting the heart upon it even moderately. But there is another and more terrible sentence in that paragraph describing another class of men, "People who want to get rich" (6:9a). These are not the people that hanker after gold, but they are the people that determine at any cost to be rich. For them there is a shorter career and a quicker descent. They "fall into temptation and a trap and into many foolish and harmful desires that plunge men into ruin and destruction" (6:9b). Beloved, if God has saved you from this snare, be careful how you ever tamper with it again.

SELFISHNESS

Selfishness was one of the banes of Solomon's life. He allowed himself to become the end of not only his own existence, but of his people's. Everything was made tributary to his power, greatness and success. Seventy thousand citizens were drafted into labor gangs which toiled in the quarries and lumber camps to supply the material for his extensive buildings and extravagant undertakings. Thousands of servants waited upon him, and whole trains of sheep and cattle and all sorts of animals were brought into his palace to administer every luxury to his table. For a while the people bore the cost of this splendid entertainment, but, after a while, they groaned under the yoke of enormous taxation, and eventually they rose against the oppression and spurned the hand that inaugurated it. Rehoboam rightly described the persecution under Solomon's reign when he said, "My father laid on you a heavy yoke; I will make it even heavier. My father scourged you with whips; I will scourge you with scorpions" (1 Kings 12:11).

A selfish life will always be an unhappy and unsuccessful life. While you are the center of your life plan and the end to which all things are made to converge, you will find yourself openly defied and disappointed. It is the law of heaven that he that saves his life shall lose it, and he that loses his life, for the sake of Christ and others, will find it (Matthew 10:39). Selfishness is the essence of Satan; love is the center of God's life and God's government, and love is the opposite of self. It, therefore, must be true that the man who lives for self is the enemy of God, and all the forces of God's government are against him. If you love your friends because they minister to your pleasure, if you pursue your love in order that you may reap the joy, if you hold your money for your own will and gratification, if you even do your Christian work for your own honor and reputation, you shall find your life will turn against you, will get out of adjustment and end in disaster. You are putting the pyramid on the wrong end and it cannot stand. We are all naturally wound around ourselves like a watch spring around its center. We need to be unwound and then fastened around God. We are naturally introverted and we need to be turned upside down and inside out, and de-centered and re-centered. Alas for Solomon! He lived for himself and he lived to find that all was lost.

FLESHLY LUST

Alas, there was a deeper depth of sin and folly. Solomon is an example of the curse of sensuality and earthly indulgence. It was partly through his pride and love of display that he surrounded himself with the rank and beauty of the world and maintained a harem of a thousand fair women from all the courts of the surrounding nations. But it was also an exhibition of the grossest self-indulgence, and the coarse unbridled passion which has so often degraded the thrones and palaces of earth into beastly menageries, and brought upon mankind the curse of Sodom and Gomorrah. Alas, it is, perhaps, the strongest and most perilous social current in our own time; and, like a fetid torrent from the sewers of the pit, it is sweeping through the social life of our own land and our own time, with a breath of license and a depth of wickedness which but too surely remind us that that fearful sign of the end. "It was the same in the days of Lot" (Luke 17:28), is at last upon us.

You may gild this sin with all the beauty of Solomon's court, you may keep it out of the low level of the street and the slums, you may hide it under the subterfuges of your deceitful social system, but it will ever prove, as it ever has, the most subtle, the most swift, the most certain highway to the lowest hell. Oh, let the young, the reckless, the tempted, ponder the awful words which this man has left us out of the bitterness of his own experience: "For her house leads down to death/ and her paths to the spirits of the dead./ None who go to her return/ or attain the paths of life" (Proverbs 2:18–19). "But little do they know that the dead are there,/ that her guests are in the depths of the grave" (9:18).

THE WORLD

Disobedience to God's law respecting marriage with the heathen and separation from the world had much to do with Solomon's fall. God had strictly forbidden ancient Israel to mingle with the surrounding nations in social life, and especially marriage; and He has forbidden us to be "yoked together with unbelievers" (2 Corinthians 6:14). Any man or woman who dares to disobey this divine command must take the consequences—an unhappy life and perhaps a lost eternity.

A spirit of easy compromise and unholy yielding to the influence of others, especially of his heathen wives, was another cause of Solomon's sin. It was bad enough to marry them and bring them into the heart of a holy nation. It was much worse to allow them to practice the heathen rites of their idolatrous religions with his consent. It was intolerable when he went so far as to erect costly temples for them for their abominable rites on the very brow of Olivet and overlooking the temple itself, for we are expressly told that he built a high place for Chemosh, the abomination of Moab, in the hill that is before Jerusalem, and the other of Moloch, the abomination of the children of Ammon. Right there in full view of the holy city were these monuments of cruel superstition which God had denounced in the most terrible terms; and in the fiery arms of the burning idol, the little children were offered in living sacrifice while their cries were drowned by the rude song of heathen music before the holy nation who had been taught for centuries to beware of these hideous rites. No wonder they called that hill the Mount of Offence.

But this was not the worst. It was but one step more for him to join in these infamous idolatries and to yield to the pleadings of the wives he loved and throw himself without reserve into their abominable excesses. Alas, it has been well said:

> Vice is a monster of such horrid mien
> That to be hated needs but to be seen;
> But seen too often familiar grows its face,
> And first we fear, then pity, then embrace.

SIN

All this was heightened and aggravated by the fact that Solomon sank into these depths of sin after he had known the Lord, and, as the sacred record expresses it, after the Lord had appeared unto him twice.

How solemnly it reminds us of the peril of backsliding after we have received the deeper life of Christ, and the second blessing of the Holy Spirit. It was very sad when Israel went back after they were saved from Egypt, but it was more sad and terrible when they apostatized after they had won the land of Canaan. "See to it, brothers, that none of you has a sinful, unbelieving heart that turns away from the living God" (Hebrews 3:12). Let us fear lest we too should become, like Solomon, beacons, useful only in the awful warning which our lives will hold forth to others. Let us shun the dangers which led him into sin and folly. Let us especially make sure to claim that which he missed, the utter surrender of our life from the world and self and sin and the indwelling life of God who is, through the Holy Spirit, within us.

And, finally, let us "Watch out! Be on guard against all kinds of greed" (Luke 12:15). Never shall I forget a picture which comes back to me from early ministry: that of a beautiful young couple with whom my life was thrown for some months in somewhat intimate acquaintance at the time when God first blessed me with the Holy Spirit. The beautiful wife was much laid upon my heart in prayer and personal effort for her salvation, but she met all my approaches with the hard and heartless impulse of a worldling. Often she used to say to me, "I love the world. I revel in it. I delight in the dance, in the horse race, in the theater. I have no sympathy with your narrow notions and puritanical ideas. I just idolize the world." One day I said to her: "My dear sister, some day you will hate the world as much as you love it now." She laughed me to scorn, but I prayed on. In a few weeks I noticed her spirit had changed. She seemed to grow depressed, bitter and cynical. One day when we were talking, she said to me, "Oh, I just hate the world," and her lips were set with the bitterness of a cynic. I reminded her of how she loved it once, and she broke out with bitter invectives and told me how everything had failed her, deceived her and how she wished she could fly from it. I tried to tell her of a better world and of a joy that would fill her heart, but her heart had been poisoned by the bane of Solomon, and she left me with the bitterness of the wormwood and gall. Next morning I was startled by an early call, and as I went to my door a messenger with pale face asked me to come down quickly. I hastened to obey and to my horror when I reached the parlor, under the white sheet lay the lifeless body of that wretched society woman. She had just been dragged from the river into which she had plunged in the darkness of night—a soul sickened of earth but unfit for heaven. As I stood beside that coffin and tried to perform the service of that funeral, it seemed to me that I was looking at a lost eternity, and I heard, like a whisper, the solemn message: "Dear children, keep yourselves from idols" (1 John 5:21).

CHAPTER 19

SOLOMON, A TYPE OF CHRIST

And Solomon ruled over all the kingdoms from the River to the land of the Philistines, as far as the border of Egypt. . . . God gave Solomon wisdom and very great insight, and a breadth of understanding as measureless as the sand on the seashore. . . . Men of all nations came to listen to Solomon's wisdom, sent by all the kings of the world, who had heard of his wisdom. . . . The weight of the gold that Solomon received yearly was 666 talents, . . . The king made silver as common in Jerusalem as stones, and cedar as plentiful as sycamore-fig trees in the foothills. (1 Kings 4:21, 29, 34; 10:14, 27)

He will rule from sea to sea
  and from the River to the ends of the earth.
The desert tribes will bow before him
  and his enemies will lick the dust.
The kings of Tarshish and of distant shores
  will bring tribute to him;
the kings of Sheba and Seba
  will present him gifts.
All kings will bow down to him
  and all nations will serve him.

For he will deliver the needy who cry out,
  the afflicted who have no one to help.
He will take pity on the weak and the needy
  and save the needy from death.
He will rescue them from oppression and violence,
  for precious is their blood in his sight.

Long may he live!
  May gold from Sheba be given him.

May people ever pray for him
and bless him all day long. (Psalm 72:8–15)

These two passages describe respectively the glory of Solomon's kingdom and the greater glory of his greater Antitype. While there will always be a few hero worshipers, yet the world cares not for men. We soon weary of the noblest ideal and long for someone more glorious and true, because man at his best estate is only man. All the lives that have lived above the ordinary plane have been but types of the only Man who can ever satisfy God or meet the needs of men, the glorious Son of man who once lived for us an ideal human life and who is coming back again as the world's true King and blessed Hope. Therefore we pass quickly from Solomon to Christ, from the son of peace to the Prince of Peace, whose coming glory was so greatly foreshadowed by Solomon's reign.

In truth, it required the united lives of David and Solomon to furnish a perfect foreshadowing of our coming King and His millennial reign. David represented rather the militant aspect and Solomon the glorious and ultimate character of Christ's promised kingdom. The former represents the conflict which Christ is waging today against His foes; the latter the peaceful and worldwide years during which He shall sit with His saints upon His millennial throne and sway the scepter of peace the world around.

HIS BIRTH

Solomon's birth and its attendant circumstances were strongly suggestive of the gracious character and purpose of the Lord Jesus Christ, our coming King. Solomon's birth was the most emphatic expression of God's mercy to David. He was born to Bathsheba after David's monstrous crime. The fact that God should choose the fruit of that union, after it became legitimate, to sit on Israel's throne at the most glorious crisis of her history, was a most touching seal of the forgiveness which He had extended to His erring child, the mercy of which Jesus Christ's mission is the most impressive expression in all the history of the world. Solomon never could forget that his very existence and destiny were all associated with the grace of Jehovah. This had already been emphatically expressed in the name given to Solomon when he was born. The Lord called him Jedidiah, which means "the beloved," and we are told that the Lord loved him. Beautiful type of Him who is the Son of His love and who comes to represent the mercy of God and stand for sinful men.

Again, Solomon was not the firstborn, but the secondborn of this union. The first had to die under the ban and doom of sin, but the secondborn lived as the child of grace. This is the very principle of the regenerate life.

The first, natural, passes away. The second is the divine and eternal. The first man Adam, sinned; the second Adam lives. The first natural generation perishes; the second birth, regeneration, brings us life and salvation. Solomon represented this, and thus the very germ and principle of the gospel is embodied and impersonated in his life.

HIS NAME

Solomon's name means "peace," and he was the fitting type of the Prince of Peace. David's reign was associated with war and carnage and therefore he was not permitted to build the temple. Solomon was a man of peace and the chief glories of his administration were the triumph of peace, prosperity and progress. David, therefore, could not represent the millennial stage of Christ's kingdom, but rather the stage of conflicts that led up to it. Solomon stands for the age of glory when He shall have put down all authority and opposition, and He shall reign over a realm of perfect love and peace. That age is surely coming. Battle flags will yet be furled, the groans of the wounded and dying will cease, earth's cemeteries shall be transformed into paradises and the curse of ages shall be turned into eternal blessing: not through human culture, not through the development of man's theories and the improvement of man's nature, but by the personal advent of the Prince of Peace of the increase of whose government and peace there shall be no end.

HIS CORONATION

The circumstances attending Solomon's coronation and the bitter hostility manifested toward him by his enemies and rivals was a striking foreshadowing of the opposition of men to the advent and reign of Christ. When He comes to reign He is not going to be accorded a public reception by the kings and nations and parliaments of earth. The second Psalm has given us a picture of Solomon's accession and Christ's coming. It was written, no doubt, with reference to both, but the temporal allusion soon passes into the higher fulfillment of the distant future. The heathen rage. The people imagine vanity. The kings of the earth are concerted against the Lord and His Christ. The license of man is grinding its teeth against the control of His authority; the proud, willful human heart is crying out, "Let us break their chains, . . . and throw off their fetters" (2:3). But "the One enthroned in heaven laughs" (2:4); and by His sure decree and strong right arm "[has] installed [his] King on Zion, [his] holy hill" (2:6), and "will dash . . . to pieces like pottery" (2:9) the nations that oppose Him, summoning them to "be wise" (2:10), and "rejoice with trembling" (2:11), and to "kiss the Son" in lowly submission before "his wrath . . . flare up in a moment" (2:12). This is the picture that we can see already developed out of the vortex of political confusion and contemporary history.

The nations are gradually and steadily withdrawing from the control of the Lord Jesus Christ. The concert of the powers which has begun is not to maintain His cause but to protect their little ambitions, aggrandizements and selfish interests; already within a year the concert of Europe has condoned enough unspeakable wickedness against the very children of God and the martyrs of Jesus to bring down upon them God's eternal curse. The end is not going to be a peaceful Christian confederation of the world, but it is going to be Armageddon, the great day of conflict of earth's kings against the Lamb of God and the saints of Jesus. All this was foreshadowed by Solomon's accession. Adonijah, his own brother, reared the standard of rebellion. Joab and Abiathar took his part and multitudes of the people were ready to join them, when by David's strong determination the opposition was suppressed and Solomon was set upon his throne. So it will be at the end: Adonijah representing the political powers, Joab representing the leaders and military forces, and Abiathar representing the corrupt Church. These are the combined forces that are to resist the coming of Christ and to be broken in pieces by the mighty hand of God, even as Daniel's stone cut out of the mountains smashed and scattered the image of earthly sovereignties and became the kingdom that filled the whole earth.

JUDGMENTS

The judgments which accompanied the inauguration of Solomon's reign were very striking and suggestive types of the events that are to accompany the return of the Lord Jesus Christ. There are many instances of men that had lived through the whole reign of David and their darkly dyed crimes had passed with impunity, but their retribution came with the accession of Solomon. One of these was Joab, who had often vexed the heart of David, whose judgment was reserved until the accession of his son. But even Joab was not hastily punished by Solomon but was allowed to show his true character at the end, by joining the standard of Adonijah in open rebellion and thus bringing upon himself at last the deserved doom that David had so often foretold.

Another was Adonijah, who was pardoned for his first act of rebellion, but he was likewise to show a little later his true character by a more subtle conspiracy against the kingdom through Abishag the Shunamite, and this brought upon him also the fate that he had already merited.

Similar was the sentence of Abiathar, who was set aside from the high ecclesiastical place that he had falsely filled, and Zadok appointed in his stead.

The most striking of all these judgments was the death of Shimei, the miserable old churl who had openly cursed David in the hour of his tribulation and who had been magnanimously spared by the king and even granted a respite by Solomon at the beginning of his reign with a definite parole and understanding that if he should break it he should forfeit his life. Shimei was true to his parole for a short time, but he also presumed to despise his pledge of honor and brought upon his own head the judgment that had been pronounced. Thus all these men passed away under the just and terrible retribution which in every case was brought upon their guilty heads by some rash act of their own.

So it will be when the greater King shall come. Then how many secrets will be disclosed! How many lives will be made manifest! How many that have long tried the patience and longsuffering of God will be brought to strict account! How many, by some such test of character, will show that they were never really true and will stand revealed and confessed among His enemies and receive His condemnation and His judgment. "Therefore judge nothing before the appointed time; wait till the Lord comes. He will bring to light what is hidden in darkness and will expose the motives of men's hearts" (1 Corinthians 4:5), for the fire shall try every man's work (3:13).

HIS REIGN

Solomon's reign was a type of Christ's millennial glory. His dominion was the most extensive and his throne the most magnificent the world had seen. All nations, it might truly be said, acknowledged his supremacy and came to pay court at his footstool. His riches were so immense that all the vessels of his court and palace were of gold, and silver was scarcely counted of value in the streets of Jerusalem. He maintained a splendid court and table, a thousand wives, innumerable attendants and a vast army wholly occupied in providing for his household. His throne was of ivory and gold and his palace of cedar and marble took 13 years in building and was a gem of magnificence and beauty. Thirty oxen and 100 sheep were daily slaughtered to supply his own royal table. Forty thousand horses formed his stable. Vast aqueducts were built from the mountains to convey water to his pleasure grounds, and paradises and parks of incomparable beauty were constructed on his vast estates. A splendid palace was reared on the slopes of Lebanon, and as he traveled hither and thither he rode in a chariot of ivory, robed in spotless white, with splendid equipage and state, and great pillars of smoking incense preceded and followed his train. As they saw him approach along the valleys of Samaria, the watchmen on the towers of Lebanon cried, "Who is this coming up from the desert/ like a column of smoke?" (Song of Songs 3:6). Vast forests were cut down and transported from Lebanon to the Persian Gulf and immense navies were built at Ezion Geber at the head of the Indian Ocean. And after a three years' voyage the ships of commerce returned from India laden with gold, silver, wood, peacocks, apes, rarest incense and spices, and all the treasures of the tropics, and the people of

Jerusalem saw the caravans day by day entering their gates and bringing their vast treasures to enrich the king and his subjects.

In the early days of his reign, the people shared in this splendid wealth and rejoiced in the sunshine of an extraordinary prosperity, dwelling, as we are told, under their vine and their fig tree in gladness of heart and cloudless prosperity. It was the golden age of Israel and the picture of the summer time of peace and benignity and blessedness which some day will dawn upon this distracted world.

HIS TEMPLE

Solomon's reign was signaled by the building of the temple. Christ's coming will be marked by the gathering of the Church, the completing of the Bride and the glorious consummation of the new Jerusalem—that edifice of living stones which Christ has been building through the ages and which some day will stand forth amid the admiring gaze of wondering worlds in all the ineffable glory of the vision of the Apocalypse, with the blended light of the jasper and the gold, the sapphire and the emerald, the amethyst and the pearl, the ruby and the diamond, while the glory of God shall flash from His face and the likeness of the Lamb shall be reflected in His glorified and beloved Bride.

ISRAEL'S PREEMINENCE

Solomon's reign was marked by the preeminence it gave to the Jewish nation. Israel was the queen of the earthly kingdoms and her supremacy was unchallenged. So it will be when He comes again. He shall restore the splendor of David's throne and the world shall acknowledge Israel as the chosen race. For this He is preparing her scattered sons today. For this He is giving them the language of the nations, the commercial ascendancy in the markets of the world, and even the literary control of journalism and the politics of nations. The time is coming soon when David shall sit upon His throne, and Israel shall sing once more in the heights of Zion. "Pray for the peace of Jerusalem:/ 'May those who love you be secure' " (Psalm 122:6).

THE GENTILES

The reign of Solomon was marked by a very wonderful influence among the Gentile nations. For once Israel outreached her ancient limits and stretched out her hands to all the people around. Her ships went to Tarshish and to India; the mighty Phoenician people in the north were her allies and her friends; Egypt, Assyria, Damascus, Hamar and Hiram of Tyre were in friendly alliance, and from the distant south the Queen of Sheba came, representing the myriad multitudes of the outlying world, to pay tribute at his feet. So it will be when Jesus comes again. Then shall the myriad peoples of earth become the subjects of His kingdom and come to pay their tribute at the footstool of His throne. This is not our expectation in this age. Our business is to bring Him to them through the message of the gospel. His business will be to bring them to Him in the conversion of the world. Today we are gathering for Him a little sample from all earth's tribes and nations, a kind of firstfruits of His kingdom; then He Himself shall claim the homage of all their millions and He shall reign from sea to sea and from the river to the ends of the earth.

HIS BRIDE

One of the most beautiful circumstances of Solomon's reign was his relation to one loving heart, to whom he seems to have given his supreme affection and who was singled out as the subject of an exquisite romance and the sweetest poem of affection that human language ever composed. It was the beautiful Shunamite of whom he wrote the song of love, the exquisite book of Canticles, and who seems to stand as the very type of the Bride of the Lord Jesus Christ, the one for whom He has prepared His kingdom and with whom He is about to share His throne. We cannot enlarge upon this, but we know that Christ is gathering out a Bride for His name, and sweetly calling the hearts that are willing to hearken and obey, to understand His high calling and to know His love and to prepare for His coming. "Listen, O daughter, consider and give ear," He cries; "forget your people and your father's house./ The king is enthralled by your beauty;/ honor him, for he is your lord" (Psalm 45:10–11).

Oh, beloved, let us not miss this lesson. Has He offered us this high calling? Has He given us the secret of His heart, the invitation to the marriage of the Lamb? Let us not miss His calling. Let us not miss the slightest whisper of His love. Let us keep in closest touch with Him in these last days of time and be ready at a moment's warning to meet Him in the air.

GREATER THAN HIS THRONE

Finally, the greatest fact in connection with Solomon's reign was that Solomon himself was greater than all his pageantry of pomp and circumstances that surrounded him. The man was more than the king on the throne. It was not to see his splendor that the nations came, but to hear his wisdom and to come in contact with his personal worth. There are very few of whom this is true. Most persons are made up of their surroundings and their dress. Real beauty when unadorned is adorned the most, and when adorned it transcends its setting. This is supremely true of Jesus only. Greater than all the greatness that surrounds Him, He Himself is "outstanding among ten thousand" (Song of Songs 5:10), and "altogether lovely" (5:16)! Oh, have we seen Him in His beauty (Isaiah 33:17)? Do we know

Him in His love? Are we longing for Him more than for all He is going to bring, and can we truly say with the old seraphic song,

> The bride eyes not her garment,
> But her dear bridegroom's face.
> I will not gaze on the glory,
> But on the King of Grace;
> Not on the crown He giveth,
> But on His pierced hand.
> The Lamb is all the glory
> In Emmanuel's land.